SightLines

Reading Contemporary Canadian Art

The cover photograph is from *Made to Measure* by Max Dean.
The page seperation photographs are details of *Interior* by Shirley Wiitasalo.

Published by Artextes editions
Artexte Information Centre

CANADIAN CATALOGUING IN PUBLICATION DATA

Main entry under title:
Sight lines: reading contemporary Canadian art

Includes bibliographical references.
ISBN 2-9800632-9-0

1. Art, Canadian. 2. Art, Modern – 20th century – Canada. I. Bradley, Jessica
II. Johnstone, Lesley III. Artexte Information Centre

N6545.S53 1994   709'.71'09048   C94-900266-6

Dépôt légal: Bibliothèque nationale du Québec
and the National Library of Canada, 2nd quarter 1994

ISBN 2-9800632-9-0

Printed in Canada

Published with the assistance of The Canada Council

SightLines

Reading Contemporary Canadian Art

Edited by
Jessica Bradley
and Lesley Johnstone

Artextes editions 1994

table of contents

sightings

crosscurrents

transitions and transgressions

In memory of Jacqueline Fry
and René Payant

PREFACE

As this anthology goes to press, several others on contemporary Canadian art are in progress or have recently been published. This activity bears witness to the multiplicity of histories worthy of our attention and their role in providing artists, critics, and their communities not only with a sense of their past but also of their place in the present. The vigorous and varied critical activity of the 1980s is at the origin of *Sight Lines*. As the decade grew to a close, the publications committee at Artexte discussed the idea of bringing together a selection of existing texts from diverse sources which would reflect the changing tenor of critical writing on art in Canada.

Sight Lines is intended as a reference for the informed reader while providing a source book on contemporary art in Canada for the general reader. The recurrent critical configurations that emerged during our research around such issues as gender and representation, the ideology of the art institution, and the role of theory in criticism determined the scope and thematic format of this anthology. Individual texts were chosen in relation to their significance at the time of writing rather than within the development of a single author's body of writing. The inclusion of texts by both English and French authors, and the translation of many of these for the first time, was based on a desire to acknowledge different critical traditions, increase their potential readership, and invite further dialogue. As this project developed within Artexte's archival and educational mandate, it was also conceived for students. With this purpose in mind, we have included a general bibliography and a selection of images to suggest the nature of the context within which these texts were written.

We wish to express our appreciation for the thoughtful comments made by numerous individuals on both the concept and the content of *Sight Lines* during its various stages of development. The project itself was initiated by the Artexte publications committee that included Reesa Greenberg, Nicole Jolicoeur, and Johanne Lamoureux, as well as ourselves. The contribution of a great number of individuals made *Sight Lines* possible. Most important amongst these are the twenty-five authors who gave us permission to reprint their texts. We are also grateful to each of the magazines for allowing us to reprint texts that originally appeared in their pages and to the many individuals and institutions who provided photographs for the visual section. The Visual Arts Section of The Canada Council contributed to the initial stages of research and pre-production, and further funding from the Writing and Publishing Section contributed to the translation of the French texts and the production of the publication. As the project developed Nathalie Parent and Martine Deslauriers provided diligent assistance with research. Don McGrath has translated the French texts with eloquence. His perseverance and humour, as well as the dedication of Marie Côté and Jennifer Allen to the difficult task of entering and copy editing texts published over a ten-year period by several different authors, were indispensable. Edward Tingley did the final proofreading and met the challenge of compiling the index. We are particularly indebted to these individuals for bringing *Sight Lines* to completion. Michel Des Jardins, Artexte's administrative director, has supported us throughout this endeavour, as has the staff and board of directors at Artexte. Their recognition of the importance of this project encouraged us through several stages of fund-raising. Finally, we would like to thank the designers, Angela Grauerholz and Réjean Myette, for their elegant presentation of the texts and images.

J.B. & L.J.

INTRODUCTION

In 1979 Philip Monk, then a free-lance writer and curator, introduced his self-published pamphlet *Peripheral/Drift* by declaring: "Criticism is in a state of drift, out of control. Its loss, however, is willed; its drifting theoretical. Initially the question is: How is criticism presently adequate to its object?" Monk's text might now be seen as a sort of manifesto, for it is, in his own words, an attempt "to sketch a re-evaluation of the values of art and theory through a critical vocabulary of intensive, shifting terms."[1] A desire for new forms of critical response and dialogue is witnessed by the remarkable increase in the range of voices that began to appear in Canada by the late 1970s. Texts such as Monk's signalled the self-conscious sense that a new critical language was required, and the presence of recently translated French and German theory, together with feminist analyses of gender and culture, provided not only the terms but also an impetus for the articulation of this language. Over the decade that followed, the production and reception of works of art were increasingly viewed as contingent upon the overlapping and conflicting discursive systems that constitute culture. And art history and criticism themselves were perceived as participating in these complex configurations of power and value.

Conditions specific to a Canadian context attended this moment of vital activity in the visual arts. The late 1970s and early 1980s marked a particularly fertile period in the contemporary Canadian art milieu whose stability and diversity had been nurtured by favourable cultural policies and generous funding for more than a decade. There was a growing self-awareness and sense of local histories throughout artistic communities across the country. For example, the dramatic increase in the number of artist-run centres (seventeen in 1976 and thirty-one by 1983) meant that virtually every city had a venue for exhibiting contemporary art. ANNPAC (Association of National Non-Profit Artists' Centres) and its publication *Parallelogramme* (both founded in 1976) became important means of exchange and communication. The historical significance of this alternative network was recognized by the mid 1980s in the *From Sea to Shining Sea* exhibition and catalogue produced by The Power Plant.

As early as 1977 Russell Keziere (editor of *Vanguard* magazine virtually until its demise in 1987) wrote an article entitled "Cdn Art Mags: Implications and Consequences of the Proliferation of Art Periodicals in Canada."[2] And at that same time a gathering of writers, artists, editors, and funding administrators was held in Toronto to take stock of this phenomenon and to assure the future of a new order of art publications. During this period, art publishing in Canada witnessed the appearance of several magazines, many of which began as modest tabloids issuing from artist-run centres or ad hoc collectives. Among those published in Toronto alone were *File* (1972–1989), *Proof Only* (1973–1974) and its successor *Only Paper Today* (1974–1980), *Impulse* (1971–1991), *Image Nation* (1972–1982), *Artist's Review* (1977–1980), *Photocommunique* (1979–1988), *Provincial Essays* (1984–1990), and *Impressions* (1970–1983) that became *C Magazine* in 1984. *Fuse* magazine was created when its predecessor *Centerfold* (first published in 1976) moved from Calgary to Toronto in 1978. In the Maritimes *Arts Atlantic* began to publish in 1979, and in Manitoba *Border Crossings* replaced *Arts Manitoba* which appeared from 1978 to 1985. In Vancouver *Criteria*, published from 1974 to 1978, attempted to offer more radical perspectives than those of the original *Vanguard*, at this time a tabloid-form house organ of the Vancouver Art Gallery. Among French language publications were *Cahiers des arts visuels au Québec* (1979–1988), *Propos d'art* (1977–1984), *Inter* (1978– . . .), and *Ovo* (1970–1983). *Parachute* was founded in 1975, and *Vie des Arts* and *artscanada* (resurrected in 1984 under its original title of *Canadian Art*) had by then a long history.

Significantly, it was frequently artists themselves who launched these publications, designed, and wrote for them, a fact that further suggests the limitations of the critical apparatus, as it had existed, to respond to the art that was being made. In 1973, Art Metropole was established in Toronto by the three-artist collective General Idea as an archive, bookstore, and international distribution centre for artist's books and exhibition catalogues. This organization also initiated some of the first anthologies on performance art, video, and books by artists. In Montréal, Artexte was founded in 1980 to provide similar services but with concentration on a wide range of Canadian publications for which neither a resource centre nor a means of distribution and cataloguing had previously existed.

Throughout the 1980s, the development of critical activity continued to the point that there is now a plethora of visual arts and interdisciplinary magazines currently published in Canada. At the same time, the exhibition of contemporary Canadian art by museums and public galleries increasingly included catalogues that surpassed their documentary purpose. By the late 1980s, many artist-run centres, too, considered comprehensive publications integral to their critical role. The net result is not only a greater breadth and depth of writing about art in Canada, but also an increased dissemination of critical points of view and a greater awareness of artists, their works, and their communities.

Concurrent with these developments was the increased visibility of Canadian artists on the international art scene. The state or "official" representation of Canadian art abroad prevalent in the 1960s and 1970s became virtually moribund following the mammoth and controversial *OKanada* exhibition held in Berlin at the Akademie der Kunste in 1982. The mounting of *OKromaZone* by the Toronto artists collective Chromazone at the same time in Berlin as a counter-exhibition to *OKanada* and the subsequent exhibition *Künstler aus Kanada* in Stuttgart both demonstrated the desire to present a less institutional view of Canadian art on an international level. A perceived internationalization of art was reflected in a preoccupation with the interweaving of local history and geographic location with international avant-garde and modernist discourses, most clearly demonstrated by the critical positions in the writings, teaching, and art production of Vancouver artists Jeff Wall and Ian Wallace.

In Toronto, Ian Carr-Harris described the art scene as undertaking an "archaeology of itself" during this period.[3] This claiming of local histories was witnessed officially by events such as the exhibition *Toronto, A Play of History (Jeu d'histoire)* (1987) and its response from Montréal *The Historical Ruse* (1988), both held at The Power Plant in Toronto. *Vancouver Art and Artists 1931–1983* mounted by the Vancouver Art Gallery was a more comprehensive historical manifestation of this same enterprise, while the *October Show*, which focused on local emerging artists, occurred in reaction to what was considered to be an official view of history. Meanwhile, in 1985 in Montréal, the newly founded Centre international d'art contemporain (CIAC) launched its first exhibition, *Aurora Borealis*, celebrating installation works by thirty artists from across the country and exhibiting them in an unused shopping concourse beneath a downtown residential complex. Subsequently, CIAC's *Cent jours d'art contemporain* placed Canadian artists in the company of their international peers in the thematic exhibitions *Lumières* (1986) and *Stations* (1987).

The simultaneous desire within artistic communities for a more engaging critical discourse that realigned the once separate tasks of the artist and the critic in a dynamic dialogue, is attested by a range of conferences, round tables, and talks in the mid 1980s that focused on criticism and the role of the critic. Prominent among these was the "Talking—a Habit" series of lectures that took place at the Rivoli Cafe in Toronto in 1982–1983.[4] Two other conferences sought to attend more closely to the critical discourses that shaped the art scene both in Canada and abroad. In 1984, *Parachute* magazine organized the international conference *Art and Criticsm in the 80s*, also held in Toronto, continuing a tradition of public events in timely response to international issues of art and criticism that had been initiated with its 1981 conference in Montréal, *Multidisciplinary Aspects of Performance: Postmodernism.*[5] In 1985 the issue of criticism was returned to the more immediate context of the critical relationship between artists, curators, and writers in Canada with the *Artists/Critics* conference organized by YYZ at the Ontario College of Art.[6]

––––––––––––

Writing in *Centerfold* magazine in 1978, Kenneth Coutts-Smith remarked:

> As the ideological dust is now clearing after the final collapse of colonialism, one particular factor crucial to our thinking concerning culture becomes illuminated, as it were, from a different direction, and begins insistently to demand reassessment. With the shift of political centres of gravity away from the old colonialist nations of Europe (and their American extensions), we may note the fact that what used to be considered world cultural history is, of course, merely the history of one small and aggressive corner of the earth.[7]

Coutts-Smith is worth quoting not because what he says seems particularly novel today, but because of the prescience of his comments. As the constitutional debates of the early 1990s demonstrated, a unifying Canadian essence neither exists nor can be legislated. The presence of a recurring identity crisis in Canada's political history reflects our own complex roots in colonialism. In the early 1970s, artists such as Joyce Wieland, Greg Curnoe, and John Boyle saw the affirmation of a unique Canadian identity as a bulwark against American cultural imperialism. While this concern for Canadian cultural autonomy continues to be of importance, the question of identity has become more complex. A new generation of artists who emerged during the 1980s—among them Jamelie Hassan, Lani Maestro, Rebecca Belmore, and Carl Beam, to name only a few—look at cultural identity in multiple terms: from the specificity of their origins, from larger spheres of cultural and political imperialism, and from the perspective of the oppression that brought them here or the repression of their cultures in Canada.

By pausing to question the validity of predominant myths of Canadian identity, the essays in the first section of this anthology, "Reconsidering Contexts and Identities," look implicitly towards issues in art practice and criticism anticipated by Coutts-Smith. The authors consider the limitations of cultural narratives that have constructed this identity, first, around concepts of nature and the north that seem increasingly at odds with the highly urbanized country this is (over 75% of Canadians live in urban centres); and second, as primarily English-speaking and central-Canadian.

Philip Fry proposes an alternative reading of Gaile McGregor's 1985 book *The Wacousta Syndrome* in reaction to her collapsing of the visual arts into painting. He examines the theme of nature, the motif of space, and the construction of Canadian identity in "strategies of avoidance and devices of mediation" by looking, instead, at sculpture and installation. Michael Dorland and Bruce Ferguson draw upon the work of Canadian cultural theorists Harold Innis, George Grant, and Marshall McLuhan. Dorland provides historical background for his claim that the Canadian cultural tradition is one of *ressentiment*, a legacy of silence, self-effacement, and, in turn, harboured resentment. In so doing he traces the evolution of the cliché of the landscape in Canadian painting to develop a theory of "reactionary modernity." Beginning where Dorland leaves off, Ferguson formulates two dominant Canadian cultural narratives, considering them in relation to modernist discourses of alienation. He proposes a postmodernist realism that is disruptive, eschews narrative seamlessness, and "noisily" insists upon the social and institutional context of artistic production.

The title of Marcel Saint-Pierre's text, "Idem," suggests a return to or a repetition of questions of cultural identity within the Québécois artistic milieu. Sketching a tradition of opposition from the *Refus Global* of 1948 through to the public debates around the exhibition *Québec '75*, Saint-Pierre examines the shift from modernism to postmodernism, re-evaluating cultural specificity in light of the internationalization of art. Kim Sawchuk's analysis of the critical reception of Don Proch's 1980 work *Field* recasts questions of regionalism into a web of complex and multiple power relations. Employing the motif of the field, with its territorial connotations, Sawchuk describes the workings of an internal critical colonialism that exists in Canada by subtle degrees rather than in blatant hierarchies.

The final essay in this section also looks at the work of a single artist in relation to questions of identity as these are compounded in the subjective and the social, in issues of authorship, as well as in cultural and linguistic difference. Engaged as it is in the realms of meaning and language, Serge Bérard's reading of Rober Racine's work insists upon difference, voice, and identity, ultimately asserting that the cultural politics of language for a Québécois artist are present even in works as seemingly "formal" as Racine's.

By the 1980s, larger museums were consistently exhibiting contemporary art, and many smaller institutions were dedicating their programming primarily to current artistic production. The artist-run centres
were firmly anchored in their respective communities, and most had
established a working structure with boards of directors, directors,
archives, and, inevitably, several employees. In addition, a larger number
of commercial galleries devoted to exhibiting and selling contemporary
Canadian art existed. Yet in the space of two years (1983 and 1984),
across the country and virtually simultaneously, a number of large-scale
exhibitions were organized by artists and independent curators in abandoned warehouse spaces and municipal buildings, as well as in the artist-
run centres. Among these were the *October Show*, the *Warehouse Show*,
and *Artropolis* in Vancouver, *Montréal-tout-terrain*, and *Monumenta*,
Chromaliving, and *The New City of Sculpture* in Toronto as well as the
massive, nation-wide *Locations/National, Sites/Locations* which included
thirty-one site-specific projects. Concurrently many individual artists were
producing their own exhibitions in alternative sites—one thinks of Betty
Goodwin, Martha Fleming and Lyne Lapointe, General Idea, and Joey
Morgan, to name only a few. A related phenomenon was the number of
independent curators, often artists themselves, who were the innovators of
temporary exhibitions or who were increasingly engaged to produce special exhibitions for museums and artist-run centres. The preponderance of
installations and site-specific works in Canada in the 1980s now appears
emblematic of the challenge to traditional institutional structures that
took place during this period. In many respects these developments constituted a tacit response to the limitations of the museum. Importantly, they
also animated local art scenes by providing an alternative critical forum.

Given the debates around the ideological significance of the museum that are a recurring theme within postmodernist theory and the burgeoning of art institutions that characterized the 1980s, it is not surprising
that the institutional context of art emerges as a subtext in many of the
essays in this anthology. The second section, "Systems and Symbols," is
devoted to considerations of this relationship between the artist, or the art
object, and the exhibiting institution.

Jacqueline Fry, Charlotte Townsend-Gault, and Kass Banning
address the ideological structure of the institution and the political use
made of artists and their works while Christine Ross presents case studies
of two major museum exhibitions of work by women artists in Québec
during the 1980s. Fry's essay offers a detailed analysis of works by artists
who specifically address the museum as a framing device. However, she
emphasizes how works of art that question the institution of art may,

paradoxically be recuperated by the museum whose values rely persistently on ideologies of exclusion and connoisseurship. Townsend-Gault examines the contradictory exhibition history of the Kwakiutl food vessel to reveal the inherent taxonomic imperialism of the museum. By questioning the legitimizing function of acts of classification, she indicates the vexed position of the contemporary Native artist in today's art system.

Kass Banning's analysis of the institutional framing of Joyce Wieland's 1987 retrospective exhibition at the Art Gallery of Ontario points to the important influence of feminism in the rethinking of institutional structures and the authority they embody. In tracing Wieland's critical reception she notes the curious displacement of the local, the female, and the "Canadianness" of her work that occurred with its institutional legitimation. Christine Ross's essay too addresses the difficulties of the institutionalization of women's artistic production. Writing at the close of the decade, she concludes that exhibitions of work by women artists must dispense with narrow formulas of feminist art production, while acknowledging both the discursive and experiential history of the feminist subject.

At the end of her essay, Fry suggests a number of alternatives to the conventional museum structure, one of which is the artist-run centre, noting, however, that it appears to have inevitably adopted a structure similar to that of the museum. Nonetheless the historical significance of the artist-run centre in the Canadian art milieu cannot be overemphasized. In her essay, Diana Nemiroff traces the political, economic, socio-cultural, and aesthetic conditions that coincided to encourage the emergence of these centres. Dating from 1983, her text is primarily concerned with the history of the first decade of such centres; however, her analysis remains pertinent today in light of the continuing institutionalization of the art system.

Postmodernism, conceived either as a rupture with formalist late modernism or a continuity with the principles of avant-gardist critical modernism, the formulation of a critical language to address works that challenge media autonomy, and the shifting relationship of art practices to their social and institutional context as well as to the spectator, are prominent amongst the concerns raised by the authors in the third section, "Crosscurrents." As each author engages with the positioning of art in current theoretical discourses, the reader is often made party to an attempt to locate a voice and a critical strategy within the act of writing itself.

René Payant, Philip Monk, and Walter Klepac variously address art works and their critical reception within a dialectic of modernism and postmodernism. Payant locates the specific dynamics of installation in the new relationship it proposed between the spectator and the work of art. In so doing he claims that installation is *the* postmodern form. Through exhibition *Art and Censorship* organized in 1985 after recurring scrutiny of the Toronto film and video community. Writing in 1983 at the height of this repressive climate in Toronto, Varda Burstyn called for the continued, varied, and active production of sexual imagery by artists, insisting that exempting art from laws governing pornography, as had been suggested, would only disarm its crucial and potentially disruptive relation to society-at-large. While the arguments in Burstyn's essay evolve from the feminist antiporn/anticensorship debates of the early 1980s, the production of multiple viewpoints she advocates prefigures more recent artistic activity around sexuality and identity politics. Guy Sioui Durand's essay turns such questions inside out, reflecting, instead, on the more subtle cultural politics of state supported art and the problems of an institutionalized self-censorship by artists as their work becomes more politically engaged.

The question of identity—both sexual and cultural—and its representation is central to the remaining three texts in this section. While Dot Tuer looks at video productions of the mid 1980s in relation to current psychoanalytic and feminist theories of sexuality and subjectivity, Monika Gagnon's monograph on the work of Jamelie Hassan considers the ways in which the artist examines the politics of representation that operate over a range of social and international sites of political oppression. Tuer's tracing of a transsexual motif in a number of video works offers a model of gender, sex, and desire that destabilizes the authority of binary terms of sexual difference. Gagnon traces the ways in which Hassan's work has attempted to make evident the interaction of identity, politics, and art-making using both feminist and postcolonial theoretical perspectives. Finally, Loretta Todd's text on the appropriation of Native imagery by non-Native artists calls for a reassessment of the appropriative techniques typical of postmodernist practice. She draws attention to the inversion of cultural autonomy, noting that what is appropriated in the final instance is the possibility of oppressed or marginalized cultural groups speaking for themselves. As Todd makes evident, colonialist attitudes may be perpetuated in an unquestioned embracing of multiculturalism or even in practices designed to promote cross-cultural understanding.

The different ways that questions of identity are raised in the first and last sections of this anthology indicate not only a realignment and expansion of critical perspectives to take into account the place of artistic production in the broader context of culture as a system of representational practices, but also a crisis in the aesthetic and political values that had formerly determined critical judgement. What can we make of the fact that a privileging of order gives way to a questioning of the ordering impulse? Or that the analysis of content in works of art is increasingly tied to a consideration of the context of production? Evaluative criticism is necessarily challenged by these shifts while interpretive acts are enriched by the recognition of contingent and contested configurations of value.

The culmination of such changes in both artmaking and critical writing, already apparent by the early 1980s, is perhaps all too easily submerged under the elusive term postmodernism. Yet a reconsideration of the meaning of authorship, history, and identity, as well as a questioning of the institutional politics of representation and the ideology of consumer culture as they affect art practices, recurs throughout this volume. Within this climate of critical inquiry, evaluative and interpretive endeavours that ignore the ideological, social, economic, and political conditions of art production become less tenable. The exercising of critical judgement throughout *Sight Lines* manifests a search for interpretive approaches that question the transparency of meaning in works of art and the institutional systems that contextualize them. Similarly, methodologies of art history that rely solely on connoisseurship and biography, and the predominance of critical debates based on aesthetic values confined to the realm of art, are subject to scrutiny and critical dismantling. A profound scepticism regarding cultural narratives that propose a progressive and rational view of history and subjectivity is prevalent in the self-reflexive character of much of the critical writing that emerged during the 1980s. The preoccupation with the act of writing itself, with the relationship between the text and the work of art—that is, with the production of meaning—evident in the texts in this anthology characterizes a shift in focus from descriptive evaluation to interpretive analysis.

Jessica Bradley
Lesley Johnstone

Notes

1.   Philip Monk, *Peripheral/Drift: A Vocabulary of Theoretical Criticism* (Toronto: Rumour, 1979).

2.   Russell Keziere, "Cdn Art Mags: Implications and Consequences of the Proliferation of Art Periodicals in Canada," *Criteria,* vol. 3, no. 3 (November 1977).

3.   Ian Carr-Harris, "Toronto, Art, and History," in Louise Dompierre, Alvin Balking, et al., *Toronto, A Play of History (Jeu d'histoire)* (Toronto: The Power Plant, 1987), 35.

4.   These lectures were published as a series of texts in *Parallelogramme* from October 1982 to Fall 1983.

5.   The conference proceedings were published as *Performance, Text(e)s & Documents,* ed. Chantal Pontbriand (Montréal: Éditions Parachute, 1980).

6.   The conference proceedings were published as *Artists/Critics,* ed. Bruce Grenville and Jeanne Randolph (Toronto: YYZ, 1985).

7.   Kenneth Coutts-Smith, "Art and Social Transformation," *Centerfold,* vol. 2, no. 4 (April 1978): 22.

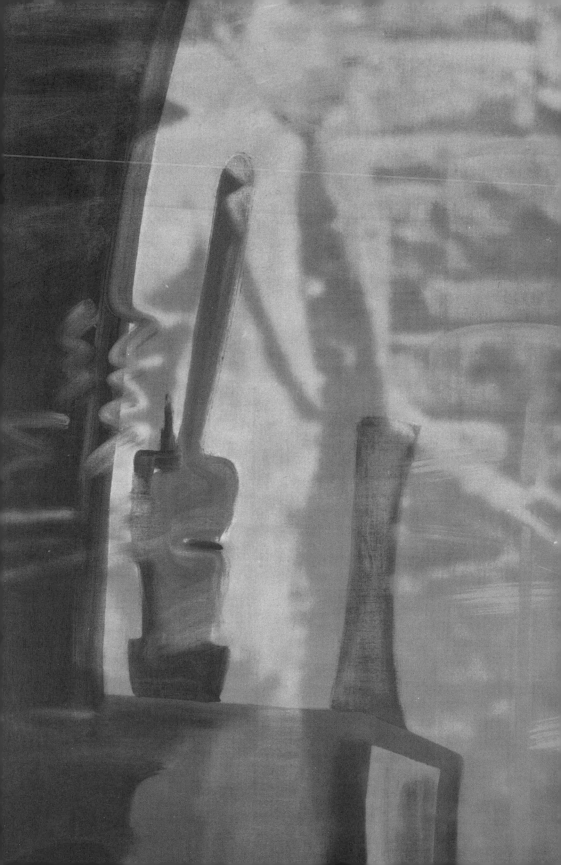

reconsidering contexts and identities

jective involvement, the issues themselves are treated with admirable discipline. Based on an analytic treatment of documents (the identification of themes and formal devices, the recognition of similarities and differences, of regularities) and constructed as a synthesis of her findings, the image of the Canadian self that McGregor offers for our consideration is clearly an abstract representation, a model. Its validity, like that of any other model, can be assessed. Seen as a tool, it should offer a coherent explanation of the evidence under study (its representative value) and provide a pattern for examining other relevant cases or examples not yet studied (its hypothetical value). In this connection, I believe that issue can indeed be taken with several substantive aspects of *The Wacousta Syndrome*, but that this does not constitute a serious enough problem to undermine the fundamental value of the work. There are, however, some questions concerning the author's use of the visual arts that I would like to dwell upon here.

It is in the first four chapters that McGregor does the actual construction work on her model by tracing out its historical manifestation and development. Her view of the Canadian self takes shape as she discusses literary works (novels, poems, critical writings) and paintings as symptoms to be analysed and interpreted. With few exceptions, the only direct visual evidence used comes in the form of painting, which leaves us to wonder what a similar study of, say, early Canadian land surveying, town planning, architecture, and photography might reveal.

This restriction of the visual component of the corpus to painting appears increasingly unfortunate as we realize how important the notion of imported convention is to the development of the book's argument.

When we reach the fifth chapter—and the middle of the twentieth century—we find that the approach shifts from the construction to the interpretative use and refinement of the model. As the interpretative mode gets under way, works of visual art are temporarily boosted to a leading, decisive position because of the "purity" with which they exemplify key notions. But, once again, the evidence is limited almost exclusively to painting, even though the argument itself fairly cries out for examples from more contemporary forms—at least photography, film, and video, not to speak of site-specific sculpture, installations, and multimedia presentations. What is also very strange is that, in the final seven chapters, we see no more of the visual arts with the exception of a few brief "cameo appearances" in conjunction with a point to be made. To me, this absence seems particularly noticeable in the chapter on authorship and the artist's self-consciousness, as well as in the context of McGregor's discussion of photography and film, not as primary evidence, but as *literary* images having to do with fact, history, and fiction.

To my mind, if these reservations about the constitution of McGregor's corpus tend to weaken the representative value of her model, they do so without tarnishing its inherent interest; what they make even more apparent is the model's value as an hypothesis, a heuristic device. A great deal of verification remains to be done, and what I propose is to begin here. As grounds for discussion, I will first outline *The Wacousta Syndrome*, reducing the display of evidence and the argumentation to a minimum (the book, with critical apparatus, is 474 pages) while emphasizing points that seem particularly pertinent to the visual arts. I will then attempt to see how the model applies to a few cases not examined by McGregor.

What, Then, is the Wacousta Syndrome?

Named after a nineteenth-century novel by Major John Richardson, the syndrome is a configuration of relations, the particular self-image that has arisen from the pioneer experience of the Canadian wilderness. The key to this configuration is the settlers' strongly negative reaction to the brute hostility of their new surroundings. Harsh, impersonal, uncompromising, nature on the Northern frontier was more than indifferent to human needs and aspirations. Living on the homestead was, to put it bluntly, very dangerous. Encompassing the pioneer like a circular barricade, limitless and impenetrable, unpredictable and chaotic, untamed, sinister, the landscape was totally alien, radically distinct from the civilized world. And there was no way out. The response to this situation was a fear, a hatred of nature which triggered a recoil into the self. With the recoil came deeply felt sentiments of isolation, of entrapment, of vulnerability: the self engulfed by the Other. Canadians, it is said, carry terror in their souls.

The main consequence of this strongly negative response to nature is that the *site* of the Canadian self, the *place* from which relationships are entertained and qualified, displays a distinct topography. Although nature is experienced as an obstacle, the situation is not envisaged as a polar relationship—represented graphically by the location of two terms on opposite ends of a line—in which the self stands outside and facing the obstacle that it attempts to overcome. The Canadian self appears as a moveable point within a circle or as a figure on a field. Familiar images rush to mind: being lost in the snowstorm or fog while trying to return home, swimming in a rough sea with no land in sight, standing alone on the immense, featureless prairie with an overdetermined horizon line curving around the back of one's head. Unlike the polarized self, which fixes its position relative to the object of its concern, the encompassed self, barri-

the encompassed self

caded within a fortress but nevertheless vulnerable from all sides, has difficulty determining where and what the obstacle is. Acting from an indeterminate place within the circle, the self experiences fundamental incertitude and is ambivalent in those relationships it does manage to establish. Correspondingly, the nonself is struck with a radical ambiguity.

The recoil reaction was not simply a temporary response to the settlers' first contact with nature. Over the years, rather than losing its power as familiarity grew, it was repressed, becoming a deep attitudinal pattern. Hidden from direct observation, its presence as an organizing factor of the self is revealed symptomatically as an insistent preoccupation with the relationship between the self and nature, between civilization and the wilderness. Overt expression of dislike or hatred of nature has been relatively rare; when it is encountered it is usually formulated by explorers or foreign visitors. Indirect expressions are, however, numerous. They take two basic forms: strategies of avoidance and devices of mediation.

Firstly, the strategies. *Simple avoidance* extends from feigned ignorance—pretending that nature isn't there at all or is just a backdrop (the big green curtain) for the human scene—to the selective exploitation of elements that are of use in human affairs. This involves a kind of short focus on pertinent details and a corresponding rejection of their context. Surrounded by what is felt to be a meaningless nature, both the Canadian and his city are located … nowhere.

Conventionalization consists in an attempt to use imported cultural forms and values (e.g., romantic sensitivity, the pastoral ideal, the myth of the Western frontier) to put order and meaning into nature. Put briefly, it is using someone else's tools to tame the wilderness. But, because these tools were developed in response to significantly different natural contexts—certainly not the wildly disordered, incomprehensible Canadian landscape—they do not work very well and fail to provide an adequate solution to the Canadian's deep-seated uneasiness. Indeed, their use runs contrary to the harder realities of pragmatic experience, thereby tending to heighten rather than reduce the self's sense of plight. No matter how enthusiastically they are adopted, such conventions remain and work on a surface level of the self, leaving the deep structure intact and opening the way to conflict between conscious expression and norms (what one says and does) on the one hand and covert values (what one really believes and feels) on the other. There is another disadvantage to this strategy: reliance on imported conventions screens and in a sense censors our reception of fresh information and works against the development of an original vision.

Domestication is a secondary, more deliberate response in which the selective focus mentioned above is used to construct a humanized environment. Based on implicit considerations about the possibility of control and relevance to human life, it paves the way for exploitation by putting things into some kind of useful order through operations such as naming, classifying, measuring, quantifying, cataloguing. But, once again, this strategy is only a way of looking away from what one fears. The hard fact is that nature is both tough and unruly. The day's work is never done, and one only dreams of living happily ever after. Anxiety is hidden under the calm regularity, the formalities of daily life and practices.

Secondly, the mediating devices. Because his or her relationship with things is problematic, instead of dealing with things directly in the American way, the Canadian, cautious and circumspect, places a great deal more attention on *how* to deal with them. (You could, after all, get hurt.) Because certain things have the ability to separate and mark the zones of the self and the other, they have a particular importance as mediating devices—the fortress, the house, the window, the box, the frame, the human body itself. Cast in their roles, these devices are ambiguous: playing against the security offered by the fortress and the house, there is the confinement proper to a prison; against the openness and order offered by the window, box, and frame, there is closure, constraint, and exclusion; within the living vitality of the body, death grows. These devices work because they all embody the form of enclosure. It would seem that, for Canadians, this form, quite independently of what it is used to present, has its own semantic resonances.

If, in McGregor's presentation, the kitchen garden is presented as an example of domestication, the landscape garden, used as mediating device in both occidental and oriental cultures, appears only indirectly through her reference to Shaftesbury and English romanticism. Her overly hasty treatment of this matter is curious.

The Canadian self-image comes into clearer focus when McGregor compares it to the American "Western Frontier" mentality. The main idea is that, in America, the pioneer saw the wilderness in the framework of the Edenic myth: although he encountered real obstacles and dangers, he nevertheless believed that he was in the Garden of Eden. By personally facing and overcoming the difficulties imposed by the land, he would find salvation, becoming the new Adam. And, once the garden began to grow in one place, he would hear the call of the Western Frontier promising the discovery of new lands flowing with milk and honey. Should, from time to time, his labour meet with failure, it was at worst a temporary set-back; with renewed effort Adam would be born again. This is a story of the individual pitted against nature in a struggle for salvation which he will surely win. Law and order, as well as the democratic process, function in this narrative to the extent that they guarantee the right to life, liberty, and the pursuit of happiness. After performing his righteous deed—which might even involve challenging not justice itself, but its application—the American hero rides off alone into the sunset. For him, there will always be a new horizon, a new beginning.

The Canadian view is radically different: the settler could never imagine the Northern wilderness as a garden. Engulfed by the hostile nature from which he could not even wrest the bare stuff of existence without the help of others, he held fast to those things that would provide at least relative security by assuring him a place in human society and by facilitating coexistence and collaboration: order, neighbourly conduct, good government. In the Canadian story, *if* the protagonist is rash enough to venture into the countryside alone, instead of accomplishing a great deed or finding happiness at the end of the rainbow, he has a harrowing experience in which he recognizes his need for others. He then heads straight back to town. He has realized that *there is nothing else*—no new horizon, no beyond.

McGregor's next step in the construction of her model consists in showing that the recoil from nature gives rise to secondary patterns of response. This process can be resumed as a sequence of psychological events: the primary reaction is so strong, it so distances nature, that the latter is neutralized, nullified, as an object of fear; without a precise object, the sentiment of insecurity, of helpless isolation, becomes generalized and free-floating; in need of a place to anchor feelings, the self seizes upon a new object. Detached from its original object, generalized, and displaced, the primary ambivalence of the self towards nature—and towards the self itself inasmuch as it is a death-bearing body—is extended to all things, including the self as object. To the self's radical doubt about others, inversion of the model adds radical self-doubt.

Returning to the comparison of the American and Canadian self-images for a moment, it is clear that in both cases obstacles can give rise to serious difficulties. But the levels at which the problems are experienced are different. The American, confident that there is some solution even if it isn't apparent, deals with difficulties on a practical level. But for the Canadian, unsure that there is any ultimate solution, a problem is an intimation of the fundamental absurdity of things and is *felt* on an existential level. Americans believe in transcendence; Canadians might like—and try—to, but it doesn't ring true in their deepest feelings. This is why, in their respective approaches to the expression of values, Americans tend to function on the vertical romantic-ironic axis of metaphor, imaging or criticizing their dream of a beyond, whereas Canadians emphasize the horizontal tragic-comic axis of metonymy, seeing each thing as a part of the whole problem of being here and nowhere else. There is, however, the confusion that arises from the massive reception in Canada of American imagery and values. Because of an overlay effect, a Canadian might attempt to identify with the American image, creating a tension between his own mostly covert self-image and the overt imported image: the covert self-image is then associated with self-doubt and negative feelings (frustration) and the imported one, with public approval and positive feelings.

Having established the basic armature of her model, McGregor devotes the remainder of her book to its application, verification, and enrichment. After the section on the visual arts mentioned above, she deals with various social relations and personality profiles as they are presented in Canadian literature: whether it involves one of the partners in marriage, parents, the figures of the fool-saint, the noble savage, or the leader as magician, the adoption of a social role thrusts the self into a state of deep ambivalence. The social image projected is correspondingly ambiguous. This indeterminacy of attitude is based on an inversion: neither nurturing nor protective, in Canada nature is assimilated, not with feminine, maternal principles, but with masculine, paternal forces. Male-typed social roles—those that involve deliberate action, order, law, reason, leadership—are therefore the object of particularly anguished sentiments: the need for and the admiration of strong, self-declarative activity are counterbalanced by fear and rejection. In general, the pattern of action that appears as desirable to Canadians can be symbolized by the passive animal, the animal that, seen as a victim of nature, survives through capitulation, submission, concealment, or disguise. Those who adopt an active role are asking for trouble. This brings us to the self-image of the artist.

Because the artist attempts to achieve self-identification through modes of activity that cannot help but challenge the passivity in which security is found, he or she appears as the quintessential embodiment of Canadian self-doubt. The risk taken is double-edged: on the one side, the commitment to art not only cuts the artist off from others, it implies directing a sort of violence against oneself and against the object of concern, giving rise to a fear of destroying (unleashing the monster within, "consuming" the object of interest); on the other, self-assertion—not only an indiscretion but also an obscenity in the Canadian context—exposes the self to a merited punishment, giving rise to the fear of being destroyed. Insecure, anxious, the artist attempts to shield the self from danger by developing strategies both to mark and to reduce his or her responsibility for creative action, producing work that is both declarative of the self and self-effacing. In literature, two important strategies are well-evidenced:

when a narrator is presented within a text (the "I" who recounts the story), various techniques are used to set up or question the narrator's identity, thereby distancing the author outside the text; when no narrator is presented, techniques such as verbal collage, borrowed structure, mixture of genres, obfuscation of viewpoint, and indeterminacy are employed to reduce the responsibility of the implied narrator. Some of these techniques would seem to have interesting parallels in the visual arts.

We are now, I believe, in a position to attempt the application of McGregor's model to a few examples not included in her corpus.

Allow me, then, to present two pieces as evidence: Charles Gagnon's *Box #6–The Window* (1962) and Michael Snow's *Authorization* (1969). These works embody and assign a particularly strong value to formal devices by which the relationship between the self and the other is mediated, and they can also both be seen in the light of the artist's *œuvre*, they reveal the use of techniques which establish a distanced or decentred authorial stance.

In the Gagnon work, several distinct devices—the box, the window, a blind, a painted "landscape," mirrors—are structurally and functionally coordinated. The box is divided into three main sections: the lower area, a flat surface trimmed with a horizontal strip of moulding, acts as a sill for the window which occupies the large central area; above this, there is another flat surface in which four circular holes have been cut.

The box presents, contains, and reveals: the sill qualifies the glass front as window pane; the window displays a blind and a painted landscape, both located on the inside of the box; and the holes reveal the viewer's eye reflected in one of the mirrors located in the upper section of the box.

A parallel is established between the window and the holes: both offer to view and focus attention upon an object while holding it at a distance thanks to an interposed physical barrier. Identified as a "landscape" as much by its relationship to other works by Gagnon as by its visual structure, the image seen through the window is, from a literal point of view, a collage unified by a loosely brushed painted surface. One of the items featured—in or on?—the landscape is an empty paint tube. Eschewing any possibility of grasping the image as a representation of a given scene, the landscape is presented—framed and contained by the box—as a product of the artist's work and marked as such, but it is left open to interpretation by the viewer. When looking through a hole in the upper section, one sees one's own eye reflected in a mirror, framed and caught in the act of looking, the eye sees the "I" seeing, that is, peering out of the box from within.

By metonymy, the structure composed of the sill, window, and blind imply the potential presence of a house, a dwelling place of the self. But because the blind is located inside the box, between the glass and the landscape, the viewer's position in regard to the house is indeterminate: if one is outside, why would the landscape be seen inside? Or, if one is inside, why would the blind be located on the outside? The set-up makes sense only if the position of the viewer is left floating. When, however, considered in parallel to the relationship established by looking into one of the holes in the upper section, this indetermination is understood to involve inversion and interiorization: as the self sees the mirrored eye as both object and subject, so the landscape is located and identified as exterior *and* interior to the dwelling space of the self.

The devices employed in *Box #6–The Window* are analogues of features that appear in Gagnon's studio work (his paintings, drawings, collages, and constructions) and photographs with sufficiently high frequency to be considered constants.

First, in regard to the studio works: if the box considered as a physical container and display tool—that is, as a literal device—appears mainly in the 1961–62 series of which *Box #6* is the final member and in two works of the 1970s, it appears implicitly throughout the Gagnon corpus as a figurative device through its formal and functional similarities to the frame and the window. In turn, the frame and the window, used literally to present and mediate images produced by the artist, also function, sometimes in the form of the related threshold images of the doorway or the archway, as motifs that, while constituting the image, mediate between its literal and figurative planes. The relationship between these planes is consistently ambiguous, indeterminate.

Now, in regard to Gagnon's photos: taken together, the devices used in *Box #6* form a kind of viewing machine not unlike a *camera obscura*; this analogy makes it possible, while paying due attention to differences of media, to trace out functional and formal similarities between the means Gagnon uses to make and/or take "pictures." If the box is understood as a room designed for the projection of images, the window (frame and pane) can be compared to both the viewfinder and the lens, the blind, to the camera's shutter, and the painting, to the image projected on the wall. In Gagnon's photos, certain aspects of the viewfinder's function are singularly marked: by using the edge to cut off portions of a figure or by permitting the intrusion of apparently extraneous elements, the visual field is made to appear *as* incomplete, *as* a portion or a segment of a wider, given whole. And, as ambiguity arises from the tension between the literal and figurative places in Gagnon's paintings, so it is produced in the photos by an open, indeterminate visual and semantic structure. Although they most frequently present ordinary, easily-identified objects or scenes, it is not clear what the photos are *about*: if they display a *given*, it is more to suggest, evoke, or intimate, than to document a fact. Or, perhaps, it is to demonstrate that suggesting is all that facts are about. As photographed by Gagnon, the world itself is a frame, a window, a threshold.

The openness or indetermination of Gagnon's work invites determination by the viewer; it also distances the artist as author of the work by reducing his responsibilities for the final outcome, the apperception of the work by the viewer. This distance is increased by Gagnon's use of studio works and photography in the constitution of one corpus. The roles habitually assigned to artists—painter, sculptor, photographer, and so forth—identify and limit what the artists as authors are expected to do, locating, as it were, their accountability within the use of a medium and its conventions. By identifying a role, we try to "put a handle" on art, tie it down, bring it closer. Gagnon's use of several distinct media *as* distinct, suggests that we situate the place of responsibility somewhere beyond or anterior to the division of roles, somewhere less attainable. As Gagnon puts it: "Art for me is at a level that is not attached to a particular discipline, nor to any particular aspects of life. It has nothing (or very little) to do with technical ability or prowess and much to do with a spiritual dimension, the ability to understand, but in a nonintellectual way."[3]

The methodological use of analogies for the purpose of clarifying the structure of Gagnon's work should not blind us to the metonymic bond by which each work is related to the world: indeed, whether painting or photograph, each work stands for the world, the whole of which it is a part. Gagnon's work is situated, then, not on the vertical romantic-ironic axis of metaphor, proposing an ideal world, but on the horizontal tragic-comic axis of metonymy, revealing the way things are. The window, the landscape itself, opens both outwards and inwards upon the void.

Turning now to the work by Michael Snow, our discussion of mediating devices is considerably advanced by Gene Youngblood's "classic" description which I quote at length:

> *Authorization* (1969) consists of five Polaroid photos taped to the surface of a mirror, four in the centre and one in the upper left corner. The four, reading clockwise, show: 1. Snow shooting the mirror with a rectangle of tape in its centre which frames Snow's reflection, thus making a "picture" of Snow making a picture; 2. The first photo taped on the mirror with Snow shooting; 3. Two photos with Snow shooting; 4. Three photos with Snow shooting. The fifth photo, taped in

the upper left corner, shows all four photographs filling in the centre rectangle and effectively obscuring Snow's reflection. This photo acts as an "announcement" of the process which is documented in the centre of the mirror, while the infinity of frames-within-frames serves as an "echo" of that process. Snow's own work is seen to be eclipsing himself, yet each element includes himself within himself."[4]

To the symptoms of the Wacousta syndrome pointed out in this description (the insistent use of frames, the embedded or "boxed-in" imagery, the shifting relative positions of the artist as subject and object, the tempering of self-presentation with self-effacement), should be added the on-going function of the mirror that frames each viewer viewing the work within a concrete environment. Through the agency of the mirror, the viewer's position (in the work and in the world) and activities are identified with those of the artist. The ambiguity of the title is thereby doubled: referring either to the self-declarative act through which a reality comes into existence or to the self-effacing reception of a permission to act, it applies equally well to both the artist and the viewer. For both, *Authorization* functions as a perceptual/conceptual machine.

Resuming, as it were, Snow's previous work—think of *Blues in Place* (1959), *Lac Clair* (1960), *Window* (1962), *Scope* (1967), *Blind* (1967), *Portrait* (1967), *Wavelength* (1966–1967)—and forecasting what was to come—*Morning in Holland* (1969–1974), *Glares* (1973), *Reds* (1974), *Plus Tard* (1977), *Rameau's Nephew by Diderot (Thanx to Dennis Young) by Wilma Schoen* (1972–1974)—*Authorization* is less a proposition about things themselves, a metaphysics, than a concrete investigation of how we know things, an epistemology. Here, knowledge is not only a mediated relation between subject and object, it is *shown* to be mediated by a technology of vision in which arbitrary, conventional forms (the mirror's frame, the taped rectangle) are functionally associated with necessary conditions of sight and mechanical instrumentality (the eye, the lens, the viewfinder). If, in individual instances, the frame is chosen, framing itself remains inescapable. The relation of knowledge is also presented as a self-affirming and self-denying constitutive process: arresting the potentially infinite recession or embedding of meaning through the imposition of a frame of reference, the subject actively forms the object; reflecting meaning in accordance with its own characteristics, the object informs the receptive subject. Dealing with knowledge as a process taking place in the real world, Snow's work is situated dead centre on the tragic-comic axis of metonymy.

At this point in our discussion, it is perhaps best to acknowledge a nagging doubt about what we have found: rather than seeing the devices we have isolated in Gagnon's and Snow's respective *œuvre* as symptoms of the Wacousta syndrome, is it not possible, and indeed more in accordance with historical information, to interpret them as consciously adopted conventions? It is, of course, clear that the themes of the window, mirror, and frame run through the history of modern and contemporary art, and that openness, ambiguity, and indeterminism are hallmarks of the modernist game plan which, as I understand it, is concerned essentially with epistemological moves. One helpful, though insufficient, answer is that Mallarmé was haunted by *l'azur* and that Duchamp kept his eye focused on the Domain of the Bride; idealists both, these father-figures situated their work on the romantic-ironic axis of metaphor. The fact nevertheless remains that the devices of contemporary art are, for a large part, consciously shared within a field of practice defined more by urbanization than by national or regional limits, with the effects that the artistic self-image appears to be international on its overt or surface level. On this level, factors relating to the concrete geosphere and biosphere in which work is produced, if they appear at all, are deemed accidental rather than constitutive. If, then, as McGregor herself points out, we wish to uncover and reveal the underlying structure, the Wacousta syndrome, it would seem to require the use of a method that is attentive to the relative frequency and intensity with which the key devices appear. Quantitative and qualitative, statistical and interpretative, the pursuit of this kind of investigation is not free of problems. For example, how can we establish whether Gagnon is more insistent upon a decentred approach than, say, John Cage? Is Snow's work more self-effacing than, say, Jasper Johns's or Robert Rauschenberg's? And, even if we are finally satisfied with the demonstration in regard to these two artists, what can be said about the extension of the syndrome to the whole field of contemporary art in Canada? McGregor seems to think of the Wacousta syndrome as a kind of determining factor of our art production. Perhaps it would be better to see it, for the time being at least, as a purely heuristic model, a tool that can help us sort out questions, identify areas of research, and elucidate works.

Here, by way of example, are a few instances that could be pursued in greater depth and detail:

The impact of Tony Brown's two multimedia installations, *Spinning House* (1981) and *Breaking House* (1983), that use the house image is perhaps due to our personal implication in the ambiguous dwelling/prison theme as well as to his exploitation of technological devices.

Sylvain P. Cousineau's "loans" or "quotations" of other artists' styles, constituting in themselves an ironic comment on an idealized practice of art, seem to be used to frame or formulate a theme of passage on the tragic-comic axis.

The displacement of Henry Saxe's *Sight-Site* (1973) from its original location on the irregular ground of a field bordered by fences and trees to the National Gallery of Canada seriously modified the visual and psycho-social conditions of its use as a sighting instrument. The pertinent question here is the degree to which the ambivalence with which Canadians view public institutions is extended to their appreciation of the works they present.

The zero point of authorship almost attained by Max Dean in *A Work* (1977) appears perhaps in a different form in his use of complex, viewer-initiated mechanisms or robots that seem to run themselves.

Stephen Cruise's installations are doubly decentred: his images rise from a dream world to which he has privileged access but over which he has no conscious control and, as these images present themselves (stand on their own feet) in context, both the images and their underdetermined relationships invite interpretation.

Through his use of evocation and a logic of the both/and type, Robin Collyer associates the viewer in his interrogation of contemporary belief systems.

The work of new Canadians might provide interesting corroborative information.

Begun when she still lived in the United States, Lynne Cohen's photographs of interiors deal with the presence and arrangement of objects in claustrophobic, boxed-in spaces, a fact that, in itself, suggests a typically Canadian preoccupation. However, until recently, her use of illumination and point of view have tended to isolate and display the objects in the box/room as receptacles of desire, idealizing them and, at the same time, situating the work itself on the "American" romantic-ironic axis. In her more recent photographs, the objects, frequently tools of social control, are strongly allusive, leading the viewer to consider actual conditions outside the box/room. Cohen, since being in Canada for a while, seems, at the very least, to have been experimenting with the tragic-comic axis of expression.

The main components of Trevor Gould's installation, *The Writings on the Wall* (1984–1985), consist of a model house, a life-sized wall relief of a gorilla, a black cylindrical object, a black artificial flower, and the word "trophies" printed in widely spaced letters on the wall. The house, held at a precarious angle off the floor, is supported by an inverted tea cup and segments of a small birch tree. On the outside back wall of the house, there are graffiti-like drawings of a table and a chair (both tilted), a revolver, and the word "error." Inside the house, a colour transparency showing a white woman dressed in a bright cotton tunic and accompanied on each side by a black man can be seen by peeking through a window. Each of the objects is, in itself, open to interpretation, and the semantic relationships established between them, if qualified by the notion of "trophy" (a structure erected as a memorial of a victory in war, anything serving as a token or evidence of victory, valour, skill, power, etc.), nevertheless remain underdetermined. One possible interpretation that is pertinent here is that, for the artist, the gorilla and the house, standing for Africa as a point of departure and Canada as a point of arrival, no doubt have autobiographical connotations. The violence of the rupture, registered in the forlorn gaze of the gorilla and the precarious position of the house, is marked by the pairing of the two other objects, what seem to be a grenade and a charred flower. For every viewer, these elements can no doubt be used to tell a different story. The point to be made for the moment, however, is that after such a short time in Canada, Gould has adopted an almost massive use of devices that accentuate indeterminacy and openness, which are, of course, symptoms of the Wacousta syndrome.

In guise of a conclusion, we should perhaps ask: What picture does the foregoing discussion sketch out for those of us who believe that the task of art is to mediate, and that our relationship with nature is in dire need of renegotiation? The answer seems to lie in this direction: if we survey the field of possible artistic activity in Canada according to a pattern suggested by the Wacousta syndrome, we can distinguish three areas of endeavour.

The first, exemplified by painting, is based on the use of conventions and techniques that predate the arrival of the settlers; imported and deeply rooted in the traditions of foreign lands, the use of art forms of this type as symbolic mediators is possible, but fraught with difficulty. The positive side of their contribution is in their capacity to predispose and aid the subject in regard to a revision or renewal of his or her views, rather than actually effect a new relationship; the negative side is the ease with which these forms become avoidance strategies.

The second area, exemplified by film and video, is based on the use of technologies and conventions that, though they may have originated elsewhere, have developed concurrently with the growth of Canada as a nation, making them, in a sense, indigenous. Designed as tools for the storage, treatment, and communication of information, these forms possess immense powers as symbolic mediators and motivators but, like the urban context of which they are an integral part, they so distance nature that an effective relationship can be established only with great effort.

The third area, represented by the landscape garden, is based on direct collaboration with natural elements and processes at the point where the geosphere and the biosphere mesh together. As yet in the process of self-definition, work in this area, rejecting the romantic-ironic possibility of a "return to nature" modelled on an Adamic rediscovery of the Garden of Eden, is articulated in the tragic-comic axis of metonymy, promoting the use of ecological principles in the renegotiation of a relationship with nature that has simply not been working.

But discussing that would be another article.

Notes

1.   Gaile McGregor, *The Wacousta Syndrome: Explorations in the Canadian Langscape* (Toronto: University of Toronto Press, 1985).

2.   Thierry de Duve provides a pertinent and useful discussion of the work of art as auto-analytical in his book *Nominalisme pictural: Marcel Duchamp, la peinture et la modernité* (Paris: Éditions de Minuit, 1984). [*Pictorial Nominalism*, trans. Dana Polan (Minneapolis: University of Minnesota Press, 1991).]

3.   [Charles Gagnon, quoted by Philip Fry in *Charles Gagnon* (Montréal: Montréal Museum of Fine Arts, 1978), 27.]

4.   Gene Youngblood, "Icon and Idea in the World of Michael Snow," *artscanada*, no. 140/141 (February 1970): 7.

Michael Dorland

A Thoroughly Hidden Country:
Ressentiment, Canadian Nationalism,
Canadian Culture

> The object is to explore the huge, distant, and thoroughly hidden country of morality.
>
> Friedrich Nietzsche

> ... the Canadian cultural obsession with victimization is the flip side of a belief in total superiority.
>
> B. W. Powe

Introduction

> ... the most terrible antidote used against ... people is to drive them so deep into themselves that their re-emergence is inevitably a volcanic eruption.
>
> Friedrich Nietzsche

With the distinguished yet qualified exception of George Grant and the writings of some Canadian historians, the theme of *ressentiment* as such has been all too neglected in the critical literature on Canadian culture—not because the theme is a minor one in the Canadian discourse but on the contrary perhaps because it is so massively pervasive by its absence. In this negative form, *ressentiment* presents profound problems in the development of cultural expression and in the formation and application of a cultural politics that would include artistic practices, their institutional orientation, and critical interpretation—in short, the problems of Canadian culture. If, as will be argued here, *ressentiment* does, in fact, constitute a dominant theme explicitly in Canadian political and cultural practices and implicitly in the administrative practices of their institutional orientation, its nonrecognition hitherto in Canadian critical writing might indicate if not interpretive timidity then at least a strategy of avoidance worth examining in greater detail.

This is a shortened version of a text first published in *Canadian Journal of Political and Social Theory*, vol. xii, no. 1–2 (1988).

Ontology of Canadian *Ressentiment*:
The Discourses of Canadian Silence

> I had come to see that everything was radically connected with politics
> and that, however one proceeded, no people would be other than the
> nature of its government made it.
>
> Rousseau, Confessions

Forty years ago, reflecting on his "unhappy experiences" at academic conferences, Harold Innis had discerned a rhetorical pattern at such meetings,
namely that Americans and Englishmen, "quickly made aware of our sen-
sitiveness," spent much of their time commenting on how much better
things were done in Canada than in Great Britain or the United States. As
Innis observed, "The demand for this type of speech implies a lack of
interest in a Canadian speaker who might say something distasteful about
domestic affairs."[1]

As Innis would go on to explain, the "lack of interest" came not
from foreign guests, in any event invited only to praise, but from
Canadians and so suggested, as Innis was aware, the presence of something
more problematic than mere lack of interest. In fact, it suggested something deeply rooted in Canadian experience, the presence, as he put it, of
"a continuous repression" of "a very great fear of pronouncements"[2] by
Canadians. Indeed, it suggested that there was something, possibly dreadful, about Canada that only a Canadian might be able to utter "since ...
non-Canadians ... could not make statements about Canadian affairs
which would be taken seriously."[3]

But if tasteful statements about domestic affairs by non-Canadians
were not to be taken seriously and if there were such a great fear of distasteful pronouncements on the part of Canadians, when they actually
attempt to say something, their only recourse would be, as Innis put it of
his own experience, "writing in such guarded fashion that no one can
understand what is written."[4] What is being maintained in silence, and
silenced to such an extent as to suggest, again, something possibly more
considerable than lapses of taste?

The notion of a distasteful statement, however, provides a clue as to
what might be involved since the idea of taste suggests, narrowly, what
goes into or comes out of the mouth (as food, drink, or words) and so
more broadly an idea of politeness, manners, i.e., culture. The distasteful
statement, then, would be the expression of a form of culture (or perhaps,
more precisely, nonculture) whose *taste* has been so affected or altered in
such a way as to have become *distasteful*. As for the nature of that distaste,

suffice it for now merely to indicate its lack of specificity by way of a potentiality that could range from the merely unpleasant through the bitter to the extremities of the poisonous or even the monstrous. More important, however, might be the question of what happens when the mouth, i.e., the organ of communication and culture, is filled with unpleasantries to the point of becoming so unspeakable that these cannot be expressed openly, or its public forms of expression must, therefore, be subjected to rigorous policing or strict morality? What happens when a nation, i.e., a territorial configuration of mouths, establishes silence as the cultural norm for domestic affairs?

This paper will attempt to begin to account, by means of a theory of *ressentiment*, for the discrepancies between Canadians' very great fear of unauthorized pronouncements that Innis indicated and the mere talk of an officialized nationalist and culturalist discourse whose *precondition* is silence, i.e., the security that comes from knowing that nothing can ever be contradicted because nothing will ever be said. And security principally because, in William Kilbourn's grim formulation, *Canadian nature* "dreadful and infinite has inhibited the growth of the higher amenities in Canada":

> Outnumbered by the trees and unable to lick them, a lot of Canadians
> look as though they had joined them—having gone all faceless or a bit
> pulp-and-papery, and mournful as the evening jackpine round the
> edges of the voice, as if ... something long lost and dear were being
> endlessly regretted.[5]

Such an account must then begin with an interrogation of the nature of Canadian silence.[6]

Writing in 1986 some months after the opening of the then current (and largely secret) round of Canada-U.S. free trade talks, *Report on Business Magazine* editor Peter Cook remarked that "there is probably no better sign of our own maturity than the fact that the average Canadian spends twice as much on imported goods as the average American without feeling bitter or resentful about it."[7] The valorization of an absence of *ressentiment* is what one might term, after Innis, a tasteful Canadian statement about domestic affairs, especially when, according to Cook, Americans by contrast are not only bitter and resentful but also "pugnacious" and "xenophobic" as a result of *their* trade deficit. However, Cook went on, if Canadians display remarkable maturity by their absence of resentment and bitterness, American "tantrums and tirades" are nevertheless "particularly vexing" for Canadians who in opening the free trade talks "made the decision that America is the trade partner with whom they want to share their future."[8]

Cook's statement illuminates what Innis meant forty years ago, at least in part, by the "distasteful," namely, bitterness and resentment. But if, on Cook's account, Canadians today possess such maturity as not to feel bitterness and resentment on economic questions, they are still capable of feeling particularly vexed on other accounts, such as being rebuffed by the *trade* partner with whom they want to share their future. In other words, and contrary to what Cook writes explicitly, Canadians *do* implicitly feel economic bitterness and resentment and so much so that in addition they feel emotionally vexed as well. But vexation, like resentment, is an emotion or a form of expression that does not suddenly surface; rather, it is slow-burning and long-term. To say something is vexed, as in "a vexed question," is to say that it has occurred again and again, that it is tormenting, and that it is something that needs to be much debated and discussed. Like resentment, and perhaps this sense becomes clearer in its French form as *re-sentir* (literally, feeling again), vexation is experienced repeatedly, repetitively, compulsively, and obsessionally: "a gruesome sight is a person single-mindedly obsessed by a wrong."[9] Furthermore, Cook's use of metaphor suggests that Canadian vexation or resentment arises from a perception of intimacy and (fear of) the rejection of that proposed intimacy by a chosen partner. As for the gender of the chosen partner, Cook makes clear, by two references to American films (*Rambo* and *Conan the Barbarian*), how he regards at least one partner in the future relationship. The gender of the Canadian partner, however, is ambivalent: "[I]f the deal is not … rushed through Parliament and Congress, we will face a fresh administration in Washington which, like a spoiled child, will have to be tutored in the ways of the world anew."[10]

Canadian *denial of ressentiment*—the cultural celebration of silence as the highest form of our modernity—thus conceals a complex interlocking of multiple resentments: (1) a resurfacing of economic resentment that is, (2) then displaced to a general emotional resentment where it recharges itself as vexation, and, (3) is displaced again as an interpersonal relationship in which fear of (and resentment of) rejection causes it to shift once more to, (4) a moral plane now, where, from rebuff to rejection, Canada emerges radiantly as master of the ways of the world. In addition, Cook's use of what one could term a gender-bound metaphor (of the family, in which resentment is processed by morality and transformed into love, the rejection of which becomes an occasion for self-pity and so further resentment) evokes similar such recurrences in Canada's past that, as with the 1986 round of free trade talks, involved fundamental relationships and orientations in Canadian history, internal and external, in which metaphors of the family encode far greater violence. The first example is

internal and refers to the long and never-declared civil war between Canada and Québec, or what Hubert Aquin in 1964 called "the theme of the shotgun marriage" in Confederation, namely "the coexistence between two nations"—might this not equally apply to Canada and the U.S.?— "seems to form a venereal relationship pushed to a paroxysm of disgust, when it is not the very image of a Christian marriage, indissoluble and in ruins."[11] The second example is external (Canada's place in imperial relations) and thus entails a reversal in venereal relationships, from the aggressive waging of internal civil war to a more passive form of commodity transfer, here from one pimp (the British Empire) to another (the American Empire). As William L. Grant put it in a 1911–1912 address on "The Fallacy of Nationalism," "I have no desire that this country of mine should be either the kept woman of the United States, or the harlot of the Empire."[12] A third example from the time of Canada's entry into the Second World War sees an American writer describing Canada as "the problem child of the Western Hemisphere," a typical product of family estrangement with an Oedipus complex, where the mother country prevents the child from ever growing up. As the writer puts it, "Canada, exploded one of her resentful intellectuals, is in international affairs not a man but a woman!"[13]

In other words, and in a concretization of George Grant's "listening for the intimations of deprival,"[14] attending to intimations of *ressentiment* becomes a way of hearing Canadian silence speak. Instead of mere silence, following the chains of Canadian resentment soon unconceals discursive fields that extend from the landscape to economics, to politics, to sociology, to technology, to the intimacies of sexuality, and to the "higher amenities" of culture. What I'm suggesting here, in fact, is that there are few areas, if any, of Canadian experience where one is not struck by the extent to which the discourse upon that experience—whether acknowledged or repressed, whether official (government and press), intellectual (academic), or cultural (literary and artistic), to make some possibly arbitrary distinctions—is a discourse of *ressentiment*. All this may sound a lot more overwhelming than it might actually turn out to be; in fact, it may simply be a guarded way of saying that, so far perhaps, Canadian experience has been intensely given over to nursing the petty wounds of the small, as Denys Arcand has suggested in films such as *Le Confort et l'indifférence* and *Le Déclin de l'empire américain* or Harold Town, in his painting *Canadian Retirement Dream,* or the many other Canadian artists who, like Nietzsche's Zarathustra, may have sighed for a homeland where they need no longer "stoop before those who are small." But Canadian artistic expression may be just as imbricated with resentment as any other dimension of Canadian existence. The point is simply that, at the outset, we cannot know without a better grasp of Canadian *ressentiment*: what is it? how prevalent is it? how does it articulate itself? what have been its effects? and, last, how does one overcome it since, according to Nietzsche, *ressentiment* does not disappear without being overcome?

Ressentiment as a Concept for Cultural Studies

In contemporary cultural studies, *ressentiment* has been curiously under-employed, though I suspect that as Nietzsche increasingly comes to be seen as the philosopher of (the overcoming of) *ressentiment*, this state of affairs is likely to change.[15] Certainly, in some of its earlier applications including Nietzsche's, *ressentiment* would appear to offer an infinitely rich terrain for cultural studies. One can cite, for instance, Nietzsche's own characterization of the entire Judeo-Christian tradition as "the very seat of *ressentiment*,"[16] or Michelet's and Taine's use of *ressentiment* as the motive of the French Revolution,[17] or Simmel's ascription of *ressentiment* as "for all time the most solid support of bourgeois morality,"[18] or even Max Scheler's observation that "there is no literature more charged with *ressentiment* than Russian literature."[19] In more recent studies, one may cite Fritz Stern's identification of "the ideology of Resentment" as having appeared almost simultaneously in almost every continental country in the last decades of the nineteenth century, including as well in certain aspects of American Populism.[20] And, in film studies, one may look to historians of Hollywood (such as the British writer David Thomson or the American businessman Benjamin Hampton) who ascribe one of the key drives in American popular culture to *ressentiment*.[21]

In other words, even a brief overview of some of the applications that have been made of *ressentiment* might, potentially at least, indicate a concept for the study of cultural formations (e.g., religion, secular ideology, and forms of popular culture such as literature and cinema) in the wide range of countries or continents that could be embraced within such notions as "the Judeo-Christian tradition" or "bourgeois morality" or the Western tradition of political, social, and cultural modernity.

Perhaps *ressentiment* has not been adopted in recent scholarship precisely because it can be used to describe so many different cultural formations. One can only wait and see how the term will be used and developed in larger fields such as cultural studies. Indeed, in an extension of the Michelet-Taine hypothesis that *ressentiment* is the content of revolution, Fredric Jameson argues that "the theory of *ressentiment*, wherever it appears, will *always* ... be the expression and production of *ressentiment*."[22]

In other words, the production of *ressentiment* as a theory cannot be distinguished (or at least only with difficulty) from the production(s) of theorists. According to Jameson, "the intellectuals …—unsuccessful writers and poets, bad philosophers, bilious journalists, and failures of all kinds— whose private dissatisfactions lead them to their vocations as political and revolutionary militants … will furnish the inner dynamic for a whole tradition of counterrevolutionary propaganda from Dostoyevsky and Conrad to Orwell."[23] However, blaming intellectuals, whether revolutionary or counterrevolutionary, for the production of *ressentiment* is only restating the theory (or phenomenon) of *ressentiment* whereby, following Jameson's concept, "authentic *ressentiment*," once stripped of its bad faith, "may be said to have a certain authenticity,"[24] i.e., that *ressentiment*, like the rose by any other name, is *ressentiment*.

But what exactly is *ressentiment*? The word has no exact correspondence in German, but a German thinker (Nietzsche) introduced it into philosophy "in its technical sense."[25] Of Nietzsche and *ressentiment*, it might be possible to say—as Nietzsche remarked of Schopenhauer, "he had only one task and a thousand means of accomplishing it: one meaning and countless hieroglyphs to express it"[26]—that there are a thousand ways of defining *ressentiment* in its technical or other senses. Walter Kaufmann, for instance, finds it impossible to define *ressentiment* other than by quoting Nietzsche who in turn variously sketches *ressentiment* as "hatred," "tyrannic will," or "picture-hating drives" (Heine as quoted by Nietzsche).[27] Similarly, Scheler refutes not so much *ressentiment per se*, which, like Simmel, he considers as the basis of bourgeois morality and modern humanitarianism, but rather Nietzsche's charge that *ressentiment* is the content of Christian (or more precisely Catholic) love; but Scheler at least sidesteps Nietzsche to the extent of providing a working definition of *ressentiment* as:

> … the experience and rumination of a certain affective reaction direct-
> ed against an other that allows this feeling to gain in depth and pene-
> trate little by little to the very heart of the person while at the same
> time abandoning the realm of expression and activity, and this obscure,
> rumbling, contained exasperation, independent of the activity of the
> ego, engenders little by little a long rumination of hatred or animosity
> without a clearly determined object of hostility, but filled with an
> infinity of hostile intentions.[28]

Ressentiment is then not so much a theory (or at least it does not begin as a theory) as a (silent) feeling. To say what kind of a feeling *ressentiment* is, however, requires transforming it from an emotion into a theory, in other words, reducing Nietzsche to a theorist of *ressentiment* when, if anything, he was its greatest dramatist—not a preacher of *ressentiment* but the poet of its overcoming. Be that as it may, the Nietzschean definition of *ressentiment* employed here is one where *ressentiment* becomes a creative revolt:

> The slave revolt in morals begins by rancor turning creative and giving birth to values—the rancor of beings who, deprived of the direct outlet of action, compensate by an imaginary vengeance. ... Slave ethics ... begins by saying "no" to an outside, an other, a non-self, and that no is its creative act. This reversal of the direction of the evaluating look, this invariable looking outward instead of inward, is a fundamental feature of rancor. Slave ethics requires ... a sphere different from and hostile to its own ... it requires an outside structure in order to act at all; all its action is reaction.[29]

Let me elaborate this definition a little by suggesting, after Nietzsche, that *ressentiment* is the emotional content of the catastrophe of modern culture. The advent of modern culture—in the form of what Nietzsche called the three M's: Moment, Mode, and Mob,[30] and to which we can add a fourth, namely, Mood (and later perhaps a fifth: Movies)—entails a great silencing of everything else that was or might have been. If for Nietzsche, Western culture is the progressive advent of ever-larger *adiaphora*—spheres of nondeterminacy or the neutralization of difference (*diapherein*, to differ)—*ressentiment* is the mood of the *adiaphora*, the "absolute silence" of any other cultural possibility save (totalitarian) Modernity, its History, its Culture, and its multinational organization as States, which "[i]n their hostilities ... shall become inventors of images and ghosts, and with their images and ghosts they shall yet fight the highest fight against one another."[31]

In what follows, rather than extrapolating Nietzsche quotations, I'd like to illustrate this theory of *ressentiment* with particular reference to the forms of the "creative no" developed by one modern state, namely Canada, in its experience with the *adiaphora* of the history, culture, and multinational organization of modernity.

Ressentiment in Canadian Discourse: Cultural Implications

> ... there is a sort of mixture of inquisition and censorship which the Germans have developed into a fine art—it is called absolute silence.
>> Nietzsche, *Schopenhauer as Educator*

The greatest melancholy of the will, even the liberating will, and thus the source of its *ressentiment* and revenge-seeking, is its inability to change the

past: "Powerless against what has been done, [the will] is an angry spectator of all that is past."[32] As a result, according to Nietzsche, history, justice,
willing itself, and "all life" become a form of suffering or punishment:
revenge-seeking but with a good conscience. In such a form of suffering or
punishment—not so much a theory but "as an almost intolerable
anxiety"[33]—this corresponds to the *written* experience of Canadian history
and literature, in a word, the Canadian experience of culture, primarily in
the form of chronicles of the (usually deserved) administration of punishment. Thus, to take what would be, in effect, the first of innumerable
Royal Commission Reports, Lord Durham's 1839 report recommended
the "obliteration" of the nation (here French Canada) out of fear that "the
mass of French Canadians" would otherwise succumb to the "spirit of
jealous and *resentful nationality*."[34] Crushing the "resentful nationalities" of
North America (first French Canada, second—unsuccessfully—the
Thirteen Colonies, and third English Canada) "seems ... to have been ...
the policy of the British Government ... to govern its colonies by means
of division, and to break them down as much as possible into petty isolated communities, incapable of combination, and possessing no sufficient
strength for individual resistance to the Empire."[35] The absence of any
kind of revolutionary (or merely combinatory) disruption (of isolation) in
Canadian experience meant that the tradition of punitive administration
assumed a deep and uninterrupted development in the form of "a continuous repression" (Innis) of Canadian cultural expression as resentful
nationality (or in the more modern administrative discourse of the
Canadian state, "narrow nationalism"). What nationalism and culture
there would be in Canada would thus be: firmly Erastian, i.e., under the
authority of the state, both in character and in organization;[36] and, if not
under the control of the state, either marginalized, fragmentary, or nonexistent; or, if neither of the above, imported. In other words, in Canada
ressentiment takes the form of the administrative practice of an absent discourse on the relationship between nationalism and culture. This absence
is structured around its preservation and by the denial of the relationship
between nationalism and culture instituted as three separations: an administrative separation (known in the discourse of cultural policy as "arm's
length") of state cultural agencies from both nation and culture; an economic separation by the state of culture into public and private administrative realms; and a cultural separation by nationality where the content
of the public realm is officially (and incrementally) Canadian whereas that
of the private realm is unofficially (and exponentially) American.[37] To put
it in a less rebarbative manner, Canadian *ressentiment* articulates itself as
the three absent discourses of a social structuring of cultural contempt: the

contempt of the administrators for those whom they administer ("Inside every Canadian, whether she or he knows it or not, there is, in fact, an American"); the contempt of middle- and upper-class Canadians "concerned with the health and viability of Canadian culture"; and, finally, the contempt of lower-class Canadians who express their *ressentiment* in preferring American popular culture ("the more low-brow an American cultural activity, the wider its appeal in Canada").[38]

What characterizes these absent discourses as absences is that each forms a discursive whole whose rhetorical strategy, but not practices, consists in the denial of its own *ressentiment*. Thus, the discourse of Canadian cultural policy is always meliorative, though its punitive characteristics do transpire. One example from the cultural realm that has a long history in official Canadian policy is cinema. Peter Pearson, then head of the principal state agency responsible for feature film and television series production, reported in a speech to the Canada/California Chamber of Commerce that, "We, the private sector, and Telefilm now are fulfilling our joint goal: to be on network prime time and playing the mainstream, not only in Canada, but like the Hollywood studios, all over the world." I won't discuss the validity of the claim other than to note its similarity to Peter Cook's vision of Canada as master of the ways of the world. According to Pearson, this world-wide expansion of Canadian cinema is predicated upon and made possible by the silencing of the nationalism that had, until this point, been the content of Canadian films, though the blame for this is attributed to Canadian youth who must now be punished: "Now this 'national glue theory' is coming unstuck. The reality is that teenagers in Canada won't go to a Canadian movie if you pay them. Unless of course they want to." But as they don't want to, making them want to would henceforth be the thrust of Canadian policy; as Pearson put it, "Canadian fannies are going to have to fill the theatre seats, and Canadian eyeballs watch the programs."[39]

Similarly, the discourse of Canadian literary culture denies its double *ressentiment* (which would otherwise be directed upwards at the literary patron, the state, and downwards onto the antinationalist and uneducated masses, the cultural consumers) and instead replaces it with theories of victimization: *ressentiment* turned in upon itself as self-punishment. The clearest form of Canadian *ressentiment* comes from Margaret Atwood's classic, *Survival*: "Let us suppose, for the sake of argument, that Canada as a whole is a victim." The supposition, of course, soon becomes self-fulfilling: "[s]tick a pin in Canadian literature at random, and nine times out of ten you'll hit a victim."[40] If the perspectives of victim-production provide Canadian literature with a discourse that is not about *ressentiment*,

ATWOOD
CANADA
IS A
Victim

the problem with victims as a literary natural resource is that supplies run out unless consciously produced. As Atwood notes, the productive resources of victimization only become depleted over time and increasingly obscure, thus creating the (state-supported) demand on CanLit to produce another Canadian staple, like fur, wheat, or hydro-electricity: the culture-victim.

> In earlier writers these obstacles are external—the land, the climate, and so forth. In later writers these obstacles tend to become both harder to identify and more internal; ... no longer obstacles to physical survival but ... spiritual survival, to life as anything more than a minimally human being ... and when life becomes a threat to life, you have a moderately vicious circle. If a man feels he can survive only by amputating himself, turning himself into a cripple or a eunuch, what price survival?[41]

With that question—what price survival?—we come to the third and most literally absent discourse in Canadian *ressentiment*, namely the absolute silence of the Canadian public itself: glacial, inert, and so totally impenetrable that it can only be represented. "Have you no public opinion in that province?" a British statesman once asked Ontario's equivalent to Duplessis, Sir Oliver Mowat, while Sir Richard Cartwright, then Minister of Finance, commented severely on the worthlessness of public opinion in the same province.[42] This absolute silence, however, is presumed by the other Canadian discourses of *ressentiment* to be the one most driven by revenge-seeking and so most to be feared and despised. Here is the (presumed) source of the "resentful nationality" that, in the administrative discourse (Durham), "would separate the working class of the community from the possessors of wealth and the employers of labour."[43] Namely, they are the inhabitants of North America who, in Canadian historical discourse, "sometimes found their greatest and most malicious pleasure in the freedom to wreak upon their superiors the long locked-up hatred of their hearts";[44] a people who in Canadian literary discourse "make up for the[ir] meekness [in the province of public criticism] ... by a generous use of the corresponding privilege in private";[45] a people that Canadian philosophical discourse (George Grant) has designated as the majority population of the continent, the last men of an achieved modernity.

To dwell in modernity might thus be assumed to be the animus of Canadian *ressentiment*. The signs of modernity (population, urbanization, technologization, or in its cultural form, Americanization) would then be experienced with something akin to panic, an unbalancing and literal dislocation that Northrop Frye, in a profound insight, describes perfectly

FRYE (circled)

when he writes that, "... Canadian sensibility has been profoundly disturbed, not so much by our famous problem of identity ... as by a series of paradoxes in what confronts that identity ... less ... the question 'Who am I?' than ... some such riddle as 'Where is here?'"[46] If one understands Canadian *ressentiment* as such a dislocation, Frye's comments would suggest that the advent of modernity is accompanied by the inability to change not only the past (as in Nietzschean *ressentiment*) but also the present and future. William Norris, a Canadian author of the 1870s, expressed it, half-seriously: "Under the present system [in Canada] there is no past to be proud of, no present to give reliance, and no future to hope for. Devoid of national life the country lies like a corpse, dead and stagnant; but not so bad as it has been."[47]

This fear of loss—of one's place in time or history and in the space of community, of nation, of culture, in short, of group values—is what Frye calls "the real terror" of the Canadian (garrison) imagination, namely, the individuation that is also part of modernity, in which the individual is confronted with nothingness. "The real terror comes when the individual feels himself becoming an individual, pulling away from the group, losing the sense of driving power that the group gives him, aware of a conflict within himself far subtler than the struggle of morality against evil." Frye does not identify with this struggle, but I would suggest that it is a struggle of *morality as ressentiment denied*. Instead of engaging with this struggle, as Frye remarks, "It is much easier to multiply garrisons, and when that happens, something anticultural comes into Canadian life, a dominating herd-mind in which nothing original can grow. The intensity of the sectarian divisiveness in Canadian towns, both religious and political, is an example."[48] Denied, *ressentiment* proliferates, rooted in the Canadian social structure: "The garrison mentality is that of its officers: it can tolerate only the conservative idealism of its ruling class, which for Canada means the moral and propertied middle class."[49] Garrisons multiply, the anticultural herd-mind dominates, and "from the exhausted loins of the half-dead masses of people in modern cities"[50] (as Frye puts it in a rare display of his own *ressentiment*), the literature produced by the garrison (but now metropolitan) society "*at every stage*, tends to be rhetorical, an illustration or allegory of certain social attitudes."[51] The literature is rhetorical, as opposed to poetic (historical as opposed to mythic, documentary as opposed to imaginative, and single-mindedly obsessed with assertion as opposed to an autonomous literature) because, according to Frye, it avoids the theme of self-conflict,[52] the theme of *ressentiment*, preferring instead the self-inflicted punishment of a good conscience.

GARRISON
INDIVIDUATION

CANADIAN CULTURE

Ressentiment and the Canadian Mind:
Innis, McLuhan, Grant

If Canadian *ressentiment* can thus be understood as strategies for the avoidance of the (national and cultural) implications of modernity—even
though as Frye remarks, "Canada is not 'new' or 'young': it is exactly the
same age as any other country under a system of industrial capitalism"[33]—
does Canadian intellectual discourse share in the avoidance of
ressentiment? Taking the three "emblematic figures in Canadian thought"[54]
of Innis, McLuhan, and Grant, one would have to say that they too practise survivalist strategies of avoidance, but primarily by way of attempts at
displacing Canadian *ressentiment* onto larger transnational and technological entities. If Innis, McLuhan, and Grant write always guardedly of
Canadian *ressentiment*, their occasional lapses are, therefore, all the more
powerful.

Innis

Innis's most unguarded text, and perhaps his most blunt, is his 1947 "The
Church in Canada." "[I]n this country we are all too much concerned
with the arts of *suppressio veri, suggestio falsi.* 'The inexorable isolation of
the individual is a bitter fact for the human animal ... and much of his
verbalizing reflects his obstinate refusal to face squarely so unwelcome a
realization.'"[55] Thus the Canadian preference for public lies, the inertia of
public opinion, the notorious longevity of the political life of public
figures, and the settling of "all great public questions" on the basis of
petty, personal prejudices had for Innis "particular significance for the
fundamental corruption of Canadian public life."[56] The uninterrupted and
counterrevolutionary tradition of the dominance of church and state
bureaucracies in both English and French Canada (which allowed the
British to govern New France, brought Québec into Confederation, and
made possible Canadian resource development by government ownership
of canals, railways, hydro-electric, and communications facilities), had also
profoundly imprinted Canadian cultural development with what Innis
termed "ecclesiasticism." This comprised a Puritanical repression of art
and other expressions of cultural life, dogmatism, heresy trials, fanaticism,
and supination before the state's incipient totalitarian encroachments
upon civil liberties in general and intellectual freedom in particular.[57]
These aspects of the corruption of Canadian public life thus made it "not
only dangerous in this country to be a social scientist with an interest in
truth but ... exhausting."

52   *Michael Dorland*

On a wider plane it is a source of constant frustration to attempt to be Canadian. Both Great Britain and the United States encourage us in assuming the false position that we are a great power and in urging that we have great national and imperial possibilities. From both groups we are increasingly subjected ... to bureaucratic tendencies dictated by external forces. We have no sense of our limitations.[58]

Without once using the word, Innis manages in this text to provide what amounts to a model or research agenda for understanding Canadian *ressentiment*.

McLuhan

Though McLuhan did not write at any length specifically on Canada, in *Counterblast* (1954) he offered the following poem on Canadian culture:

> Oh BLAST
> The MASSEY REPORT damp cultural igloo
> for Canadian devotees of
> TIME
> &
> LIFE
> Oh BLAST . . . . (t)he cring-
> ing, flunkey spirit of Canadian culture, its
> servant-quarter snobbishness
> resentments
> ignorance
> penury
> . . . .
> BLESS
> The MASSEY REPORT
> HUGE RED HERRING for
> derailing Canadian kulcha while it is
> absorbed by American ART & Technology.[59]

In other words, Canadian culture, as one particularly resentment-charged idiom in the residues of European nationalist print-culture, would be (deservedly) punished for its *ressentiment* by being joyously ground into "cosmic talc" by the American crusher of art and technology. McLuhan's flight into the cosmos of the technological Pentecost of universal under-standing and unity[60] is thus but another version of the denial of Canadian *ressentiment* by a moralizing fantasy of world (or now cosmic) proportions.

In this sense, McLuhan, as Arthur Kroker has written, by the time "he became fully aware of the nightmarish quality of ... his thought ... he was ..., in the end, trapped in the 'figure' of his own making. ... In a fully tragic sense, ... he was the playful perpetrator, and then victim, of a sign-crime."[61]

Grant

In Grant, Canadian *ressentiment* is not denied qua *ressentiment*; on the contrary, it is universalized as the psychology of the "last men who will come to be the majority in any realized technical society."[62] (Saved perhaps by the "nemesis" of its aspiration to nationhood or at least protected by religious remnants of an identification of virtue and reason, Canada, for Grant, as for Frye, is not a realized but a "decadent" technical society.[63]) The will's despair at being unable to reverse or change the abyss of existence—life experienced as public and private fields of pain and defeat—becomes the spirit of revenge against ourselves, against others, against time itself. But the central fact about the last men is that because they cannot despise themselves, they can thus inoculate themselves against existence: "The little they ask of life (only entertainment and comfort) will give them endurance."[64] Because they *think* they have found happiness, the last men of the northern hemisphere in the modern age have not overcome *ressentiment* but "want revenge ... against anything that threatens their expectations from triviality."[65] Impotent to live in the world, "in their self-pity [they] extrapolate to a nonexistent perfection in which their failures will be made good." They are the last men because they are the inheritors of a decadent rationalism, the products of (resentful) Christianity in its secularized form.

Thus Grant's celebration of the defeat of Canadian nationalism in *Lament for a Nation*—"I lament as a celebration of memory"[66]—might be seen as a model for the overcoming of *ressentiment*, a Nietzschean exercise in *amor fati*: a willed deliverance from the spirit of revenge. In the realization that this "last-ditch stand of a local culture"[67] was not a trivial issue (unlike the branch-plant culture of the last men) but actually involves "the diamond stuff of which nationalists must be made in these circumstances," Grant suggests a heroic or noble acceptation of defeat:

> Perhaps we should rejoice in the disappearance of Canada. We leave the narrow provincialism and our backwoods culture; we enter the excitement of the United States where all the great things are being done. Who would compare the science, the art, the politics, the entertainment of our petty world to the overflowing achievements of New

York, Washington, Chicago and San Francisco? ... This is the pro-
foundest argument for ... break[ing] down our parochialism and
lead[ing] us into the future.[68]

But is this acceptation not, as Grant remarked of his "incomprehension"
of Nietzsche, simply too much demand? Would the defeat of Canada's
local culture be, in fact, an overcoming of *ressentiment* to the core of the
modern, technical civilization? For Grant, *amor fati* "seems to me a vision
that would drive men mad—not in the sense of a divine madness, but a
madness destructive of good."[69] In this sense, Grant implies that accepting
the defeat of Canadian nationalism would be such a form of madness—
destructive of the good. But what then would be the "good" of Canada's
local culture? Here, rather than further exploring Grant's writings, I
would like to submit that such a definition would be the (gratuitous)
undertaking of Canadian culture itself, in the Applebaum-Hébert Report's
sense that "the largest subsidy to the cultural life of Canada [has] come ...
not from governments, corporations or other patrons, but from the artists
themselves, through their unpaid or underpaid labour."[70] Defining the
good of Canada would thus be a "gift" to the nation from its artists.

Ressentiment and Canadian Visual Arts: The "Clichéization" of the Landscape

> One must guess the painter in order to understand the picture. But
> now the whole scientific fraternity is out to understand the canvas and
> the colours—not the picture.
>
> Nietzsche, *Schopenhauer as Educator*

Dennis Reid has suggested that "of all the arts in Canada, painting is the
one that most directly presents the Canadian experience."[71] However, if
there is any consistency to Canadian experience (and I have argued that
there is), the experience has been predominantly characterized by *ressentiment* and the quest for its relocation by distancing in a *meta*-Canadian
moralism, a *pan*-Canadian nationalism, and a *trans*-Canadian land-
scapism. In this sense, rather than directly presenting Canadian experience, Canadian art continues along the same trajectory of relocation that
one encounters in Canadian philosophy, historical writing, and literature.
As Vancouver artist Robert Kleyn has put it:

> Plagued by questions of identity, Canadian art often proposes prescrip-
> tive frameworks which easily lead to deciphering rather than interrogat-
> ing the authority of the representation behind the presentation. This
> identity is posed in terms of recognition, recognition outside Canada.[72]

That recognition, however, would be made possible, in D.G. Creighton's bitter observation, only "by abandoning a part, or the whole of [the artist's] own tradition or special point-of-view. ... A Canadian artist ... could either leave Canada for the metropolitan centre of his choice, or he could give up Canadian themes, except those ... regarded as quaint or barbaric, and therefore interesting, in the artistic and literary capitals of Western Europe and America."[73] But, in fact, there was another, and more intricate, possibility for the development of Canadian art as a strategy of avoidance of Canadian *ressentiment*, and I'd like to term this the "clichéization" of the landscape.

Between Confederation and the end of the nineteenth century, Canadian art followed no direction save that of "pleasing the public."[74] If most Canadian artists approached painting in the spirit of the age—to become rich fast—that spirit would increasingly be one marked by the development of mechanical (or photo-chemical) means of reproduction. The impact of the camera on Canadian art would be decisive as part of the "pragmatic materialism and commercialism [that] permeated the *whole fabric* of Canadian life."[75] Three elements may be singled out in a total transformative process affecting Canadian art: the *institutionalization* of art, the *commercialization* of artists, and the *mechanization* of vision.

The institutionalization of art, began with the Ontario Society of Artists, the Royal Society, and the Royal Canadian Academy of Arts. By the 1870s, this institutionalization was directed by the state (the Marquis of Lorne as Governor General) and modelled on the creation of "little replicas of British cultural organizations."[76] The process of stratification was distinguished by outbursts of *ressentiment* or a "marvellous amount of bitterness and bad language; half the artists are ready just now to choke the other half with their paint brushes."[77]

The commercialization of art amounted to the subordination of painting to photography and the rise of photographic firms such as William Notman of Montréal, Notman and Fraser of Toronto, and later the other commercial studios such as Toronto's Grip, the Brigden Organization and Phillips-Gutkin Associates in Winnipeg, and Graphics Associates in Toronto, all of which played essential roles in the development of modern Canadian art and film.[78] One example of the general subordination of painting to photography (though, according to Harper, photography would "indirectly encourage ... the spread of painting through Canada") may be found in the decision made by the Ontario Society of Artists' to hold their first exhibition (in 1873) at the Notman and Fraser Photographic Gallery in Toronto.

The aesthetic of Erastian institutionalization combined with commercialization produced a photographic vision or realism that, at its best, aspired to be "a precise clear reflection of the world." In Canadian terms, this vision meant the search for ever wilder Canadian terrain, a search that would culminate in the work of the Group of Seven. At its worst, such photographic realism was "pedestrian and laborious." In between, it led to a Canadian national style whose beginnings would be the production of the double volume entitled *Picturesque Canada* (1882). In this publication, a "veritable army" of artists, including American newspaper illustrators who had worked on the earlier *Picturesque America*, "made available to public and artists alike the first great series of locally produced Canadian scenes ... at a time when nationalism was being aroused on all sides."[79]

The problem posed by the "clichéization" of the landscape involves a major (and I'm tempted to say absolute) displacement. In part, this displacement is the media problem of the shift from landscape as a literary figure to landscape as a backdrop or cliché (from the German, *kitsch*, lump or mass, and thus its aesthetic, *kitsch*). In other words, this displacement may be understood as the shift from figure to image that Walter Benjamin understood as the annihilation of metaphor by the advent of "the long-sought image sphere ... the world of universal and integral actualities, where the 'best room' is missing—the sphere, in a word, in which political materialism and physical nature share the inner man."[80] To put it another way, the transition from literary to mechanized medium involved a double displacement of the Canadian landscape: first, the *objectification* of the vacant landscape (whose evacuation is an effect of *ressentiment*) as *reality*; second, the deterritorialized nonspecificity or *universalization* of a vacant reality by mechanical means. If American newspaper illustrators could readily produce Canadian scenes, American film crews would within a few years produce *Canadian* features shot entirely in the U.S., just as Canadian film producers would one day come to specialize in making *American* features shot entirely in Canada.

The annihilation, or at least uni-dimensionalization, of metaphor by the "clichéization" of the landscape thus naturalized Canadian silence to a degree that Canadian letters (or any literary medium, including newspapers) could never attain. Like the ownership of the land by the Crown, the development of Canadian communications would be a state-monopoly. But before making further references to modern media, I would like to examine the *ressentiment* produced by the Group of Seven's attempted revolt against the clichéd landscape.

If the members of the Group were "the first to speak loudly as consciously national Canadian painters,"[81] the search for something Canadian in painting had been the objective of several Toronto painters since the

1890s. But as Jock MacDonald said of one of his teachers ("the Canadian in him is not quite dead"), this objective kept getting "switched off the tracks,"[82] and the Group was no exception. Interruptions included World War I; Lawren Harris's training in Germany; Tom Thomson's dependency on photographs; and the "tremendous" impact of a 1913 exhibition in Buffalo of Scandinavian painting seen by Harris and MacDonald. The actual origins of the Group's "cult of Canadianism" (Harper) need not concern us here; what matters was that they felt they were painting *Canada*, and the *ressentiment* that such a presumption unleashed.

As Harper puts it, "Toronto critics in particular were so indignant that an observer could but assume they had been personally insulted." Harper also writes of an "incredible flood of adverse publicity," "massive criticism," and he cites Harris's claim that the first Group show (May 1920) produced whole pages in newspapers and periodicals of "anger, outrage, and cheap wit that had never occurred in Canada before."[83] Critics (and writers like Hugh MacLennan) saw alarming expressions of terror and violence in their work. Hector Charlesworth felt that the Group's work was detrimental to Canada's foreign image because it was likely to discourage immigration. Members of Parliament joined in the bitter criticism, hurling abuse and humiliation at the director of the National Gallery of Canada for his choice of Group of Seven paintings sent to the British Empire Exhibition at Wembley in 1924.[84] The Royal Canadian Academy "resented the Gallery's involvement in the organization of an international exhibition."[85] But the collective resentment suddenly evaporated when overseas critics pronounced that the Group's work was the most vital painting of the century. Within two years the Group was the acknowledged centre of serious art activity in Canada. By 1931, the year of their last group exhibition, "their supremacy was acknowledged—both grudgingly and willingly—right across the country."[86]

Perhaps the most problematic effect of the "clichéization" of the landscape—and in this sense Group *Canadianism* failed, becoming a suffocating artistic orthodoxy by the 1930s and well into the 1950s—is that it was the neutralization of the only valid emotional outlet for Canadian *ressentiment*.

Conclusion: Modernity, the Reactionary Landscape, and the Bias of *Ressentiment*

On a wider plane, it is a source of constant frustration to attempt to be Canadian.

Harold Innis

Is it possible to begin to situate Canadian *ressentiment*? I believe it is, if only to attempt to put the tormented question of Canadian *ressentiment* to, by now perhaps, a much deserved rest.

Since the Second World War, since Canada's full-scale integration into the American empire after a decade of proto-nationhood, there developed in Canadian literature and in literary criticism principally—more broadly speaking within the instrumentalization of the humanities—a largely southern Ontario school with a curious kind of awareness of the Canadian literary landscape. "I have long been impressed in Canadian poetry," wrote Frye in his 1965 conclusion to a literary history of Canada, "by a tone of deep terror in regard to nature."[87] Compare this statement with an observation of Emily Carr's: "I have often wondered what caused that fear, almost terror, of New York before I saw her."[88] I would like to suggest, therefore, that in the Canadian imaginary *nature* and *modernity* are one and the same, and both evoke an identical response: terror experienced as *ressentiment*. Terror is admitted in some cases, but more often, in what Gaile McGregor terms "the Wacousta syndrome,"[89] it is denied because it is terrible. However, the consciousness of terror, I would suggest, makes *ressentiment* the primary characteristic of the Canadian imaginary, *ressentiment* which is displaced or projected onto the landscape and so denies its own existence. Given that the landscape, or rather representations of the landscape, by their indexicality or referentiality can claim to point to, to refer to, or to show a "natural" or "objective out there," it may be possible to say that the landscape is the least mediated or noninstitutionalized form of Canadian ideas of modernity itself. Thus, the Canadian "identity" can only be said to be "fully integral to the question of technology," as Arthur Kroker has written,[90] in the sense of being dissimulated in the attempt to displace itself beyond the *ressentiment* occasioned by modernity. If McGregor is correct in defining Canadian being as "a kind of normalized duplicity,"[91] it becomes almost impossible to make a distinction between a threatening externality (for instance, technology or modernity or nature) and the internal core of that being itself (terror). Indeed, is it possible to assign limits to an imaginary?

But, for the sake of argument, taking the external threat as such (nature as terrifying), what this produces is Frye's garrison mentality or the reinforcement of institutionalization. If space is, as McGregor says, "the identifying feature of the Canadian interior,"[92] then it is space-binding institutions and techniques (nationalism, the state, communications, and culture) that are privileged as a result—but only to silence that space by binding it. The institutions of overcoming space are themselves subject to the same normalized duplicity. McGregor, analysing Canadian literature, uncovers a similar ambivalence, or as she terms it, "institutionalized ambivalence" with respect to institutions. "The state," she remarks, "is simply *alien,* and that's what makes it dangerous ... *society* in Canada is viewed as fearful specifically because it is *not* machinelike, predictable, mechanical but [because it is] prey to confusion and disorder. ... In Canadian literature ... the public world is somehow demonic, an utterly foreign element."[93]

If nature in Canada is terrifying and the Canadian social world is demonic, then what is safe? What becomes completely safe is precisely what is *genuinely* foreign, "machinelike, predictable, mechanical"—technology, or the empty will to will. But just to be absolutely preserved from experiencing Canadian *ressentiment,* this technology and this willing are preferable in their imported as opposed to indigenous (i.e., absent or silenced) forms. As McGregor puts it, "Judging by our literature ... many Canadians believe ... that for us ... symbolic capitulations to the victimizing forces are liberation"[94]—because capitulation, symbolic or real, is liberation from Canadian *ressentiment.*

I said earlier that these views of nature were characteristic of a largely southern Ontario school, i.e., were formed in the intellectual and cultural centre of Canadian modernity. However the "stable and restrained society of Ontario," as geographer Cole Harris remarked in an essay on the myth of the land in Canadian nationalism, "developed in an environment which has been less a challenge than a neutral backdrop."[95] If "the land," as Harris insists, "did not create tensions," then the landscape itself becomes the primary cultural myth of Canadian avoidance of its own modernity, namely, what the Canadian art historian David Solkin has termed "the landscape of reaction."[96] Canadian *ressentiment* would thus be the fullest form of the expression of Canada's *reactionary modernity*; it is a form of nostalgia that is itself a (purely mythical) dimension of modernity.[97]

If this is so, and in the light of what I've examined here, it may be enough to raise some questions in terms of both the pregnant interpretations and practices of Canadian cultural existence. Such a questioning would clearly, I think, bring to the forefront what I have argued is the dual displacement of the nature and institutions of modern Canadian nationalism and culture by a reactionary *ressentiment.*

If Canadian thought has excelled in comprehensive analyses of the biases of communications (Innis) and technology (Grant, Kroker), it would seem that this enterprise could be complemented only by an understanding of the bias of the culture that connects them. Then, and only then, might something of this huge, distant, and thoroughly hidden country of *ressentiment* emerge finally into view.

Notes

The epigraphs are from Friedrich Nietzsche, *The Genealogy of Morals,* trans. Francis Golffing (New York: Doubleday, 1956); Bruce W. Powe, *The Solitary Outlaw* (Toronto: Lester and Orpen Dennys, 1987); and Friedrich Nietzsche, *Schopenhauer as Educator* (South Bend, Indiana: Regnery/Gateway, 1965).

1.   Harold A. Innis, *Essays in Canadian Economic History,* ed. Mary Q. Innis (Toronto: University of Toronto Press, 1956), 383.

2.   Ibid., 386.

3.   Ibid., 387.

4.   Ibid.

5.   William Kilbourn, *Canada: A Guide to the Peaceable Kingdom* (Toronto: Macmillan of Canada, 1971), xiv.

6.   This approach is also the starting point for Marc Henry Soulet's study of the Québec intelligentsia, *Le Silence des intellectuels: Radioscopie de l'intellectuel québécois* (Montréal: Éditions Saint-Martin, 1987).

7.   Peter Cook, *Report on Business Magazine,* September 1986, 15.

8.   Ibid.

9.   Friedrich Nietzsche, "On the Adder's Bite," *Thus Spoke Zarathustra* in *The Portable Nietzsche,* edited and translated by Walter Kaufmann (Harmondsworth: Penguin, 1959), 180.

10.   Cook, *Report on Business Magazine,* 6.

11.   Hubert Aquin, "Le Corps mystique," *Blocs erratiques* (Montréal: 10/10, 1982), 105.

12.   William L. Grant, *Imperialism and Nationalism, 1884–1914: A Conflict in Canadian Thought,* ed. Carl Berger (Toronto: Copp Clark, 1969), 60–61.

13.   John MacCormac, *Canada: America's Problem* (New York: The Viking Press, 1940), 32.

14.   George Grant, *Technology and Empire* (Toronto: Anansi Press, 1969), 141.

15.   "Nietzsche's whole vision of history, his historical master narrative is organized around this proposition [*ressentiment*]." Fredric Jameson, "Authentic *Ressentiment*: Generic Discontinuities and Ideologemes in the 'Experimental' Novels of George Gissing," *The Political Unconscious* (Ithaca: Cornell University Press, 1981), 185–205.

16.   Friedrich Nietzsche, *The Will To Power,* edited by Walter Kaufmann and translated by Walter Kaufmann and R.J. Hollingdale (New York: Vintage, 1967), 100–101.

17.   Jameson, *The Political Unconscious,* 201.

18.   Georg Simmel, *Le Bourgeois*, trans. V. Jankelevitch (Paris: Payot, 1926), 411–412.

19.   Max Scheler, *Über Ressentiment und Moralische Werturteile* (1912), translated to French as *L'Homme du ressentiment* (Paris: Gallimard, 1970), 49, note 1.

20.   Fritz Stern, *The Politics of Cultural Despair* (Berkeley and Los Angeles: University of California Press, 1961), xx–xxi.

21.   See David Thomson, *America in The Dark: The Impact of Hollywood Films on American Culture* (New York: William Morrow, 1977), *passim*, and Benjamin B. Hampton, *History of the American Film Industry: From Its Beginnings to 1931* (New York: Dover, 1970), esp. ix–x.

22.   Jameson, *The Political Unconscious*, 202. Emphasis added.

23.   Ibid.

24.   Ibid., 205.

25.   Scheler, *L'Homme du ressentiment*, 11.

26.   Friedrich Nietzsche, *Schopenhauer as Educator* (South Bend, Indiana: Regnery/Gateway, 1965), 91.

27.   Walter Kaufmann, *Nietzsche: Philosopher, Psychologist, Antichrist* (New York: Meridian, 1956), esp. 319–325.

28.   Scheler, *L'Homme du ressentiment*, 11.

29.   Friedrich Nietzsche, *The Genealogy of Morals,* 170–171.

30.   Nietzsche, *Schopenhauer as Educator*, 69.

31.   Nietzsche, *Thus Spoke Zarathustra*, 213.

32.   Ibid., 251.

33.   Margaret Atwood, *Survival: A Thematic Guide to Canadian Literature* (Toronto: Anansi Press, 1972), 33.

34.   Cited in Anthony Wilden, *The Imaginary Canadian* (Vancouver: Pulp Press, 1980), 71. Emphasis added.

35.   Durham Report (1839) also cited in Wilden, 43.

36.   Innis, *Essays in Canadian Economic History*, 384.

37.   See for instance *Report of the Federal Cultural Policy Review Committee* (Ottawa: Information Services, Department of Communications, Government of Canada, 1982), 15. "We start from a view of Canadian society that sees it as an aggregate of distinctive spheres of activity. Each of these has its own values and purposes and its own network of institutions, interacting with one another in myriad ways but equal in their social importance. The political order—the state—is one of these great spheres and institutional systems; the cultural world is another." See also Theodor W. Adorno, "Culture and Administration," *TELOS*, no. 37 (Fall

1978): 93–111.

38.	John Meisel, "Escaping Extinction: Cultural Defence of an Unde-fended Border," *Canadian Journal of Political and Social Theory*, vol. 10, no. 1–2 (Winter/Spring 1986): 248, 252.

39.	"Telefilm Fund Ready to Make 'Movies,' Not 'Films,' Sez Pearson," *Variety*, December 3, 1986, 32. A certain sense of *déjà vu* or perhaps *déjà entendu* was echoed by the *Variety* writer's lead paragraph: "As it makes its decades-old pitch again to 'strike a new deal' in the international film industry and unhitch the 'old hegemony' of Hollywood, Canada is getting ready to make 'movies' rather than 'films.'"

40.	Atwood, *Survival*, 35, 39.

41.	Ibid., 33.

42.	Innis, *Essays in Canadian Economic History*, 386. See also A.R.M. Lower, *Colony to Nation* (Toronto: Longmans, 1946), 399.

43.	Wilden, *The Imaginary Canadian*, 71.

44.	D. G. Creighton, *Dominion of the North* (Toronto: Macmillan of Canada, 1967), 217.

45.	Sara Jeannette Duncan, *The Imperialist* (Toronto: McClelland and Stewart, 1961), 61–62.

46.	Northrop Frye, *The Bush Garden: Essays on the Canadian Imagination* (Toronto: Anansi Press, 1971), 220.

47.	William Norris, *The Canadian Question*, 1875, cited in Wilden, *The Imaginary Canadian*, 123.

48.	Frye, *The Bush Garden*, 226.

49.	Ibid., 236.

50.	Ibid., 135.

51.	Ibid., 231. Emphasis added.

52.	Ibid.

53.	Ibid., 135.

54.	Arthur Kroker, *Technology and the Canadian Mind: Innis/ McLuhan/Grant* (Montréal: New World Perspectives, 1984), 15.

55.	Innis, *Essays in Canadian Economic History*, 386.

56.	Ibid.

57.	Ibid., 385–389.

58.	Ibid., 392.

59.	Cited in Wallace Clement and Daniel Drache, *A Practical Guide to*

Canadian Political Economy (Toronto: James Lorimer & Co., 1978), 24. The poem does not appear in the Canada Council grant–supported subsequent editions of *Counterblast*: Toronto (1969), New York (1969), and Montréal (1972).

60.   See Kroker, *Technology and the Canadian Mind*, 80.

61.   Ibid., 86.

62.   George Grant, *Time as History* (Toronto: Canadian Broadcasting Corporation, 1969), 33.

63.   Ibid., 34–35. See also Grant, *Technology and Justice* (Toronto: Anansi, 1986), 100; and Joan E. O'Donovan, *George Grant and the Twilight of Justice* (Toronto: University of Toronto Press, 1984), 4, 87.

64.   Grant, *Time as History*, 33.

65.   Ibid., 40.

66.   George Grant, *Lament for a Nation: The Defeat of Canadian Nationalism* (Toronto: McClelland and Stewart, 1965), 5.

67.   Ibid., 66, 76.

68.   Ibid., 88.

69.   Grant, *Time as History*, 46–47.

70.   *Report of the Federal Cultural Policy Review Committee*, 4.

71.   Dennis Reid, *A Concise History of Canadian Painting* (Toronto: Oxford University Press, 1973), 7.

72.   Robert Kleyn, "Canadian Art or Canadian Artists?" *Vanguard*, vol. 14, no. 1 (February 1985): 29.

73.   Creighton, *Dominion of the North*, 578.

74.   J. Russell Harper, *Painting in Canada: A History*, 2nd ed. (Toronto and Québec City: University of Toronto Press and Les Presses de l'Université Laval, 1977), 180.

75.   Ibid., 181. Emphasis added.

76.   Ibid., 183.

77.   W. Stewart McNutt, *Days of Lorne* (Fredericton, 1955), cited in Harper, *Painting in Canada*, 184. See also Karen Davison-Wood, "A Philistine Culture? Literature, Paintings and the Newspapers in Late Victorian Toronto" (Ph.D. diss., Concordia University, 1981), 121.

78.   Harper, *Painting in Canada*, 182–183. See also Gene Walz, "Flashback: An Introduction," in *Flashback: People and Institutions in Canadian Film History*, ed. Gene Walz (Montréal: Mediatexte Publications, 1986), 9–15; John Porter, "Artists Discovering Film: Postwar Toronto," *Vanguard*, vol. 13, no. 5/6 (Summer 1984): 24–26.

79.   Harper, *Painting in Canada*, 180, 183, 194.

80.   Walter Benjamin, "Surrealism: The Last Snap-shot of the European Intelligentsia," trans. Edmund Jephcott, in *Reflections*, ed. Peter Demetz (New York: Harcourt, Brace, Jovanovitch, 1978), 192; see also Abraham Moles, *Psychologie du kitsch: L'art du bonheur* (Paris: HMH, 1971).

Benjamin ←

81.   Harper, *Painting in Canada*, 288; see also Ramsay Cook, "Landscape Painting and National Sentiment in Canada," *The Maple Leaf Forever: Essays on Nationalism and Politics in Canada* (Toronto: Macmillan of Canada, 1977), 158–179.

READ ←

82.   Cited in Harper, *Painting in Canada*, 264.

83.   Ibid., 263, 279.

84.   Ibid., 288.

85.   Reid, *A Concise History of Canadian Painting*, 151.

86.   Ibid., 152.

87.   Frye, *The Bush Garden*, 235.

88.   Emily Carr, cited in R. Cook, *Maple Leaf Forever*, 158.

89.   Gaile McGregor, *The Wacousta Syndrome: Explorations in the Canadian Langscape* (Toronto: University of Toronto Press, 1985).

READ

90.   Kroker, *Technology and the Canadian Mind*, 12.

91.   McGregor, *The Wacousta Syndrome*, 53.

92.   Ibid., 13.

93.   Ibid., 173.

94.   Ibid., 229.

95.   Cole Harris, *Nationalism in Canada*, ed. Peter Russell (Toronto: McGraw-Hill, 1966), 27–46.

96.   Neil McWilliam and Alex Potts, "The Landscape of Reaction," *The New Art History*, ed. A.L. Rees & F. Borzello (London: Camden Press, 1986), 106–119.

READ SOON

97.   R.K. Crook, "Modernization and Nostalgia: A Note on the Sociology of Pessimism," *Queen's Quarterly*, vol. 73, no. 2 (Summer 1966): 289–283. "Nostalgia is a morbid activity which does not require the presence of a set of past events which did in fact occur, in the sense that one experienced them in their pure form at some previous [sic] time period. To be nostalgic is to enter the world of half rememberance and half fantasy in which uniquely created images refer to carefully cherished and mainly mythical interpretations, but which provide a secure retreat from present realities."

NOSTALGIA Q
useful for films

Bruce W. Ferguson

Northern Noises

The grand narrative has lost its credibility, regardless of what mode of unification it uses, regardless of whether it is a speculative narrative or a narrative of emancipation.

Jean-François Lyotard

Until recently, Canadian artistic practices provided two exemplary narratives of historical modernism.[1] The first of these stories might be called "The Grand Silence." In this story, the basic alienation of a single subject, which is the very core of Western modernist thought, manifests itself in two aesthetic legacies. Through iconography, the landscape schemata are employed and privileged, from early nineteenth-century military watercolours all the way to present-day regional representation. The lonely "survival" (Atwood's term for the cognitive style of most writing) of a pioneer existence in a harsh environment that has haunted Canadian literature and poetry is symbolized by a single pine tree clinging tenaciously to a rock, the cipher of the nationally famous Group of Seven. This first enduring instance of modernism, then, is romantic documentary in style and is characterized by a break with the *natural*, a schism between man and nature made comprehensible only by artistic descriptive control. From the position of one of the "solitudes" (French or English) a *loss* is inscribed in a narrative that pits the voyeuristic tourist sensibility against unassailable and forever willful forces of flora and fauna, conquered only in the mediated form of art.

In its second enduring instance which begins later but, as the first, continues to the present day, "The Grand Silence" again privileges the alienation of the individual in a narrative of *loss*—this time from motivated and dominant social forces. It is written here along two opposing stylistic lines. Existential abstraction, employing either geometric or organic schemata of hermeticism, responds to an increasingly mechanically-determined social environment by emphasizing subconscious structures or feelings. This imported school demonstrates a private-language humanism—an élitist and idealist reaction to popular culture's impositions and perceived degradations by uses of subjective critical standards. It is Canada's closest version of an international avant-garde and thus represents its most

Versions of this text were published in *Vanguard* (December/January 1987–1988) and in *Northern Noises* (Winnipeg: Winnipeg Art Gallery, 1987).

radical volunteer colonialism. Urban shamanism, on the other hand, unlike its name's suggestive origins in the symbolic and ritualistic, is characterized by *logical* attempts to deconstruct dominant social forces through figurative and media-representational modes increasingly dependent upon imported textual explanations—yet another volunteer colonialism. Such works attempt to exorcize rationally naturalized social politics while remaining bound to traditional contexts of art production and distribution. In both these responses—abstractions and shamanisms informed by the existentially subjective and the academically tenured—styles and subjects are often borrowed, and ambitions are modest. The effects of the frequently sad laments of "The Grand Silence" are most often conservative enough to create an ideological space easily reterritorialized by official culture's rhetoric in the names of nationalism, regionalism, or even, as in Toronto, localism.

The second of the Canadian stories might be called "The Technological Empire." Here, the subject is inscribed by and enmeshed in an environment of (past) transportation and (present) telecommunications in a country always in the hopeful state of becoming a unity through institutional networks. "The Technological Empire" finds the subject of its discourse more complexly alienated from the country due to its sheer cultural diversity and overwhelming physical dimensions. One scenario tries to overcome the rupture by utilizing positivistic measures of technocracy. Or, conversely, the expanded technocratic system is seen as the very cause of social alienation. However, in both the technophilic and the technophobic responses, "The Technological Empire" remains the more fully articulated narrative of Canadian modernism to date. Its versions are told by active liberal and conservative politicians and bureaucrats, as well as artists and aesthetic theoreticians: men (it must be said) like Harold Innis, George Grant, Marshall McLuhan, Edward Carpenter, Glenn Gould, Pierre Elliot Trudeau, Pierre Juneau, Michael Snow, Robert Fulford, Jeff Wall, David Cronenberg, Leonard Cohen, to name just a few. For them, there is either a communications problem and/or solution. For some, it is *always* an empire that can be conquered by just one more national commission, one more underground cable, or one more on-line satellite hook-up. For others, it is *always* an empire that has been created and would be maintained by radical policies—delimiting technoservices in order to preserve a difference of innocence from the centralized dynamo of America. In "The Technological Empire," technological dependence and progressive state independence are intertwined in complex scenarios of competing visions.

Both of these discourses have historical exceptions that cannot be pursued here, historical instances of resistance, but both still have a pre-

dominant currency in discussions of art in Canada.[2] "The Grand Silence"
and "The Technological Empire" are both documentary and nationalistic
in tone, with artists recreating the unimaginable space of a nation (or
region or town) through iconographic ideology. At first look, the two narratives seem polarized in relation to one another: the natural privileged in
one and the cultural (technologies, languages, bureaucracies), in the other;
the exterior experience in opposition to the interior experience; the passive
lament versus the active ritual, and so on. Yet, they are in fact mirror
images, homogeneous at another level—the level of their accommodation
to the modernist notion of alienation in general and to the negative totalizing effects of outside forces (reductive determinisms) in relation to the
subject in particular. Both narratives seek and find alienation as a guiding
motivation for aesthetic responses, and both are jingoistic in their
affiliation to a national construction of this alienation. But both are forms
of reductive determinisms, discourses that converge precisely because they
do not allow for the intersubjectivity of experiences, do not allow for the
ways in which subjects resist their melancholy authority.

However, convincing arguments have suggested that the break from
the "archaic" to the "modern," which has dominated consciousness for a
few centuries, has been superseded or eclipsed by another rupture widely
understood as significant enough to deserve the term "post" in relation to
the modern. This rupture, as the Lyotard quote at the opening suggests, is
signalled in a globalizing culture by a diminished purchase on the ideology
of the bourgeois liberal notion of the individual separated from the claustrophobic idea of progress *per se*. The premises and parameters of this
postmodernism are thoroughly debatable, and theoretical and textual for
the most part. But it is what it seems to mean for art in recent Canadian
practices that its importance lies here.[3]

> The Canadian discourse is neither the American way nor the European
> way, but an oppositional culture trapped midway between economy
> and history. This is to say that the Canadian mind is that of the in-
> between: a restless oscillation between the pragmatic will to live at all
> costs of the Americans and a searing lament for that which has been
> suppressed by the modern technical order. ... Canadian thought forces
> the question of what is the most appropriate response to the technolog-
> ical dynamo.[4]

Arthur Kroker's provocative claims, always exaggerated and always insight-
ful, provide another entry into the classical Canadian narratives. In his
summation of Canadian modernism by three of its principal theoreticians,
he suggests three tangents within the Canadian experience which he
names "technological dependency" (Grant), "technological humanism"

(McLuhan), and "technological realism" (Innis). By Kroker's isolation of the theses it is possible to see that if modernism is reperceived or "over" or heightened to another qualitative stage, then both the dependency and humanist theories, despite their important contributions historically, are inadequate to today's conditions. Both are registers of an idealism now defunct. The special alienation claimed for modernist artists has been eclipsed by a spectacular reception of their art forms as luxury entertainment and capital investment, and alienation itself is maintained as the very necessary base of all consumer activity. And progress is circumscribed: by past and continuous violence to humans and land on progressively massive scales on the one hand; with the ever-present threat of the future as complete techno-annihilation on the other. Even utopia as self-transformation has little credibility on a new fully cynical agenda, and utopia as folly has been the grim post–World War II reality. Thus, a kind of "realism" is what is available as a response today, a realism that includes the very contingencies unavailable to the idealism of the modernist avant-garde programme.

If the model of Innis's realism is helpful in suggesting a reconsidered realism in Canadian aesthetics, it is because his own intellectual example offers the very oscillation between sentimental European history and pragmatic American power, between theory and practice, emotion and cognition, or between philosophy and politics necessary for a balance today between such predictable extremes. Such intellectual tight–rope walking was as risky as Jean-François Gravelet's (Blondin) walk over Niagara Falls in 1859 from the American to the Canadian side of the rapids, but it was Innis's achievement to provide a sustaining example of rigorous coordination against normative vertigo in his studies of the biases of communication. Without considering here his important empirical work on economic history through staples theory, it is in his particular argument concerning the necessity to recreate the attenuations against pure logic, most importantly through poetics, that he offers an inspiration to the realism imagined here. In his own words it is *dialogue* in which "the life and movement of dialectic opposed the establishment of a finished system of dogma" that must be sustained. It is in his sense of the oral (of sound and noise), in which the "individual continued in a constant struggle with language and brought about constant adjustment" against written "definitive forms," that a realism not of "descriptive control" is relevant to today's productions.[5]

Or, more specifically, it is Innis's sense of restoring *time* to a culture dominated by space (or spatial management) that is critical to this emergent art. Duration is now privileged in offsetting linear classification and its consequent monopolies of knowledge. Such oscillation, which then includes para-language (historical moments, a speaker's gestures, postures, nuances of colour, gender, class, and contexts of reception, etc.), denies progress and does not privilege individual perception as much as it demands of each communication act a renegotiated and precarious balance to be achieved for effectiveness. This realism is thematized here in relation to an art that engages processes over products, experiences over texts, and heterogeneous responses over unity.

In saying this I am deliberately posing "realism" as an oscillation and confronting Kroker's and many others' use of such artists as Alex Colville, Christopher Pratt, or Ernest Lindner as "realists," as well as those who use "realism" to describe a whole documentary tradition well-known in Canadian film and photography. There is another lesser-known documentary, "realist" moment in the modernist fine arts of Canada, which includes the conceptual works of the N.E. Thing Co. and even the conceptual abstractions of Ron Martin. His painstaking record of painting procedures and materials forms an interesting but consistent version of the traditional "realist" position. What I am arguing here is that these older "realisms" are ones of descriptive control, giving precise, completed, and static images to what is only and must remain a process, an ongoing movement.

If there has in fact been a rupture in these discourses (without going into either its disputable causes or its contested terminology here)—a disaffiliation with the romantic individualism or the positivist progressivism of those technological versions of modernism within an imaginary nationhood—then it is beginning to be identifiably registered in a newfound and redefined realism that responds complexly to these new impulses and demands. This other art is being called "Northern Noises" here, referring to noise in both the literal and the metaphorical sense by virtue of the works' grating relationship to previously correct and closed discourses. This realistic model is being presented to represent best the situation today against the convergence of the silence and the empire. The work presented in this exhibition disrupts the comfortable reception expectations of the two classical narratives outlined above and is, by contrast, particular, intersubjective, incomplete, contradictory, and performative.

> The utopia in great art is never the simple negation of the reality principle but its transcending preservation (*Aufhebung*) in which past and present cast their shadow on fulfilment. The authentic utopia is grounded in recollection.[6]

It is perhaps not peculiar nor coincidental that a marginal economy, one of the principal subjects of Innis's work, is historically responsible for the conditions that have allowed such artistic practices to develop critically in Canada. Government intervention, the necessary mainstay of a politically dependent nation, has provided an economic system and network of artistic support during the past decade which in turn has developed to provide a counterproposition to the rigidities of this government's own tendencies towards cultural icons. Art in Canada has matured in the past decade primarily due to artists' own efforts and their own counterinstitutions outside a commercial market or, more specifically, outside of the considerations of a privately moneyed collecting system and outside of the centres of media power. Similarly, this alternative system has evolved counterpractices to traditional museums, in terms of values and forms, emphasizing artists' concerns for the contexts of distribution. The results have been a very significant kind of work that deals with its own conditions of presentation and its relation to audiences without suffering the pressures of the fashions of commodity art.

The kinds of inversions available in the works of Kim Adams, Eleanor Bond, Roland Brener, Geneviève Cadieux, Wyn Geleynse, and Barbara Steinman are substantive precisely because they open themselves to critical engagement through drama and contingency in the nature of their installations. Bond, for instance, inverts the nineteenth-century "bird's-eye view" of property description imagery by positing the image in the future (perhaps the near future). The private pride in the subject of both the patron and artist in the nineteenth-century genre can become an ironic public space in the twentieth. Bond's pictures are a future memory (a vision of the saturation of technology into a region's natural resources) fused to the present by escaping the scopophilic ideology, but not the precision, of past iconographical methods. Or Geleynse can re-render the spectacular privacy of movies through technological interventions that allow the rooms for his projections to remain light and public and introduce his personal memory (a home movie) as an indice of the social memory. Steinman's work in this exhibition is a direct appeal to social memory by re-presentation of absence. The technologies of classification and social subjugation are subtly reused by her to force presence from absence, remembrance from reification, and poetry from rhetoric.

Cadieux dramatizes the act and institution of seeing, of voyeuristic control of the subject, and of its links to a real *polis*. She aggrandizes the documents and dramatizes the act of "capturing" at a scale at which intimacy becomes public knowledge. Brener literalizes "noise" through radio frequencies, tuned to the present conditions of the viewer, and movement in the same space. Although his salvaged materials pay homage to formalist modernist sculpture as a skeletal base, his methods rupture the absolutist and static in favour of the literal and temporary. And Adams's works likewise pay ironic tribute to earlier abstract sculptural traditions while incorporating the banal and everyday materials of industrial products into the moving (often literally) and suggestively connotative spaces of the social. In the full fluorescent light of postmodern reality Adams suggests the possible interrelation between art and life in a productive encounter.

Innis argued persuasively that institutions and bureaucracies are biased in favour of space with all of the powerful implications of the hegemony of the visual that it implies. The new-found realism is, by contrast, a reminder of the "lived tradition" which takes place in time. Long before postmodernism became popularized, McLuhan described Innis's view of progress. It was, he wrote, "a theme that would have brought out his wit and humour, and his entire writing stands as a testimony against this popular assumption."[7] The argument for an orientation to time that will counter an orientation to space, taken in microscopic terms at the level of art institutions, is an argument against museological and art historical priorities towards the autonomy of the image.

The renewed realism, which is being discussed here, forces museums and their professionals to account for tactility (which confronts the modernist stricture "do not touch"), movement (which confronts the latent religiosity in still pictures and sculpture), sound *per se* (which destroys the hushed and reverent environment so much like the church it replaces), the technical/mechanical (which confronts curatorial and conservationist distancing by demanding active maintenance), and performance (which produces unexpected and sometimes disruptive audience responses). *Northern Noises* attempts to overcome the schisms of Canadian modernism's alienating narrative of loss by favouring a renewed perceptual and social ground through the staging of "events"—rich with intentions and interpretations, volatilities, revisions, and resistances. There is an emphasis on process producing the noise of change in this reconsidered realism of poetics, a deliberate abdication of certainty in favour of a contingent object that begins the oscillation back to time and, thus, to common ground. There is a concentrated and conscious vulnerability here that is now an indispensable cultural response to prior historical reifications.

Notes

The epigraph is from Jean-François Lyotard, *The Postmodern Condition: A Report on Knowledge*, trans. Geoff Bennington and Brian Massumi (Minneapolis: University of Minnesota Press, 1984).

1.   This text combines two versions of "Northern Noises," the first published in *Northern Noises* by the Winnipeg Art Gallery for the 1987 São Paolo Biennial, and the second published in *Vanguard*, vol. 16, no. 6 (December/January 1988): 10–13. The exhibition included the works of Kim Adams, Eleanor Bond, Roland Brener, Geneviève Cadieux, Wyn Geleynse, and Barbara Steinman.

2.   Most of these exceptions would be fairly recent and might include specific pieces rather than whole bodies of work (e.g., Betty Goodwin's *Rue Mentana*). But a partial list of Canadian artists whose work exemplifies specific traits of this resistance through "poetic realism" includes Lyne Lapointe and Martha Fleming, Rita McKeough, Max Dean, Michael Fernandes, Joey Morgan, Mowry Baden, Tony Brown, Carol Wainio, Raymond Gervais, and Al McWilliams, plus a full complement of performance and video artists over two decades. For a fully realized articulation of just two artists working with contingent means, see Russell Keziere, "Hermes in the Agora: Art and the Erotic Life of Meaning," *Vanguard*, vol. 16, no. 3 (Summer 1987): 18–23.

3.   For a list of the "posts" that surround the field of consideration see Dick Hebdige, *Hiding in the Light: On Images and Things* (London: Comedia, 1987). Also see Hebdige, "A Report on the Western Front: Postmodernism and the 'Politics of Style,'" *Block*, no. 12 (Winter 1986–1987): 4–26. I would add to his list the computer POST (preliminary operating systems test) which is performed before the user's "read and write" memory (RAM) is available for "volatile manipulation." Lyotard intuits this use of "post" when he associates the beginning of postmodernism with "the computer revolution dating from 1965, with the new generation of IBM 360s." From R.M. Ashby, "La Seconde Génération de la micro-électronique," *La recherche*, vol. 2 (June, 1970): 127 ff.

4.   Arthur Kroker, *Technology and the Canadian Mind: Innis/McLuhan/Grant* (Montréal: New World Perspectives, 1984), 7.

5.   Harold A. Innis, *Empire and Communications*, revised by Mary Q. Innis (Toronto: University of Toronto Press, 1972).

6.   Herbert Marcuse, *The Aesthetic Dimension: Toward a Critique of Marxist Aesthetics* (Boston: Beacon Press, 1978).

7.   See Innis, *Empire and Communications*, particularly chapter four "The Oral Tradition and the Roman Empire."

Marcel Saint-Pierre

Idem

Under the present circumstances, any attempt to deal with Québec's cultural identity may initially cause a certain amount of surprise, for the very timeworn nature of this question now creates the impression that it just popped out of the blue. The present period seems so ill-inclined to draft a collective project, especially one that has a nationalist agenda, that the legitimacy of the issue has been compromised. Rare is the politician who can even mention it in a speech without losing some of his or her credibility. The difficulty one encounters in trying to revive this issue—this legitimate issue, one should say—is symptomatic of the apparent dissolution of the social contract for the sake of its individual constituents, of the loss of that consensus which, until recently, enabled a community to launch itself into the future or to represent itself in an emancipatory light. Recent assessments of the preceding period and its nationalist project have voiced feelings of disenchantment, spoken of the end of illusions and of a "lost community."[1]

Given the current decline of just about every kind of "empire," the crisis of social vision is not restricted to Québec. The general climate in this *fin de siècle* tends to favour reaction. In the field of art, in the ten years or so that have elapsed since the end of formalism's hegemony, this climate has led to the return of the repressed. By the latter I mean, among other things, figuration and neo-expressionism, under whose tutelage the most exacerbated forms of subjectivity (forms which were apparently of no use to the preceding period) have returned to the fore, paradoxically bringing to light a whole range of already-familiar forms and content. I am not implying that we should see this as an inane projection into the past, one that would take the place of alternatives focused exclusively on a collective future—an ideal to be attained or a project to be implemented—because this new attitude is also shared by artists who, in returning to the same repressed materials, take a critical, if not contrary, stance towards these avatars and do not confuse novelty with tradition or, to speak in art market terms, periodic influxes of "antiquities" with transformations of our cultural heritage. In this realm, as in others, the notion of history as future- or progress-oriented is opposed by a so-called posthistoric vision of the modernist system of avant-gardes and their social function, while the

This is a translation of a text first published in *ETC*, no. 1 (1987).

inexhaustible wealth of multiple pasts and the fruitful exploitation of their heritages have tended more and more to provide the material for both trendy retrograde work and truly experimental approaches to artmaking.

It is not up to me to pass judgement on all these familiar, overly numerous variations; let me say, however, that it is not uncommon to find, in the markets that cater to them, distributors who in the name of novelty make nationalist or even regional claims for work whose producers were, for the most part, interested only in taking up concerns and reconquering territories that had been set aside by modernism. These reappropriations, which it has suddenly become imperative to situate somewhere beyond the avant-gardes punctuating the history of modern art, have enabled some artists to rediscover earlier subjects and allegories, while others, in trying to scale down the burden of their past, have advanced a Berlin style of art; meanwhile, in Italy, similar readaptations are promoted to the rank of the trans-avant-garde. This, all too briefly, is what distinguishes the current attitude from the view that, for more than a century, based its notion of the avant-garde on the founding myth of modernity, on the hope of a historical or, perhaps, even "revolutionary" project.

Thus it is not surprising that the current step backward is a disillusioning experience for some. The aspirations that formerly shaped avant-garde ambitions have been replaced by an expansion of the market to encompass antiquated national characteristics and local colour. Such resurgences, however, do not come without a measure of worrisome regression. By indiscriminately legitimating almost every kind of product, the market substitutes the proliferation of novelties for those "values in action"[2] that, according to Pierre Gaudibert, the concept of "the new" represented for the avant-garde. In response to the cultural imperialism and consumer strategies of large market economies, the current view rejects the modernist logic of the avant-garde with its talk of rupture and the latter's corollary, revolution.

Contrary to the stylistic uniformity engendered by the modernist model, particularly the cultural standardization instituted by mass communication and the complexities of modern technology, resistance today is defined by the affirmation of subjective differences, appeals for stronger regional identities, and the revival of local issues; all things considered, it calls for a return to an art bound up with such national characteristics as place, language, and tradition. This is why we should not be surprised by the fact that contemporary art discourse has again made it fashionable, above and beyond any conceivable political or collective vision, to traffic in the romantic myth of the artist and his/her inalienable singularity.

Not so long ago, barely a decade in fact, a good many of us—if not an entire generation—were content to see our various artistic practices as stylistic, if not theoretical, extensions of neo-plasticism as well as a sur-rational automatism. Independently of this connection (it wasn't the only one) and the "para-automatist" label, and regardless of the occasionally mechanistic or often plainly simplistic interpretations of this "position-ing," developments then taking place in the international avant-garde made it important for us to inscribe our work and its foreign influences within the specific context of Québec. However uncertain it may have been, this perspective is diametrically opposite to today's brand of one-way re-examination. If I may be permitted to situate the most recent revision of past art outside of history, the forms this revision has taken obvi-ously allow no room for any artistic programme for anything resembling the community values that have been espoused so far—I mean the kind of values associated with an art that, by definition or "almost by definition," saw itself as revolutionary and tied its capacity for formal renewal to the possibility of a better world.

Despite the many accomplishments to their credit, this political view with the very belief in progress now find itself without support. Its career exudes the musty smell of lost causes! The bittersweet glance cast nowadays upon this dissolution of links susceptible of forming organic bonds between artists and art collectives, or between artists and larger social movements, reminds me of a chapter in my own life, of a past in which the future loomed large. I am not, however, saying that this period was entirely taken up with the future or with blind idealism; it is just that the social issues that came to the fore, like certain things one felt obliged to overcome (by means of perpetually new artistic strategies), made up the fabric of a common history. For most of us back then, this was the history of a small community [un "petit peuple"][3] which, in seeking to cast off its fears (the "links in the chain"), envisioned the eventual birth, in a revolt[4] that would be more or less "quiet," of the "collective hope" of liberation from ancient servitude.

Thus it happened (at least with the events of 1968–69 and with the challenges to institutions issued by *Opération Déclic*)[5] that the unrest of the moment drew upon this first sociocultural revolt and paved the way for a "tradition of opposition"[6] descended directly from Borduas's *Refus global*. Now, it is in this crucial period of our very recent history, when the question of cultural identity was the order of the day, that we must also situate the henceforth celebrated polemic engendered by Marcel Rioux's division of Québec's ideological climate into survival, "catch-up," and lib-eration ideologies.[7] Begun before the invasion of the "international style" of the 1970s, this debate cut through the morass of upcoming and fash-

ionable trends and was unmistakably the event that defined, for a time a
least, the situation of the fine arts in Québec. But the terms in which the
debate was framed, as well as the cultural identity issue bound up with it,
were also misconstrued in the neo-nationalist context—that is, if they
hadn't already been distorted or poorly articulated as a result of François-
Marc Gagnon's opting for an *art brut*[8] in opposition, apparently, to the
successive catch-up measures denounced and carried out with reference to
the New York and Paris schools. This point of view was certainly debatable. It became, for good reason, a bone of contention among concerned
Québec artists, for it threatened to make the spectre of perpetual lateness a
characteristic trait of our cultural identity—as if we were fated to seek our
roots elsewhere, with the motherland or with Uncle Sam, as if our past
were still too young, its modern legacy far too limiting. In short, this was
the state of affairs only a few years after the 1967 reassessment which *Parti
pris* made in the *Aliénation et dépossession* issue devoted to "culture from
here."[9]

All this, echoes of which were evident in *ti-pop* (1966–67)[10] as well
as in the *Poèmes et chants de la résistance* (1968 and 1971),[11] was subsequently to receive a substantially more partisan political interpretation
that oscillated between nationalism and Marxism. As such, it was to have
further repercussions in the disputes of the *Front commun des artistes et des
créateurs* (1969)[12] and the *États généraux de la culture* of Vaudreuil
(1972),[13] as well as in the public debate surrounding the *Québec '75* exhibition.[14] The publication of Laurent-Michel Vacher's *Pamphlet sur la situation des arts plastiques au Québec* (1974)[15] also helped to fan the flames of
this heated polemic. (This time, however, the crux of the debate was
artists' social and political commitment.) The *Péquiste* period of 1976 was
also the time of the "extreme left," a time of rallies of every conceivable
stripe, of the political mobilization of groups and of organized struggle
aimed at the creation of a would-be workers' party. The incorporation of
the question of identity into the framework of the class struggle and prole-
tarian internationalism was a surprising development, even for the time;
yet whatever contradictions they may have harboured, the new terms of
this cultural debate, a debate considered by many to have played itself out,
were symptomatic of the new state of affairs that divided the art community in the mid 1970s.

As Fernande Saint-Martin wrote, it looked as if "the lame hypothesis of struggling to catch up was quickly transformed into a simple desire
to be up-to-date; except, of course, for those individuals who, believing
that Québec artists were for once abreast of events, now thought it possible to work at home by building upon true cultural foundations. These

members of what could be called the *autonomist axis* attempted to go beyond the basic orientations of contemporary Québec art."[16] Without entering into the specifics of this "axis" or separating out the various strands of the opposing "cosmopolitans," let us say that this polarization had the advantage of distinguishing emerging forces specific to Québec from those that represented adaptation to international formulae. Again, Saint-Martin: "In opposition to the autonomist axis, which is not that of the avid nationalists [les *nationaleux*], another group of young artists has tried to base its values and concerns on art produced outside Québec—yet in a manner vastly different from the traditional relationships that existed between colonies and metropolises. This approach is characterized mainly by immediate reaction to the circulation of art information picked up in the media or through personal experience."[17]

Unlike this direct line to every manifestation of the international scene (typified here at home by the dynamic alternative gallery Véhicule Art Inc.), it is under the umbrella of postmodernism that the lure and appeal of intricate approaches and cosmopolitan influences (exemplified by *Parachute* magazine) is beginning to fade, to lose ground to the above-mentioned resurgence of interest in regional characteristics, in the local colour of certain cultural groups, and even, for some countries, in national schools. An unexpected phenomenon, a complete turnabout, this would have been completely inconceivable in the 1970s. This return of the art-historical repressed is not without its share of contradictions and ambiguities, but all such revivals prefer the particular to the general, favour discontinuity over continuity, tradition over rupture.

From studies by art historians and curators of the reactions that followed the "artistic revolutions" of the turn of the century, we are aware of the many entrenchments to which these advances in modern art have led. The rediscovery of these "steps backward" has obviously facilitated the latest fandangos of international art. Faced with the cultural imperialism of formalism, of American postminimalism and its impact on the marketing of the new German fauvists, some, such as Achille Bonito-Oliva[18] a few years back, have tried to set themselves apart by drawing upon a reinvigorated Italian iconographic tradition.

In France, this latest alliance has met with an opposing strategy which, in an effort to break the hegemony of Italy, Germany, and the United States, has rallied around the country's incontestable tradition of abstraction. Figures such as Alain Jouffroy, Michel Ragon, and Jean-Marc Chalumeau[19] have banded together to denounce this collusion. Reacting to the power of the young American tradition, some, like Guy Scarpetta,[20] have even argued for a "European identity" based on the principle of longevity. Caught up in this whirlwind of resistance, and taking advantage of a widespread tendency to become inward-looking, people are turning to their own cultures and local traditions, even to their regional schools, in the hope of winning back a share of the market or, perhaps, of rekindling the sparks of their identity.

Judging by the resistance avant-garde strategies are encountering in almost every quarter, it should be legitimate for us to set our own tradition of nonfigurative abstraction against the most prominent of the neo-expressionist transfigurations. The clarity with which our own cultural distinctiveness would emerge against this international backdrop should enable us to understand the analogies between our culture and the new crisis of identity which, above and beyond all the avant-gardes and the defensive reactions engendered by every form of imperialism, seeks to cast its specific products and their cultural connections in a positive light by abolishing the longstanding confusion between the value of works and their price index.

Today's institutions certainly cannot compare with those of the past, and it is a fact that the framework in which our local market operates is defined less by competition than by a form of "free trade" dominated entirely by outside forces. Unless we are prepared, whatever the cost, to confuse the genuine fruits of our culture with a few choice plums, it is much more important to ask what our cultural identity would consist of today. Given that this is composed of something new together with something old, with the latter extended to encompass aboriginal cultures as well as the contributions of the dominant cultures, it is not a question of our forecasting the event that would restore market equilibrium, or of predicting the appellations of those national novelties likely to make it to the art stock exchange. Nor is it a question of plotting our progress in the international proceedings of postmodernism or the trans-avant-garde. But the moment we stop seeing ourselves as unlikely to amount to anything, as perpetual followers of events beyond our ken—then, I believe, each artist or art critic will assume his or her responsibility to contribute to our cultural distinctiveness and to develop whatever measure of originality he or she may possess. Despite the total openness characteristic of the Québec scene during the 1970s and 1980s, we must still beware of reverse chauvinism; for provincial submission to outside fashions, like the self-indulgent withdrawal into oneself, today constitutes a threat not only to the identity but also to the cultural development of every nation.

The desire for a radical renewal of our cultural identity, a desire that emerged in the wake of our retreat before yesterday's avant-gardes and today's postmodernism, proceeds by re-evaluating local tradition and by recognizing the most heterogeneous contributions. Whether they stem from the vanguard of feminism or from a resurgent interest in symbolic form, whether they originate in the United States or abroad, these eminently accessible influences will only be assimilated when there is a desire for qualitative change vastly different from the limited uses now being made of the most varied heritages.

In short, while we obviously must assume responsibility for our local tradition with all that it has to offer, the new interest in cultural autonomy, particularly in traditional forms and the knowledge contained therein, is not entirely free of a reactionary attitude marked by entrenchment behind established values. On the other hand, it is also possible to see this "re-rooting" not as a provincial form of withdrawal but as a re-evaluation of our cultural identity in the light of experiences and encounters with other types of culture. Québec's cultural heritage, like Borduas's "poetic treasure" of humanity, would have to be "transformed to be transmitted."

Such transformations are discontinuous and as indeterminate as the very idea of cultural identity. By definition impossible to achieve, the process of cultural identity is, in its analytical and dialectical workings, interminable. Because of the allowance it makes for change and movement, this conception of both identity and history runs counter to most of today's consoling returns to familiar values. Behind their postmodern art objects and their second-order cultural borrowings, such returns restore concepts whose "historicity" (as Benjamin Buchloh puts it)[21] too often leads to stock responses or to a formalism revised and edited by systematic quotation. Of course, the ultraliberalism of the current art market is the real beneficiary of revivals that bring about the end of the avant-garde and, by the same token, legitimate the return of the repressed. This type of legitimation is diametrically opposed to the kind that predominated during the 1960s and 1970s; for all intents and purposes, the latter saw the legitimacy of its most advanced ideas as residing in the contributions they made to the development of a history specific to art and, consequently, to the advancement of its heritage.

Let us hope that the temporary suppression of the legitimate question of cultural identity can soon manage to come round to itself without, in the process, becoming simply a local (and eternal) return of the same old thing.

Notes

1.   Jean-Marc Piotte, *La communauté perdue* (Paris: VLB Éditeur, 1987).

2.   Pierre Gaudibert, *Du culturel au sacré* (Paris: Casterman, 1981).

3.   Paul-Émile Borduas, *Refus global* (Montréal: Mithra-Mythe Éditeur, 1948).

4.   [The author specifically uses the word *révolte* instead of *révolution*, although the latter is the term usually employed with reference to Québec.]

5.   See *Québec Underground 1962–1972*, vol. 1 (Montréal: Éditions Médiart, 1973), 350–375.

6.   Marcel Saint-Pierre, "Art et politique (Montréal 1975–1980)," in *Art-Société 1975–1980* (Québec: Éditions intervention et Musée du Québec, 1981), 10–35.

7.   Marcel Rioux, "Sur l'évolution des idéologies au Québec," in *French-Canadian Society*, ed. Marcel Rioux and Yves Martin (Toronto: McClelland & Stewart, 1964), 95–124.

8.   François-Marc Gagnon, "Mimétisme en peinture contemporaine au Québec," in *Peinture canadienne-française: débats*, ed. François-Marc Gagnon and André Jasin, Conférences J.A. de Sève, no. 11–12 (Montréal: Presses de l'Université de Montréal, 1971), 57–60.

9.   *Parti pris*, vol. 4, no. 9–12 (May–August 1967).

10.   *Québec Underground 1962–1972*, vol. 1, 100–114.

11.   *Chansons et poèmes de la résistance* (Montréal: Éditions d'Orphée, 1969).

12.   See *Québec Underground*, 370–374.

13.   See *Revue Médiart*, vol. 1, no. 2 (October 1971) and the following videos: *Bobo-z-arts Vaudreuil* (Conference, October 15–17, 1971), by Charles Binamé and Normand Thériault, production Vidéographe and the National Film Board, black-and-white, 60 minutes; and *États généraux de la culture au Québec* (Vaudreuil, June 15–17, 1973), by Jo Laforce and Mimi Simard, production Vidéographe, black-and-white, 30 minutes.

14.   Normand Thériault, *Québec '75/arts* (Montréal: Institut d'art contemporain de Montréal, 1975).

15.   Laurent-Michel Vacher, *Pamphlet sur la situation des arts plastiques au Québec* (Montréal: VLB Éditeur, 1974).

16.   Fernande Saint-Martin, "La situation de l'art et l'identité québécoise," *Voix et images*, vol. 2, no. 1 (September 1976): 25.

17.   Ibid., 25.

18.   Achille Bonito-Oliva, *The Italian Trans-avantgarde*, trans. Michael Moore (Milan: Giancarlo Politi Editore, 1980).

19.   Jean-Luc Chalumeau, *L'art au présent* (Paris: Union générale d'éditions, 1985).

20.   Guy Scarpetta, *L'impureté*, Collection Figures (Paris: Grasset, 1985).

21.   Benjamin H.D. Buchloh, *Formalisme et historicité/Autoritarisme et régression*, trans. Claude Gintz (Paris: Éditions Territoires, 1982). "Formalism and Historicity" was published in English in *Europe in the Seventies* (Chicago: Art Institute of Chicago, 1977) and "Figures of Authority, Ciphers of Regression" was first published in *October*, no. 16 (Spring 1981): 39–68.

Translated from the French by Donald McGrath.

Kim Sawchuk

Shifting Fields:
Art Within the Context of Colonialism in Canada;
The Work of Don Proch

> As notions that serve an analytical purpose, otherness and sameness are more use-ful when they are viewed not in terms of dualities or conflicts but in terms of degrees and movements within the same concept, or better, in terms of differ-ences both within and between entities (differences between First and Third—if such naming serves a temporary purpose—and differences between First, within Third—if such differences can be temporarily fixed). Otherness to the outsider or insider is necessarily not the same as otherness from these positions, and in their encounter the two need not conflict with each other nor merely complement each other. Exploring oneself and one's culture in its interaction with other selves and other cultures remains a vital process when understanding is creating—is creation.
>
> Trinh T. Minh-ha

First Field

I start with this quote by filmmaker, writer, and composer Trinh T. Minh-ha because she makes an important point on the experience of colo-nialism as a question of degrees—otherness as not simply a duality between two oppositional terms, but as degree and movement within a concept, within a field—a field of force.

It is within this reconceptualization that I would like to frame my discussion of Manitoba artist Don Proch and my discussion of regionalism in Canadian art. Before I do this, I would like to reverse fields, so to speak. I would like to examine Proch's 1980 work, *Field*, as it relates to the topic of this paper and this volume: "How can we consider colonialism within the context of art in Canada?" I would like to turn this question around and ask: "How can we consider art within the context of colonialism in Canada?" This change is more than simply a deconstructive flip-flop into alterity.

Colonialism is not simply a subcategory of art. Whether it deals with colonialism explicitly or implicitly, art in Canada occurs within a field of colonial and imperialist relations of power and domination. In reframing the question, I want to examine the fields of force suggested by Proch's work, and in the Canadian art scene. In doing so I don't want to

This text was first published in *Provincial Essays*, no. 8 (1989).

ON HINTERLAND
DOMINATION

CANADA AS A
COLONY
NATIVES mentioned   see fn.'s

83

fix an interpretive meaning to the work. Rather, I want to spin off its suggestive nature.[1]

The richness of Proch's *Field,* as well as of his earlier works, particularly his masks, allows one to think through the degrees and movements of dependency, domination, and colonialism, of sameness and difference articulated by Trinh. This experience of dependency cannot be framed within a simple dialectical model of oppressor and oppressed, but is again a question of degrees between regions and forces, between the Maritimes and central Canada, between the North and central Canada, between the Prairies and central Canada, between classes, races and racist categories, linguistic groups, and sexes within these regions, etc.

Proch's *Field,* [over] ten years old, continues to speak to a colonialism, an internal colonialism, which is as much a part of the fabric of this country as the language issue. Art in Canada is produced within the context of an internal colonialism represented by the axis of Montréal, Toronto, and sometimes Vancouver, which have a gravitational pull on the production of art in marginal areas such as the Maritimes or the Prairies or the North. There is obviously more money, more buyers, more galleries, and the perception that there are more audiences and opportunities in the centre. While art cannot be reduced to these economic and political criteria, this economic and political centralization has an effect on artistic production and the generation of culture.

This is not to claim that to be from the Prairies is the same as being from Latin America, India, or other countries undergoing the painful process of decolonization. It is not the same as being from the North, or living as a Native person in this country, incarcerated on reserves. However, if I may quote Trinh again, "No system functions in isolation. No First World exists independently from the Third World; there is a Third World in every First World and vice versa."[2] The Prairies is not the Third World, but it contains its third worlds, and there is a relationship of difference, of domination and dependency which exists in the Prairie experience, articulated within the tradition of Canadian political economy, but rarely spoken of in relation to artistic, intellectual, or other forms of cultural production. I would like to close this gap, or at least juxtapose these discourses.[3]

Second Field

To be from the Prairies is to have a Canadian identity marked by a regional affiliation: not an identity based on an essence, but a difference based on geography, politics, history, a personal history connected to one's family, as well as one's imaginary and real relation to central Canada. As well, because of the history of settlement in this country, it often implies that a specifically "ethnic" component is part of one's regional identity.[4] Like the so-called "negative" Canadian identity in relationship to the United States, part of a regional identity of the Prairies is based on the relationship of otherness that one has in relation to the metropolis—in this case the urban centre.

To be from the Prairies is to realize that the *Toronto Globe and Mail* is not our national newspaper, and to realize that only a newspaper from the centre could make that claim—for the *Winnipeg Free Press* to declare itself our national newspaper would be as surprising as hearing men collectively begin to subsume themselves under the category of women. While unemployment and poverty are not as chronic in the Prairie hinterland as in the Maritimes, Newfoundland, or the North, largely because of the intervention of past socialist provincial governments in regional development in Manitoba and Saskatchewan, to be from the Prairies is to realize your political nonimportance in relationship to the rest of Canada because of numbers, dollars, and population.

The 1988 federal elections were a fascinating and discouraging experience for a former Western Canadian. After the numbers came in from Ontario and Québec, the winners were declared by the Canadian Broadcasting Corporation, our national radio station. The results from the rest of the country were moot—I realized I could retire to bed. The most salient occurrence was the split, not between English and French Canada, but between central Canada and the other regions of Canada in the Canadian hinterland, except Alberta. A new economic and political future for Canada was determined by a particular region with particular interests—access to the United States and other global markets at the expense of protecting certain key staple industries such as mining, lumber, fishing, and agriculture located at the margins.[5]

Because of these disparities, exile is a continual feature of the Prairies, both past and present. As Susan Musgrave once wrote, "Exile is in our time like blood."[6] Many of the early settlers were exiles, displaced by war and poverty in other parts of the world. And now there are many who do leave or must leave because of economic stagnation, for educations, for jobs, and sometimes even because of the cold or out of boredom. Sometimes we come back, but often we don't, and, if we do stay in the East, we often feel the difference between ourselves and those who were born and bred in central Canada. Our biggest export has been people, including a number of writers such as Margaret Laurence and Gabrielle Roy, artists such as Suzanne Gauthier, and many intellectuals, particularly a large chunk of the left-wing intelligentsia. However, to be an exile from the Prairies isn't as visible as being an exile from another country. One can assimilate easily; the differences aren't as apparent. One can lose one's accent, get used to paying premiums for medicare and exorbitant prices for automobile insurance.

However, there are some things one never loses. The landscape appears to be predominantly two-dimensional, governed by the sense that one can literally see all around oneself in 360 degrees. One's perception of spatial and temporal relations is governed by these horizons and created by this interaction.[7] This sense of the proximity of the rural, in particular of the absolute flatness of the region, is not simply an economic relationship, but a symbolic and imaginary relationship—a part of our otherness. In the Prairies the horizon can always be seen, and the rural is not so far away. Thus, a sense of proximity and dependency on an agricultural base is always within visual perception, even if one's roots are predominantly urban.

The work of Don Proch is fascinating for the exile because of its obvious inspiration from this specifically geographic topographical experience of the full presence of Prairie nothingness—nothingness, that is, to the outsider. Proch's works from the early *Asessippi Tread* play between two-dimensional and three-dimensional surfaces; the body of a cyclist is flattened into a two-dimensional surface while underneath, in three dimensions, the spokes of the tires, as furrows of the plough, eat at the soil. Proch's drawings include such familiar themes as the uneasy relationship between technology and nature, rural and urban life; his compositions include elevators, furrowed fields, and cascades of billowing clouds that one sees only on the Prairies; and his materials are also drawn from the Prairies—harrows, baler twine, chicken bones, soil, as well as references to his own Ukrainian ethnicity.[8]

Proch's work is not a romantic pastoral depiction of this experience of horizon. His sculptures, in particular his masks sculpted between 1972 and 1976, deal with complex philosophical questions on the interrelationship of landscape, nature, technology, the body, and subjectivity. The inscriptions on the outside of these virtual helmets are important works in themselves because they link the technologically sophisticated space helmet with traditional icons such as Easter eggs, and they visually depict Prairie brush fires, birds, and other familiar features of a Prairie landscape. Fields drawn in silverpoint form a large part of the composition of these masks. Nature features prominently in these works, but increasingly it is technology and capital that link the two and are the inspiration for a violent mediation.

These helmets play with the borders of the inside and outside, of interiority and exteriority. Like the experience of an endless horizon, one's position as subject is constantly shifting in relationship to the masks. One can view the mask from the outside looking in, or from the inside looking out. The fields on the outside of these masks as well as their very structure suggest that even in their beauty this subject positioning is about securing the field of the imagination. As Brian Massumi has written, the parameters of our lives are now defined less by what we think or believe or desire or imagine than how we are secured. "Social control is learning to forgo internalization. It is locating itself directly at the boundary, on our own skin, and at our doorsteps. ..."[9] The securing of borders, a colonization of the inside through the outside, a spatial domination are thematic continuums in Proch's work.

Thus Proch is a "Prairie artist" whose work is more than regional, although it has a regional basis. He is also an artist who has chosen to remain and work within the province—a problem because there are few parallel galleries in Winnipeg, indeed few throughout the Prairies. To choose to stay in Winnipeg is a choice few artists or intellectuals either make or can afford to make because of a relation of structural inequality.

Third Field

In 1979 Proch was asked to participate in *Pluralities/1980/Pluralités*, an exhibition at the National Gallery of Canada. His work entitled *Field* was created for this exhibition, which commemorated the gallery's centennial celebration.

Field was a resin reproduction, made from a plaster cast, of a field near Headingly, Manitoba. The large piece, a 28-by-16-foot oval of resin representing furrowed earth, filled an entire room of the gallery. In the centre of the field was a large crop of wild prairie bunch grass, made from unravelled and cut baler twine, surrounded by the narrow oval of the resin field. At the edge of the oval a pair of farmer's work boots with the back shorn off was embedded in the earth. Interestingly, the photographic documentation of the piece, as integral to the piece as the installation made for the National Gallery itself, included a live element, so obvious it was missing from almost all of the critical descriptions of the work—the security guard ever present in the National Gallery.

Pluralities did not meet with critical acclaim, and Proch's work was labelled as the "weakest" of these works. I will not examine in detail the criteria of these judgements.[10] Instead I will return to the question of fields and its multifarious meanings in relationship to our initial question of colonialism as a relationship not of dialectical opposites but of movement and degrees.

Fields are not simply sites of agricultural production. The term itself is exceedingly rich in semiotic proliferations. In fact when asked what the piece was called, Proch himself insisted that it would not be called *The Field*, simply *Field*.[11] To call the piece *The Field* would have implied that only one reading, one based on the obvious connection between the art work and the Prairies, is possible. We speak of fields in relationship to knowledge; in sexual parlance, we speak of playing the field. A field is a site demarcated for contestation, a battle zone, or the ground upon which a game is played. Field is a common term in scientific terminology, particularly in the terminology of particle physics where it describes the threshold where interactions between fundamental particles can occur thereby securing the structure of the material world.[12]

Finally, in marketing research, "field" is the term used to delineate what is outside the office walls. The field is where the consumer/audience is located, be it shopping malls or the home. It is the place where data is accumulated, where evidence is found to support the conclusions we want to make, to reinforce the opinions we want to generate. A field is a space where relations of power are played out. Like colonialism, it is the staking out of a territory, be it political, economic, or symbolic. And fields, like all relations of power, are not simply static but are often shifting.

Like the fields depicted on his masks, Proch's *Field* plays with these notions, for the ritual involved in its production was as important as the final object. Proch literally recreated the scene of the National Gallery in the field near Headingly. First, he built in the field a frame of the walls of the room of the National Gallery, including a replication of its exact dimensions and the lighting. Finally, he hired a security guard to oversee the event. In creating *Field*, Proch recreated some of the symbolic elements, often invisible, that structure the institutional edifice governing the conditions of his work: the activity of framing the field, of the doubling of reproduction of the gallery inside the field, of the field inside the gallery. In other words, the terrain of the nation was brought home in the creation of *Field*. Thus Proch's own position at this time, like the possibility of alterity in terms of positioning oneself inside/outside the virtual helmets, was played on the field of *Field*. Yet it is not simply a reversal of two equal terms. The security guard signifies the presence of the continual policing of the art world by canons, not only formulated outside of Canada but also decided centrally in the country—in artistic, political, and economic terms, the reproduction of power at the centre.

It is this structural system of unequal exchange between regions that is the primary cause of regional underdevelopment—a poor return for staples such as agriculture and mining. In terms of political economy, the hinterland perspective points out the economic inferiority of the hinterland because of the price system which favours financial powers in the metropolis.[13] As a friend once put it, farmers are the only producers who must buy their commodities at retail prices and sell them wholesale. Canadian political economists have noted:

> Typically peripheral areas are led to specialize in the production export of raw materials necessary for industrial expansion in the centre. In this regard Canada has stood in the same relation first to England and then the United States as the Atlantic region has stood in relation to the central provinces, and, at a different level again, the rural areas stand in relation to the urban centres.[14]

Like the Toronto-Montréal art world which is governed by a colonial and imperialist relation of power to Britain and the United States, colonialism in this context, the system of unequal exchange and the securing of territories or markets, is a question of degrees, not of fixed positions within the world economic order where neat hierarchies can be delineated.

However, in pointing out the internal relationship of colonialism within Canada and the Canadian art scene, one cannot simply romanticize the Prairie experience of dependency. It is worthwhile stating, as Ken Hughes notes, that Proch's *Field* had at its centre wild Prairie bunch grass, and not wheat as some of Proch's critics mistakenly thought—for agriculture is not akin to nature but is closer to the experience of culture and has always been implicated both in technological rationality and the bureaucratic control of territory at the founding of Canada as a nation.[15] The unwound twine, which another critic thought looked like the wig of a Barbie doll, represented not only bunch grass but also the synthetic, mediated nature of the field itself. And why not Barbie? It is only a problem if one assumes that a Prairie artist would "naturally" be representing a field full of wheat. As well, the oval-shaped border around this carpet-like mass of "hair" is significant because it is in the shape of a race track and not simply a furrowed field.[16] *Field* is not the bombastic, obvious piece that critics originally claimed, but has a complex understanding of the role of agriculture, of Prairie culture. This deconstruction of agriculture is another major theme in Proch's works.

To continue, agriculture has a paradoxical role in relation to colonialism and technology for it did mean the domination of the landscape, through the cultivation of previously uncultivated land. Agriculture was instrumental in the beginning of Canadian development as a tool of the state for securing our national borders. Canadian economic "development" deliberately and consistently used agriculture as a basis for building an economic and political empire. As Paul Phillips notes, it served as an instrument for empire in different ways "according to the requirements of place and time":[17] first, as a means for the defence of territories and trade routes; second, as provisioner of the great staple trade; and third, as a provider of investment opportunities in the agricultural frontier. Within the framework of the economic and political life of this country, agriculture was in the paradoxical position of providing a livelihood for countless European peasants who fled their homes during and after the First World War—at the same time the colonization of the West, and of Canada in general, meant the annihilation of Native culture and economic life.

Farmers have been the unwitting tools and pawns of state power, based in merchant capital in the East in the twentieth century, and now finance capital, again predominantly Eastern based. The power of farmers, including the prices they could get for their wheat, has varied in proportion to the contribution that agriculture could make at any given time to the cause of commerce, finance, and industry. This, in some respects, accounts for the widely different responses to the boots placed at the edge of the field in the final installation. While some critics thought them inviting, others saw them as menacing. Indeed, who would want to step into these boots? The disunity and economic division manifest in the 1988 election is part of this country's long history of inequality between metropolis and hinterland. For as Fowke pointed out in the 1930s, "Canadian merchants never paid much attention to the international boundary. If the Canadian capitalist had been able to cash in on the [U.S.] frontier development, there probably would have been no Canadian nation."[18] In other words, the economic powers that be are willing to use the state when it is convenient for securing market protection. As Phillips writes, while the development of the Canadian West "was truly a counter-imperialism to American imperialist designs on western British North America, it was imperialist nevertheless."[19]

Fourth Field

Within the current academic fashion to talk about the "discourse of colonialism" there are some important reasons not to overlook the term imperialism. Within the literature of political science, colonialism was an historical phenomenon related to the founding of colonies which secured territory. Colonialism transformed indigenous political structures *and* social relations for economic and political gain. Imperialism, on the other hand, has been tied to a tradition of Marxist theory which looks exclusively at

economic relations. The weakness of the theory of imperialism is that it became dominated by Lenin's theory of imperialism as "the highest stage of capitalism," and it never took into account domination on the basis of race or colour or sex, i.e., the cultural sphere. However, the term colonialism, on its own, is inadequate because one does not have to occupy a country in order to control it. One can do it economically through debt, as the United States has done through institutions such as the International Monetary Fund and the World Bank.

The new "national" policy, free trade, means that the state doesn't have to legislate warmer relations with the United States—it is done through culture, through the marketing and selling of commodities and useless consumer goods. In this scenario, artistic production will more and more be seen as a product to be marketed, like shoes.

The new security apparatus of business and the state, of the New Business States, is not simply the enforcement of a certain official art policy, but the securing of the consumer's imagination through the massive system of advertising. It is this internal colonization of the imagination that the artistic imagination draws to our attention and hopefully combats. As Proch's virtual helmets visually depict, it is the realm of the imagination that makes life bearable. The desire to turn this into a more privatized free-enterprise country means precisely an erosion of the public into audiences, and communities into interest groups.[20] In this our exterior and interior landscapes are perceptibly shifting.

Even our language is subjected to the processing of the economic imperial order. In this schema, English or French will not matter. It is the language of numbers that will count. It is already happening in that other field, the field of marketing research which is becoming more and more integral to the multinational corporations who want to track the rapid eye movements of the consuming population.

In this virtual world, reality is called support, but, because it is support, because it is fictive, doesn't mean that it is not real—it is hyper-real. What counts is not the performance of the product, but its image and our ability to remember this image.[21] Proch's fields, on his helmets, in the National Gallery, are a testimony of our transition into this new phase of postindustrial, postmodern, late capitalist life where the real world is the virtual world. More and more our subjectivities are being secured by thorough and continual testing of the population for drugs, for AIDS, for image consumption. Through the medium of the television superconductor populations are blasted with information like miniature particles in collision. The field of "marketing research," a massive security system, is about the extension of power into consumer populations and of corporations into themselves. While the National Gallery's own history has never been independent of those with economic, social, and political power, ironically, its symbolic power was bolstered with the opening of a new building at a time when, economically, the nation is being eroded through the policy of free trade.

The security guard present in Proch's work represents not only the state but also the private armies of security guards who help secure and maintain private property and the circulation of capital. He represents, as Ken Hughes so eloquently writes, security guards, the RCMP, the armed forces, the regular police, and policy makers. Thus, perhaps Proch's choice of a field near Headingly where the provincial jail is located isn't so coincidental after all.

To return to our beginning, the notion of field, the territorial demarcation and subsequent policing of a certain terrain, isn't simply a relationship of metropole to hinterland. Colonialism, within the context of Canada and Canadian art, is a complex relation of degree and movement. Canada is a peculiar colonial nation—founded as a colony by Great Britain, currently under the economic sway of the United States, determined at this moment to exert economic force over other nations. And like many other nations, it must contend with its own north-south question, Native question and relations of political, economic, and cultural dependency and underdevelopment between its urban central regions and its marginal areas, between the privileged classes in these regions and its disadvantaged and dispossessed cultures.

In all of these cases the question is one of securing boundaries to ensure the continuation of relations of power. *Field* spoke a certain truth about contemporary Canadian plurality—that our liberalism and tolerance, our notions of "pluralism" and "multiculturalism," often mask internal relations of power. For, as Ken Hughes points out in his analysis of *Field*, the whole structure built in the field pointed eastward. If *Field* were to be rebuilt today, the security guard would be a television screen, or a video camera, and the field would be pointing south.

Notes

The epigraph is from Trinh T. Minh-ha, "Of Other Peoples: Beyond the 'Salvage' Paradigm," in *Discussions in Contemporary Culture*, ed. Hal Foster, Dia Art Foundation Discussions in Contemporary Culture, no. 1 (Seattle: Bay Press, 1987), 138–141.

1.   See Tom Hill, "First Nations and Museums," *Muse*, vol. 6, no. 3 (Fall 1988): 2. In his excellent editorial in this special issue devoted to the question of

Native art, culture, and Canadian museum policy, Hill argues that "museums have been manifestations of colonial society for too long." In the same issue, Julia Harrison of the Glenbow Museum in Calgary and curators of other Canadian museums protest that Native concerns are narrow and political, and that "museums must remain independent of external political pressures" (p. 12). In this debate it is interesting to read how traditional humanist values of freedom of speech and freedom from suppression are used by the curators, ignoring the fact that most "artefacts" in these museums were collected while Native culture was being systematically destroyed and, in this particular instance, that the Glenbow Museum had received a grant from Shell Oil for the exhibit *When the Spirit Sings* (1987). Shell is one of the multinationals drifting for oil on the lands of the Lubicon Lake Cree.

2.   Trinh, "Of Other Peoples," 138. There are many outstanding Canadian artists whose work deals directly with colonialism and imperialism, such as Dominique Blain and Barry Allikas, two Montréal artists whose work uses art to tease out the interconnections between First World artistic production and the Third World (Blain), and the abuse of the environment by industry in Canada (Allikas).

3.   See Myrna Kostash's essay "Domination and Exclusion: Notes of a Resident Alien," *Border Crossings*, vol. 5, no. 4 (Fall 1986): 65–71. *Border Crossings* is an arts magazine from Winnipeg and deals with artistic and intellectual questions on/from the hinterland experience/perspective.

4.   As Kostash writes, to be an "alien is not a simple condition. ... The concept of otherness—social, political, sexual—is freighted with prejudice," and there are often multiple exclusions based on race, class, gender, ethnicity, and region.

5.   Mark Duncan, "The Hinterland Strikes Back: Localizing Critical Pride," *Border Crossings*, vol. 7, no. 3 (June 1988): 9–11.

6.   Quoted in Robert Enright's editorial in the special "Exiled Imagination" issue of *Border Crossings*, vol. 7, no. 4 (Fall 1988): 4.

7.   Sometimes these interventions of remembrance are subtle. As Suzanne Gauthier recounts, "With my work I deal with this illusion of depth, or I'm dealing with this very shallow space. I really do think it's a conditioning from the Prairies. Of course in the winter it's so much more striking. You've just got dark and light." From Hilary Michaels's "Black and White and Light: The Photographs of Suzanne Gauthier," *Border Crossings*, vol. 7, no. 4 (Fall 1988): 65.

8.   It is interesting to note that many of Proch's masks, such as *Manitoba Mining Mask* and *Night Flight, Pincushion Man* (*Wearing Brushcut Listening for Buffalo Mask*), illustrate explicitly industrialized, economic concerns. Kenneth Hughes's monograph *Don Proch* (Winnipeg: Manitoba Arts Monographs, 1980) is the most complete account of Proch's work.

9.   See Brian Massumi's proposal for a special issue of *Copyright* on the

theme of fear. [This issue has been published as a book. See *The Politics of Everyday Fear*, ed. Brian Massumi (Minneapolis: University of Minnesota Press, 1993).]

10.   *Field* was compared to Walter de Maria's *Dirt Room*, and the work of British artist Mark Boyle. This comparison between an art installation in New York and a British artist would be the topic of another paper, however it does once again indicate the lines of forces operating within the Canadian art world. Kenneth Hughes has written an angry analysis of these criticisms and an interesting interpretation of *Field* in his monograph. See Hughes, *Don Proch*, 221–250.

11.   Ibid., 245. According to Hughes, Proch was aware of these implications in the work, and fields of force became a metaphor for the structure of the Canadian federal system.

12.   Ibid. See also *Superstrings: A Theory of Everything?* ed. P.C.W. Davies and J. Brown (Cambridge: Cambridge University Press, 1988), 27.

13.   Paul Phillips, "The Hinterland Perspective: The Political Economy of Vernon C. Fowke," *Canadian Journal of Political and Social Theory*, vol. 2, no. 2 (Spring/Summer 1978): 74.

14.   Henry Veltmeyer, "Dependency and Underdevelopment: Some Questions and Problems," *Canadian Journal of Political and Social Theory*, vol. 2, no. 2 (Spring/Summer 1978): 60.

15.   See Phillips, "The Hinterland Perspective."

16.   Machines that provide speed, such as bicycles and motorcycles, also figure in much of Proch's work. See in particular *Asessippi Tread* and *Asessippi Laser Racer*.

17.   Phillips, "The Hinterland Perspective," 74.

18.   Ibid., 82.

19.   Ibid., 86.

20.   Martha Rosler provides an analysis of this distinction in "The Birth and Death of the Viewer: On the Public Function of Art," in *Discussions in Contemporary Culture*, 9–15.

21.   Philippe Nicolas, "From Value to Love," *Journal of Advertising Research*, vol. 28, no. 4 (August/September 1988): RC8.

Serge Bérard

Rober Racine,
or the Work of Deconstructing the Dictionary

Rober, the *Petit* Robert

One day I asked Rober Racine why he had such an unusual first name,
how, in fact, he came to "lose" his "t." He replied that it happened while
he was working on his signature. "Working" on one's signature is something that many of us are familiar with, either from or before adolescence.
As if, after the mirror stage, each individual were to pass through a "signature" stage in which "his" body and "his" name joyfully confronted each
other via the blank page. It was, therefore, in signing his name that
"Robert" found himself a name (a highly unusual name, let me repeat); it
was while "affirming" his name that it changed and while symbolically
affirming his uniqueness that he found himself such a unique name. It
happened quite simply. While Racine was signing his name, proceeding
undoubtedly with great speed ("Robert Racine," "Robert Racine," "Rober
Racine"), "Robert" and "Racine" drew ever closer together and, as the
speed with which they were yoked increased, the "t" in "Robert" was
absorbed into the stem of the "R" in "Racine." (Thus "Robert Racine,"
"RobertRacine," "RoberRacine" led to "Rober Racine.") Here, then, is the
origin or root [*racine*] of "Rober." It turns out that this "work" on his signature was not really "work" after all, since it happened by itself, indeed
almost without Racine's willing it.

I am not trying to turn this biographical detail into a key to the
work; rather, I want to point to a particular concurrence involving, on the
one hand, a certain uneasiness with regard to the question of identity (in
its muffled, emotional manifestation via Rober Racine's signature) and, on
the other hand, the work of Rober Racine which, intuitively yet methodi-
cally, formalizes and extends this question. Racine's practising of his signature, with its rather exceptional outcome, was surely not an artistic gesture
but a graphological diversion that may be symptomatic of fleeting existential anxiety. Note, however, that it *could* have been an artistic gesture not
unlike the existential affirmations of On Kawara. What the experience
lacks, rather, what it needs in order to be artistic, is such an *intention* on
the part of someone who had already proclaimed himself an artist, even if

This is a translation of a text first published in *Parachute*, no. 62 (1991).

only to himself. In such a case, the signature would issue from a duly authorized hand, from a "signatory," and would represent a kind of commitment instead of a simple affirmation. Since conceptual art at least, we have been familiar with the type of questioning that pushes self-referentiality back to the person of the artist.

But getting back to this question of a concurrence between a youthful action and an artistic work, a further question comes "naturally" to mind when one considers Racine's work on the *Petit Robert*. Why did he choose this dictionary? Why not the *Larousse*, the *Littré*, or even the *Grand Robert*? The latter, one could object, would have represented an interminable task. But is it not in the nature of Racine's "work" that it be interminable. (I will come back to this later.) Isn't there a connection between Racine's insecurity, over the writing of his given name (since all obsessive behaviour points to insecurity, and nothing is more obsessive than this repetition of a signature) and his choice of the *Petit Robert*? What I mean is that there may be a link *chez* Racine, that is, at that place in Racine [*en Racine*] where his identity is rooted [*s'enracine*], a link between anxiety concerning his personal identity (what I mean by this will eventually become clearer), an anxiety symptomized by the transformation, the *diminution*, of his signature (since there is a loss), between this and the fact that he opted for the *Petit Robert* instead of the *Grand*, the *Petit Robert* as in "pauvre petit Rober(t)," or "poor little Rober(t)."

In order to answer this question (the sole purpose of this essay), I will make liberal use of a text that Racine wrote to mark the publication of a book on his work with the dictionary.[1] I believe that this text offers numerous partial and, from the artist's standpoint, almost inadvertent clues that will shed light on the connection outlined above.

Very early on in his text Racine states that his work on the dictionary consists of two parts, *Le Terrain du dictionnaire A/Z* (1980) and *Les 2 130 Pages-Miroirs* (1979–1988). Yet this is not all, since the *idea* or *dream* of a "French Language Park" is mentioned—if only in order to be excluded from the work and relegated to the ambiguous location of the origin. Yet isn't this "Park" also a "work"? Does it not also constitute a third element or part of the "work" on the dictionary? Of course, ideas and dreams are two very different things—indeed opposites, if one goes by psychoanalytic theory. Still, Racine's text mentions an idea *and* a dream.

> It all started on October 29, 1979, in the Saint-Martin quarter of Laval. It was there that I got the *idea* for a French Language Park, that is, a permanent park or garden where panels inscribed with all the words in the French language, along with their definitions, would be set in the ground. They would be distributed in different word areas,

with each category identified by a specific colour. I *dreamt* of a public place where, in order to learn new words, the reader/stroller would have to move about physically from one word to another, from, for example, the L zone to the I zone and from the Rs to the Es.[2]

Note the lack of effort, the extreme passivity in this passage. The idea of a park was not something Racine had to work hard at, was not the result of any hypothesis, experiment, or trial and error. On the contrary, the idea simply came to him. The language here is suggestive of a "visitation"; indeed, as if to confirm the supernatural nature of the experience, Racine states that it came to him in a dream.[3] And he goes on to pursue this (received) idea, again in a passive vein, musing or dreaming about it. ("I dreamt," he says, "of a public place.") There is, however, a paradox here because it is work he is dreaming about. Indeed the park involves work, both in its development and in the enjoyment of the finished product. The words are to be *inscribed* on panels that would then be *distributed* in different word areas and *set* in the ground. Each word category would be *identified* by a certain colour that would have to be specified. Likewise, those who happened to go to the park in order to passively take in what it has to offer (to contemplate it) would have to *move about* physically because their purpose in being there would be precisely to *learn* the words. Thus, amid passivity, Racine is haunted by work.

Going from this park which "visited" Racine (in the process effecting a role reversal), from this ideal to what it became, one comes up against the problem of incompleteness. For it was not the park that was completed, but two projects which constitute the negative imperfects of the dream. That is, whereas the park was to encompass words and their definitions, Racine's *Terrain* contained only words, and his *Pages-Miroirs*, only definitions.

In making his idea a (partial) reality, in fleshing out his dream, Racine was faced with an enormous undertaking. For a whole year he worked from eight to ten hours a day (p. 6), meticulously cutting around the edges of the 55,000 words that would make up *Le Terrain du diction-naire A/Z*; and, for the *Pages-Miroirs*, he spent nine years marking, inscribing, and performing other operations on the 2,130 pages of the *Petit Robert*.

Whose Deconstruction?

Before explaining my interest in the question of identity and the concept of work exemplified by Racine, I must first point out what I consider to be the horizon of this work. I believe that what Racine does in art can truly be called deconstruction. But the concept of deconstruction is currently so hackneyed that a certain degree of explanation is in order.

The word "deconstruction" is now used in the way that "critique" or "dialectic" once were. Such linguistic fashions—pardon me, such "fashion effects"—should alone suffice to cast suspicion on the efforts of the intelligentsia (another erstwhile fashionable term) and lend credit to the discourse of Richard Rorty, a writer intent on showing that the "great" philosophical questions are actually illusions produced by the very vocabulary used to frame them. In short, the word "deconstruction" often serves as a pretext for an excess of extremely muddled theorizing. One deconstructs in situations that merely call for critiques. This remark may apply more to Anglo-Saxon than to French discourse, particularly to what comes out of the United States where the craze for deconstruction, especially in literary theory and cultural criticism, has generated an extraordinary variety of deconstructions of every description. Of course, this remark pertains less to academic philosophy which, with the well-known exception of Richard Rorty, is fiercely opposed to Derridean theory. Art criticism is in a similar situation. If one goes by many of the interpretative essays that have appeared in recent years, art practice is now in a deconstructivist period (which, by a strange coincidence, is also a postmodernist one—as if the two attributes were interchangeable.) I, too, used to believe that deconstructive concerns were generally at work in visual art practice.[4] I should, in passing, point out the great variety of "objects" of "deconstruction" in art discourse, given that artists themselves have developed the habit of working interpretive strategies into their praxis. This may, for example, involve "deconstructing" the medium (photography, painting, sculpture, etc.) to which their work belongs; or it may mean deconstructing an external "reality," particularly (and this will explain the quotation marks) that constructed by the mass media. Now we can see that simply by replacing "deconstruction" with "critique" (without making the text any less intelligible—if it ever was intelligible!), the concepts appear to be interchangeable. Does this mean, then, that deconstruction is just another "type" of critique? I believe that the answer (if one is possible) lies in the definition of the object targeted by deconstruction.

Those familiar with Derridean theory know how extremely problematic, infinitesimal, and almost "objectless" this "object" actually is. The clearest definition of the object of Derridean deconstruction occurs not in Derrida but in the following somewhat turgid passage by Marjorie Grene:

> The sound (the *signifiant*, those sounds the grown-ups make and the child learns to make too), designates, points to, a concept, or thought—or thinking—in the mind (that thought, or thinking is the

signifié). But that thought in turn reflects or expresses a reality, an object of thinking, which is luminously and evidently present to the mind in its thinking and as (so to speak) it speaks. The correlation of *signifiant* and *signifié* is of course conventional, as is the correlation of words and things in the Augustinian story. But what is conventionally correlated in this account is sounds as "inner" processes, and the relation to reality—to "things"—makes its appearance (or is said to do so) only in that presence of Being to the mind which is expressed (or is said to be expressed) by the speaker in living speech.[5]

This object (of thought) is, then, the object of Derridean deconstruction. It is an object with remarkable, almost divine attributes, which alone should make it suspect. In the first place, it is hardly an object at all but a purely mental entity. It is in no way affected by the physical universe, not even by something so marginally physical as language. For example, the fact that the concept or idea of "two" is expressed as "two" in English, "deux" in French, and "zwei" in German in no way changes its meaning. It seems to exist independently of all supporting context, linguistic or otherwise. This last characteristic is the source of supplementary qualities: the concept is universal, univocal, and always identical to itself. It also seems to maintain an extremely intimate rapport with consciousness. Indeed, their closeness is such that the concept seems to be the unique incarnation of consciousness, and even appears to constitute individuality or identity as they are experienced singly by individuals. This purely mental (or ideal) object is also metaphysical; in itself it constitutes the entire field of inquiry of metaphysics. The mental object comes into play because it is called upon, because it is the object of an act of volition on the part of consciousness. Consciousness *perceives* the mental object because it is consciousness that summoned it, that intended it in the first place. Metaphysics, therefore, is always voluntarist metaphysics.

It is generally known that Derrida's critique of this metaphysical conception proceeds via the concept of writing [*l'écriture*]. Since a lack of space prevents me from tracing the development of this critique here, I will merely give a brief outline of its results. Derrida states categorically that such mental and metaphysical content was never present to perception[6] because this content, with all of the above-mentioned characteristics, is an illusion, as is the ideal purity of the interior speech said to animate it. This illusion of the presence of a mental (ideal) content is what constitutes the metaphysics of presence. Writing replaces, or takes priority over, speech or the interior voice. In an extremely metaphorical fashion, Derrida's concept of writing must be seen as embracing all "physicality," that is, everything that eats away at the ideal characteristics of mental content. Language is one such exponent of the physical. The fact that "two" is "two" in English and "deux" in French suddenly becomes very important. Now it would be quite feasible to extend this concept of writing (Derrida unfortunately does not) to other domains such as neurology, where hormonal balances are just as important as conscious willpower in determining the assortment and nature of the Subject's mental content. The "transcendental Subject," supposedly situated beyond the world, considered pure because it manipulates pure concepts, is "decentred" in the sense that it has lost absolute mastery over its mental content.

It seems to me that there are very few works that exemplify the kind of deconstruction just described. Racine's work is, I believe, one example. And the "work" of John Cage also springs to mind, for its concern with intentionality places it within the horizon of Derridean deconstruction. Yet in order to evaluate the remove Cage's work produces, it remains to be shown how "logocentric" music, that is, all music before John Cage, can signify, bear meaning [*vouloir-dire*]. Of course it will be understood why, in this context, I have placed parentheses around Cage's "work"; for Cage worked in order to eliminate all work—conscious work, that is—on his part. Finally, we are familiar with the ambiguities generated by those works in which Cage chose not to make choices and, in a more radical move, partially determined the indetermination in his pieces by setting certain parameters for them and by being more partial to certain results. The same ambiguity is a fundamental feature of both Racine's work[7] *and* Derrida's theory. I will come back to this point at the end.

Deconstructing the Dictionary

The reader may have already sensed how the link between Racine's signature experience and his work can be articulated within the theoretical horizon just outlined. Like Cage, Racine practises the effacement of his (conscious) will before his "material." Unlike Cage, whose works always appear to emerge spontaneously, Racine insists on the effort involved, does everything in his power to ensure that it is visible. But this effort is— and the qualifier is important—purely "mechanical." As in the case of the signature, it proceeds without the creative intervention of consciousness, and it is mindless. Thus Racine does not only practise self-effacement before his material; he does so before his task as well. Now, one may ask, what exactly is this task?

These tasks, one should say, since there are two outcomes. The first, *Le Terrain du dictionnaire A/Z*, is quite simple. It consists in cutting out the 55,000 entries in the *Petit Robert* and gluing them on small, blue cards mounted on tooth picks. In the text cited above, Racine says that this work is a form of writing, indeed that it is a text—"a 'written' text produced at a rate of eight to ten hours per day" (p. 6). If Racine highlights the adjective "written," it is because he knows his claim to be precarious. Indeed, does he actually have a text? Can a succession of words without the slightest articulation constitute a text? Is he really engaged in *writing* at all? Yes and no, he explains, because what is involved is *an/other* form of writing: "What happened in that instance—again note the extreme passivity—was another form of writing. A form wherein I did not actually, calligraphically that is, form even the slightest letter or word" (p. 6). Writing, as opposed to the *other* form of writing, is defined here in terms of its action, its calligraphy—in short, by the physical gestures involved. What is omitted is writing in its relation to the metaphysics of presence. In fact, one of the purposes of writing (according to a definition in the *Petit Robert*) is that it enables us to "in one form or another express our thoughts by means of written language." In other words, what is missing in the definition of writing that Racine gives us is expression, the desire to say something, express a meaning [*vouloir-dire*]—to use the term that Derrida borrows from Edmund Husserl. The *other* writing, the writing practised by Racine, is the writing of the Other, that is, of that part of oneself that does not belong to one's self but pertains rather to an active exteriority that weakens (the existent's) interiority.

Having completed *Le Terrain*, Racine began work on the *Pages-Miroirs*. The material for this project consists of the same pages that provided the entries for *Le Terrain*. The work is composed of a series of additions and subtractions that place "Racine" or, more precisely, his conscious will, at a further remove from his material and his task. It is, therefore, a deconstruction of the metaphysics of presence since the latter primarily and inevitably involves an exercise of the will. Indeed, for this second task Racine considers the dictionary as a musical score to be interpreted or performed (p. 13), thereby underscoring the absence of intentions on his part. For the text is already written, Racine is merely its humble executor, and all desire for expression is nullified. The *Pages-Miroirs* initially involved cutting out paper from beneath the words in such a way that the gaps between them became visible. Do these gaps, then, represent the absence of meaning's self-presence, the predominance of the letter? A mirror positioned behind the pages enables viewers to see their own faces at the same time as the other side of the page; thus the self-questioning (as well as uncertainty and lack of self-assurance) symbolized by the mirror is combined with the materiality of language, as symbolized by the thickness of the page. The mirror functions in such a way that "the text is suspended precisely between one's true face and the motivated reflection of it" (p. 19). "True face"? Does this rather curious expression denote self-perception as that pure interiority whose ideal existence is challenged by the *barrier* of words that reflection requires, and wherein motivation, intention, and expression are sullied by the active (that is, efficacious) empiricism of words? Would there no longer be any motivation, only *motivation*,[8] a contamination of interiority, of the interior by the exterior.

Racine goes on to punch tiny holes in the paper directly beneath each letter in those authors' names that appear in the definitions. For Racine, these perforations are another way of underscoring a certain reality by directing attention to the pores of the page, the skin of the dictionary. He points out that each hole is also a "void, the opposite face of a period," its invisible side; moreover, he suggests that "a little invisibility under an author is not a bad thing" (p. 16). Note that this "death" of the author— every instance of invisibility is a kind of death—is inextricably bound up with increased emphasis on the materiality of the dictionary and is in keeping with the spirit of deconstruction (and structuralism) for which the interplay of textual structures, as perceived by the reader, replaces the omnipotence of the author.

Thus the place occupied by "Racine" becomes minuscule. Whereas the Subject (or the author) formerly occupied the place of a king, the seat of consciousness and signification, the decentred Subject (or author) becomes only one of the elements in the process of signification. In the place of a *grand Rober*, a *Rober-roi*, one finds a *petit Rober*, a fallen Subject. Once there were no longer divinities (or the divinity, the divine) to function as the bearers of signification, the Subject was hastily installed in their place and promoted to the rank of receiver and source of all signification. But if the process of signification *must* be deconstructed, with its sources disseminated so far afield as to include zones of unconsciousness, of "pure" matter, this "Subject" must in turn suffer the ultimate humiliation of its dethronement. It becomes only one element among a host of others; to the extent that a "one" exists, it exists only in the "other." This bitter fate may explain why Racine gilds some of the letters,[9] a gesture that goes back to ancient illuminated manuscripts. The pill of deconstruction, of the constant refusal of the Subject's sovereignty and the acceptance of intrusive alterity, is certainly a bitter one to swallow. Perhaps Racine is trying to gild *it*. Doesn't the practice of manuscript illumination go back to the heyday of "logocentric" thinking, to a time when the connection between the world of ideas and the world of the divine was considered natural?

In a journal that Racine kept while he was working on the *Pages-Miroirs*, and which contains jottings on ideas inspired by the project, there is an imaginary dialogue written on April 5, 1985. This dialogue has long fascinated its author, who felt that it "settled quite a few things" for him.

> Yes, to be quite frank, somewhere within myself I wanted to discourage viewers with the P.M. [*Pages-Miroirs*], to take it so far that they would say, "it makes no sense, it's completely absurd." Yes, I wanted this fervently.
>
> But why?
>
> To show that I could get into something that is not really me, but that nevertheless corresponds to me.
>
> Isn't this paradoxical?
>
> Yes, but I have always worked in a paradoxical manner, against my own grain. And the P.M. is my latest work on this paradox.
>
> Why did you do it?
>
> … In order to exaggerate.

Thus the entire "meaning" of Racine's work is disclosed. Discouraging viewers by presenting them with "absurdity," Racine destroys, or seeks to destroy, the logocentric assurance (of the presence of meaning). Working against himself, he sees to it that the conscious or independent entity in which this assurance is grounded is, as a consequence, shaken; in a way, he works at affirming that all this is not (really) him.

Racine has said that this work demands "rigour, discipline, patience, self-abnegation, and almost obsessional foolhardiness" (p. 11). It is curiously similar to his signature experience, the obsessional nature of which I have already spoken. Obsession used to be correlated with the idea of possession by a demon and represented the opposite of clarity or purity. (The expression, "the demon of writing" aptly conveys the idea.) Here, too, a kind of possession is at work, an invasion by a foreign body alien to the self-identity of ideal mental content. Racine's work is truly interminable, and he admits that he is captivated by the idea that it can never come to an end (p. 11). There is, as well, the following admission: "Interminable. This was the word that sprang most often to mind during the nine years or so I spent on the *Pages-Miroirs*. It is an unbearable word, like 'phagocytosis.' To phagocytose is to absorb, engulf, destroy, and it is the destruction of the all-powerful Subject that the work of writing accomplishes. The product of bodily rigour, a scriptorial rigour more physical than ideal (or mental, or pure), the *Pages-Miroirs* derived mainly from physical labour in which the entire body was invested, as well as invaded."[10] To such an extent that only the body was left, without any mind whatsoever. This explains why Racine exhausts himself in a struggle [*corps à corps*] between his body and the body of language, a struggle that is at the same time a strange fusion of these two "matters" against the metaphysics of presence.

Why this fascination with the interminable? The answer to this question also sheds light on the ambiguity in the notion of work exemplified in the work of Racine, just as it helps to determine the precise scope of Derridean deconstruction. What I have said so far regarding Derrida's theory and Racine's praxis seems to imply that the metaphysics of presence (of the existence of a mental or conceptual universe independent of all physicality) should be replaced by an affirmation of materiality (of writing, language, or any other manifestation of the physical). My statements could easily be taken to mean that it is simply a matter of replacing one set of founding parameters by another. Accordingly, notions such as writing, the trace, difference, and the empirical would be substituted for others such as the interior voice, the concept, identity, and transcendence. However, all this represents only one facet of Derridean theory. Such a replacement does not, in fact, constitute deconstruction. Deconstruction does not advocate choosing empiricism over transcendentalism. As Derrida puts it:

> *That is why a thought of the trace can no more break with a transcendental phenomenology than be reduced to it.* Here as elsewhere, to pose the problem in terms of choice, to oblige or to believe oneself obliged to answer it by a *yes* or *no*, to conceive of appurtenance as an allegiance or nonappurtenance as plain speaking, is to confuse very different levels, paths, and styles. In the destruction of the arche, one does not make a choice.[11]

This work is interminable because it always "falls back on the metaphysics of presence." There is, in the strategy inscribing the *Pages-Miroirs*, something closely resembling a lapse into metaphysics. It occurs in what Racine refers to as the *phrases harmoniques*. This is how he explains the method used to generate these phrases from underlined words:

> I proceed as if the page were a sound and each word on the page the harmonic phrase, its harmonics. This is a way to make the page speak. It whispers a secret. Each phrase must have a meaning, must be grammatically correct (with agreements of verbs and participles, etc.). On the other hand, with respect to punctuation, a certain degree of … liberty is permitted. Nothing in the phrases is left to chance. They are not exquisite corpses. Everything is worked out, subject to a decision, either kept or rejected. (p. 21)

"Everything is worked out." "Each phrase must have a meaning." Here one can see the extent to which Racine distances himself from his previous pronouncements on the validation of the nonsensical and the literalness of his material. His desire to "make the page speak" becomes an attempt to exclude it from the jurisdiction of writing. The "harmonic phrases" operate on the same level as the gilt that Racine applies to his pages; they signal a retreat with respect to the work of deconstruction because Racine once again *desires*, wishes for, a meaning. He seeks to impart a meaning to matter, wants to translate (that is, to confer meaning on, invest) what he originally sought to present as nonsensical. Unable to resist the temptation of intentionality, he gets caught in a double bind.[12] The concept of double bind is essential for an understanding of Derrida's thought (which does not, as I have already said, advocate replacing transcendence with empiricism). Every act of understanding a text or discourse, every attempt at translation,[13] requires a belief in something like a "transcendental signified," in other words, in the existence of univocal mental objects untouched by the materiality of language or, for that matter, anything else. In the acts of understanding or translating, these objects must be susceptible of being extracted from the text or discourse to be understood or translated, and they must be capable of being transported into another text or discourse where, reformulated, reworked, and transformed, they can take up residence "in a new body." Yet this transformation must preserve a "constant," otherwise neither understanding nor translation can be said to occur. Now, reflection on writing undermines this notion of a constant, of a univocal meaning always identical to itself. Thus every attempt at comprehension or translation is taken up in an interminable struggle between the desire for (the metaphysics of) the presence of this univocal meaning and the barrier constituted by the materiality of writing.

This is what underlies Racine's attempts to recover, through his harmonic phrases, *one* meaning from the plurality and dissemination of meanings represented by a page of the dictionary. "Each phrase *must* have a meaning," he says, and nothing escapes this demand for uniqueness, not even "Rober" who throws himself into the fray [*corps-à-corps*] (because ultimately, unable to resist, he gives into it body and soul [*corps et âme*]).

Appendix: Politics of the Dictionary

Derrida's theory may be seen as being in a position analogous to that of Hegelian philosophy in its relation to Marxist theory; in other words, in order for his theory to have any meaning or relevance, it must be flipped over and restored to an upright position. It is in this light that we must view approaches as diverse as those of Gayatri Spivak, Edward Said, and a host of others for whom the "Other" ceases to be a strictly philosophical concept and manifests itself in questions as concrete as sexual differentiation and cultural relativity. Much could be said about this shift, which raises serious obstacles for "translation." At the same time, one could see Racine's work assuming a political dimension since the dictionary he has worked on is, after all, the dictionary of the *French* language. For all work on the materiality of language requires that one distance oneself from the formal system of language (*langage*, and take up a position vis-à-vis a specific *langue* (Saussure), that is, a "natural" language. Anything having to do with the question of language obviously has political resonances in Québec and leads invariably to other considerations regarding the question of identity. In this respect, Racine's work is anything but innocent; indeed, it shows how work as "formal" (?) as his can be caught up in the whirlwind of political affairs.

Notes

1.   Rober Racine, *Le Dictionnaire*, including excerpts from the *Le Terrain du dictionnaire A/Z* (1980) and *Les Pages-Miroirs* (1979–1988) (Montréal: Les Éditions Parachute/Galerie René Blouin, 1988).

2.   Racine, *Le Dictionnaire*, 5. Emphasis added. [Further references to this volume are made in parentheses in the text. This and all subsequent translations from Racine are by the present translator.]

3.   See Racine, *Le Dictionnaire*, 10. Also on page ten, Racine explains that, in an audio cassette he made to explain his project to children who might visit his *Terrain*, the project came to him in a dream.

4.   See my "Paysage culturel" in the catalogue *Paysage* (Montréal: Galerie Dazibao, 1987). I believed in the *need* for art practice to be deconstructive since it could no longer maintain a simple, noncritical relationship with reality.

5.   Marjorie Grene, "Life, Death and Language: Some Thoughts on Wittgenstein and Derrida," in *Philosophy In and Out of Europe*, ed. Marjorie Grene (Berkeley: University of California Press, 1976), 143.

6.   Derrida's "celebrated" statement that "[t]here never was any 'perception'" is also probably the least understood, as well as being the one that generated the most hostility. See Jacques Derrida, *Speech and Phenomena*, trans. David B. Allison (Evanston: Northwestern University Press, 1973), 103. For an example of such incomprehension, one does not have to go farther than Laurent-Michel Vacher's *Pour un matérialisme vulgaire* (Montréal: Les Herbes rouges, 1984). Yet this book deserves to be read because it proposes a convincing (and, unfortunately, frequently unheard) alternative to the generalized craze, particularly in Québec, for every kind of symbolic system, particularly structuralism. On the basis of the above-quoted statement, Vacher concludes that, "in the most classical way possible, Derridean discourse joins in the strategy of undermining empiricism" (Ibid., 122). What he means is that Derrida, by refusing all perception of the *real*, takes refuge

in metaphysics. Now Derrida's remark signified the very opposite. Instructive in this regard is the following excerpt from Newton Garver's preface to *Speech and Phenomena*: "This is, of course, not a rejection of any familiar everyday experience, but a rejection of a concept, a concept that is an idealized and, one might say, logicized abstraction from our common everyday experience. It is the concept of perception, not as an awareness of circumstances in which we live and move and have our being, but rather as the pure immediate awareness of a sensory content which … has no *intrinsic* reference to any such actual circumstances" (Ibid., xxiii).

7.   It is possible to see an affinity between Racine's work and the work of John Cage. The literalness of language of the one is matched by the literalness of sound of the other; in both there is a refusal of the process of signification. Take the *Pages-Miroirs* as one example. The way that Racine isolates the names of musical notes within words in the dictionary and uses them to generate musical scores—a process I will not go into here since it appears to be not entirely germane to my interpretation—is fundamentally the same as Cage's approach to "composition." Such scores are completely devoid of "meaning."

8.   "The immotivation of the trace ought now to be understood as an operation and not as a state, as an active movement, a demotivation, and not as a given structure." Jacques Derrida, *Of Grammatology*, trans. Gayatri Chakravorty Spivak (Baltimore: Johns Hopkins University Press, 1974), 51. [Note that "motivation" plays on the French *mot*, which means word.]

9.   The letters and closed numbers of the words in italics: a, b, d, e, g, o, p, q and 4, 6, 8, 9, 0.

10.   "… to tell you that the *Pages-Miroirs* were first and foremost physical labour, an undertaking in which my whole body was both invested and invaded." Racine, *Le Dictionnaire*, 18.

11.   Derrida, *Of Grammatology*, 62.

12.   "One is obliged to translate and not to translate. I am reminded of the double bind presented by YHWH when, with the name of its choice, its Babel name, so to speak, it simultaneously *does and does not lend itself to translation*. Since its first appearance, the double postulation has been unavoidable." Jacques Derrida, "Of an Apocalyptic Tone Recently Adopted in Philosophy," *Oxford Literary Review*, vol. 6, no. 2 (1984): 10.

13.   Derrida develops the concept of the double bind in the context of reflections on the question of translation. This question is taken up in several texts, among which we find: "Of an Apocalyptic Tone Recently Adopted in Philosophy"; "Freud and the Scene of Writing," *Writing and Difference*, trans. Alan Bass (Chicago: University of Chicago Press, 1978); and *Ulysse gramophone, Deux mots pour Joyce* (Paris: Galilée, 1987).

Translated from the French by Donald McGrath.

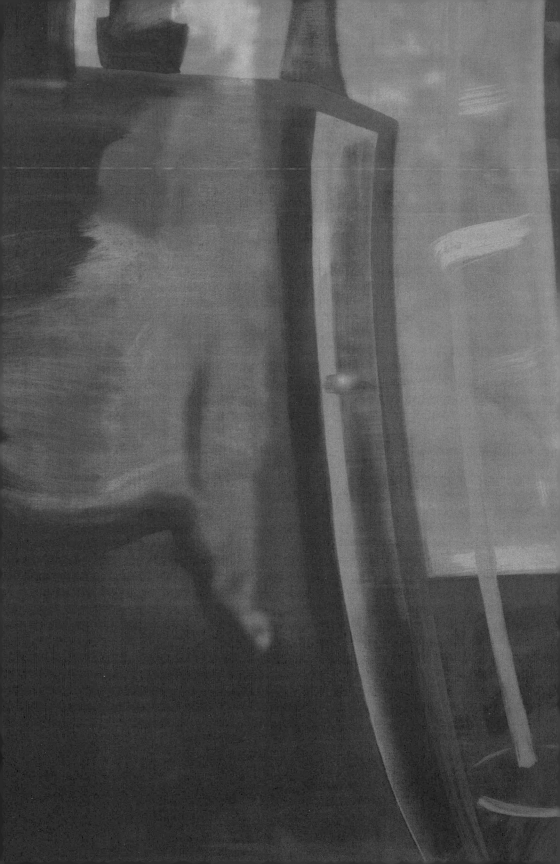

systems and symbols

Jacqueline Fry

The Museum in a Number of Recent Works

Much has already been written about the calling into question of that public service institution known as the museum. Or, to be more precise, the art museum. Aside from the many conferences, events, and seminars that have issued from this development, countless related visual critiques have been made, and diverse associations formed. The problem that has produced all this debate, in the process engendering the most extreme ideological positioning, is a monolithic or barely relativist view of culture that has been with us since the end of the nineteenth century. And it is in the contemporary art museum that the challenge to museology is most acutely felt. One could even claim that the very conception of the contemporary art museum constitutes the crux of every cultural problematic having to do with institutional mechanisms. Insofar as this type of museum sanctifies the exemplary images of a world unknown to most of its visitors (that is, those outside the small world of art circles), the contemporary art museum draws attention to the whole array of ideological and professional functions of museums and cultural institutions in general.

I will attempt neither to analyse nor to trace a history of museological criticism, and I am even less concerned with that double or shadow constituted by the critique of art and its social function.[1] Instead, I prefer to extract a few specific questions and study them carefully in order to arrive at further observations, thus avoiding the kind of unwieldy and precarious concoctions that lead to generalizations.

Can works that refer (whether in form or content) to museums tell us anything about the role of the contemporary art museum or the function of contemporary art wings as fragments of museographic wholes? Do such works, taken individually in their material specificity, manifest diverse attitudes towards the institution, and could such diversity help us to pinpoint the contradictions in the duo "contemporary art/art museum"? Finally, do such products of the imagination reveal anything about dominant or subservient ideologies, and are they indicative of future roles?

Three exemplary types of work will serve as a springboard for my inquiry. Two of them take on the world of the museum, while the third steers away from it. The former are represented here by the work of Daniel Buren and Hans Haacke, while the latter is exemplified by the

This is a translation of a text first published in *Parachute*, no. 24 (1981).

practitioners of sociological art. Once I have looked at these examples, I will be better equipped to elucidate the subtleties of certain Canadian works.

Daniel Buren

For roughly a decade, using uniform, equidistant stripes painted on paper or canvas, Daniel Buren has made museological space the focus of an interrogation from within, while from without he has been examining the gaze brought to bear on the so-called work of art. "The greatest difference," he has written, "between a given Pollock and a neighbouring Monet in the Museum of Modern Art is ... 3.5 metres." This statement serves to focus attention on the viewing space of the art object.[2] Buren's object, his X, his plastically constant painting/sign, questions every space in which it is shown and, in doing so, brings out another constant, namely the lack of autonomy of the art work due to its dependence on the museum. Whether acquiescent or indifferent—or indeed complicit—the artist is invariably eclipsed by museum curators working on behalf of *their* museum, *their* space, the place where they contrive to present the work. As Buren puts it, "The work has no place outside this place, does not take place without it" [*En dehors du lieu, l'œuvre n'a pas lieu*].[3] The architecture of the building in question, its specialized galleries, the specific character of each room, the walls, doors, corners, columns, plinths, light switches, spacing of works, exit signs, and so on all come into play in exhibitions. The exhibited object (in Buren's case usually a painting) is not seen as a thing in itself since the gaze is channelled by discreet mechanisms that are increasingly refining our supposedly innocent viewing conditions. Much has been written on Daniel Buren, and he is himself a prolific writer. His texts are an integral part of an œuvre that must be understood as experimental. It has remained faithful to a key concern initially formulated in the 1960s and expanded during the 1970s, that is, the exposure of the visual mechanisms that serve the ideological programmes of museums. In this, Buren is more concerned with finding ways of disengaging painting—intended, apparently, as a stand-in for all art—from the grip of obscurantists, than he is with waging a political struggle against the system. His interest in pinpointing the "painting effect" reflects the approach of a philosopher *plasticien* rather than that of a sociologist. Buren made this quite clear when he said:

> I deal with the visible. ... My work is not that of the sociologist or critic. What interests me is the way the museum leaves its mark on the objects it exhibits. I have never been "anti," whether antisculpture, antipainting or whatever. Indeed, I always end up making paintings.[4]

Artémisia, an exhibition organized in 1979 by the Galerie Yvon Lambert in Paris, also included a book/catalogue[5] which may be viewed as one of the objects in the exhibition. Or it could even function as a double of the gallery itself since it exhibits texts (such as Evan Manzia's explicitly titled *Autoportrait en guise de peinture*), as well as textual fragments, notes, extensions of various works, and a soundtrack. Participants in the exhibition were invited to draw upon their particular expertise to make a work based on Artemisia Gentileschi's *Judith and Maidservant with the Head of Holofernes* (c. 1625).

Daniel Buren made good use of the opportunity, and his contribution to the event was representative of his specific brand of visual polemics. Equally exemplary was the relation he established between visual and textual strategies. Before proceeding to base a piece on the Gentileschi, Buren showed how things stood with the work itself, that is, he disclosed the mode of existence and material conditions of a painting that, he remarked sharply, had probably been seen by few besides himself. (What art historian or critic could fail to feel the sting of this remark?) Buren tells us just what one has to do in order to see *Judith and Holofernes*. After Kafkaesque bureaucratic procedures in Florence, we come upon it finally in the Corridoio Vasari of the Uffizi, a section closed to the public! It is "the last one to the right, on the wall directly opposite the entrance to the Caravaggio Room, and it is attached to the wall by a large ring extending beyond the top of the frame." Visitors to the Paris gallery discovered a white space standing in for the missing painting. "Framed" white spaces indicated the simultaneous presence and absence of neighbouring works. In the book, information about the works was conveyed by means of "souvenir photographs"[6] and by drawings that showed the order in which they were hung. Buren's object implacably underscored the lack of the real object and suggested an analogy with another lack, namely, the lack of visibility of the painting, owing, in subtle ways, to its treatment at the hands of the museum.

Ponctuations, statue/sculpture was inaugurated in November of 1980. The work is of relevance here for a number of reasons. First, it was sponsored by the Nouveau Musée of Lyon, a museum that did not actually exist—rather, it did exist but as a team, programme, and office. Second, the objective of *Ponctuations* was to display the kind of work most typically found in museums (i.e. statuary) in quintessentially public contexts outside museums. Third, also pertinent is the guidebook it produced to statuary in and around Lyon.

The pedestals of all the statues "dotting the squares, avenues, and public gardens of Lyon and Villeurbanne"[7] were wrapped in Buren's

Chocolate Master) exhibition held at the Paul Maenz Gallery in Cologne (June 1981), displays proof of collusion between the administrative apparatus of museums and that of a much larger institution which controls the very ways in which we live and think. The generous donor or distinguished collector of modern and contemporary art, who is also a president or member of some board of trustees, is seen in a light other than that of the cultural benefactor. As head of a multinational corporation—a *maître de forges* or ironmaster, as they were once called in France—he leads an organization that, in the course of its operations, is not particularly concerned with the living conditions of workers, the plight of those under the sway of colonialism or neocolonialism, or the resolution of conflicts that threaten world peace.

For examples of Haacke's early works, I will begin by mentioning a project that was rejected by the director of the Guggenheim Museum in 1971 (it revealed much about the real estate system). This was followed in 1972 by the *John Weber Gallery Visitor's Profile 1* and *Profile 2*. These were studies carried out in May and September of that year to determine the number of people visiting a contemporary art gallery (John Weber). In March 1974, New York's Stefanotty Gallery exhibited data that Haacke had collected on the members of the Solomon Guggenheim Museum's Board of Trustees; this data delineated members' family ties, their connections with large companies, and their cultural roles. Subsequently, Haacke's *Manet-PROJEKT '74*, exhibited at Cologne's Paul Maenz Gallery after being refused by the city's Wallraf-Richartz Museum, retraced the trajectory of Manet's *Bunch of Asparagus* (1880) through the hands of its various owners—biographies of the latter were attached. One of these revealed that the last owner, president of the Friends of the Museum and himself a generous donor, had not, during a certain period, shown himself to be particularly anti-Nazi. Finally, in *Social Grease*, shown at the John Weber Gallery in 1975, six photo-engraved magnesium plates bore statements on art made by prominent figures from various cultural, political, and financial institutions.[11] Starting with the museum as the operational crux of the art system, and tracing the activities of the same players and structures, Hans Haacke has recently concentrated more on corporations in the strict sense of the word. Of course, they are all part of the same system, but there has been a shift from one apparatus to another, or from part of a mechanism to a larger structure. *We believe in the power of creative imagination* (Ghent, Museum van Hedendaagse, 1980) targets the weapons manufacturer Herstal and its arms shipments to South Africa.[12] *Upstairs at Mobil: Musings of a Shareholder* (John Weber Gallery, February 7–March 4, 1981) takes aim at the various machinations of Mobil Oil.[13]

Der Pralinenmeister requires closer examination.[14] In a thin pamphlet serving as a catalogue, fourteen pages of text and photographs trace the politico-cultural and economic avatars of one Peter Ludwig, head of the multinational chocolate manufacturer, Monheim.[15] Above each text and its title are two photographs: the one on the left is of "the boss," while the one on the right shows a typical work situation. (The chocolate makers resemble nurses, and everything seems bright and clean.) Below each text, at the bottom of the page, are photographs of chocolate boxes. The texts tells us how the company has grown nationally and internationally, in a process that can best be compared to a spreading oil slick. We learn about the harsh working conditions of the employees, most of whom are unskilled immigrant women. We are also apprised of the systematic, parallel expansion of Peter and Irene Ludwig's modern and contemporary art collection since 1966. A system of long-term deposits and donations has enabled Ludwig to be appointed to key positions on boards of trustees and acquisitions committees. Ludwig's ever increasing influence in art circles reached its apotheosis with projects for a "Ludwig Museum" (slated to begin construction in Cologne in 1985) and for a "Ludwig Foundation for Art and International Understanding." The responsibilities that Herr and Frau Ludwig have taken upon themselves with respect to nearly the entire professional decision-making apparatus of the foundation are good indicators of the authority they wield in art circles, whether regional, national, or international. Hans Haacke has set himself the task of studying and exposing the ideologically camouflaged mechanisms underlying these cultural activities.[16] From this perspective, of course, the museum is clearly a target.

The works of Daniel Buren and Hans Haacke are exemplary in their exposure of museological manœuvres. However, a further step has been taken, one that takes us beyond the exclusive domain of the museum. This approach, which may be seen as an intervention within an art field painstakingly cleared of institutional (and particularly museological) pressures, is the one adopted by sociological art.[17] The fragmented field of art practice should, according to this perspective, be able to break out of the official incestuous channels comprised of artists, museums, markets, and art coteries, and strike out on a quest for productive and cooperative creative freedom. "As far as I'm concerned," says Fred Forest, "contemporary artists no longer need museums. Let me explain. I mean that any place can become a site of creation, action, and distribution for a given time. … I also believe strongly in information exchange mechanisms, a network in which the museum may be only one element."[18] The *Institut international d'arthérapie* (Jean-Paul Thénot, 1972), *Hygiène de l'art*

(Hervé Fischer, 1972–1974), the *Bureau d'identité utopique* (Hervé Fischer, 1975), the *École sociologique interrogative* (founded by the *Collectif d'art sociologique* in May of 1976),[19] the *Société civile immobilière du mètre carré artistique* (Fred Forest, 1977), which was succeeded by the *Territoire du M² artistique* (1977)—all these represent so many alternative vocabularies, works, and situations meant to signal a turning away from the museum. Movements such as these, with their penchant for parody in naming, transform the status of the artist. Becoming a "manager," "concierge," human relations coordinator, master of ceremonies, and catalyst of individual and collective imaginations, the artist willingly gives way to collective authorship. As Jean-Paul Thénot puts it, "canvas is succeeded by the social fabric."[20] The theory informing sociological art does not derive from texts, from sociological and communication theory, but from the specifics of a practice which, while steering around the museum, does not cease to question it.

Jean-Paul Thénot

During the International Book Festival which took place in Nice in May 1978, Jean-Paul Thénot and Jean-Pierre Giovanelli invited visitors to the kiosk of the Palais des Expositions to "become coauthors and co-owners of a book to be written, printed, and autographed during the Festival." Entitled *Nous sommes tous des écrivains*, the project attracted a large audience. The size of the press run was equivalent to the number of participants. The existence of the book, which was actually printed and autographed on the same day, attested to the kiosk's success. Indeed, this was "the only place at the Festival where people were actually writing." The event engendered numerous critical challenges to myths about creativity, production, and distribution; the title itself was suggestive in this respect. Beyond the initial echoes of "We are all German Jews," a slogan repeatedly chanted on Parisian boulevards in May 1968, it seemed to bear a second connotation implying that "We are all artists." "Have we not," participants at the fair must have wondered, "have we not produced art (writing) in the form of an object (the book), and done so in and for a place (the Festival, not the museum) that is open to everybody? And didn't we do this together, as one?" *Hommage aux artistes inconnus*, a symbolic memorial erected at the University of Lund (March 27–April 21, 1981), extended the perspectives opened up by the previous event.[21] In order to build this monument, the parodic nature of which posed a challenge to both art history and the museum, temporary offices were set up in various cities and given the task of receiving plans, drawings, photographs, project proposals, and models. Earlier, in his *Art-Étalon* project (November 1980), Thénot had come up with the idea of a sort of inverse parodic tribute. "Art prototypes," designed after a series of interviews, would be "produced out of specially tested material" and "placed in museums in specially made boxes that would maintain them in optimum conditions of temperature and humidity." Finally, "because of the same concern for preservation, and in order to avoid any damage or detrimental change, the pieces could only be viewed if fifty people (or less) asked the museum to see them. In such cases, the museum would undertake to display the prototype or prototypes to the public. Eventually, only a projected image of these would be available; it could be viewed using an apparatus designed expressly for the purpose." Taking aim at consumer culture (for example, the few obligatory seconds put in viewing the Mona Lisa), Jean-Paul Thénot became the prophet of a certain style of museology.

Fred Forest

Fred Forest comes across as a strategist of mass communication techniques, systematically employing those that counter the closed communicative means of museums and art coteries. "Providers of services, intermediaries who establish networks of critical information"[22]—this is how Forest sees today's artists.

Since 1972, Forest's approach has evolved through various forms of action. His preferred medium is video, although he does not restrict himself to it.[23] After initially setting out to investigate the collective imagination, challenging both it and the institutions that enclose it, he has moved on to a second stage. He has found himself a fixed vantage point, a theatre that is at once a foundation and a community; a simulacrum of the system and its institutions, it is a place for play, a symbolic and experimental space as well as a territory, the *Territoire du M²*.

One must, however, take into account several of the many activities Forest carried out during the ten-year span that preceded his *Territoire*. Take, for example, his series of blank spaces. We can start with the white squares he invited newspaper readers to use in visual interventions (see *Le Monde*, Paris, January 1972 and the *Tribune-Matin,* Lausanne, November 1972). We can continue with the greyish-white rectangles seen during a minute of silence on French national television (January 1972); after twenty seconds without sound or image, the voice of Fred Forest was heard to declare, "Do not adjust your set. Take this time for yourself …" Finally, we could consider the blank placards carried around the streets of São Paulo during the 12th Biennial (November 1973). These pieces in the

newspapers, on television, and in the urban environment sought to provoke a level of awareness that museums barely approximate. "The museum of the day is out of touch, does not investigate. ... I can choose to
exhibit in newspapers, on television."[24] This is not to say, however, that
the museum is always excluded, for it can serve as a relay. This is indeed
what happened in November 1972 and 1978 when a museum in
Lauzanne exhibited newspaper pages with blank spaces that were subsequently filled in by readers. Also, of the many video works in Fred Forest's
career, we should note his *Famille Vidéo*, shown in Cologne in June
1976.[25] The rooms of an apartment were equipped with individual video
monitors that showed fragments of the occupant's daily activity. (Only in
the living room, which was provided with an extra monitor, was it possible to see the regular lineup of programmes broadcast by the main television station.) The succession of monitors gave rise to a series of questions.
The apartment housing the event served as an extension of the alternative
gallery system, which was originally a critical substitute for art museums.
Within this apartment, Forest's *Famille Vidéo* functioned as a mirror, one
that raised questions. Problems with respect to art and the museum were
discussed.

Forest's *Promenade sociologique* (December 1973) was yet another
instance of a museum (the São Paulo Museum of Contemporary Art) serving as a relay. Accompanied by twenty-five people who had signed up for
the adventure, Forest took a "sociological" bus tour that had been adver-
tised in the newspapers. As well, thirty duly numbered seats standing in as
witnesses for the museum were taken along by the apprentice "sociolo-
gists" as they set out to explore a neighbourhood. Having served either
symbolic or practical functions, the seats were to end up eventually back
in the museum; there they would resume their basic roles as instruments
of rest, aids to individual contemplation, or decorative fillers.

The provocative side of Forest's work operates more subtly in the
Territoire du M² artistique. To find this parodic structure one must travel
to Anserville, forty-five kilometres outside of Paris, and enter the grounds
around the hunting lodge of the Château d'Anserville, for it is here that
one finds the solitary enterprise along with the outer wall delimiting the
Territoire. The administration building includes a documentation area and
a conference room; already partially built, the latter comes equipped with
a throne reminiscent of some company chairman's seat. Outside, beyond
an incomplete entrance, is a plot of land divided by a grid into a thousand
parcels identified by boundary markers. These parcels, some of which have
already been sold,[26] function as canvases, surfaces waiting to be painted.
Set down in seven articles, the founding charter of the *Territoire* confers

on Fred Forest, "in his dual capacity as artist and manager" of the *Société civile immobilière du M² artistique*, responsibility for the management of the *Territoire* in its guise as a bureaucratic body. The reverse side of this administrative façade reveals certain utopic features that are still in a process of development, for here is the domain of the much-touted freedom of imagination permitted inside the outer wall. From this perspective, the solid brick wall may be viewed as a fiction that can at any time be penetrated from within by the utopic element in a quest for other, vaster surfaces. This is very different from the type of territorial occupation we find in museums, which hem in outward impulses. With the *Territoire du M²*, anything is possible. It seems that Georges Perec, choosing a thousand words, one for each plot of land, will create a semantic field that will blend in perfectly with the other fields generated by the interplay of other owners' projects. As Fred Forest reiterates, "Anything is possible. One could write a novel, hold elections or even take hostages (somewhat reluctant ones, that is)."[27] The *Territoire du M² artistique* gives every indication of constituting a long-term challenge to the art system and those museums that harbour images from that system.

Hervé Fischer

In addition to work by Fred Forest and Jean-Paul Thénot, the early 1970s saw the beginnings of Hervé Fischer's critique of art and its institutional underpinnings. Like his counterparts, Fischer has tended to sweep aside the limits that tradition has imposed on artistic practice. However, the body of theory he has developed in support of his activities is significantly vaster and more elaborate than that of his fellow militants in sociological art. Yet the latter's comparative lack of theory is, it should be noted, entirely calculated. With respect to Fischer, I will not dwell on texts produced in book form; rather, I will be looking at a number of works that manifest critical perspectives *vis-à-vis* the museum.[28] Fischer's *Hygiène de l'art*, a theory-supported practice worked out between 1971 and 1979, came to occupy the place of Art History.[29] In his *Hygiène du musée* (1972), an invitation card was used to make a point about the moribund character of museum spaces. *Hygiène de la galerie* (1974) extended this targeting of the support structure for Art. Using pictorial means to draw attention to the walls of a village street near Nice, Fischer transformed an everyday place into an art gallery. He did so, he claimed, in order to instigate a rupture between the sacred and the profane. In 1976, he produced *Les Trois portes du Palais du Louvre*, a visual document that disclosed a global institutional structure that we are used to seeing in fragments, which we then take for the whole. In his *Pharmacie idéologique*, variations on *Hygiène de l'art* that took place between 1975 and 1976, Fischer invited people to sit down with him at a table identified as a pharmacy and used a set of questions and answers to determine the appropriate pills to be prescribed for each person. These pieces, which brought Fischer into contact with an extremely diverse range of people, also drew upon such highly different places as public squares, private apartments, boutiques, theatres, art galleries, museums (the Musée Galliera in Paris and the São Paulo Museum), and even an actual pharmacy.[30] Occurring at the site of production itself, the dialogue between the producer and the public was pushed to its limits, oscillating between plain avowals, psychological testing, and the exchange of information.

During the International Symposium on Environmental Sculpture in Chicoutimi, Québec in 1980, Hervé Fischer and Alain Snyers organized a parallel event designed to meet a host of disparate objectives.[31] What one retains from *Citoyens/Sculpteurs*, a workshop meant to compete ideologically with other workshops and the symposium itself,[32] is the foregrounding of a previously untapped imaginative reservoir, namely, those city dwellers on whom (on whose territory) landscaping projects tend to be imposed. Their collective imagination constitutes the theatre of operations of sociological art, which thereby overturns traditional museological pedagogy with its scant regard for questioning.

If I have spent so much time on the works of Daniel Buren, Hans Haacke, and the proponents of sociological art, it was not so much to retrace the history of the art in question (museums included) as to juxtapose a set of philosophies and practices which, like the three doors of Hervé Fischer's Palais du Louvre, tend to be approached outside the context of the unique architecture that houses them. The procedures employed to demystify, to divest the museum of its supposed innocence, are all the more effective as they come from authors deeply attached to the production of a communicable visual order. From a world of material production whose axes all converge on the museum, I have selected only the most exemplary of polemical works.

I will now attempt to deal with a number of recent Canadian works that also seem to be situated within the problematic of the museum.

Irène Whittome

The reference system of Irène Whittome's *Le Musée blanc* is already evident from its title.[33] The artist did not leave viewers the choice of making interpretations solely on the basis of her work. One need only read the various critiques generated by the two best-known works in the series, *Le Musée blanc I* and *Le Musée blanc II* (both 1975), or listen to the comments of visitors seeing these museums for the first time, to realize that the museological reference draws upon a body of knowledge evoked by the title. The immediate connotation is not of a white museum but, rather, of something exotic and vaguely anthropological, a "column of totemic figures." Or, if it is not exotic, it is psychoanalytical, alluding to "phallic figures." Yet, for those who keep to the constraints imposed by the title, the artist's points of reference become increasingly clear. Irène Whittome, one sees, exposes museological values. She does so using assemblages, friezes of slender columns in string and moulded paper constructed on museographic principles rendered visually explicit. Such principles include the serial ordering of objects in accordance with classification schemes and the isolation and display of such series behind protective glass. Each component of *Le Musée blanc* not only is presented as a glass box reminiscent of museum display cases but also functions as a box inside a box, a sort of mini-museum. The museum that Irène Whittome lays out for us is a white, ordered environment that is both pure and neutral, wherein a history emerges from the juxtaposition of objects.

The five *Musées blancs* shown in Montréal in 1975 gave but a glimpse of a much greater whole, an immense white museum comprising various shapes and sizes of display cases exhibiting constantly changing assemblages of objects.[34] This white museum may eventually lead to a black museum envisioned by Whittome as a sort of necessary complement. Transparency would be supplanted by a screen of darkness that would impede immediate access to the ordering system involved. While the artist plays with her two favourite colours, in accordance with an imaginative logic that is all her own, the tribute she pays to the museum remains a constant feature of her work. For Irène Whittome pays homage to the museum, that memory-place wherein her personal sense of time becomes indistinguishable from the general passage of time attested to by the objects on display. The museum remains a cultural site where the artist discovers the aesthetic, material traces of the world. The rules governing order and visibility serve as models.

Michael Snow

Irène Whittome's quotation of the museum is, as it were, allegorical. In contrast to this, Michael Snow's *Plus tard* (1977), a series of twenty-five colour photographs of landscapes by the Group of Seven, is a literal quotation from a collection once housed on the third floor of the National

Gallery of Canada in Ottawa. Behind Plexiglas, in their wood frames, these images emphasize the intervention of the artist/photographer. The blurred quality of these arrested images is of particular interest since this is what indicates that the quotation is quite complex. While it does appear to be literal, it is not, for all that, any less ambiguous. Approaching *Plus tard* in this manner, one admittedly falls into the trap of seizing on an isolated segment of Snow's work; I am aware of the difficulties involved here. For *Plus tard* is but one element in Snow's entire corpus, and it is to this corpus, in its entirety, that one must look for the very substance of his approach.[35]

The discrepancies between the photographic images and those in the paintings in the National Gallery (landscapes that are already representations of the vision of the Group of Seven) support the conclusion that Snow was concerned with both the problematic of representation and the problem of grasping space and time by means of a carefully orchestrated apparatus. Faithful to my particular interest in locating quotations from the world of the museum, I discover that I can, through the photographs, almost reconstruct the National Gallery's Group of Seven Room from the wall spaces above, below, and between the works; for these give precise indications of the location and sequence of paintings, ceilings, floors, corners, lights, frames, labels, and so on. I can also reconstruct the itinerary of a hypothetical visit. Yet the sequence of the photographs is not intended to duplicate the trajectory dictated by the arrangement of paintings in the room. This is quite clear from the artist's written specifications. Ideally, he says, the photographs should make maximum use of the space in the room. He adds, however, that "if necessary, the frames could touch. ... *Plus tard* could be mounted on two walls or even three, in a straight line, from numbers one to twenty-five; but it is not necessary to start with number one." The important thing is to reproduce the sense of movement experienced during a gallery visit, and to maintain the discrepancy instituted by the motion of the camera between the painted and the photographic images and imposed on the eye and mind of the visitor. Michael Snow places viewers in situations in which they can discover themselves as viewers and assume whatever consequences this discovery may have for perception.[36] The viewer does not escape the artist's irony, which is but one of the effects produced by the blurred quality of the images.[37] As a perfect place for artistic reflection and an actual locus for conversation and for exhibiting the work of the Group of Seven, the Gallery here functions as a magnet. Once the reference becomes clear, it determines the focus of reflection, calling pictorial stability into question. Quotation shades over into interpretation. Is Snow's citation nationalistic? Is he paying tribute to the Group of Seven, casting its members as young revolutionary painters, as explorers of the wild landscapes of the Canadian Shield, or as artists passionately involved in capturing the transformations of nature?[38] In *Plus tard*, the phenomenon of interpretation *in situ*, as experienced by museum visitors, is literally induced by the openly ambiguous nature of the image that is doing the quoting.

"Their work and its exhibition in that one room at the National Gallery are culture, cultivation."[39] Clearly, by thus explaining his sense of the Group of Seven, Michael Snow also expresses the way he feels about the museum as a place of discovery and enrichment. While they occur in completely different visual works and strategies, the museological references of both Michael Snow and Irène Whittome share a common inscription within the traditional ideology of art and the museum.

General Idea

To mark its centennial in 1980, the National Gallery of Canada hosted the *Pluralities/1980/Pluralités* exhibition. Among the exhibitors was General Idea. Since 1968, the essentially interdisciplinary activities (performance, installation, video, film, printmaking, the publication of *FILE* magazine, and the establishment of Art Metropole) of the three founders of the group have concentrated mainly on a single project, the Miss General Idea Pavilion. This work functions as a parodic mythology of Western postindustrial culture, the models of which can be found in artistic production.[40] The project consists in getting the Pavilion ready for 1984, employing, for the purpose, a wide range of objects and events. Some of the events, such as the election of Miss General Idea, are repeated. "The Search for the Spirit of Miss General Idea" is a way of realizing all the rituals associated with the world of fashion, the latter understood as a cult that saps all our intellectual and imaginative energies. General Idea's methodology is greatly indebted to certain studies on thought processes carried out by Claude Lévi-Strauss, Michel Foucault, Roland Barthes, and others during the late 1960s and early 1970s. While waiting for 1984, the open-ended approach of the Pavilion facilitates the execution of projects that are consistent with "the general idea" of each new site.

Thus, for a time the National Gallery of Canada became synonymous with the Pavilion, in the form of *Three Information Booths in the 1984 Miss General Idea Pavilion* (1980). The booths were placed in key locations: the foyer leading into the exhibition, the contemporary art gallery on the fifth floor, and the top floor with the cafeteria.[41] The latter was, of course, a space where one could just eat, drink, and talk, a place one could go to simply for the fun of it, without being obliged to visit the other floors with their inevitably taxing exhibits. The booths, light metal constructions, were equipped with telephone receivers that one could pick up to obtain information; on the walls of the booths were photographs relating specifically to the Pavilion project. On the ground floor, visitors were provided with a guided tour and a recording of someone reading a fictional brochure on the physical features of the Gallery/Pavilion. The recording in the fifth-floor booth played off against Claes Oldenburg's *Bedroom Ensemble* (1963), thereby infusing new life into an object in the National Gallery's permanent collection. In a tone reminiscent of *belle époque* celebrities or television advertising stars extolling the virtues of shampoo or make-up, the suave voice of the guide halted visitors at the threshold of the "private apartments of Miss General Idea." Oldenburg's bedroom with its snob modernism was conducive to a more intimate acquaintance with Miss General Idea. Behind closed doors that kept the public out, it provided a haven for "the myth concealed behind the image." The booth on the fifth floor introduced visitors to the art of consuming. In the *Colour Bar Lounge*, conceived as a sort of "cultural laboratory," "aesthetic cocktails" functioned as "new cultural elixirs." With this, the circuit was complete. In this parodic reconstruction of the rituals of the artistic and intellectual "establishment," the art museum naturally found its place. As a substitute for the Pavilion, itself a substitute for the fickle world of culture, the National Gallery was drawn into an exercise in irony that ultimately doubled back upon itself ("mirrors mirroring mirrors").[42] The museum was revealed as being no different from other versions of the Pavilion; rather, it derives from the same general idea, and this "general idea" translates into art terms, is realized on art's turf.

Three other works in *Pluralities*[43] particularly drew my attention. Two of these, Don Proch's *Field* (1980) and Max Dean's *Made to Measure* (1980), invited one to share an experience that involved the situation of the museum. The third, *Allocations* (1980) by Garry Neill Kennedy, seemed akin to the polemical approaches to museums looked at above.

Betty Goodwin

For methodological reasons it may be worthwhile, before looking at Don Proch's *Field*, to dwell a moment on a second "field" located on the same floor of the National Gallery during the *Pluralities* exhibition. Betty Goodwin's *Passage in a Red Field* (1980) created a sort of chamber that was both intimate and accessible, as well as highly aesthetic and abstract. The piece as a whole was complex, with its red walls and steel surfaces, its paraffin and graphite partitions, its passageways and set of three corridors, one of which (left of centre) soon became a dead end. The narrow middle corridor was lit by a neon tube suspended just above a reddish violet floor. ("The colour red," Goodwin has said, "is the very soul of painting."[44]) Still another corridor, perpendicular to the centre one, flanked a long window normally concealed by a false wall. Goodwin cut an opening in this wall and spread a fabric screen over the windows; the result was a field awash in diffuse, natural light that could be seen from afar. At one end of this luminous field, a mirror "blocked off the corridor but made it possible to imagine the light continuing beyond it."[45] Audible crackling sounds from the electrical utilities room contributed to the character of this area and set it off from the rest of the gallery.

The field that concerns us here is simultaneously a physical construct and a mental space arising from an idea that Goodwin describes as "undefinable and private."[46] In her estimation, its isolation, apparent autonomy, and concealed windows made the area of the gallery she chose the only suitable place for an installation. What is more, it was also the only real possibility since, without it, she would not have gone ahead with her project. These considerations are ample proof of the close interrelationship subsisting between museological space and the artist. In this case, however, the museum appears as simply one space among others. Other places, private apartments, natural sites, etc., could serve just as well. Yet, while the current range of available exhibition spaces reduces the exclusivity of the museum, it does not call institutional prestige into question, and it is even less critical of cultural policy in general.[47]

Don Proch

Don Proch's field targets literal representation. The approach described here involves the convergence of two objects—a room at the National Gallery, in which the work was to be shown, and a field in Manitoba. Proch constructed a model of the room outdoors in the Manitoba field, then placed it inside the actual room at the National Gallery. Inside the model, he placed *Field*, a broad, squat oval of thick, untidy grass-like material surrounded by a dark, ploughed border. This mass occupied almost the entire floor space, leaving visitors barely enough room to walk around. Pointing into the centre from one end, the toes of a pair of work boots (cast by Proch from the feet of a friend) seemed to invite visitors to slip their feet into them. The blond mass was obviously meant to represent a field, a piece of prairie sprouting out of a parcel of tilled soil.[48] The central image consisted, then, of this piece of "land" with moulded fibreglass boots and simulated resin puddles in "grass" made from unravelled ends of packing string. Left of the entrance to the next exhibition space, six photographs depicted the work's frames of reference in Manitoba. Further to the left, the grille of an air conditioner was painted in red ochre, that is, the colour of the walls during the preceding exhibition. For Proch's exhibit, the walls were painted black. Along them at regular intervals, thin rods of unpainted wood recalled the construction in the real field visible in the photographs. Thus two spaces were simultaneously present and (re)presented.

The piece was actually inspired by the first space, the National Gallery room assigned to Proch for *Pluralities*. It built upon a casting project already underway in the artist's studio. After he had carefully inspected the room, noted its dimensions and light sources, and selected a provisional colour for the walls, Proch returned to Manitoba. He took back with him an image of a prestigious ideological space reserved for displaying historically sanctioned objects. For Proch, as an artist from Western Canada and (more specifically) from Manitoba, the National Gallery stood for something else entirely. He saw it as a space that should really represent the entire country in all its diversity, a diversity attested to by the wide range of objects assembled within its walls.

The second space was, of course, the above-mentioned field situated near the village of Headingly, west of Winnipeg. This is the site of the rural life which, Proch claims, will remain an inexhaustible source of material for his work. Onto this field, Proch plotted the notations he had made in Ottawa. The space of the exhibition room was recreated using a structure of posts connected at the base by a thick swath of flour that designated the floor. The ceiling was represented by horizontal beams. The locations of doorways and spotlights were respected; for the latter, electrical generators were used. A reconstructed, air conditioner grille was also visible, and a uniformed guard was hired for photo sessions.[49] As the projected object of an exhibition, the field itself was marked off by a double line of wooden pickets that formed an oval. In the virgin prairie soil, they took on the appearance of booby-traps.

The events that occurred near Headingly, at the National Gallery and—with a work pause—in the artist's Winnipeg studio did not constitute a work of protest or philosophical reflection but one that was somehow ethical. Not only did this work function as a visual relay for a human landscape (with its material specificity and its values), but also everything about it pointed to a desire on Proch's part to represent each space to the other, to foster mutual respect, to bring about an impossible moment of recognition. What the photographs failed to document and what, in my view, made the work even more significant was the existence, in Headingly, of a public that prefigured the one at the National Gallery. Proch built his structure close to a main road that made it accessible to local farmers as well as his friends.

This field,[50] then, attests to a specific form of interaction between the National Gallery and a "regional" artist. For Proch, who was twenty when he first visited a museum, museums are not highly stimulating or affecting cultural sites; rather, they are workplaces, parcels of land to be worked, prospective exhibition venues to be explored, places where one can exhibit things that represent an extension of—as opposed to a break with—life. The amazing thing is the trust manifested throughout this approach. It turned out, however, that this trust was betrayed. "I wanted the activities of the field," Proch said, "to be as important as the object in Ottawa."[51] Yet the transition from one social space to another went unrecognized.

Max Dean

Visitors to the *Pluralities* exhibition were confronted by Max Dean's installation the moment they stepped in the door. Before them were three 1971 Ford Pintos, parked in the right half of the room. The opposite side was empty, and, through a small door to the left of the far wall, one could catch a glimpse of a square of fluorescent adhesive tape mounted on a mirror.[52] Whether one discovered a part of the system by watching the previous visitor cross the room and exit through the small door that led to a service corridor, or simply observed the empty room under the watchful gaze of a guard posted at the door, one was clearly witnessing a break with the contemplative mode of the standard museum visit, a break already heralded by other pieces in the show.[53] The installation did much more than engage the dynamics of the body or make visitors aware of the space, it went far beyond a simple summons. A barrage of contradictory feelings may well have assailed those visitors who walked past the three Pintos and, by climbing onto the platform behind the little door, activated an electric motor that drove the cars to within centimetres of the far wall. Yet the overwhelming impression for an interested observer was undoubtedly the sense of being projected outside the building into the street, of witnessing the establishment of a singular exchange between the two places. Without delving into technical details,[54] let me just say that an initial relationship was set up between the human environment (the intersection of Elgin and Albert Streets) and the building located there. This relationship was effected via the small door, which led to a corridor (normally off-limits), the outer wall of which had windows. One could see outside! The relationship became more defined the moment one looked at a video monitor placed at the viewers' disposal; this was coordinated with another monitor set up for casual passers-by outside in the street. The reciprocal scheme of the experience was, therefore, played out both inside and out and involved the visitors, the advancing and retreating Pintos, the streets, the pedestrians, and, again, the gallery visitors, all of which represented an attempt to break out of a condition of isolation.

Max Dean's work is concerned with the Other. His meditation on the situation of the artist is a call for action addressed to both himself and the public within the specific context of exhibitions. People are asked to make decisions.[55] *A Work* (1977) was the first of Dean's pieces to display a firm resolve to unmask the indifference of museums with respect to artists and the public. For this piece, Dean built a sort of empty mini-museum of chipboard and corrugated tin directly under the glass roof of the first-floor entrance to the gallery. And in this shed, for six weeks, he waited for those who had the temerity to slide open the latch on his door. Certain features of this piece would be akin to Hervé Fischer's pharmacy, had the latter shown an interest in examining the notion of artistic practice from within the confines of the museum. As an animator and catalyst, Dean gave visitors a chance to act by transforming the space of his shed into an information exchange and, at times, a site of production, since objects and projects did materialize.

In *Pass it On* (1981), visitors found themselves in a room, in the centre of which stood a bathtub with toiletry articles. Through this room, located in a medical building, Dean seemed to be demanding that viewers become aware of their situation as viewers. Photographed at regular intervals by an automated instamatic camera, they were free (if they wished) to take the photographs with them. The snapshots were presented on the end of a narrow tray attached to the camera. Such a sudden inducement of awareness is typical of Dean's work; his goal is not to raise far-reaching questions about the museum or the social structure but, using dramatic means, to take the players in this system to task. However, he is also interested in the museum as an exhibition space, one wherein the (real or potential) public and the artist, as a producer and source of discussion, have no chance to progress together. "The institution," he says, "tends to neutralize."[56] For Dean, the museum is not only a site for reflection but also a space to be organized, to be shaped detail by detail in accordance with a theme or viewpoint. It is not surprising that, having worked as a full-time technician at the Vancouver Art Gallery from 1971 to 1974 and, more sporadically, at the Winnipeg Art Gallery, Dean has drawn a number of lessons from his experience. These have prompted him to reflect on the situation of the artist and of his/her work in the institution. He has tended to expand the parameters of the kind of art work shown in traditional museums. If the ideological limits of the creative act can be reached by parcelling it out, by transforming it into a collective act, they remain nonetheless subject to institutional conditions that Dean's work does not seek to change.

Garry Neill Kennedy

Garry Kennedy is another artist who is unconcerned with changing institutional parameters. Following in Daniel Buren's footsteps, many of Kennedy's works are apparently designed to highlight the role played by the exhibition space. In *Locating* (1979), for example, he plotted the positions of the uprights in the gallery wall.[57] Other works such as *Page Fourteen, Page Seventy* (1979)[58] combined text and images in an ironic identification system focused on the élitist world of art. In a public space housing an art gallery, loudspeakers were used to draw attention to advertising in the art market.[59] Or—to take the example of *Untitled,* shown at the Dalhousie Art Gallery[60]—visitors were caught up in a continuous exchange between the artist's studio and the gallery, in the opening up of a space between the two sites. *Allocations,* Kennedy's contribution to the *Pluralities* exhibition, was apparently designed to function as a critique of the relations subsisting between the museum administration and the artist.[61]

For *Allocations,* visitors stepped into an empty room where they were given copies of the page in the exhibition catalogue that dealt with Kennedy's work. They were informed that the gallery administrators had rejected the artist's submission and that this empty space and these texts were a substitute for his original project.

A closer look at several of Kennedy's pieces shows that his work owes more to conceptualist theory than it does to any political philosophy.[62] (Kennedy has, moreover, underlined his affinities with conceptualist theory; it determined the direction the Nova Scotia College of Art and Design was to take after he became its president in 1967.) The following is Kennedy's description of an untitled piece presented in Lethbridge in 1978: "Using a brush and two coats of acrylic artists' colour red oxide paint, three walls of the small gallery of the Southern Alberta Gallery were painted by a general paint contractor." The opposition between commercial and fine art painting was brought out through the use, by a commercial painter, of iron oxide paint and an artist's brush.

Three walls of the gallery were literally awash, not in signed painting, but in a reddish paint that normally serves as an undercoating. Kennedy promoted this work as painting, enabled it to assume its place in the world of "painting." Now, all this may seem quite familiar and one could easily conclude, among other things, that the commercial painter and the "artist" overlapped at this point and that the very walls conspired to destroy the barriers between what is and isn't "fine art." In the *Recent Paintings*[63] show, Kennedy recorded the positions of paintings in the exhibition immediately preceding his own by drawing lines around the paintings before they were taken down. Again a commercial painter was called in to apply a coat of acrylic paint, an artist's yellow oxide, over the remaining rectangles. This, too, may seem equally familiar since it draws attention to the constrictive materiality of museum spaces and museographic systems of intervention. It seems to suggest that one should stop to think about those painters normally not considered to be "artists."[64] The last two examples illustrate the ambiguity in Kennedy's work. While recognizing concerns akin to those that have occupied Daniel Buren since the late 1960s, one can also see that there are features derived from other sources. For Kennedy, the important thing about his piece in the Southern Alberta Art Gallery is also what ties it in with the overall concern of his work, that is, the exposure of the conditions governing painting.[65] Aside from being an obvious statement about the gallery,[66] *Recent Paintings* was about the materiality of painting, about its very being.[67] In the continuous exchange of the two paintings involved, visitors literally witnessed the material life of painting, for the artist employed a system and a type of surface that enabled him to show the actual physical accretions of paint as it builds up over time.[68] The striking thing about Kennedy's work is its fidelity to the pictorial tradition of modernism, his constant preoccupation with Painting and Art History. This preoccupation is, it would seem, first and foremost a family matter within the art world, and one that in its own way takes account of recent thinking about the museum. The substance of the work does not, though, reflect any meditation on the ideological aura of the museum, or on that structure's political reality—its role, that is, in a form of social control indistinguishable from political power. By the same token, Kennedy does not create polemical objects standing in opposition to historical authority, nor does he seek to break out of the small world of art circles.

When artists become concerned with specifying the responsibilities of the art world with respect to the human world of which it is merely a fragment, and when this concern is translated into concrete practices that create enough distance between artists and the art world for the focus of thought and action to shift into the larger human sphere, then we find ourselves in the realm of the practitioners of sociological art. From this standpoint the museum (which could for certain above-mentioned artists become a locus for critical exploration without seeing its privileged institutional and cultural role called into question) begins to be eclipsed, gives up its place and becomes the target of demystifying strategies.

Brian Dyson and Paul Woodrow

In his introduction to the work of Brian Dyson,[69] Paul Woodrow notes the tendency of many artists, in the evolution of the art of the 1970s, "to become involved directly or indirectly with the social aspects of art as an educational tool directed towards either themselves or the community." He goes on to say that "one of the most interesting recent developments is the concept of the individual as a group."[70] This attitude is characteristic of the stage in which the artist's work first began to move outside institutional parameters.[71]

Paul Woodrow and Brian Dyson elected to live in Calgary, a very American kind of city that underwent rapid economic development. This augured a parallel development of the arts in accordance with models furnished by art criticism and official national and international institutions. These artists' decision to opt for sociological art led to involvement in effective local action that ran counter to the models then popular. Woodrow and Dyson are firm on this point. As one of them put it, "I have no use for an art gallery; I am not interested in museums."[72] The parodies Dyson made of Marcel Duchamp, the other objects/statements he fabricated for his *Canadian(s) Pacific Company*, his data collecting activities for *LE.LA* (a mutual provident society), and his *Pharmacies des Marchepieds* are all experiences that now seem far in the past. A year and a half as curator of the gallery of the University of Alberta's College of Art (1978–1980) prompted Dyson's departure for a life devoted to community action. He belongs to an association representing both isolated individuals and families from different social backgrounds (middle class, working class, the elderly, etc.) spread across two Calgary neighbourhoods, one of which is his home. The association works to improve the material and cultural living conditions of its constituency. As leader of various related workshops that include a graphics studio functioning on commercial, artistic, and political fronts, Dyson is, in a sense, the person responsible for cultural projects in the city. He has also received a mandate to participate in a municipal study to determine the impact of Rapid City Transport, a project that threatens to disrupt the community.

While at the University of Calgary and as a member of the WORKS group, Paul Woodrow, whose experience closely resembles Dyson's, produced a number of works that illustrate his relationship to the museum.[73] However, it was in his 1977 exhibition at the University of Calgary that Woodrow most clearly affirmed the direction of his work. The *Bureau of Imaginary Exchange*—with its echoes of another bureau, namely, Hervé Fischer's *Bureau d'identité utopique*—was an installation that made use of an office format to bring two individuals face to face for questioning. On the walls of a *Theory and Propaganda* area partially separated from the office by low partitions, white stickers inside empty frames bore provocative statements about art. ("Art discriminates," for example.) Together with these frames, unframed canvases formed a figure made up of rows of question marks. On a questionnaire compiled by Woodrow, visitors were asked to indicate the colours they liked or disliked, the things they considered most valuable, the work of art they would like most to possess, and, finally, the type of social service likely to have an exchange value equivalent to it. The very process of interrogation, the nature of the questions, the character of the installation, and, indeed, its presence in an art gallery (and a university gallery at that) all stem from a practice aimed at reorienting the role of the institution and altering museum space to suit a utopic function.

All these practices, which are motivated by the desire to stimulate the imagination, to expose the ideological mechanisms of social life, and to elicit responses through confrontation and questioning, originated with the artists using various aesthetic means. Turning their backs on sanctioned exhibition venues such as museums and galleries (and parodying some of them), they have set their sights on the way stations of daily life. A sizeable portion of video art shares this perspective. It draws on the energy of numerous artists who, if pressed to work in other media, would probably find themselves engaged in interventions somewhat similar to several of the works described above.[74]

At the end of this extended survey it seems quite clear that, by targeting the museum in general or by rejecting it or repositioning it in the world, contemporary art paves the way for a problematic specific to the art museum. It also appears likely that the collapse of museological privilege, particularly with respect to the representation of history and culture, has shaken the foundations of art museums and the latest of their progeny, the contemporary art museum. The latter undoubtedly has not even had time to consolidate its position. It is not only history or art history that is being questioned, but also the very responsibility of cultural institutions. If art history is founded upon ideological choices that deny or ignore the imaginative experiences of most social groups, then the museum along with those who finance, administer, maintain, and present it can only be seen as a cog in a system that makes choices on behalf of people it knows nothing about. Let it be recognized that art presents representations of the world. While conceding that the choices museums have made with respect to past representations could be revised or reinterpreted in light of the temporal remove and critical distance that now separates the present from the past, one must admit that the same does not hold for contemporary art. For it, all distance appears to be abolished. Louise Letocha, formerly director of the only existing Canadian contemporary art museum, was particularly sensitive to this effect of distance which allows for the protective refuge of history. For her, the way in which the symbolic function of the museum clashes with the reality of the contemporary art museum is paradoxical.[75] In presenting contemporary art works the latter cannot— and here I am interpreting—perform the sacred function of other museums. "Criticism," says Letocha, "has no ground to stand on."[76] So not only can the contemporary art museum not play a role similar to that of other museums, but also the whole interpretative apparatus employed by the others, with more or less success, no longer functions when it comes to contemporary art. Finally, the contemporary art museum assails us with questions posed with a brutality unparalleled by any other source.

If the public contemporary art museum did not exist in its present aristocratic form and if an ideological critical apparatus were not relatively available through semiofficial or underground channels, the current situation of art and its public would have nothing remarkable about it, would not generate such a range of polemical reactions. Preindustrial and industrial Western society has always manifested a rupture between the "creative artist" and the rest of society insofar as the former works on certain ideas and materials, access to which is highly exclusive. Today, the contemporary art museum houses objects produced by contemporary artists who benefit from the confusion between it and historical museums.

The contemporary art museum tends to share in the prestige of historical museums, and artists whose works are collected by those in control of the economy and culture believe that they enter thereby into the annals of history. At the same time, however, their works qualify as interesting commodities for a specialized market and move away from the core of social life. Such confusion undermines the contemporary art museum.

In art dealing with institutions, today's museum workers recognize the very image of this confusion. The works analysed above, whether by Daniel Buren, Hans Haacke, the proponents of sociological art, or by the heterogeneous mix of Canadian artists, show that there are two ways of envisioning the museum. Like artists faced with the choice of working within or outside the museum system, museum workers can choose to work for change inside artistic and museum circles or opt for working outside in projects free from the burden of tradition and other prevailing pressures. Louise Letocha, for example, makes common cause with the "open museum" of the late 1960s and early 1970s[77] when she says that the contemporary art museum should be first and foremost a critical, experimental space that shies away from retrospectives and hagiographic "solo" exhibitions, that it should be impervious to pressure from the arts community and support pluralistic programming. It should, in other words, be more like a site of interventions than a museum.[78] From this vantage point, a break with the museum model could only be beneficial to contemporary art. In place of the museum, one could have experimental public spaces with varying degrees of flexibility, associated with or independent from the more frequently visited historical museums. (The latter would also have to be reconsidered.) It seems desirable to come up with alternatives without, however, falling into the trap of parallel galleries that merely reproduce the conditions of the museum.

The route that leads outside the museum links up with the path taken by Pierre Gaudibert at the end of the 1960s. Both approaches have been driven by the desire to avoid falling under the sway of dominant ideologies. They have aimed at a type of cultural action liberated from all central administrative power and integrated into local communities, one that would break down the walls separating "artists" and "artisans," professionals and amateurs, in order to work in an extramuseological context with those whom Gaudibert calls "the makers of images and objects."[79] One could go even further and undertake a process that would sink its roots in the very flux of everyday social life.

Since the early 1970s, the world of the museum has been questioning its role in a society characterized by increasing contradictions. While some opt for facelifts, others make profound structural changes. And there are those who move well out of range of the controlling ideological system. At the same time, certain artists display similar concerns through their works.

By questioning the workings of art and the museum in a way that differs from the kind of analysis employed by the standard history and criticism of art and official museology, one hopes to gain insight into what these works have to tell us about museums today. It is an attempt to move forward along an autonomous path, a shared task that makes museums in general and art museums in particular the focus of a meditation on cultural behaviour and its consequences.

Notes

1.   A sociology of the development of museographic institutions and antimuseum movements remains to be worked out. The many existing versions of the better-known stages include: Marc Le Bot, "Le temps qui est le temps des musées," *Peinture et Machinisme* (Paris: Éditions Klincksieck, 1973), 35–40; Jean Clair, "Erostrate ou le musée en question," *L'Art de masse n'existe pas*, 10/18, no. 903 (Paris: Union générale d'éditions, 1974), 185–206. In *L'Histoire de l'art est terminée* (Paris: Balland, 1981), Hervé Fischer outlines the history of critical approaches to the museum. His summary of the development of antiart begins with the nineteenth-century anarchists and takes in Futurists, Constructivists, Dadaists, Marcel Duchamp, Fluxus, the Situationist critique, and artists' museums (particularly those of Marcel Broodthaers). In a special issue of *L'Art vivant* devoted to challenges to the museum, an article by Irmeline Lebeer recounts a number of adventures of the "Galerie légitime" founded by Robert Filliou (1961–1962). See *L'Art vivant*, no. 35 (December 1972–January 1973).

2.   Daniel Buren, "À partir de là," *NDLR. écriture-peinture*, no. 2 (Fall 1976).

3.   Daniel Buren, *Rebondissements* (Brussels: Daled and Gevaert, 1977), 14. Also quoted by Georges Roque in an article dealing with the museum's co-opting of painting. See "L'Avant-garde, récupération, Buren, etc. Quelques notes," *Parachute*, no. 11 (Summer 1970): 46–49.

4.   Interview with the artist, 28 March 1981.

5.   *Artémisia, Mot pour mot* series, no. 2 (Paris: Galerie Yvon Lambert, 1979).

6.   The subjective connotations of the term "souvenir photographs" distance these photographs from the notion of documentary truth.

7.   Daniel Buren, "Ponctuations," *Ponctuations, statue/sculpture* (Lyon: Éditions le Nouveau Musée, 1980).

8.   On the relationship between his work in the plastic and written media, see Jean-François Lyotard, "The Works and Writings of Daniel Buren: An Introduction to the Philosophy of Contemporary Art," trans. Lisa Liebmann, *Artforum*, vol. 19, no. 6 (February 1981): 57–64.

9.   Unfortunately I was unable to visit Daniel Buren's *apartment number* (March 28–April 18, 1981). It appears that this *High Rise Installation*, which was set up in conjunction with A Space and presented the work of seven artists in succession, is only one example of the logical (or fashionable) move from the gallery to the apartment. One has the impression that, for most of the artists involved, the work did not issue from any theoretical considerations regarding the museum.

10.   "Exhibitions and *mise en scène*" was the subject of a debate between artists (including Daniel Buren) and museum curators; it took place at the Centre Georges Pompidou, on April 27, 1981. I stayed for only part of the debate which

appeared to be somewhat dull; Daniel Buren had trouble making himself understood!

11.   Two of these plates are reproduced in Tony Brown, "Artist as Corporate Critic: An Interview with Hans Haacke," *Parachute*, no. 23 (Summer 1981): 14–15.

12.   See David Craven, "Hans Haacke and the Aesthetics of Legitimation," *Parachute*, no. 23 (Summer 1981): 5–11.

13.   Tony Brown, "Artist as Corporate Critic."

14.   Translated as "The Master of Assorted Chocolate," *Der Pralinenmeister* loses some of its bite. "Praline master" constitutes a clever allegory, since the carmelized sugar coating the almond is suggestive of the seductive envelope of cultural pretexts surrounding the bitter core of economic and social life.

15.   The confectionary Comète Ltée in Saint-Hyacinthe, Québec, is owned by Monheim.

16.   In the suggestively titled article, "Working Conditions" [*Artforum*, vol. 19, no. 10 (Summer 1981): 56–61], Hans Haacke specifies the conditions governing all polemical or sociopolitical artwork issuing from an art world influenced on all sides by the increasing involvement of big business in building art collections and mounting exhibitions. Art provides large companies with a shining and profitable aura of altruism, a situation that directly affects museum policies.

17.   The term "sociological art" [*art sociologique*] had to fight hard for acceptance. Wilhelm Flüsser, however, found it perfectly satisfactory since, he claimed, it referred "to two truths that mirror each other and, in the process, cancel each other out." Quoted in Fred Forest, *Art sociologique: Vidéo*, 10/18, no. 1188 (Paris: Union générale d'éditions, 1977), 387.

18.   In a letter by Fred Forest dated 16 January 1981.

19.   After 1976 the *Collectif d'art sociologique*, founded two years earlier by Hervé Fischer, Fred Forest, and Jean-Paul Thénot, defined its relationship with certain Canadian groups that included Karl Beveridge, Carol Conde, and others in Toronto, as well as Paul Woodrow and Brian Dyson in Calgary.

20.   Jean-Paul Thénot, "Trois expériences d'art sociologique," unpublished manuscript (Paris, November 1980).

21.   Here I should note how the Galerie St-Petri defined itself on its invitation cards: "The Gallery, which exists since 1971, represents an unusual research experiment in contemporary art, stressing as it does borderline creative work of particular interest from the standpoint of the sociology, psychology, and history of art."

22.   Interview with the artist, 21 April 1981.

23.   On Fred Forest's use of video, see Wilhelm Flüsser, *Art sociologique: Vidéo*, 10/18, no. 1188 (Paris: Union générale d'éditions, 1977), 414–428.

24.   Interview with the artist, 21 April 1981.

25.   Wilhelm Flüsser, "L'espace communiquant: L'expérience de Fred Forest," *Communication et langages*, no. 18 (2nd Quarter 1973): 81–92.

26.   In purchasing an artistic square metre (once the development project for the land has been accepted by the manager), the purchaser acquires original artistic property rights "equivalent in value to a work of art."

27.   The Political Science Department of the University of Berkeley planned to study ways of starting a revolution on the territory!

28.   See Hervé Fischer, *Théorie de l'art sociologique, Synthèses contemporaines* series (Tournai: Casterman, 1977). Also see, by the same author, *L'Histoire de l'art est terminée* (Paris: Balland, 1981). Situationist critical theory seems the closest to that of Hervé Fischer insofar as the museum appears as the point of rupture between life as it is experienced and life as it is represented by history. Taking up Guy Debord's comparison of the museum to a cultural bazaar, Hervé Fischer sees André Malraux's "Imaginary Museum" as the cultural bazaar *par excellence*. Although it denies history, Malraux's "Imaginary Museum" also denies life. Also see Guy Debord, *La Société du spectacle* (Paris: Éditions Buchet/Chastel, 1967). [English translation published as *Society of the Spectacle* (Detroit: Black and Red, 1983).]

29.   Dictionaries define hygiene as a health science that sets out the rules one must follow to improve the functioning of body organs and to avoid illness. Given that the evolutionary and materialist theories of history are moribund, Fischer proposes a metaphoric form of intervention.

30.   The *Pharmacie idéologique* (1974), as well as the *Bureau d'identité utopique* (1977) which marks the following phase, were set up in Vancouver, Calgary, and Toronto.

31.   See Phillipe Fertray, *Citoyens/Sculpteurs: Une expérience d'art sociologique au Québec* ([n.p.] Parism Éditions SOGEDO, 1981). In addition to a group publication, this experience led to an exhibition of documents at the Canadian Cultural Centre in Paris from April to May, 1981.

32.   See Francine Périnet's article, "Chicoutimi, été 1980," *Parachute*, no. 20 (Fall 1980): 51–52.

33.   See Jacqueline Fry, *Irène Whittome, 1975–1980* (Montréal: Montréal Museum of Fine Arts, 1980), 7–13; also, see René Payant, "Irène Whittome—Le discours blanc: De l'invention du classement au classement de l'invention," *Parachute*, no. 7 (Summer 1977): 10–15.

34.   Ten *Musées blancs* had been completed by 1977.

35.   In this connection, see *Michael Snow* (Paris: Centre Georges Pompidou, 1979); Chantal Pontbriand, "Plus tard, plus tard ... Michael Snow," *Parachute*, no. 17 (Winter 1979): 49–55; and René Payant, "Bricolage pictural:

L'art à propos de l'art, 2e partie, citation et intertextualité," *Parachute*, no. 18 (Spring 1980): 25–32.

36.   In Michael Snow's own words: "… *Plus tard* where the movement of the still-camera during the exposure made abstractions of images which were already abstractions of nature. It was partly a kind of painting with the camera. … It is a motion recorded, just as visible brush strokes are a recording of motions. … The title refers to the time gaps between the painting of the several landscape paintings (they are *realistic* recordings of subjects which existed) and their installations together in a room of the National Gallery of Canada and my personal photographic recording of them *in situ* and the spectator's personal present in seeing the final superimposition of these times." See Pierre Théberge, "Conversation with Michael Snow," in *Michael Snow*, 42.

37.   "I was conscious of the joke/implication that this is the way an average viewer looks at paintings. …" Letter from Michael Snow dated 9 June 1981.

38.   See J. Russell Harper, "Nationalism and the 'Group,'" *Painting in Canada: A History* (Toronto: University of Toronto Press, 1966), 265–306.

39.   Letter from Michael Snow dated 9 June 1981.

40.   See these and other texts on General Idea: Chantal Pontbriand, "General Idea," *Pluralities /1980/ Pluralités* (National Gallery of Canada, 1980), 61–66; Michael Morris, "The Artist as Curator of Imagination," *artscanada*, no. 220/221 (April/May 1978): 41; "1984, A Year in Pictures," *FILE*, vol. 4, no. 1 (Summer 1978).

41.   [Please note that the National Gallery of Canada moved in 1988. The descriptions and locations correspond to the former building on Elgin Street.]

42.   General Idea, "1984, A Year in Pictures," 12.

43.   It is no accident that the *Pluralities* exhibition provides numerous examples of work concerned with the museum. It is also certainly no coincidence that the exhibition was generally condemned by critics who were not amused by the fact that it did not reflect their own models. One Toronto critic even reproached the curators for their lack of direction. See Philip Monk, "A Clearing House of Trends," *Maclean's*, 28 July 1980, 50–51. Misadventures of this sort crop up in the brief history of contemporary art. *Québec '75* comes to mind [*Québec '75/Arts*, (Montréal: Institut d'Art contemporain, 1975)].

44.   Interview with Betty Goodwin, 9 July 1981.

45.   Ibid.

46.   Ibid.

47.   *Passage in a Red Field* signals Betty Goodwin's return to the museum. For Goodwin, the museum is a less temporary site than Mentana Street (where her previous project took place from 1978–1979) or Art Park (from 1978, where a sculpture situated between a craggy cliff and a river "bed" suggested the idea of the

abandoned bed in the Mentana Street project). The Clark Street project (1977) had been closed to the public. Betty Goodwin is a good example of current practices used in creating installations and environments. The phenomenon of expansion beyond the museum's walls into "natural" geographic space takes us back once again to the late 1960s; however, I will not pursue this line here since it would take us too far from the topic.

48.   In my opinion, this blond mass inevitably conjured up associations with a field of wheat. In the original manuscript of a text titled *Don Proch* (Winnipeg: Manitoba Arts Monograph, 1980), Kenneth Hughes correctly remarked that the almost universally negative commentaries devoted to this piece were noteworthy in their failure to give it serious consideration. Hughes wrote: "[M]ost important of all, [Proch] did not create a centre part of 'synthetic wheat.' Using unwound binder twine, Proch simulated *wild prairie bunch grass* in the centre ... under no circumstances, one would have thought, could the unwound binder twine tangled together as bunch grass be confused with wheat."

49.   Photographs of the field and museum guards were exhibited, in addition to being published in an exhibition catalogue. See Karyn Allen, *Rituals: The Winnipeg Perspective 1981* (Winnipeg: Winnipeg Art Gallery, 1981).

50.   Much could be said about the comparisons made between *Field* and earthworks, particularly Denis Oppenheim's *Gallery Transplant* (1969). As always, comparisons tend to turn critiqued works into derivative objects; no attempt is made to situate the constituent factors, whether constant or variable, within their proper context.

51.   Interview with the artist, 8 June 1981.

52.   The piece is meticulously described by Dean himself and amply illustrated with photographs in *Parachute*, no. 20 (Fall 1980): 10–11. [For a description in English see *Impressions*, no. 27 (Spring 1981): 18–19.]

53.   For example, see Mowry Baden's *Ottawa Room* (1980) which leads the viewer into an angular wooden structure occupying a space that connects the fourth and fifth floors of the Gallery.

54.   See Dean, *Parachute,* no. 20.

55.   On the works of Max Dean, see Philip Fry, "Max Dean: Three Projects and the Theory of Open Art," *Parachute*, no. 14 (Spring 1979): 16–23 and Willard Holmes, "Max Dean," in *Pluralities/1980/Pluralités*, 51–54.

56.   Interview with the artist, 23 July 1981.

57.   Eye-Level Gallery, Halifax, 1979.

58.   A Space Gallery, Toronto, 1979, in two separate publications.

59.   Harbourfront Gallery, Toronto, 1979.

60.   *Untitled,* Halifax, 1978.

61.   For more on the works mentioned here, see especially: "Garry Kennedy, an interview with Alan Barkley," *Parachute*, no. 13 (Winter 1978): 14–17; Allan MacKay, "Garry Neill Kennedy," in *Pluralities*, 73–78.

62.   "My arriving at painting came out of conceptual art pieces. ..." See "Garry Kenedy, an interview with Alan Barkley," 14.

63.   Galerie Optica, Montréal, 1978.

64.   With respect to *Recent Paintings* and its potential irony, Kennedy comments, "I am very sensitive to that and I don't want it to be seen that way. ..." "Garry Kennedy," 17.

65.   With respect to this exhibition, Kennedy states "[T]hat's consistent with my object painting, with the way I apply paint. The clearest use of the material—paint as material—is the way it is used commercially. In all my work I use that feature, that is, the paint consistency. ..." Ibid.

66.   "Only it is going into a space and commenting the space—the space of a gallery, the activity of a rotating show, the size of paintings today, etc." Ibid.

67.   "It's the oxideness that I want, not necessarily the yellow. But it's a change from the red. ..." Ibid.

68.   The work is described and photographs of it are represented in "Garry Kennedy," 16–17.

69.   Paul Woodrow, "Looking Both Ways at Once," *Parachute*, no. 11 (Summer 1978): 43–45.

70.   Ibid., 43.

71.   Between 1965 and the late 1970s, artists were involved in many kinds of ecological, social, and political work in which the "natural" or human landscape and the community became sites of aesthetic practices. Such actions include: N.E. Thing Co. Ltd. founded by Iain and Ingrid Baxter in 1966; The Image Bank (1968) managed by Michael Morris (founder of the Western Front Society in Vancouver) and Vincent Trasov; the Creative Playground Workshop (1972)—a playground project, with sculptures in the village of Silton near Regina—led by Russ Yuristy; and the presentation of a candidate from the Peanut Party in the 1974 electoral campaign for the office of mayor of Vancouver (John Mitchell and Vincent Trasov).

72.   Interview with Paul Woodrow and Brian Dyson, 16 June 1981.

73.   A report—WORKSCOPORT (Cullompton, Devon, United Kingdom: Beau Geste Press, 1974–1975)—produced by WORKS mentions a number of interventions involving museum space as such. For example, "Gallery Isolation" (University of Calgary Art Gallery, 1973), organized by Clive Robertson, "uses the gallery as a 'nonliving space'. ..." For almost two days, Clive Robertson submitted to self-imposed restrictions "on food, drink, freedom of choice, amusement, and many other life ingredients that we enjoy outside the

room." The sort of self-alienation expressed by the author of this intervention derived from the very nature of the art gallery.

74.   Pierre Falardeau and Julien Poulin, for example.

75.   Interview with Louise Letocha, 9 July 1981.

76.   Ibid.

77.   See for example, "Le Musée ouvert: Entretien avec F. Althaus," *L'Art vivant*, no. 24 (October 1971): 8–10 and Yann Pavie's interview with Pontus Hulten, "Vers le musée du futur," *Opus international*, no. 24/25 (May 1971): 56–63.

78.   Interview with Louise Letocha, 9 July 1981. The term "intervention" is also systematically used by Normand Thériault ([then] curator of contemporary art at the Montréal Museum of Fine Arts), whose view is best summed up by the title of an interview I had with him, 8 July 1981: The museum puts a gloss on everything. [*Le musée polit tout.*]

79.   See Pierre Gaudibert's postscript to his, *Action culturelle: intégration et/ou subversion*, 3rd ed., *Synthèses contemporaines* series (Paris: Casterman, 1977), 143–176.

Translated from the French by Donald McGrath.

Charlotte Townsend-Gault

Kwakiutl Ready-Mades?

As the work of Canada's Native artists becomes more visible, and their concerns more audible, the ways in which the work of their predecessors is valued and classified becomes a matter of cultural and political significance. If it is also a matter of aesthetic significance then it is time to look more closely at how that particular designation has been arrived at.

The French anthropologist Pierre Bourdieu has said that "every period arranges art representations as a whole according to an institutional system of classifications of its own."[1] There are some signs that the cultural community in Canada (exactly what *that* means also needs a closer look) is becoming more aware of what its "institutional system" is and equally aware of some of the mechanisms by which one person's art is another person's artefact and a third person's ... or, as Bourdieu would put it, the system is making us account for mechanisms "problematizing the activity of reference."[2]

The retroactive classification of, say, Kwakiutl food vessels as art needs careful examination because it amounts to a species of aesthetic imperialism over the cultural past of the Kwakiutl of the present. Such classification is in more urgent need of deconstruction since it not only represents the superimposition of an alien aesthetic but also lends a spurious importance to the materiality of Native cultural production.

If "we" are going to call it art we need to understand whose model of art is being used—Jacqueline Fry's, Benjamin Buchloh's, Michael Ames's, Jeff Wall's, Marcel Duchamp's, or some other? And where do their models come from? Also, the question as to whether it is necessary or possible to separate "aesthetic" from "cultural" or "political" with reference to any given work applies here with particular force.

The Museum—Classification Site

Before our eyes assumptions are being paraded and traded. The provocative spectacle of *The Spirit Sings* [held at the Glenbow Museum in 1987] has brought into focus the claim that spirituality inheres in certain objects, and also the barefaced paradox of corporate sponsorship. Next year [1989] the new Museum of Civilization opens with the promise to "exhibit

This text was first published in *Vanguard* (November 1988).

Indian creativity in an art gallery setting which will demonstrate the range, diversity and ingenuity of artists/craftsmen."[3] Meanwhile, at the new National Gallery, the reconstituted Rideau Street Chapel, the silk-hung walls for Canaletto, and the hanging urinal in the Duchamp room present a range, no less extraordinary for being common enough in any museum, of "things" to take into account. Faced with their disjunctions one either settles for surrealistic somnolence or is provoked to the provenance of the value classifications that have got them into the building.[4]

There is a well-defended view that museums are inimical to art and to the interest of artists. It was expressed during the colloquium *Artists and Museums* (1988), which preceded the opening of the National Gallery of Canada: museums sanction dead classifications and kill art. However, there is also some appreciation of the fact that the National Gallery is, at least in part, a political creation and that this must affect the way in which the works inside are received. Well, good. Of course. But this doesn't suggest death so much as the realization that there never have been ideal sites for ideal viewing. Rather, the contemporary museum makes it impossible to overlook the problems of art and its reception and thus makes it possible to examine those problems in the world as well as in the recondite, if necessary, pages of critical theory. The problems are the eternal ones: What are we looking at? What do we need to know about it? Who are "we"?

One example: at the time of the opening of the National Gallery, art historian Thierry de Duve made it clear, and it was rightly reported in *The Globe and Mail*, that it was time to ask again whether the Duchamp readymades really are art. No doubt others were asking the same thing too, if from rather different perspectives. To say that the question has been asked before would be an understatement. But one is provoked to ask it again in these elegant new surroundings where they have been so lovingly installed. This grand, planned, context has changed the holy cows, again.

Another instance would be the reception accorded Hans Haacke's *Voici Alcan* (1983) installed in the contemporary galleries. The photographic triptych, framed in cheap aluminium windows, has photographs of Montréal Opera productions sponsored by Alcan flanking the devastating photograph of Steven Biko's face bearing the stigmata of his torture and murder by South African police. The work was evidently not laundered, as some would suggest, when it became part of the collection. Pity that the gallery used this line in self-defence, since it is one of the few public institutions with the courage to acquire one of Haacke's "political" works. Nor, despite the avant-garde's habit of flagellating itself for its useless élitism, has it lost all its political clout. Alcan is implicated, and clearly Alcan, in asking for the work to be removed from the gallery, feels implicated. The object that hangs on the gallery walls has brought with it a socio-political context, some knowledge of South African apartheid policies and of multinationals and the world economy. Because "political art" cannot be instrumental in all spheres does not mean that it is not instrumental in some.

Kwakiutl Food Vessels

Food vessels of the Kwakiutl are made from wood, commonly alder, either carved or kerfed.[5] They vary in size from a few centimetres to two or more metres, intentionally the scale of a small canoe. Their forms are those of the bodies of either animals, humans, or the spirit beings of Kwakiutl cosmology. The bowl itself is the hollowed out stomach or back. As physical objects, food vessels are only one group amongst others found on the Northwest Coast—storage boxes, blankets, staffs, rattles, masks—all of which were an inextricable part of a complex that equally involved intangibles—ceremonial titles, songs, family histories, myths, dances, and privileges of various sorts. None of them is only a physical object. What distinguishes food vessels is their role in the ceremonial display and sharing of food, a key trait for these cultures and for the Kwakiutl in particular. For this reason, they are implicated, even where material culture as such is not being specifically discussed, in the many readings available in the extensive literature on the Northwest Coast culture.

Because of the close relationship between food and the animals, or the food quest from which it is derived, and between food and the ceremonies associated with the giving and receiving of status, the category of food vessels can be identified as emblematic of a complex of ideas and practices. In Native terms they are not reducible to either a use factor or cosmological references. They can be seen as shifting back and forth between functional object and spiritual representations, culturally meaningful as both. They are physically, and conceptually, ambiguous.

Food vessels are in a perpetual state of transformation, between their double existence as container and representation, between their significant objecthood and significant representations, between their use value and their symbolic value, between the power of the wealth they contain and the power of the seal, wolf, *Dzonokwa* or *Sisiutl* they embody. Meanwhile the food they contain is itself transformed from its use value as nourishment to possessing symbolic value as spiritual wealth. The connection between the life of the vessels as objects and their metaphorical existence is made through their ability to transform. How else could the contradiction in terms that spirits have bodies be represented? The Kwakiutl conception of transformation makes redundant a dichotomy between material and spiritual or between the socio-economic and the cosmological.

In other words, these "things" do not lend themselves to a one-dimensional interpretation. Thus they were seen to be the subject of disputes about inheritance, the blazons of a name newly acquired, the transporters of abundant food wealth, the endorsement of their owner's right to perform in a winter dance society; they might denote the continuity of a social group in its ranked position or connote the fact that negotiations were in progress which could lead to a rise in the group's status. The concern with status was an obsession. Status came with wealth. It meant the accumulation of maximal amounts of power; that power, which pervaded the Kwakiutl lifeworld, was their reality and was manifested in an object like a food vessel. To gain power, property was desired, and, for this reason, it was valued.

The simplicity of this scenario is engaging but improbable. There were plenty of factors that complicated the situation, created tensions and ambivalences, made power harder to get. Marking and activating social transactions, food vessels were "good to think with" because as objects and in use, they shaped and represented the complexities and ambiguities, personal and social, that lay beneath the deceptively orderly presentation and serving of food.

The crucial point is that, in Kwakiutl society, features that anthropologists identify as "inheritance disputes," "control of resources," "assertion of rights," etc. had to take physical form in order to be made real. Food vessels themselves, as what may be termed spiritual objects (not really a contradiction in terms), both illumine and help to shape, not merely reflect, the contexts in which they operate. In short, there is a correspondence between the ways in which food vessels are made and used, how they are classified, and the way they look.

Classified Objects—Duchamp and Dishes

The dialectical relationship between an object and the context that classifies it is well-illustrated with the example of an historical Native object, such as the food vessels of the Northwest Coast which can be seen in museums all over the world, displayed, *inter alia*, as art objects. There is no reason to spare them the same questions that the ready-mades prompt in 1988: what are we looking at? what have other people thought they were looking at? what do we need to know about it? who are "we"? Even partial answers reveal a complex web of classifications, of interdependent values. Any understanding of Native artefacts can only be extended by tempering it with an understanding of how they have been, and are, classified. By asking, for instance, on what grounds a totem pole is sculpture? or a Kwakiutl food vessel an art object? The answers have some bearing on the relationship between contemporary Native artists and their history, and also their relationship with contemporary art in general.

Food vessels are typical of the sort of things that have been included in numerous exhibitions, in published surveys of the "art" of the region, are an essential part of any museum display concerned with the area, and so on. Because they are well-known and well-documented and because they have always hovered uneasily between the interpretative efforts of at least two fields of inquiry—art and anthropology—and because they are, in one important respect, clearly functional, these dishes have been worried over in the aesthetics versus function debates in both fields.

One may object that to consider a Kwakiutl food vessel and Duchamp's snow shovel together is historically irresponsible, the worst kind of ethnocentrism, and pointless. On the contrary—juxtapositions of the kind we find in, and between, contemporary museums should force historical and anthropological considerations, not obliterate them. The harder thing is to keep them apart. The time is past for a simple art/not-art classification. What the dish and the shovel have in common is that they both can and must submit to a multiple classification. Does this mean a dose of pluralist irresponsibility? If not, what exactly are the consequences?

Our interest in Duchamp is of two kinds. One attempts to recover the historical climate in which the ready-mades were originally conceived and received. The other urgency, as expressed by de Duve, is to work out how they look, what they mean today when they inhabit a museum context that juxtaposes them with Kwakiutl food vessels and hundreds of other supposedly aesthetically classified objects. In one sense, both were mundane objects in the culture of origin—in advance of a broken arm, in advance of messy eating. Now both are subjected to focused attention in a designed environment because they have been reclassified as art. If it must be asked whether the snow shovel taken from a hardware store to a gallery in 1915 is art in 1988, and what makes this so, then it must also be asked of these "ready-mades" from the coastal rain forests of British Columbia. The reclassification of food vessels from potlatch to pedestal has been, if more gradual, no less drastic.

This process itself owes not a little to Duchamp's historical gesture which has had well-known consequences on subsequent classifications-as-art and on the development of a critical response. Its consequence on the nomination of objects of precontact, Native manufacture as art has not been worked through. Put simply, Duchamp pointed out some of the contradictions involved in paying close attention to one kind of object in a particular setting. Thus, in a museum/gallery, attention is first drawn to food vessels by what might appear to be a "natural" fascination with intriguing, hand-wrought objects, which are also, in many cases, representations of various real and imaginary beings. Such fascination is in fact totally culture-bound. The "natural" acclamation given to a class of so-called aesthetic objects—paintings in an art gallery—was one of the biases to which Duchamp opposed the snow shovel, bottle-rack, and other manufactured "givens." Surely it is more accurate to align the food vessels with the shovel than with the paintings it usurped? To allow the modernist paradigm to engulf them is to sacrifice too much.

This is the significance of de Duve asking the fundamental question, again, about the ready-mades just when it might have looked as though they, and the rest of the contents of the National Gallery, were settling in for an eternity of acceptance as art, good or bad.

The Classification of Dishes

Walter Benjamin's view that history is lost to us and that all we have is a set of shifting constructs is well-illustrated by the "history" of classification of artefacts of Native manufacture in the postcontact period. Shifts in classification took place over a 200-year period through the efforts of explorers, traders, missionaries, collectors, government agents, and anthropologists—all prepared to classify the products of the area in their own ways.

Captain George Dixon was one of the first white men to be in contact with the people of the Northwest Coast, and one of the first collectors. In 1787 he took away with him a carved wooden food vessel amongst other pieces from the Haida. It is now in the British Museum. Marking the beginning of the plunder of the area on behalf of private and public collectors around the world, the removal of the objects also began a series of "outsider" classifications of artefacts which continues to the present. These classifications proceed from the curios—the "artificial curiosities" of the time of the Cook expeditions—through specimens of scientific interest arranged typologically, to ethnographic objects arranged "in context" as evidence of the otherness of the other (during what William Sturtevant has called the "museum age" of anthropology, 1880–1920), to, finally, "art."[6] Some of these versions are quite bizarre in terms of the Native memory and ethnography of precontact times.

In the case of the Kwakiutl, the literature does not add up to a con-

things. The first is to appreciate the complexity of their role within indigenous culture—this of course is an anthropological axiom—but with a clearer idea of the variable classifications through which we see them. The second is to have at hand a more satisfactory model for an anthropology of art. This model is able to encompass, because they can now be seen to match, the current endeavours of both fields of discourse, both modes of inquiry, anthropology and art.

Notes

1.   Pierre Bourdieu, "Outline of a Theory of Art Perception," *International Social Science Journal*, vol. 20, no. 4 (1968): 593.

2.   Ibid.

3.   This is one of the stated purposes taken from a working paper provided by the Museum. The others are: to illustrate the presence of an Indian art tradition from prehistory to the present; to augment exhibits in the Native Peoples Hall; to provide a reference base for the study of contemporary Indian Art; to educate the visitor by providing a wider focus on the objects and themes that will be presented in the temporary area of the Native Art Gallery.

4.   Work by Louise Lawler, Michael Asher, and Daniel Buren has drawn attention to these juxtapositioned categories. When *Museums by Artists* was at the Glenbow Museum in Calgary in 1983, Buren had the model of a fully caparisoned "cowboy's" horse moved into the exhibition of contemporary works, while the horse's original base, in the Western display area, was papered over with stripes.

5.   The term is used to describe a box or bowl that has been formed from a single thin plank of wood, steamed, and then bent, at the kerfs, so that its ends join at one corner of the rectangle. The Kwakiutl excelled at this technique for making watertight containers.

6.   Douglas Cole, *Captured Heritage: The Scramble for Northwest Coast Artefacts* (Vancouver: Douglas and McIntyre, 1985).

7.   Two examples: Franz Boas, *Primitive Art* (1927; reprint, New York: Dover, 1955); Raymond Firth, "Tikopia Art and Society," in *Primitive Art and Society*, ed. A. Forge (London: Oxford University Press, 1973).

8.   See Philip Drucker, *Indians of the Northwest Coast* (Garden City: Natural History Press, 1955); Audrey Hawthorn *Art of the Kwakiutl Indians and Other Northwest Coast Tribes*; and Hilary Stewart, *Artefacts of the Northwest Coast Indians* (Vancouver: Hancock House, 1973).

9.   Jacqueline Fry implies something rather similar in her article "Contemporary Inuit Art and Art from Other Tribal Cultures," *American Review of Canadian Studies*, vol. 17, no. 1 (Spring 1987): 41–46.

Kass Banning

The Mummification of Mommy:
Joyce Wieland as the AGO'S First Living Other

I think of Canada as female. All the work I've been doing is about Canada.
                                         Joyce Wieland, *Take One*, 1972

So far as I am aware, Wieland was the first Canadian artist to state flatly, about eight years ago, that there is both female art and male art and that they are separate and distinct—neither complementary nor contradictory, just different. It seems odd, for the idea is so generally accepted today.
                                         Doug Fetherling, *The Canadian Forum*, 1976

... there was something pointedly pathological in Joyce Wieland's treatment of the North in *Reason Over Passion*, just as there was something pointedly dishonest about her treatment of it in *The Far Shore*.
                                         Douglas Ord, *Cinema Canada*, 1977

Consideration of Joyce Wieland's retrospective at the Art Gallery of Ontario in 1987 unleashes a troubling paradox, a vertigo of checks and balances, engendering a mixed reaction—namely, vindication and negation, with its necessary corollary, suspicion. Initially, one cannot help but applaud; it's about time the AGO granted a female artist the same authorization her brothers have enjoyed since time immemorial. It is about time that recognition was bestowed on such a "deserving" and *living* artist.

Leaving aside the settling of scores, one nevertheless feels compelled to ask some disruptive questions, to engage in what Julia Kristeva has called vigilant analytic dissidence. Why *this* time, at this critical moment, and why this particular artist? What forces—historical, critical, partisan, or otherwise—induced the AGO to designate Joyce Wieland as their representative "first Other"? In other words, why was it Wieland's time?

The timing of her retrospective brings to light a number of pressing concerns. It is within the pages of the exhibition's catalogue that these problems crystallize.[1] The catalogue is problematic not only in and of itself, but also in the way in which it echoes the consistent reception of Wieland's work in the past. This retrospective repeats and extends, albeit in a refashioned manner, what I consider to be a problem of the hermeneutics of interpretation, a problem that pervasively informs, in spite of recent attempts at feminist contextualization, *the analysis of female*

This text was first published in *C Magazine*, no. 13 (1987).

artists in this country. This particular context, of a woman artist, living in Canada and taken up by feminism, inadvertently raises a startling number of contradictions that are not easily rectified.

Wieland offers a pertinent case study, as her position within the art field was original; she was one of the first female artists in this country to gain recognition. It is the particular nature of that reception that demands elucidation, exposure, and inquiry. Looking back at Douglas Ord's comments in the above quote from *Cinema Canada*, it is easy to feel smug. On the surface, it appears as if we have travelled a great distance from such fatuous criticism; in hindsight, it looks as if we have made great strides. But have we? For what emerges from the AGO catalogue on Wieland is simply a series of reversals: denigration transforms into reverence. Yet, good intentions aside, the end result is the same. Ultimately, Wieland's difference—local, female, Canadian—is confined through authorization.

Looking Back

The contradictions engendered by this retrospective cannot in any way deny Wieland's impressive history: her contributions to Canadian art and the attendant art "scene" are both unique and far-reaching. Many of Wieland's practices anticipate artistic workings that are now commonplace. Among these "firsts" was the incorporation of political or social content into her practice. Not only did Wieland cast her gaze backwards and rework and re-present Canadian history, as evinced in such titles as *Laura Secord Saves Upper Canada* (1961), *Confedespread* (1967), and *Montcalm's Last Letter* (1971), but a political immediacy informs many of her works, especially during the late 1960s and early 1970s. The politics of the moment were realized in several of her films: in *Solidarity* (1973), Wieland depicts the Dare cookie strikers of Kitchener as a series of marching feet; the well-known *Rat Life and Diet in America* (1968) relates the tale of two gerbils who escape U.S. imperialism to take up organic gardening in Canada; *Pierre Vallières* (1972) presents the lips of a Québec revolutionary who makes the claim that both Québec and women suffer a similar form of state oppression. Such work, along with Wieland's activism, her early involvement with CAR (Canadian Artists' Representation), and her vehement stand on ecological issues, for example, exemplify a praxis: a commitment in and outside of the studio.

Wieland, more than any other Canadian artist, plays with our myths, those edifices of identity that are constructed to ameliorate the anxiety of difference. The 1971 National Gallery exhibition, *True Patriot Love*, for example, is entirely devoted to this practice. The piece entitled

Arctic Passion Cake is exemplary. Canada is represented as a huge landscape that supports "The Spirit of Canada"—a woman who suckles her offspring, twin beavers, one French, the other English.

Most critics have mistakenly perceived such works as simple, playful representations and have designated Wieland's role as one of "mythmaker." Robert Fulford slots her into a limiting patriotic position in his piece "Giving Us a Sense of Ourselves":

> … Joyce Wieland wants also to be a Canadian mythmaker. In her films
> of the Canadian landscape, in her quilts made up of patriotic emblems
> and slogans, in her embroidery pieces related to Canadian history, she
> is now moving into the position as the visual poet of 1970s Canadian
> nationalism.[2]

But this description is inaccurate. Through parody (which not infrequently can slip into bawdy humour), whatever medium she uses—whether lithographs, film, oils, plastic assemblages, or fabric collages—Wieland decodes the fixed consignation of sameness and thus points to the inherent contradictions underlying our engraved national consciousness. Her works never comprise simple celebrations of identity. This practice is particularly evident in the film *Reason Over Passion* (1967–1969) where she accentuates the rhetoric of nationalism through distortion and juxtaposition of text and image, which she reworks into the fabric of the natural. In other media—the embroidered mouths of *Squid Jigging Ground* (1974), the written text of *Josephine's Last Letter to Napoléon*, and the quilt *Laura Secord Saves Upper Canada*—Wieland utilizes text in unconventional settings, thus producing tension, throwing naming into relief. Again, Wieland's application of lettering and text onto her varied canvases prefigures its current wide usage. The use of narrative in the cartoon oils and in the sequential grid-like disaster paintings of the mid 1960s (*Car Crash* (1966), *Double Crash* (1966), and *Tragedy in the Air* (1963) to name but a few) anticipates the massive attention to narrative evident today.

In *Reason Over Passion* pans across the Canadian landscape are frequently interrupted to include such iconography as the Canadian flag, the national anthem, Pierre Trudeau's words "reason over passion" (537 permutations of the phrase are superimposed over the landscape images) as well as Trudeau himself. Wieland does not fetishize Trudeau, offering a paean; she is putting him on for his Enlightenment-like overvaluation of reason.[3] Through rephotography she literally breaks down Trudeau's face; the graininess of the image underlines the gaps in his façade—he appears as icon. In this way, Wieland distinguishes the "real"—the man Trudeau or the land itself—from the imaginary—the mythologies we construct to represent ourselves. Wieland provokes, she does not name. She calls these fixed myths into crisis and transforms them, urging the viewer to re-examine the relationship between the symbol and the landscape (the signified of Canada).

Images of Canadian topology often converge with Wieland's delightful obsession with the erotic and with sexual difference. *O Canada*, a 1970 lithograph made up of lipstick impressions of Wieland's lips as she mouthed the words "O Canada" is the prototype for this alignment. As early as the 1960s, Wieland prefigured the current production of, and critical obsessional engagement with, sexual difference.

An oft-repeated male/female dichotomy provides a formal tension, which additionally engenders a thematic sexual tension within the works themselves. Sexual difference in Wieland's case offers dialectical tension, the essential requisite to the art work. This gender division informs the formal demarcation of space, where tension is magnified due to the lack of depth relations. The painting *Captain* (1963), with its filmic devices, offers an exemplary illustration. The continual images of the captain in right profile, which "move" to the right of the canvas, are followed by a woman in left profile "moving" in the opposite direction to that of the captain's. This male/female figural dichotomy is present from her earliest 1956 abstract oils, *Lunch Time* and *Morning* for example, where the male and female figures are designated to the opposite sides of the frame, through to the most recent mythologically-informed paintings. *The Phenomenal World* (1983), *The Wanderer* (1984–1986), and *Paint Phantom* (1983–1984), from the 1980s, all repeat, albeit in a more muted, mystical manner, the same theme—the division of the sexes.

A and B in Ontario (1984), a recently completed film, reiterates this play with difference through its formal construction. The film is composed of Hollis Frampton and Wieland, each armed with a camera, playing a cat-and-mouse game pivoting around the point-of-view shot. Separately, each views the other; they rarely share the same space or frame. Such titles as *Heart-on* (1961), *Balling* (1961), or the phallic hot dogs of the film *Patriotism* (1964) playfully evoke a concern with the sexual. In the 1963 painting, *Nature Mixes*, a hand evolves into a flower, then into a phallus.

What further separates Wieland from other artists of her generation is the constant attention to, and representation of, elements that comprise a feminine and often domestic concern. Many of Wieland's works engage the possibility of the *parler femme*, with its analogical relation to feminine sexuality and its deconstructive potential regarding representation and the social. The 1960s stain paintings, produced by Wieland imprinting herself directly on canvas, provide an unprecedented realization of *écriture fémi-nine*. Similarly, in the film *Water Sark* (1964–1965) Wieland films herself filming through the use of mirrors and prisms and engages with her own body as a site for self-discovery.[4] *Handtinting* (1967–1968), a film com-prised solely of images of women, through the point-of-view shot and the suturing effect, provides a site for a feminine imaginary.[5] This female world was again evoked in the omnipresence of goddesses in the exhibi-tion of coloured pencil drawings *The Bloom of the Matter*, in 1981, at the Isaacs Gallery in Toronto.

Wieland's evocation of the feminine was not limited to the female imagery of lips or womb-like shapes. Through the incorporation of objects found around the home, such as cloth or plastic (made into quilts or home totems), Wieland exceeded the limitations of Pop Art and broke down the division between high and low art. This practice realized Walter Benjamin's hope that art begins to engage with social relations, that a "recasting of forms, a melting down in which many of the oppositions in which we have been accustomed to think may lose their relevance"[6] might occur. The collage *Clothes of Love* (1960–1961), with its wire clothes-line and hanging rags, or the Nevelson-like constructions such as *Cooling Room II* (1964), with its four coffee cups placed along the bottom shelf of a box-like construction, are illustrative of the encroachment of the domes-tic into the social. Once set in the gallery context, the arena of art, these craft-like constructions widened the parameters of the normative, restric-tive conceptions of "art."

The Presence of the Now—The Double Bind

> History is the subject of a structure whose site is not homogeneous empty time, but time filled by the presence of the now.
>
> Walter Benjamin, "Theses on the Philosophy of History"

In spite of these ground-breaking contributions, what is of most concern here is the overriding sense that this commemorative retrospective is out of sync with the spirit of Wieland's past achievements—it lacks a sense of immediacy because it does not engage current, local critical practice. Most of Wieland's "breakthroughs" occurred twenty years ago. Her output does span thirty years, the same thirty years that witnessed the ascent of North American feminism and, more locally, the rise of Canadian nationalism. The convergence of these two historical movements "naturally" has informed her work and, more infrequently, its subsequent reception. Both "isms" stem from a liberal heritage and share its attendant positivist impulses. It is noteworthy that the nationalist cause immediately claimed Wieland, whereas the feminist one did not. This limping metadiscourse (so pervasive in the 1960s and 1970s) has waited until now to make its claims. Hence, there is little evidence that Wieland's œuvre has been lifted into the critical climate of the 1980s.

Like most retrospectives, this one demonstrates how an institution such as the AGO often confers legitimacy on an artist only after that artist has returned to a more conventional form, in Wieland's case, the "art" of painting. (Wieland is tainted by her varied career; her move through divergent practices and media, including a feature film, has lessened her claim to serious consideration within the art field.) This retrospective also demonstrates how validating institutions such as the AGO, through their efforts to match the art object to a "fitting" critical complement, often stretch too far back and too far away. That is, the contextualization given to Wieland in the exhibition's catalogue restores the tenets of 1970s American feminism. And through the limitations of its critical engagements this consolidation paradoxically merges the past with the present, conflating America with Canada. This reads like a regression—it is also familiar.

An immediate corollary to this retrospective is the effect of validation on Wieland. Elevating an artist whose two-fold marginality, Canadian and female, formerly engendered a troubling presence—a presence that disrupted epistemological fields and exceeded the strictures of several recognized "traditions" (the structuralist film canon and the modernist credo, to name two)—has its subsequent effects. (It is ironic that Wieland's exclusion from New York's Anthology Film Archives precipitated her return to Canada in 1971. The Archives was formed to institutionalize and consecrate experimental filmmaking, but in Wieland's case it functioned as an expelling agency.) It is now a commonplace, given the recent pervasive influence of Adorno, that the art object, once institutionalized, is drained of its autonomy and becomes contained, bound, and drained of its outsider potential or difference. Within this economy, women are locked into a double bind. For the cost of entry into the realm of the "art star" has considerable symbolic resonance. Joining the canon and playing inside has its costs. Remaining outside in eternal cyclical time, benefiting from the imaginary's poetic disruptive effects, demands isolation and the risk of crossing over the borderline into incommunication. Women granted recognition, especially those formerly deemed "bad girls," once fetishized, are transformed into phallic mothers. Taking up the position of figurehead demands that one exchange the swirling circles of the imaginary for the phallic sceptre. The particular source of the validation in this

case, however, strips, dispossesses, and forces Wieland to represent a representation—she becomes a site for displaced meanings.

One could argue that Wieland is not, nor ever was, an outsider. It is
not as if Wieland has not been recognized. She has exhibited in group
shows, often as the only woman artist, and the solo exhibitions *The Bloom
of the Matter* and *Joyce Wieland: A Decade of Painting* (1985) are recent.
Wieland has had several retrospectives, all within a three-year period, from
1968 to 1971. *True Patriot Love* (1971) was the first retrospective given by
the National Gallery to a living woman—another first for Wieland. Yet it
is telling that this retrospective did coincide with the year Wieland
returned to Canada. The validating aura of America had to last for a long
time; since her return we have waited sixteen years for this next retrospective. Nevertheless, in the face of this attention, or perhaps because of it,
the critical complements that attend Wieland's work, the residual effects,
do not provide adequate documentation—they do not account for the
subversive potential inherent to her practice.

Lest We Forget

> Joyce Wieland, the Toronto painter, quiltmaker, and filmmaker is buy-
> ing herself a smashing new scarlet and cream coloured satin gown to
> wear next Thursday.
>
> Frank Raskey, *Toronto Star*, 1976

This retrospective provides an excellent opportunity to redress history
through the catalogue essays, to initiate a revision of past interpretive
hegemonies as the former critical reception bestowed upon Wieland's
work offers an exemplary instance of critical "malepractice." There is a
negligible amount of critical writing on her contribution in any medium.
The past reception of Wieland's work in both the popular press and the
art journals surely demonstrates the insidious nature of bias within cultural designation.

Hostility and systematic critical neglect, of course, are not unique to
work by women, but the sustained neglect—the totally evasive and inadequate literature on Wieland—gives one pause. There are a number of reasons for this, but the most evident is the inadequacy of past conceptual
frameworks in which to situate her work. All of Wieland's texts demand a
closer reading; they raise problems, directly or implicitly, of all sorts—his-
toriographic, aesthetic, and political—which demand revision. These past
inadequacies underscore the resolute "strangeness" of her work.

Wieland's visibility in the popular press has contributed to the commonly held view that she is a known figure—but known for what? Whether relegated to the women's, entertainment, or ecological news section of the newspaper, one facet emerges as dominant—Wieland makes a good human interest story. This journalistic prominence reinforces her persona as the familiar. That is, the sheer number of pieces contributes to this familiarity, and the tone breeds a familiar turn as well. Generally an overattention to biography informs the reviews, comprising an aberrant form of canonization—as if her persona alone could legitimize her work. She is there yet not there, familiar but strange.

Such a preoccupation with the personal is not solely relegated to the dailies. Marshall Delaney (also known as Robert Fulford) of *Saturday Night* even coined the term "Wielandism," maintaining that "it's a full-blown personal aesthetic" and categorized Wielandism as possessing assumed female attributes—"innocence, naive and sentimental charm, sexuality, melancholy romanticism, blatant symbolism, parody, ecology, and art."[7] Harry Malcolmson's crude affirmation in *Canadian Forum* is typical of the generous reviews: he employs such phrases as "spontaneity … warm and loving treatment … child-like fascination … and naive quality"[8] as a palliative description of Wieland's work. In his book *Contemporary Canadian Painting*, William Withrow (then Director of the AGO) unnecessarily describes Wieland as "a short, plump woman, unmindful of her appearance, Joyce Wieland was born in Toronto. …"[9]

The other stream of criticism, the one that bypasses physiology, deals with the works themselves:

Obviously influenced by the work of her husband, painter Mike Snow, Wieland. … Mrs. Snow has so completely infused the film [*Reason Over Passion*] with relentless motion that it has become totally static. … Mrs. Snow ends up bullying the viewer completely. The approach is completely clinical, utterly without warmth or humanity of any kind, with a sense of detachment that is a little frightening. Is this what Canada looks like? Or is this simply one lonely friendless woman's view of the world around her? Canada, Mrs. Wieland seems to be saying, is one vast nothingness at which one can poke fun by having the national anthem performed by a series of tuned flatuses.

The writer is Jacob Siskind of the *Montréal Gazette*,[10] and his hostility does not need further elaboration. His tone and selectivity is similar to that of Douglas Ord's, who uses *Reason Over Passion* as a sounding board for what he perceives to be wrong with Canadian film. Such phrases as "pathetically provincial … terror stricken flight … borderline hysterical … and we'll thank Joyce Wieland to keep her paranoid visions to herself,"[11] are typical not only of Ord's criticism, but of the derision of female artists in general. Art historians are not exempt from such put-downs. When Barry Lord charges that Wieland engages in "cosmetic feminism" and "reduces cultural symbolism to the most trivial level,"[12] he subtly denigrates, using adjectives with female connotations.

These examples of "critical writing" are more ethical than analytical. As we have seen, there are tendencies either to idealize or to devalue (fetishize or sublimate) Wieland. This pro/con relegation to the extreme ends of the scale attests to the fact that Wieland can take up numerous positions in the representational field. Such an overdetermined contextualization stems from the fact that there is no tradition of either critical or feminist writing to draw from in this country. The problem becomes magnified, or it reads differently, when gender is considered, and this paradigm has further marginalized female artists in Canada. Such absences increase the difficulties in appraising difference. Conflation provides the solution—it contains and eases the unsettling effects of Wieland's work.

The Ties That Bind: Here We Go Again

Even before reading the AGO catalogue, one's response may approach stupefaction when it is learned that two of the three essays were written by Americans. This choice presents the penultimate irony, given not only Wieland's former allegiance to place, the insistence on the local, but also her once-pervasive anti-American sentiments. (Wieland is still the artist who drew the cartoon *First Bombing in English Canada* (1972), where characters abduct pro-Americans to a "Canadian Content Camp.") Our colonization by Americans is a consummate concern in many of her works.

The choice of critics provides the last word on colonization: a conspiracy now engineered by ourselves (in this case, presumably with Wieland's consent). This reaction is not informed by a single-party imperative, of the nationalist navel-gazing variety. Nor does it endorse the homogeneity of stagnant, local advocacy. It stems from a desire to fight off the claims of the past and witness the latent possibilities that were imminent in a reconsideration of Wieland, possibilities that needed the (seemingly oxymoronic) maintenance of borders to guarantee heterogeneity.

The nationality of two of the critics could make one wary as to their ability to contextualize locale, as ignorance of the place of enunciation could narrow the scope of inquiry. Because of this, the writers could not read Wieland in a multiplicity of contexts, particularly those contexts that could lead to considerations of specificity. Such specificity and contextualization would exempt Wieland from the normative consolidation—feared from this direction—emanating from south of the border.

Confirmation of this anticipatory scepticism about the catalogue occurred early for this author. As a "Wielandphile" I enquired of the AGO as to who had written the catalogue essays. While I was put on hold, I could hear, "who is that famous woman from New York, the art critic?" "Famous" and "New York" say it all; she is Lucy Lippard. I do not wish to diminish Lippard's achievements; she is a competent critic and has written numerous books, including *From The Center*[13]—the paradigmatic American feminist art text that paved the way for a generation of women artists. Nevertheless, the American involvement does bring to the fore one of the contradictory strains evident in the Wieland paradigm. The essay on Wieland's films was written by the American academic, Lauren Rabinovitch, who wrote a doctoral dissertation on Wieland and other women filmmakers. Marie Fleming, formerly of the AGO, writes the art historical perspective on Wieland.

In the face of the reservations mentioned above, a central paradox emerges. How does this form of validation, a marginalized discourse itself—American feminism—speak to Wieland's local context? On the other hand, we have no indigenous discourse to replace it. If one considers Wieland's claim that she is Canadian, in addition to her twice-delegated "first Other" status, this places Wieland in the position of absolute signification. She represents all of the Others. How do we avoid conflation?

There are inherent dangers in appraising an individual artist. The lure of placing an individual's work solely within the matrix of the biographical beckons insistently. This easily leads to an overvaluation that places the artist on the side of the original and unique, often explaining production through personality. This trap is especially appealing when it comes to Wieland. It is difficult not to scramble for personality, to opt for the obvious methodological choice when there is no critical discourse laid out. And we cannot deny that Wieland is original and unique. Barthes and Foucault, among others, have signalled the decline in the status of authorship, of textual authority. The author whose "death" they announce, is, of course one long revered in Western culture (and still fetishized in many quarters—not the least of which the art field). That is, the author as master, as phallic will-to-power over the text. The suggestion of the possibility of another author emerging, one conditioned by the principle that is decidedly not phallic and not bound by conflation, was but one of the critical challenges these critics failed to meet in the catalogue. Of course, within the Canadian context this is impossible—there is no history to de-authorize, just as there are no authors to speak of. In this light Wieland is a first.

New critical currents, those arising out of recent considerations of the text, could have provided a way of addressing the troubling paradox arising when sympathetic individuals approach the individual female artist. The writer's desire to redress the past, to inscribe a place in linear history, is set against the knowledge that this is no longer the task of criticism. Affirmation can easily tip over into the realm of positivism.

Unfortunately no one rose to the challenge. The catalogue realizes every fear for it: it bites the lure of biography, falling into the same trap as its predecessors, the popular press. Through the persistent pursuit of questions of intention and biographical context, Fleming and Lippard attempt to pin down their subject by naming her as eccentric and determined.

Fleming takes up this interpretive model, based on the analogy between the work and its maker, with a vengeance. She makes her claims for this practice early; she announces that biographical references enrich the readings of the works.[14] Perhaps this is so, but her wholesale utilization of this method steers into the absurd. Fleming traces the life with the works, neck and neck. A pattern emerges. She draws from Wieland's personal history, extracting a prevalent mood or feeling from a particular time, and she illustrates this through examples in the art works. Next she turns to Wieland for substantiation. Such disclaimers as "Wieland has denied this intent" (p. 22) or "while Wieland did not consciously intend such a reading, she concedes that it could nevertheless have been unconsciously incorporated" (p. 31) are pervasive. Fleming, however, is extremely thorough; she consolidates the general line of Wieland rather elegantly. She takes stabs at outlining the artistic movements that influenced Wieland, and some of these connections, such as those with Miró and de Kooning, are informative. Nevertheless, statements that narrowly prescribe how Wieland should be interpreted severely mar the essay. Her claim that Wieland's work "is not directed at theoretical aesthetics or ontological problems" (p. 45) holds no credence within the current critical climate. Fleming echoes the popular press in her reliance on personality and does not provide a way out of the biographical conundrum. The words "intuitive," "personal," and "originality" appear consistently. Similarly, the naming of "feminine sensitivity (delicacy, paleness, lyricism)" as "that irritant to feminism" (p. 44) demonstrates precisely how she does not grasp that feminism is a generic term of semantic complexity.

When exhibited in the public domain, a work's meaning cannot be commanded by the artist but is at large, in circulation. The artist is one viewer among others. Her reading may be better than most, but it is not definitive. The intrusion of otherness into one's discourse, produced by exhibiting, manufactures meanings that are unbeknownst to her. Seen in this way, Wieland's original self becomes an illusion, an imaginative function constructed to augur the anxiety that is engendered by excess.

The desire to emphasize and construct a self additionally derives from the restorative imperative of feminist revisionism. Such efforts at validation are understandable, indeed commendable, given the past exclusions—there were very few selves to speak of. The cry of "the personal is political" informs this approach, a strategy that was obviously seen to redress past exclusions, absences, and inadequate contextualizations. What must be remembered is that this cry for equality and the validation of difference, without considering its effects, arose out of the particular contingencies of an era. "Me-too-ism," fetishistic counterpower, must be reconsidered, given that equalization has not produced its desired effect—social equality—in spite of orders to the contrary.

These observations do not endorse the dreaded disease of postfeminism, a disease that some find lurking within the "excesses" of theory. They are informed by a knowledge of the dangers in appraising an artist solely through gender. And Wieland's "femaleness" is often the sole criterion by which she is defined in these essays. The authors "flip" the "personal is political" imperative in order to personalize Wieland's art objects. Such categorization provides an aberrant form of legitimization—it ghettoizes.

Lippard's essay is guilty of this practice. Her valorizing pen delightfully places Wieland as an eccentric, building up a case for greatness. This particular brand of American feminism, with its affirmative rhetoric, is not problematic in and of itself. It becomes something else once transposed to a Canadian context and displaced onto Wieland. Inadvertently, this approach becomes an agent of colonization, by conflating the differences between women artists in different countries.

Rabinovitch's essay also suffers from its place of enunciation. The repeated use of the phrase "in Canada" reminds the reader that she is speaking at us from afar. Feeble attempts are made to include specific Canadian references, but this is thwarted by data that is simply not true. For example, her claim, in an effort to differentiate *Reason Over Passion*, that Canadian television in the 1960s and 1970s provided no in-depth analysis of nationalist concerns, is simply unfounded. Rabinovitch places Wieland within a feminine aesthetic context, then describes the films within the tradition-bound experimental film category, walking through the structuralist preoccupation with form. She points out that Wieland has feminine sensibility and that her works are political, but without examining the effects of these engagements. Rabinovitch ends with an adequate description of *The Far Shore* (1976). But *The Far Shore* is by no means Wieland's last film, and this oversight is certainly telling—the essay's "staleness" becomes magnified. Missing is a discussion of Wieland's most recent films: *A and B in Ontario, Birds at Sunrise* (1985), and *Peggy's Blue Skylight* (1985).

By not acknowledging the difficulties inherent to an analysis of a female Canadian artist, and Wieland in particular, the authors repeat the ways in which the feminine has been made a fetish by male writers. This is compounded by the manner in which they echo the cultural context of America's dispossession of Canadian production. They provide a fetishistic reification of the feminine in and of itself and thus repeat the cycle of the Eternal Feminine—as if a colonized culture could afford to go "cosmic." And in this way they unwittingly repeat what they have set out against. They recreate the fantasy of the phallic, all powerful mother through which women reconnect with the very Law they had set out to fight.[15]

Instead of challenging historicism's link to the paternal function, these essays invent their own brand of historicism by attempting to construct a new canon. In an effort to provide a formal consistency that would match her brother artists, or her American sisters, they bind and conflate Wieland into sameness. Joan Copjec's warnings against simply inverting the terms of the traditional canonical economy of literary writing are apposite here:

> What must be questioned is not the incompleteness of a list which can then simply be added to, nor, alternatively, the covering up of a separate and autonomous tradition of women writers (a feminine canon) which can then be simply uncovered. Instead one must analyse the way male-transference histories take their form (and not just their "facts") from their exclusions of women. The whole radical effect of feminism would not be the admitting of women, finally, into existing disciplines but the breaking up of the concordant epistemological fantasies which are their support and limit. The plain observation that a text takes up a sexist position is much less instructive (and much less effective) than the analysis of how this position is enabled from within the theory in which it arises.[16]

The catalogue ricochets between a historicism on the one hand and a transhistorical Feminine on the other. This double desire bespeaks an "I want it all" attitude—a mutation: the right to remain both inside and outside. And in this way, this retrospective encounters Wieland, but at the same time, it paradoxically exiles her. The relativizing agency of America has donned the unlikely masquerade of the Eternal Feminine, and thus mythologized that which Wieland demythologizes: representation and identity. Naming, a practice that Wieland threw into relief, ironically became the agent that cloaked the contradictions. Grafting, not interrogation, and affirmation, not analysis, become the order of the day.

American feminism has paradoxically occluded specificity here: gender is privileged over other, local differences. Unfortunately, Kristeva's hope "that having started off with the idea of difference, feminism will be able to break free of its belief in Woman"[17] was not realized. Same-sex choice, in this case, has paradoxically conflated, and thus limited, the number of considerations we could bring to bear on a reading of Wieland's work. This same-sex contextualization has enabled history to repeat itself. The girls are still playing with the girls, and the Americans are still on top.

It is the Canadian fate to live with the grim reality (after Thucydides) of "having consciousness of much but the ability to do nothing about it"; then it is also the Canadian circumstance to be in a privileged position to take full measure of European scepticism and American hyper-pragmatism without surrendering to either fatalism or ecstasy.[18]

It takes Arthur Kroker to name the Canadian dilemma. However, it is up to the analytic dissidence typical of feminism—a feminism that is in process—and a concentration on the local to deal with the paradox engendered by the authorization of our women artists. Examining the layers of this paradox points out some of the differences that are being smothered by this retrospective's conflation of Joyce Wieland. Perhaps with this knowledge, we can begin to articulate the specificity she deserves.

Notes

1.   *Joyce Wieland*, (Toronto: Art Gallery of Ontario and Key Porter Books, 1987).

2.   Robert Fulford, "Giving Us a Sense of Ourselves," *Toronto Star*, 10 July 1971, 55.

3.   In conversation with the author, June 1985, Wieland claimed that she was "taking Trudeau on."

4.   See Kay Armatage's discussion of *Water Sark* in relation to French feminism, "The Feminine Body: Joyce Wieland's *Water Sark*," *Canadian Women Studies*, vol. 8, no. 1 (Spring 1987): 84–88.

5.   See Kass Banning, "Textual Excess in Joyce Wieland's *Handtinting*," *CineAction*, no. 5 (Spring 1986): 12–14.

6.   Walter Benjamin, "The Author as Producer," *Understanding Brecht*, trans. Anna Bolstock (London: NLB, 1973), 94.

7.   Marshall Delaney, "Wielandism: A Personal Style in Full Bloom," *Saturday Night*, May 1976, 76–77.

8.   Harry Malcolmson, "True Patriot Love—Joyce Wieland's New Show," *Canadian Forum,* June 1971, 17–18.

9.   William Withrow, *Contemporary Canadian Painting* (Toronto: McClelland and Stewart, 1972), 122.

10.   Jacob Siskind, "Joyce Wieland's *Reason Over Passion* at Loyola Experimental Film Festival," *Montréal Gazette*, 4 July 1969, 22.

11.   Douglas Ord, "An Essay on Canadian Film," *Cinema Canada*, no. 39 (Summer 1977): 40–44.

12.   Barry Lord, *The History of Painting in Canada* (Toronto: NC Press, 1974), 212–214.

13.   Lucy Lippard, *From the Center: Feminist Essays on Women's Art* (New York: E.P. Dutton, 1976).

14.   Marie Fleming, "Joyce Wieland: A Perspective," in *Joyce Wieland*, 11. Further references to this volume appear in parentheses in the text.

15.   Julia Kristeva, "Women's Time," *Signs*, vol. 7, no. 1 (Autumn 1981): 33.

16.   Joan Copjec, "Transference: Letters and the Unknown Woman," *October*, no. 28 (Spring 1984): 76.

17.   Kristeva, "Women's Time," 33.

18.   Arthur Kroker, "Mediascape," *Canadian Journal of Political and Social Theory*, vol. 10, no. 1–2 (1986): 63.

Christine Ross

History of a Rupture

For the purposes of this text, let us consider *Art et féminisme* and *Femmes-Forces* to be the two exhibitions that open and close the history of feminist art exhibitions in Québec during the 1980s. This fragment of history will thus be primarily museological. It begins in the spring of 1982 with an exhibition, at Montréal's Musée d'art contemporain, of works by forty-one women artists, and ends in the fall of 1987 at the Musée du Québec, with an exhibition of works by thirty-five women artists.

But this fragment of history was also more particularly the rupture and closure of a history. And it was *Femmes-Forces* that was responsible for this act of dissociation, the first signs of which became apparent in the vagueness of the show's intentions. Strangely enough, *Femmes-Forces* focused neither on the art system nor on the question of the status of women artists, nor did it seek to shake up the ideology of the feminine, that is, to frame feminism in terms of critical difference, as it was understood by Rose-Marie Arbour at the time of *Art et féminisme*. Rather, *Femmes-Forces* was an exhibition that abruptly—but perhaps to no great surprise—reversed steam, opacified and transposed difference in order to create an exhibition by women at the expense of women, invalidating women artists in the name of art.

Femmes-Forces was a bringing together, then, of what shaped up to be both a beginning and an end, as well as the beginning of the end—a bringing together, indeed, for *Femmes-Forces* constructed a simulacrum of feminist memory and brought about a lack of continuity, a break and rupture with a memory, the history of which now needs to be written. Upon closer inspection, this juxtaposition of these two exhibitions turns out to be a twofold substitution. First, there was the replacement of *art-as-feminist-discourse* by *art-as-woman* [*un art-femme*], a term that will be clarified later.[1] Secondly, in correlation with this development, the concept of art understood as communication was overturned by a conception of art understood as unmediated expression. There were, then, two consubstantial substitutions without any transition, transformation, or development between them—a clear case of a split or breach between two events, a case of (I choose my words carefully) the obliteration of the one by the other.

This a translation and edited version of a text prepared for the Universities Art Association Conference, Montréal, 1990

1. Art et féminisme

The conjunction in the title is not fortuitous but was inserted only after careful consideration. Its purpose was to establish a discursive distance between two practices, between art on the one hand and feminism on the other. Arbour, curator of the exhibition, specifically outlined an "art-as-feminist-discourse" to be differentiated from both "feminist" and "feminine" art.

> This exhibition is not the place to establish the formal criteria of a typically feminist art; rather, it is an occasion for raising questions about new criteria concerning the effectiveness of communication through art. ... To divide women artists into movements and groups exclusively on the basis of formal and stylistic characteristics would be to do them a disservice. ... Thus the question of knowing "what exactly feminist art is" relegates the artists' own objectives—increasing women's awareness through art, expressing their creative experiences—to a position of secondary importance.[2]

Thus, in the early 1980s a feminist exhibition in an institutional setting could advocate "art-as-feminist-discourse." But what does this expression really mean? It means precisely this: an art devoted to communicating, making people aware of, the situation of women. The feminist message would be inscribed in, available through, art. This was an art that was, while not opposed to expression, primarily referential (p. 12), an art that, in line with the postulates of the historical avant-garde and the *Refus Global* of the *automatistes*,[3] sought to relate the personal and political, art and life, the artist and the public—to relate them, certainly, but in a way that would be fundamentally critical, drawing directly upon the programme of the Women's Movement. For example, a number of works in *Art et féminisme* challenged or denounced the notion of the feminine, whereas others attempted either to trace historical links among women or to propose alternative models. In doing so, art-as-feminist-discourse sought to translate the unspoken in concrete ways existing "beyond verbal language" (p. 12).

Art et féminisme was, overall, a feminist critique of the feminine but one that was articulated in many different ways. Arbour was firm on this point: it is essential, she said, to fight against the "reductive bipolarity" of the dichotomies underlying the differentiation of the masculine and the feminine, that is, against the gendered separation "of instinct and reason, body and spirit, practice and theory" which "reflects the opposition between the sexes ... in order to perpetuate a [dominant] order."

Stereotypes are what we must fight against, those afflicting male-female relationships and, to take another example, the stereotype of the "eternal feminine." The work of these artists is, to some degree, shaped by the refusal of sexual determinism. It bears the signs and traces, not of a celebration of "femininity," but of a critical distance with respect to the traditional model imposed on women, a model whose criteria have been accepted and interiorized by a majority of women of various social classes and origins. Such criteria would include passivity, heterosexuality, narcissism, masochism, and sentimentality. (p. 9)

Very well then. But through its critique of female stereotypes, and this brings us to a second important aspect of art-as-feminist-discourse, *Art et féminisme* also became a forum for calling art itself into question. By drawing upon women's experiences and making use of forms and figures "taken from the outside world," it ruined the self-referentiality of modernist art (p. 4). It is along these lines that we must interpret Arbour's statement to the effect that "art-as-feminist-discourse is connected to the experience of *the artist as a woman*" (p. 6, emphasis added). Thus, while the discourse would bear generally on the condition of women, it would be an *artist's* discourse, a discourse emerging from the experiences of women—on the condition, of course, that the women in question be first and foremost recognized as women artists engaged in exploiting and exploring critical strategies inherent to their respective media and practices.

The third and final aspect, implicit in the concept of discourse, is the notion of *difference.* For Arbour, there can be no question of specificity or authority in feminist art, just as there is no room for a "normative description of a certain type of women's art" (p. 9). Her repeated warnings about the dangers of categorization and normalization, which become increasingly emphatic as she proceeds, especially when she tries to establish relationships between the works, do not go so far as to dispense with the question of difference. Because difference does indeed exist. It is, Arbour declares, even "subversive" to the extent that art-as-feminist-discourse articulates difference on the basis, not of the feminine, but of feminism. Arbour writes: "In general, feminist artists do not affirm the same aesthetic values as male artists; what draws the former together is a vision of a different world" (p. 6). Thus it is feminism, the historical specificity of feminism, not the fact of being a woman, that creates difference, both from and in the masculine. This recognition of a fundamentally feminist discourse is indispensable if connections are to be made between the various works in *Art et féminisme,* be it on symbolic, technical, or iconographic grounds. And it is only in the light of feminism that reference to the body can function as a paradigm; it is through feminism that the body will reveal itself as alienated, exploited, oppressed, wounded, and fragmented, that it will be possible to emphasize the "gestures, dispositions, and behaviours, the clothing and fabrics, the physical contacts and the techniques of covering the body" deployed in the works (p. 11). In short, by its manifold references to the body, "to its collective and intimate experience and the objects that leave their imprint on it," art-as-feminist-discourse communicates in a critical manner. It transmits forms and symbols that "do not in themselves define the terms of art-as-feminist-discourse," but "constitute a point of reference and bear a salutary communicative power" (p. 11).

2. Femmes-Forces

Elsewhere I have pointed out how this exhibition represented an anti-intellectual shift for the Musée du Québec, a turnaround symptomized primarily by the choice of a collector and self-styled art lover as curator.[4] I will not belabour the point; rather, I will deal with the substitutions that *Femmes-Forces* brought about with respect to *Art et féminisme*, substitutions apparent not so much from the choice of works but from the critical foundation laid for the exhibition, specifically via the texts in the catalogue. These substitutions took shape around the notion of difference. Let us read what curator Réal Turcot had to say about the matter:

> It would be impossible today to mount another exhibition like *Art et féminisme*. … Artistic production has changed, the problematic has changed; while feminism persists, the concerns are different. One cannot, with some exceptions, make *a priori* distinctions between the work of women and that of men. There is no such thing as women's art.[5]

This passage is crucial in that it articulates the two key statements underlying the ideological orientation of *Femmes-Forces*. First, says Turcot, if feminism persists in 1992, it does so in a changed state. And this change is elucidated in "Femmes-Forces: le retour aux valeurs du sujet," a text in which Michelyne Caouette supports the theory of the "complementarity of opposites" advanced by the French feminist Elisabeth Badinter. According to Badinter, men and women have come to resemble each other to the point that *one has become the other*.[6] In this view, today's feminism is characterized by the disappearance of gender differences. Accordingly, we no longer need to fight for the emancipation of women, and the communication of gender-specific experiences, such as we saw in 1982, is completely out of the question, for, as Caouette puts it, the woman of today "knows." But what exactly does she "know"? We will come back to this question later. For now, suffice it to say that this "knowledge" is both her power and her strength, is what makes her like a man; and it is precisely this "relationship of equality," this absence of "disparity" between men and women artists, that *Femmes-Forces* seeks to establish.[7]

In the second of his two key statements, Turcot claims that there is no such thing as women's art. Was this fact not already stressed by Arbour a number of years before, with *Art et féminisme*? Then why is it emphasized here, if it is not meant to imply that, if there is no women's art in this exhibition of works by *women artists*, if difference (feminist or feminine) no longer exists, it is because, in the end, there is only *art*. This may appear to be a facile conclusion, yet it is reinforced in Caouette's analytical essay, which shows us the extent to which the true *raison d'être* of *Femmes-Forces* must be sought elsewhere, that is, neither in the feminine nor in feminism, but precisely in those strong women [*femmes-en-forces*] who have known, who *know*, how to define and explore art in terms of a "return to the values of the subject."[8]

Let us be more precise. While *Art et féminisme* drew upon the feminist subject for its critique of modernist art, and, in its desire to communicate women's experience, *Femmes-Forces* promotes a "neo-romantic art," a "reflection of artistic freedom," an art permeated by the expressive energy of women seeking in the past and in ancient mythology a fundamentally "tormented" subject with a view to "defining the identity of the present" and suggesting new models of "readaptation."[9]

With respect to the works or, more precisely, their interpretation by Caouette, this art is a return to the "*forces* of nature" (Francine Larivée) (p. 17), to "human presence" (Suzelle Levasseur) (p. 16), and "emotion" (Ilana Isehayek) (p. 15); it is, as well, an art that celebrates "freedom of transformation" (Betty Goodwin) (p. 16), the regeneration of humanity (Michèle Assal), the divinization and *heroization* of the subject (Dominique Morel and Josette Trépanier), and, finally, the hybridization of birth and rebirth (Claire Beaulieu, Sylvie Croteau, and Christine Palmieri) (pp. 15–18). Strength, liberty, presence, life cycles—what concoction of knowledge and power is being evoked here if it is not the knowledge of "the essentials," that is, a *female knowledge of essences* from which women's new power would supposedly emerge (p. 11).

There is every reason to wonder whence women derive this privilege of knowing the essence of things, especially in light of Turcot's contention that *Femmes-Forces* was more about art than about feminine knowledge or power. Indeed it is at this level of *art* that the exhibition demanded to be received. In other words, the heuristic of the (strong) woman's knowledge of essences derives from the ultimate (and ultimately desirable) effect of

Femmes-Forces, which consisted in "establishing a relationship between the work, the artist, and the public" (p. 12)—that is, in ensuring not only the art's accessibility but also the democratic ideal of the museum doing the promoting. Let us focus on this rather explicit passage from Caouette's text:

> The function of the human quality present in each of these works is to establish a meeting point between the viewer and the artist. The works exemplify an eminently accessible art form that is turned like a mirror upon the world, one in which joys and fears reveal the times in which we live. (p. 18)

Accessibility comes, then, by way of *woman* [*la femme*], in her essence. It proceeds through her as the site of emotion and expressive energy, through the woman artist whose unmediated energy permeates her work, through woman as that maternal site that, in offering protection, reassures us and delivers us from the postmodern shattering of the subject. All this, of course, hinges on Caouette's view of *Femmes-Forces* as a "model of readaptation" and a "hope for the future, as much on the artistic plane as on the social" (p. 19). If *Art et féminisme* sought to communicate women's experience through a critique of the feminine, *Femmes-Forces* gives rise to a hybrid form where, as in an apparition, the work and the female body are fused. "There is no such thing," Turcot insists, "as women's art." In actual fact, however, *Femmes-Forces* does not have to do with a specifically female type of art but, rather, with art defined as an appeal to the feminine. *Art is like woman* is the operative metaphor here. Deployed in the form of a postmodern *gynesis*,[10] it inserts woman into discourse by constituting a space coded as feminine, reserved for an "other-than-herself." (Again we have Badinter's hypothesis that one is the other, but not the reverse.) This operation invalidates women and their experience, dissolving the historical female subject and relegating it to the surface. Alice Jardine:

> The object produced by this process is neither a person nor a thing, but a horizon, that toward which the process is tending: a *gynema*. This *gynema* is a reading effect, a woman-in-effect that is never stable and has no identity. ... At the most fundamental level, this interrogation operates: first, metonymically in discourse *about* women; and second, metaphorically in discourse *by, through, as* woman. The problem is that within this ever-increasing inflation of quotation marks around the word "woman," women as thinking, writing subjects are placed in the position of constantly wondering whether it is a question of women or woman, their written *bodies* or their *written* bodies.[11]

Women's experience, which was important enough in 1982 to serve as a foundation for the feminist critique of art and society, was no longer worthy of consideration just five years later. Such was the schism that *Femmes-Forces* generated. The curating, the site plan, and the catalogue (as well as some of the works) simply eliminated the unspoken element that *Art et féminisme* had drawn upon. This was accomplished simply by suspending the question of gender (for here, remember, one has become the other) while paradoxically orchestrating a sexual division by restricting the exhibition to women artists. From the beginning, this endeavour was an exercise in self-denial since the way in which it used women to defend the accessibility of museum-sponsored art was costly in terms of their own self-actualization.

Whence the inescapable question: Didn't *Femmes-Forces* ultimately reveal a certain insufficiency, or deficiency even, on the part of feminism? In other words, can we, do we want to, continue with feminist exhibitions? Are artists still producing work involving feminist discourses? Are such discourses still relevant? Is art-as-communication still possible?

In actual fact, *Femmes-Forces* has provided at least a partial response to these questions. By projecting a surface image of *woman* [*la mise en surface de la femme*] and by undermining her experience, it has forced us to take a more critical look at *Art et féminisme*. Consequently, one wonders whether the belief in an art conceived as communication was not premature back in 1982. The surface image of women projected in 1987, that is, the insertion of *woman* into discourse at the service of a feminine definition of art, is indicative of its failure of communication. Communication would necessarily entail the transmission, through art, of a message from sender to receiver and, already in 1982, certain works in *Art et féminisme*—Joyan Saunders's *Phone* (1980), for example—attested to a breakdown in communication between the respective poles, to an erosion of difference between experience and mass media images, between empirical woman and the woman of the *photo romances*. Saunders's piece perfectly exemplified what I mean by surface; it set forth a reality in which the I and the image become indistinguishable, where distinctions between the subject, the message, feminist critique, and mass media stereotypes failed to materialize.

If art-as-feminist-discourse was measured by its communicative character, what are we to make of it now that depth—the temporal depth of history or memory as well as those depths formerly guaranteed by dichotomies inherited from metaphysics (hermeneutics, Marxism, psychoanalysis)—has been replaced by surfaces? The notion of "surface" received ample treatment in Fredric Jameson's influential article, "Postmodernism, or the Cultural Logic of Late Capitalism."[12] Here we need only concern ourselves with his essential point, which is that postmodernism is characterized by an absence of depth, a "new depthlessness," that the subject it places before us is adrift in a perpetual present amid signs s/he no longer knows how to interpret and is unable to take up any perspective, position, or viewpoint with respect to them.

To speak of a world of surfaces is to recognize, along with Bernard Tschumi, the impact of technological developments on our perception of objects. The city of today is a proliferation of special effects; form and function, the signifier and the signified, are articulated in such a state of instability that the first no longer manages to represent the second. Permanence is continually abolished in a flood of immaterial representations of abstract systems (video, computers, etc.) that eliminate distance as a time factor. The accidental rules; speed compresses space and diminishes the distance between subject and object. And this same space, having lost its cohesion and having fragmented, calls forth interpretations of interpretations *ad infinitum*. The current state of cities and architecture, of subjects and objects, is best described by prefixes such as *ex-*, *dis-*, and *de-*; hence "*ex*-centric, *dis*-integrated, *dis*-located, *dis*-jointed, *de*-constructed, *dis*-mantled, *dis*-associated, *dis*-continuous, *de*-regulated."[13]

Let us attend also to what Mario Perniola has to say. For him, the world of the mass media is synonymous with the establishment of the instantaneous and the hollowing out of the present. Such a society constitutes itself through a constant deployment, not of the new, but of remains and residues supplied with artificially revived façades; it is, in short, a marketing of images for immediate, simultaneous, and indiscriminate consumption.[14] Here we find echoes of Jameson, for the world of the mass media is a world of appearances versus things, the ephemeral versus the accessible, consumption versus conservation, assimilation versus difference, the current versus the present, the instantaneous versus memory.

There has been, therefore, a loss of depth and, as *Femmes-Forces* so forcefully reminds us, a loss of feminist memory, historicity, and the empirical body, combined with the processing of feminism by the mass media. For let us remember that, in 1987, the present denied the past just as it denied women's experience and settled down, finally, into this rupture. In this regard, it is significant that some of the works in *Femmes-Forces* bore directly on the disjunctive phenomenon of surface images of women. Thus Brigitte Radecki's *Nature morte avec crâne* (1986–87) is less a "complementarity of opposites" than a swallowing up of reality by appearance and illusion. The violently contrasting colours relentlessly flatten what would otherwise be volume, just as the heavy outlines and shadows end by nullifying the object, reducing it to the level of an image.

Consider also the transformed banner of Lise Nantel, which shows how the memory of the early feminist struggles in which she waved her own first banners—shown, by the way, in *Art et féminisme*—has persisted, but out-of-sync now with respect to its subject. In *La mémoire du rose I* (1984), shown in *Féministe-toi-même, féministe-quand-même* at *La Chambre blanche* in 1984 in Québec City, this memory of feminism, translated into banners leaning against a wall, was presented *on the same plane* as its subject. With *Une chambre à soi* (*A Room of One's Own*) (1986) in *Femmes-Forces*, the memory-banner arches over a place it can no longer manage to circumscribe. Constructed by a process of spreading and stacking (fabric-image) that apparently leads nowhere, doomed to perpetually starting over, the work attests to the difficulty of articulating desire or postulating a future. Nantel explains this difficulty, which concerns the creative act, as follows:

> A room of one's own as a metaphor. ... The time/space required by desire. ... My project consists in showing the difficulty of securing a place and a time for creating. ... You start with an image and quickly run out of breath trying to capture it. Your feet get caught in the rungs of the ladder leading to it. Suddenly, it is within reach. Upon contact, however, it disintegrates into the dust dreams are made of. And with this dust it must be built up again and preserved. Soon, however, another image comes to mind and ... again you are breathless, trying to. ...[15]

As we can see, feminist exhibitions will have to say goodbye to history and art-as-communication, at least in the way these have been understood so far. Depth, no longer where we sought it, can be conceived only in terms of the Surface, but this by no means implies that feminist exhibitions must do without the subject or the empirical body. We have seen how, in *Art et féminisme*, the body could function as a paradigm, both in its capacity as a body to be communicated within a critique of the feminine and insofar as art could simultaneously refer to it and distinguish itself from it. This distinction was, however, already being eroded in the exhibition before its final collapse in *Femmes-Forces*. Still, are we not now faced with the imperative put before us by Rosi Braidotti? Are we not confronted with the need to (re)connect strategically—in different ways this time, however—the symbolic and empirical, the conceptual and corporeal (as a "field of force"), as well as the discursive and experiential?

> The "body" in question is the threshold of subjectivity: as such it is neither the sum of its organs—a fixed biological essence—nor the result of social conditioning—a historical entity. The body is rather to be thought of as the point of intersection, as the interface between the biological and the social, that is to say between the socio-political field

of the microphysics of power and the subjective dimension. ... This vision implies that the subject is subjected to his/her unconscious; the driving notion of "desire" is precisely that which relays the self to the many "others" that constitute his/her "external" reality.[16]

The body. So be it. Feminism has always insisted on it. But what do we mean when we say "(re)connect in different ways"? How can we talk about corporeal experience in the world of the Surface? In a work titled *Au creux des apparences*,[17] Michel Maffesoli advances the thesis that, across this Surface, the reality of the body derives not only from its nature as an appearance but, as well, from its capacity to link together the subject and the object, establishing connections whose merit (or ethics) it is to *signify* on behalf of the subject. Defined in terms of appearances and hence of the *body*, the subject adheres to whatever presents itself as an image, not in order to ensure its own identity or to set itself off as different, but to establish an identification with the other, thereby instituting what Maffesoli calls *linkage* [*la reliance*], a sort of depth of the surface articulated in an emphatic melding with the Other perceived as an image. And, since appearances in mass media societies change constantly, such identification is *de facto* ephemeral and always liable to, sooner or later, be replaced by another and possibly contradictory manifestation.

In this crucible [*creux fusionnel*], this depth of identification with appearances, there is room for a feminist exhibition. In its very organization and structure, and *with* the works it could bring forward, such an exhibition would crystallize the imagery of a single second, constitute a body of ephemeral identifications susceptible to complexifying difference. The essential thing is that such an exhibition be able to manifest, and generate interaction among the empirical, multidimensional facets of women and the equally multidimensional character of feminism, in other words, be able to effect a reopening of the questions of meaning and of the subject. Why? Because the current subject in feminism has acquired complexity at the expense of definition (or distinction), instability at the expense of foresight, imagery at the expense of corporeality.

The problem of memory, however, remains unresolved. For the model of *linkage*, while allowing for connections, attractions, and a form of solidarity between myself and the Other, is inscribed within an ephemeral order that seems doomed to reinforce the amnesia of an event such as *Femmes-Forces*—unless, of course, feminist memory lies elsewhere; unless we have continued looking for it where it is now or soon to be absent; and unless memory is no longer a record of transformation and development, no longer a perfectly negotiable path that leads us inexorably from point A to point B. Let us simply say, then, that feminist memory lies somewhere close by the banners of Lise Nantel, that we must look for it there, within a developing structure [*structure en procès*] situated, so to speak, off to the side, above, on another plane. In other words, in a waiting state. Unforeseeable. A virtual memory, then, present but waiting to be actualized. A memory made ever more complex: this is the context in which the (re)thinking of feminist exhibitions and the positioning of corpo-empirical linkage (as described briefly above) will have to be inscribed.

Notes

1.   [In the original, the author makes a point of mentioning that the hyphen in *art-femme* is a sign that a metaphor (art-as-woman) is being constructed.]

2.   Rose-Marie Arbour, "Art et féminisme," in *Art et féminisme* (Montréal: Musée d'art contemporain, 1982), 4, 11. Further references appear in parentheses in the text.

3.   See Peter Bürger, *The Theory of the Avant-Garde*, trans. Michael Shaw (Minneapolis: University of Minnesota Press, 1984). For Arbour's reference to Borduas, see "Art et féminisme," 13.

4.   See Christine Ross, "Femmes-Forces: Les enjeux du Musée du Québec," *Vanguard*, vol. 17, no. 1 (February/March, 1988), 14–18. [*Amateur*, the term used in the French, designates a person whose interest in art is nonprofessional but idiosyncratic and highly dependent on individual taste.]

5.   Réal Turcot, quoted in Lise Bissonnette, "Réal Turcot: De l'art de ce temps, un ami intime," in *Femmes-Forces* (Québec: Musée du Québec, 1987), 8.

6.   Micheline Caouette, "Femmes-Forces: Le retour aux valeurs du sujet," in *Femmes-Forces*, 12. For Badinter's theory, see Elisabeth Badinter, *L'un est l'autre* (Paris: Odile Jacob, 1986). [English translation: *The Unopposite Sex: The End of the Gender Battle*, trans. Barbara Wright (New York: Harper & Row, 1989).]

7.   Caouette, "Femmes-Forces," 17, 19.

8.   [This is an explicit reference to the title of Micheline Caouette's text, "Femmes-Forces: Le retour aux valeurs du sujet."]

9.   Ibid., 18, 12, 16, and 17. Further references are made in parentheses in the text.

10.   Alice Jardine, *Gynesis: Configurations of Woman and Modernity* (Ithaca: Cornell University Press, 1985).
ROSENBURG's
- ARTICLE
IN PUBLIC
CULTURE

11.   Ibid., 36–37.

12.		See Fredric Jameson, "Postmodernism, or The Cultural Logic of Late Capitalism," *New Left Review*, no. 146 (July/August 1984), 53–92.

13.		Bernard Tschumi, "De-, Dis-, Ex-," in *Remaking History*, ed. Barbara Kruger and Phil Mariani, Dia Art Foundation Discussions in Contemporary Culture, no. 4 (Seattle: Bay Press, 1989), 267. Italics mine.

14.		Mario Perniola, "Virtualité et perfection," *Traverses*, no. 44–45 (Paris: Éditions du Centre Georges Pompidou, 1988), 29–31.

15.		Lise Nantel, in *Femmes-Forces*, 70.

16.		Rosi Braidotti, "The Politics of Ontological Difference," in *Between Feminism and Psychoanalysis*, ed. Teresa Brennan (New York: Routledge, 1989), 97.

17.		Michel Maffesoli, *Au creux des apparences: Pour une éthique de l'esthétique* (Paris: Plon, 1990).

Translated from the French by Donald McGrath.

Diana Nemiroff

Par-al-lel

I wish to approach the subject of the artist-run centres through the words that have been used to describe them. It is my contention that these words—parallel, alternative space, artist-run—are rooted in specific economic and socio-cultural conditions that illuminate the phenomenon of these spaces. It is not their supposed uniqueness that interests me but those features they have in common with other institutions of the period in which they emerged. I do not see the following remarks as definitive. They are notes towards a definition, intended to be speculative and provocative.

Shortly after ANNPAC [Association of National Non-Profit Artists' Centres] was founded in 1976 the parallel network of artist-run centres began a process of rationalization or routinization, a process of self-definition that marked the moment of maturation or institutionalization. That the older, utopian, anti-institutional ideals of the artist-run centre as a globalizing alternative did not disappear is witnessed by the rhetorical inhabitation of the museum in Glenn Lewis's *Living Museum Network* proposal put before ANNPAC in 1977. It is a gloriously perverse attempt to institutionalize the anarchistic, decentralized "eternal network" by installing a head office. In general, however, the discourse at this time took on a distinctly pragmatic character, motivated, as indeed Lewis was on behalf of ANNPAC, by a bid to appropriate power.

The first term to go was the colourful, if ambiguous, designation "parallel." Introducing the first *Parallelogramme Retrospective* (1976–1977), Barbara Shapiro wrote:

> The term [parallel galleries] has always been somewhat of a misnomer, for the centres are neither "galleries" in the traditional sense, nor do they run "parallel" to any existing institutional art system. Each centre operated rather as an artistic complex, supporting new art in all disciplines. …[1]

Jo-Anne Birnie Danzker, reporting on the conference "The New Artsspace," organized by Robert Smith of the Los Angeles Institute of Contemporary Art and held in Santa Monica in April 1978, has suggested that a problem with the term "parallel"—"something similar which is continuously equidistant"—is that it does not adequately define the artist-run

This text was first published in *Parallelogramme* (Autumn 1983).

centre as an alternative, that is, "mutually exclusive, available in place of another, and a group of persons disassociating themselves from conventional social practices."[2]

I feel that there may be another reason why "parallel" became unpopular. The current, more neutral term "artist-run centre" reflects the pragmatism emerging in the later 1970s as the recession deepened and the government showed itself less committed than in the early 1970s to policies of economic stimulation. In 1978, for instance, the Canada Council announced a freeze in its funds for the coming year. Although it promised that cutbacks would be avoided, the threat of no-growth, for a movement intrinsically based on proliferation as the artist-run centres were, was equivalent to starvation. As the well began to show signs of drying up, it became increasingly important to stress the *central* position occupied by the centres in regard to contemporary art. Parallel, with its connotations of "running alongside of," though it might originally have been coined to integrate the galleries into the Council's funding programmes without changing the structure of the latter, conveyed alarming redundancy and correlative dispensability.

The new climate of scarcity is reflected in some of the judgements contained in an interview by France Morin with Brenda Wallace, who had just left the Canada Council where she had been in charge of the aid to galleries programme, for the position of director of P.S. 1, an alternate space in New York. In response to Morin's question whether the artist-run spaces were moving away from their original *raison d'être* of responding "to very experimental work that has no audience other than perhaps an immediate community of artists," Wallace agreed that, "over the last three years, not very much new work has been surfacing in the alternate spaces."[3] The general thrust of her remarks echoes the spirit of critical assessment that the Canada Council was directing at the artist-run spaces. Her remarks betray an impatience with fears of becoming institutions, an emphasis on good management and professionalism, and more than a hint of admiration for the competitiveness and hustling of the American alternative spaces.

But, although they came at a time when the Council was calling into question the management and community relations of certain artist-run spaces by withholding funds, Wallace's words did not seriously challenge the need for the parallel galleries. After all, a certain routinization of community at this point would seem inevitable. As one observer has remarked of radical organizations in general:

> They move from an almost religious enthusiasm to an almost bureaucratic routine. Some of the characteristics that radicals liked about

counterinstitutions, such as flexibility and informality in the definition of roles and functions, may have been due as much to the youth of the organization as to the radicalism of their ideology.[4]

Precedents

Beginnings are sometimes *too* simple. Is it enough to state that A Space got started because a couple of American artists who were resisting the draft came to Toronto, found the art scene narrow and limited, and decided to do their own thing, taking advantage of the availability of government money; that Véhicule was the brain-child of a group of anglophone artists teaching at Sir George Williams University (now Concordia) and the Museum School of Fine Arts who felt isolated from the French-speaking art community and wanted to bring to Montréal some of the art they were reading about in the English-language art press; or that the Western Front arose out of the need for cheap studio and living space as downtown Vancouver underwent the throes of urban renewal? (Here I am simplifying to the point of caricature, as those who were there at the time will know.) Still, fortuitous combinations of people and circumstances should not be underestimated in importance. Yet a question arises here. Why were the bureaucrats ready to lend a sympathetic ear to those first enthusiastic proposals? Why was the money available?

There were predecessors. Funding for nontraditional venues for art had become available in the second half of the 1960s when the Canada Council expanded its traditional criterion. In addition to recognizing excellence in creative activity, it added "democratic" considerations of broadening access and accepted the principle of seed money for experimental endeavours where immediate value was difficult to assess. The first to benefit was a group called Intermedia in Vancouver, which received a grant of $40,000 in 1967 to "establish and operate a multimedia workshop." A similar undertaking in Montréal, Fusion des Arts, received $19,500 at the same time. The 11th Annual Report of the Canada Council for 1967–68 states that:

> Next in importance to the grants for individuals are those which provide facilities for the creative person in the visual arts. Our most important undertaking this year in experimental areas was a grant to Intermedia in Vancouver. This venture, essentially a workshop adaptable to any experimental requirements, gives embodiment to the long felt desire of many artists to bring the different arts together … our new venture has already attracted international attention and become a focus for considerable activity in Canada.[5]

Intermedia went on to get grants of a similar level for the next two years. It was joined in 1969 by 20/20 Gallery, established as a cooperative by a group of artists in London, Ontario. The Council's new concern with widening access—from which groups like Intermedia, but also more traditional workshop situations benefited—came out of a policy of democratization and decentralization, dictated, as Susan Crean has observed in her book *Who's Afraid of Canadian Culture?*, by the political necessity of justifying ever larger government expenditures in the arts through an emphasis on the social role of the arts.[6] The most important thing about these early ventures, despite their short life spans, was that they established that the money was there, that it could be made available in fairly substantial quantities, and on an ongoing basis.

Political and Economic Climate

For the full emergence of the artist-run centre qua alternative space, at least three factors—politico-economic, socio-cultural, and aesthetic—had to come together. The political and economic climate of the late 1960s and early 1970s was charged with tensions. The Quiet Revolution of the early 1960s in Québec had given rise to separatism, culminating in the events of the October Crisis of 1970. The bright nationalism of 1967, centennial year, yielded to a preoccupation with national unity. Québec nationalism had its role to play in bringing cultural aspirations to the forefront of public consciousness. At the same time the federal government was meeting pressure for greater regionalization from all the provinces, which meant that the older cultural formula of touring major exhibitions from central Canada as a means of disseminating culture was less satisfactory. Equally important was the problem of unemployment, which the government was confronting by a commitment to expanding job opportunities.

With the OFY (Opportunities for Youth) and LIP (Local Initiatives Programme) schemes initiated, respectively, in 1972 and 1973, the Liberal government concentrated on achieving its aims for national unity and job creation by focusing on the grassroots level of community-initiated projects. The LIP grants had a decisive effect on the early artist-run spaces. Through these programmes, both A Space and Véhicule obtained substantial amounts of money which permitted the employment of artists, ensuring the establishment of a committed base of people and allowing the development of facilities—for community access video in the case of A Space and for printing facilities (which eventually became Véhicule Press), a documentation centre, and educational programmes for Véhicule.

Because the programmes were community oriented, they encouraged artists to define themselves in practical terms as a community. This orientation in turn affected the way in which the artist was able to perceive his/her role *vis-à-vis* the larger community, displacing to some extent the image of the artist as marginal entrepreneur with a product to sell in favour of the artist as a specialist with communication skills to offer.

The Counterculture

The second factor of very great importance in shaping the alternative ideology of the artist-run centre was the widespread sense of social crisis which stimulated, particularly among the youth, a wave of utopian yearning for a new order. While the events that precipitated this millenarian spirit were on the whole not specifically Canadian, they were shared via the mass media, through the influence of such voices of dissent as the draft resisters who sought refuge in Canada, and via the axis of communication that existed along the West Coast, between the U.S. and Canada. The spirit gave rise to a whole generation of "counterinstitutions" which included communes, cooperatives, free schools, "underground" newspapers, grassroots community organizations, and so on. "Power to the people," a slogan of the times, aptly encapsulates the essential aim of these organizations. The perceived failure of the dominant social and cultural institutions was accounted for in two ways: firstly, their power rested in the hands of laymen removed from the realities they were supposed to deal with; and secondly, their structures were intrinsically flawed.

In place of the existing hierarchies, the counterinstitutions advanced the ideal of the organization as a community.

> Social relations were to be direct and personal, open and spontaneous, in contrast to the rigid, remote, and artificial relations of bureaucratic organizations. The organizational community, moreover, was to be participatory and egalitarian. It would make decisions collectively and would eliminate or at least reduce hierarchy by keeping to a minimum distinctions of status and power between leaders and members, or professionals and non-professionals.[7]

The implementation of a democratic jury system for choosing exhibitions, a feature of most artist-run centres, is a concrete example of the antihierarchical attitude.

Focus on the ideal of community is articulated by the eight artists who had bought the Western Front (an old Knights of Pythias lodge), in their membership drive letter of 1973 which stated:

> This building has the potential of being a centre for the fraternal order

that has long been developing in Vancouver on the subliminal; an association of people with a certain consciousness in common. It is better not to try to define that consciousness too exactly, but over the past few years it has been manifesting itself through the works of many individuals and groups involved with communications media, the arts, and in general with the cultural ecology of our time.

A question that may arise in the context of the counterinstitution is the putative radicalism of the artist-run centre. Revolutionary vanguardism and aesthetic vanguardism have often made common cause in times of social upheaval—one might think of the not so distant events of May 1968 in France. But the alliance is usually short-lived. Adversarial radicalism was rarely a force in the artist-run centre. The revolution to which their members sometimes referred was usually the revolution of consciousness and as such was predicated upon "the idealist assumption that changes in perception and consciousness are the principal motors of historical transformation," as one ethnographer has observed.[8]

In general, their alternative was of an exemplary, rather than oppositional, nature. That is, they sought to exemplify in their own structures and conduct an alternative set of ideals, assuming the direct and independent realization of their ultimate values, within the circumference of their own activities.

The inevitability of the narrowing of the distance between exemplary features and the norm provokes some interesting thoughts with regard to the present position of the artist-run spaces. A degree of convergence has already taken place in response to pressures from within and without: survival necessitates the implementation of better business practices; some specialization and hierarchization must occur. Yet in spite of a growing willingness on the part of artist-run centres to appropriate institutional postures—one thinks for example of the *Living Museums Network*—marginality remains a threat. This marginality is economic rather than ideological, reinforced by the resistance of the funding bodies themselves to the "institutionalizing" of the artist-run centres. That is to say that these spaces are being maintained at inadequate funding levels where their ability to challenge the larger institutions is compromised by insufficient (paid) manpower.

The limits on growth are also antipathetic to another aspect of the artist-run centres which is related to their communitarianism, their conception of themselves as a network. The term, adopted from Robert Filliou's characterization of correspondence or mail art and its practitioners as "the eternal network," suggests a decentralized and ever expanding system. This network, which does not share one physical space, is akin to the abstract idea of community. It finds its literal physical expression in the crowd. Here Elias Canetti's remarks on the nature of crowds are illuminating:

> As soon as it exists at all, it wants to consist of more people: the urge to grow is the first and supreme attribute of the crowd. It wants to seize everyone within reach, anything shaped like a human being can join it. The natural crowd is the open crowd; there are no limits whatever to its growth; it does not recognize houses, doors or locks and those who shut themselves in are suspect. "Open" is to be understood here in the fullest sense of the word; it means open everywhere and in any direction. The open crowd exists so long as it grows; it disintegrates as soon as it stops growing.[9]

The so-called institutionalization of the artist-run centres is akin, in Canetti's terms, to the transformation from an open to a closed crowd. Of the latter he observes,

> The closed crowd renounces growth and puts the stress on permanence. The first thing to be noticed about it is that it has a boundary. It establishes itself by accepting its limitation. It creates a space for itself which it must fill. ... Once the space is completely filled, no one else is allowed in. Even if there is an overflow, the important thing is always the dense crowd in the closed room; those standing outside do not really belong.[10]

Aesthetic Tendencies

To refer to the network of artist-run spaces as a crowd, whether open or closed, is to speak metaphorically. Yet the image suffices to link the social and structural characteristics of the artist-run spaces and their aesthetic tendencies. From their inception these centres have been associated with interdisciplinary, multimedia activity. Although this activity can be associated with the explosion at the end of the 1960s of traditional categories in the visual arts, it is also true that the avant-garde has always shown itself hospitable to collaboration amongst the arts. A phenomenon of the avant-garde as much as of romanticism, the *Gesamtkunstwerk* has expressed its hostility to traditional boundaries, whether social or artistic. By extension then, interdisciplinary activity suggests the liberation of the subject.

It would appear that these multimedia assemblies, with their scorn for aesthetic boundaries, are the aesthetic equivalent of Canetti's crowd. They provide a fitting symbol of the expansive philosophy of the artist's network. In practical terms as well, the appeal of visual artists to artists from other disciplines to join with them in the artist-run spaces—for example, Véhicule's founders' intention to "integrate the work of people in other disciplines (such as music, poetry, dance, and theatre) who have similar needs and desires for an alternative to existing institutions"—was a means of swelling the numbers of their crowd and enlarging its boundaries. Related to this is the umbrella philosophy of the new institutions, their wish to be comprehensive enough to offer a microcosm of the professional world to their members. It is the perennial utopian theme of self-sufficiency.

From the beginning, the artist-run centres declared their enthusiasm for new media and their fascination with new communications technology. Even earlier the utopian theme of the socially redemptive value of technology had characterized such ventures as the *Experiments in Art and Technology.* In practical terms, artists grouped together in artist-run centres were in a good position to make a bid for the establishment of video access centres when money became available. In a sense video was the perfect technology for artists—portable, requiring minimal initiation, and, with its ability to capture the transient and provide instantaneous feedback, it was the ideal instrument for the self's exploration of its environment. It seemed most fully to realize Marshall McLuhan's prediction of the communications media as extensions of our senses. In a most literal way, it made art of the environment, bringing art into life and life into art. "Video," as Peggy Gale once wrote, "has captured our imagination."

On a more concrete level, the engagement of the artist-run centres with video could be pointed to as evidence that they were fulfilling their mandate of being involved with work of an experimental nature. With time, a tendency has been developing within the artist-run centres, and particularly on the part of ANNPAC, to define experimental in an increasingly concrete, measurable way. This can be seen in the presentation which Al Mattes, as spokesperson for ANNPAC, made before the Applebaum-Hébert Committee in 1980, in his description of the key role the new technologies have played in the artist-run centres. Now it seems that computer technology is about to supplant video in ANNPAC's imagination. Mattes explicitly links the incipient technologizing of ANNPAC itself to the activity by artists he has described:

> In keeping with this engagement ANNPAC currently has an application pending for the implementation of a computer-based data network designed to enhance our communications potential and to promote the activities of contemporary artists while recording important historical developments as they occur.[11]

If Robert Filliou's "eternal network" and William Burroughs's "image bank" were the software, computer technology is the hardware with which

ANNPAC is promising to wage and win the consciousness revolution.

The fascination with technology which the ANNPAC presentation reveals is not a new phenomenon in and around the artist-run centres. The impractically grandiose conception of a computer-based data network represents the recurrent desire to appropriate the outward symbols of power of the profit-making communications empire, analogous to earlier expectations that video artists would eventually invade network television.

One final word I've come across recently in the context of the artist-run spaces: co-opt. Emanating from within the milieu of the centres, it may register dismay at the process of convergence that I mentioned earlier. If the artist-run centres are truly co-opted, they lose the ideals they have stood for: control by the community itself, flexibility, openness, an aware-ness of and commitment to new work of many kinds by young artists. This form of co-optation seems unlikely to me. Most of the artist-run cen-tres I know are articulate and clear enough about their aims to resist this.

The context in which I ran across the word co-opt suggested some-thing different: anger with the larger institutions for stealing their ideas, their art. The phrase, if I remember it correctly, went something like this: Read about it in *Parallelogramme*, see it later at the AGO. In sentiments like this one I see evidence of a territoriality which distresses me. It is a long way from the spirit of collaboration that saw Véhicule-sponsored exhibitions, for instance, at the Musée d'art contemporain or the Saidye Bronfman Centre in Montréal, or the Vancouver Art Gallery. Let me return for a moment to the problems of growth and marginality that I mentioned earlier. In the present, postscarcity period, the indefinite expansion of the parallel network seems unlikely. Rather, what is needed is more adequate funding for those that already exist. At the same time more and more of us seem to be talking only to ourselves and a small commit-ted group of devotees, even while deploring the stagnation in several of the large, public institutions in our communities. I suggest that it is time to rethink the question of growth and the problem of marginality, and work at broadening our community, at both ends of the spectrum. Artist-originated projects abroad, for instance (I'm thinking of the show Chromazone organized in Berlin), have a credibility that our official cul-tural exports are lacking. Artist-run centres can penetrate the institutions with exhibitions or events originated or cosponsored by them, and more can be done in informal neighbourhood contexts—not new ideas, but strategies which need to be re-emphasized now.

ANNPAC could serve the artist-run centres far better by focusing on and articulating strategies to realize such concerns than by trying to become the hub of a parallel high-tech communications network.

Notes

1.   Barbara Shapiro, *Parallelogramme Retrospective* (Toronto: ANNPAC, 1977), 6.

2.   Jo-Anne Birnie Danzker, "Reconsidering Parallel Galleries," *Vanguard*, vol. 7, no. 5 (June/July 1978): 5.

3.   France Morin and Brenda Wallace, "On Parallel Galeries," *Parachute*, no. 13 (Winter 1978): 48.

4.   Paul Starr, "The Phantom Community," in *Co-ops, Communes and Collectives*, ed. John Case and Rosemary C.R. Taylor (New York: Pantheon Books, 1979), 269.

5.   *The 11th Annual Report of the Canada Council* (Ottawa: The Canada Council, 1967–1968), 34.

6.   Susan M. Crean, *Who's Afraid of Canadian Culture?* (Don Mills: General Publishing, 1976), 136–137.

7.   Starr, "Phantom Community," 245.

8.   Judith E. Adler, *Artists in Offices* (New Brunswick, N.J.: Transaction Books, 1979), 26.

9.   Elias Canetti, *Crowds and Power*, trans. Carol Stewart (New York: Continuum Press, 1981), 17.

10.   Ibid.

11.   Al Mattes, "Presentation Made on Behalf of ANNPAC to the Appelbaum-Hébert Committee in Toronto," *Parallelogramme*, vol. 6, no. 6 (July/August 1981): 4.

sightings

A selection of images conceived as a visual
complement to the texts published in *Sight Lines*.

Joanne Tod, *Self Portrait as Prostitute,* 1983. Acrylic on canvas. 137 x 147 cm.

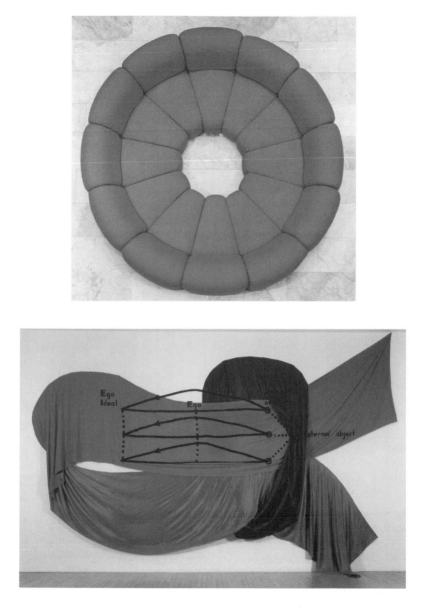

Ken Lum, *Red Circle*, 1986. 672 cm circumference. Collection: Galerie Daniel Buchholz, Cologne.

Mary Scott, *In You More Than You S:D:M:K:F: II*, 1990.
Silk, bias tape, embroidery, floss. 338 x 344 cm.

Michel Goulet, *Motifs/mobiles*, 1987. Mixed media, steel, lead. 230 x 137 x 600 cm.
Collection: Musée du Québec, Québec.

Will Gorlitz, *The Distant World* (installation detail),
1984. Mixed media.

Edward Poitras, *Little Big Horn Medicine,* 1988. Mixed media. 61 x 46 x 6 cm.
Collection: Thunder Bay Art Gallery, Thunder Bay.

Don Proch, *Field,* 1980. Site-specific installation at the National Gallery of Canada, 1980. Mixed media.

Tanya Mars, as Queen Elizabeth I in *Pure Virtue,* 1984. Performance.

General Idea, *AIDS,* 1991. Project for Amsterdam trams. Amsterdam, Holland.

Ian Carr-Harris, *Untitled* 1984–1985. Mixed media audio installation. 221 x 200 x 901 cm (variable). Collection: Art Gallery of Ontario, Toronto.

Jamelie Hassan, *Meeting Nasser* (detail), 1985–1986. Gelatin silver prints, colour video.
Collection: Canada Council Art Bank, Ottawa.

Jan Peacock, *Whitewash*, 1990. Colour videotape, 14 minutes.

Vera Frenkel, *The Last Screening Room: A Valentine*, 1984. Black-and-white video, 44 minutes.

Colin Campbell, *Dangling by Their Mouths*, 1981.
Colour video, 60 minutes.

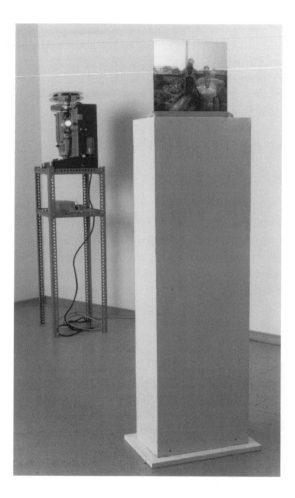

Wyn Geleynse, *Family Portrait*, 1986–1987.
Mixed media installation with 16mm film loop. 178 x 46 x 203 cm.

Jocelyne Alloucherie, *Specchio, Spéculaire (Pas encore et déjà),* 1989. Mixed media installation. Collection: National Gallery of Canada, Ottawa.

Roberto Pellegrinuzzi, *Le naufrage,* 1988. Black-and-white photographs, wood. Photo: 180 x 243 cm; table: 90 x 112 x 78 cm.

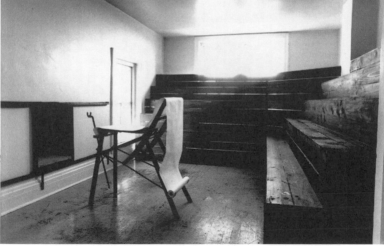

Liz Magor, *Production,* 1980–1985. Mixed media. Installed for the Centre international d'art contemporain de Montréal, 1985. Collection: National Gallery of Canada, Ottawa.

Martha Fleming & Lyne Lapointe, *Le Musée des Sciences,* gynecological examination room, 1983–1984. Site-specific installation in an abandoned post-office, Montréal.

204

Robin Collyer, *What Affects*, 1987. Mixed media. 77 x 185 x 232 cm. Collection: Art Gallery of Ontario, Toronto.

John Scott, *Second Strike*, 1981. Oil stick, graphite, varsol on paper. 244 x 244 cm. Collection: National Gallery of Canada, Ottawa.

Tony Brown, *Two Machines for Feeling*, 1984. Mixed media. Robot: 230 x 130 x 5 cm; ballerina: 267 x 155 x 155 cm. Collection: National Gallery of Canada, Ottawa.

Sandra Meigs, *The Scab Pickers* (a painting in two parts), 1984. Acrylic on linen. 300 x 730 cm.

Shelagh Alexander, *Untitled* Part 1 (panels 3 and 4), 1983. Black-and-white photomontage. 102 x 127 cm.

Rebecca Belmore, *Rising to the Occasion*, 1991. Mixed media. 213 x 122 x 122 cm.

Joey Morgan, *Fugue: A Representation of Direct and Circumstantial Evidence in Three Parts*, 1984. Site-specific audio installation in a derelict warehouse, Vancouver. Collection: Vancouver Art Gallery, Vancouver.

Melvin Charney, *Les Maisons de la rue Sherbrooke,* 1976. Installed for *Corridart,* Montréal. Wood, steel, concrete construction. 16.4 x 15.8 x 12 m.

Renée Van Halm, *Escaping History,* 1986. Oil, wood, plaster, cloth. 275 x 609 x 152 cm.

212

Eric Cameron, *Alice's Rose (3065)*, as of September 1, 1988. Acrylic gesso and acrylic (3065 half-coats) on rose. 15 x 41 x 25 cm. Collection: Glenbow Museum, Calgary.

Alain Paiement, *Anatomique*, 1988. Wood, polyster, metal, black-and-white photograph. 273 cm in diameter at its length.

Barbara Steinman, *Borrowed Scenery*, 1987. Mixed media installation with video. Installed at the New Museum of Contemporary Art, New York, 1990. Collection: Musée d'art contemporain de Montréal.

Robert Fones, *Erratic 1*, 1987. Black-and-white photograph on plywood.
101 x 108 x 15 cm. Collection: Art Gallery of Ontario, Toronto.

Michael Snow, *Plus tard*, 1977. One of twenty-five framed Ektacolor prints. 86 x 107 cm each.
Collection: National Gallery of Canada, Ottawa.

Bernie Miller, *Future Use*, 1985. Mixed media. 260 (variable) x 488 x 366 cm. Collection: Art Gallery of Ontario, Toronto.

Roy Arden, *West* (detail), 1988. Copper-plated steel, hand-coloured black-and-white silver prints. One of six panels, 84 x 53 cm each. Collection: Walter Phillips Gallery, Banff.

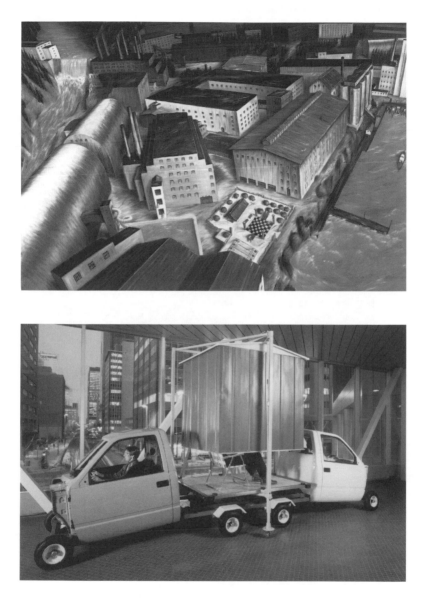

Eleanor Bond, *Work Station, IV—Converting the Powell River Mill to a Recreation and Retirement Centre,* 1986. Oil on canvas. 248 x 360 cm. Collection: Canada Council Art Bank, Ottawa.

Kim Adams, *Two-headed Lizards and a Single Shot,* 1987. Mixed media. 305 x 183 x 315 cm. Collection: National Gallery of Canada, Ottawa.

Janice Gurney, *For the Audience*, 1986. Photostats, plexiglas, found painting. 112 x 193 cm installed. Collection: Winnipeg Art Gallery, Winnipeg.

Shirley Wiitasalo, *Interior*, 1981. Oil and photo-emulsion on canvas. 152 x 183 x 3 cm. Collection: National Gallery of Canada, Ottawa.

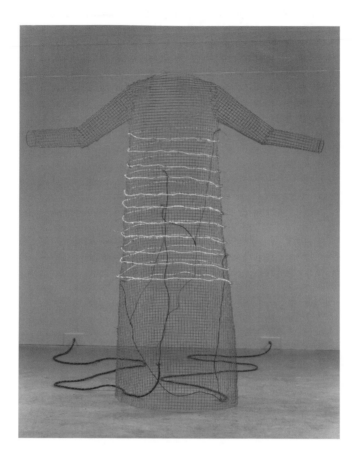

Jana Sterbak, *I Want You to Feel the Way I Do . . . (The Dress),* 1984–1985.
Live electrical wire, wire mesh, text. 145 x 122 x 46 cm.
Collection: National Gallery of Canada, Ottawa.

Rober Racine, *Page-miroir: rose/1 730/rossinant*, 1980–1988. Paper, ink, graphite, gilding, mirror. 33 x 33 cm (with mirror).

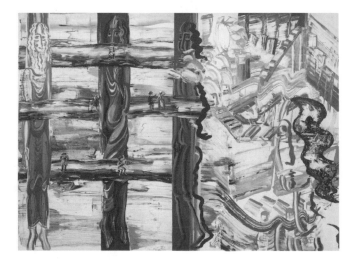

Robert Wiens, *All the Work That's to Be Done*, 1985. Steel, wood, rope, rock salt.
Cart: 210 x 430 x 150 cm; table: 200 x 150 x 150 cm.

    Carol Wainio, *Dropped From the Calendar,*
    1984. Acrylic on canvas. 152 x 206 cm.

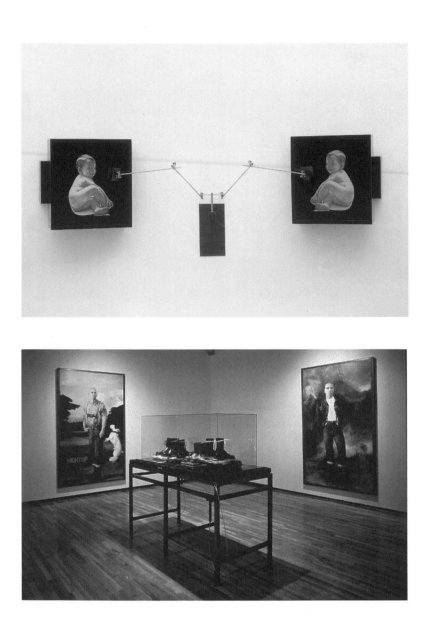

Kati Campbell, *Magnet,* 1989. Mixed media. 72 x 229 x 37 cm. Collection: Art Gallery of Ontario, Toronto.

Attila Richard Lukacs, *True North* (detail). 1989. Mixed media installation with four paintings. Collection: Seymour Collection.

Betty Goodwin, *Black Words,* 1984. Pastel, oil, charcoal on paper. 58 x 71 cm.
Collection: Banque nationale, Montréal.

Joyce Wieland, *Artist on Fire,* 1983. Oil on canvas. 108 x 129 cm.
Collection: Robert McLaughlin Art Gallery, Oshawa.

223

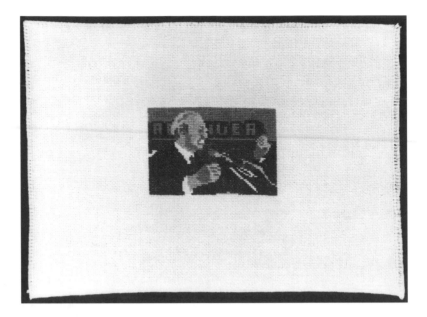

Colette Whiten, *Kurt Waldheim* (detail), 1986. Plywood, glass, cross stitch cloth, embroidery thread. 160 x 76 x 29 cm.

Nicole Jolicoeur, *La vérité folle,* 1989. Detail of the installation at Dazibao, Montréal. Two colour photographs, brass, gouache. Mural: 309 x 609 cm.
Collection: Canada Council Art Bank, Ottawa.

Jeff Wall, *Outburst,* 1986. Cibachrome transparency, fluorescent light, display case. 229 x 319 cm. Collection: Vancouver Art Gallery, Vancouver.

crosscurrents

René Payant

The Shock of the Present

> As always, the crux and scope of the work are to be sought in the finer workings of the mechanism. […] is a postmodern artist. In his view, neither the representation of large themes nor the expression of his interiority is sufficient to legitimate his art. Like the rest of us, he experiments.
>
> Jean-François Lyotard

> Life as art, plus fiction tending towards degree zero.
>
> Robert Filliou

The following observations may be appended to the "notes on performance"[1] I have already enunciated. Both are related in that the observations in question adhere to my hypothesis regarding performance; yet they are also separate insofar as these observations will try to expand the field delimited—somewhat tactically, moreover—by the "notes." Let me recall, and emphasize, that in the previous discussion the problematic was approached mainly from the viewpoint of criticism, that is, from the perspective of one who, like myself, aspires to speak about performance or, more accurately perhaps, to *speak* performance. And it has been suggested that this viewpoint, this necessary exteriority, does not exist in performance such as I have defined it, because every "viewer" is already an integral part of it. Thus, it may be that reflecting on performance, like reflecting on certain contemporary art described as postmodern, is the same as reflecting on one's own position as a critic or viewer.

Keeping to my initial hypothesis, I would like now to reformulate it, to test it against a category of work that was excluded from my initial analysis. This same work is what Lyotard sought to classify as *installation*. My own options are as follows: either I accept as performance only those works that strictly imply the physical presence of an artist or performer, or my previous observations regarding performance may also apply to what commonly goes by the name of *installation*. In the latter case, the distinction between the two would be strictly formal (the presence or absence of an element) and therefore of no relevance for the question of postmodernity. Leaping ahead to my conclusion, I will say at this point that the issue of postmodernity hinges on the fact that *the viewer constitutes the problematic of the work*. In other words, an element long considered extrinsic to

---

This is a translation of a text first published in *Performance Text(e)s et Documents* (Montréal: Éditions Parachute, 1981).

229

the work—having been superseded by either the artist (expressionist interpretation) or the object (modernist interpretation)—has now come back in the guise of a question. This explains why it is not uncommon to see the role of the viewer *materialize* in art, in works that explicitly call for viewer participation. We will see how this question is merely an expression, in synecdochic form, of postmodernity's interest in art institutions. The purpose of these remarks has been to underscore a fundamental aspect of contemporary art neglected by a certain type of criticism and to bring out those subjective features that, in the art of the last ten years, have been opposed to formalism. (Readers will bear with the obviously rather excessive or reductivist character of this statement.)

Three recent works by Canadian artists will serve to support my argument. They were chosen both for their singular character and for the fact that they seemed to lend themselves to a clear articulation of the problem that concerns us here. They are Irène Whittome's *Vancouver* (as seen at the Montréal Museum of Fine Arts in 1980),[2] Betty Goodwin's *Passage in a Red Field*, and Max Dean's *Made to Measure*. (The last two appeared in *Pluralities/1980/Pluralités*, an exhibition held to mark the centennial of the National Gallery of Canada in 1980.)

Duchamp's Lesson

The three works in question could be introduced in a variety of ways. I initially thought that I would adopt a chronological approach, trace their historical connections, provide socio-cultural profiles of those places in which one finds "installations." In the end, however, I opted for the approach that best suited my fancy. (The following preliminary remarks need no introduction.)

We all know the story of how a certain sculpture was refused by the organizers of the 1917 *Independents* show in New York. While I will not recount that event here, I will, however, draw attention to the *composition*, however minimal, of this sculpture, for it involves two distinct planes of the work and entails operations of displacement and condensation. Photographs taken at the time, as well as all subsequent exhibitions, show the urinal resting on a base. This *form* of presentation changed the original, natural position of the object, deprived it of its function. Although the object was transformed, divested of its plumbing, removed from the sphere of private life, rotated ninety degrees, and placed on a base, the urinal's (lost) functions would continue to be invoked insofar as they prove that it is now actually a *fountain*.[3] The title or proper name of the sculpture was thus also the title of *this* composition which involved an angle of presentation and a base. With this we are justified, I believe, in calling the urinal a *transformed* ready-made.

Aside from the status it bestows on objects, the base, by virtue of its very presence, has a meaning all its own. In fact, the disappearance of the base is a key feature of modern sculpture—as in, for example, the works of Brancusi and Tatlin. *Fountain* does not, however, break with tradition and eliminate this historical element which has become superfluous and detrimental to the formal specificity of sculpture; on the contrary, by showing the effect of the base, it points to the potency of this tradition. In other words, the base confers the legitimacy of "sculpture" on the object it presents. The very nature of the object in question—a prefabricated object promoted to the rank of sculpture despite the fact that it is in certain respects incongruous and troublesome to look at,[4] is an object outside its usual frame—is what enables *Fountain* to draw attention to what frames and supports the urinal. A transformed ready-made, yes, but especially as a *transplanted* object, *Fountain* designates the existential conditions of the work of art. These conditions exist prior to the work, and they lay the foundation for its transmission and reception. In short, as metonomy (conceptually representing the totality of the museum) or as synecdoche (concretely partaking of all that surrounds and supports objects deemed to be artistic), the base in this case becomes emblematic of the museum, of tradition, and of the *art institution* as a whole. Thus, *Fountain* dramatizes the deictic role of the base. The latter simultaneously shows the object it elevates in an artistic light and designates, or singles out for notice, the place where this operation occurs.

A frontal view of *Fountain* reveals, on the lower left rim, what initially appears to be a signature and a date: *R. Mutt 1917.* It is well known that this signature is a pseudonym, a mask. I, however, want to highlight what can be read *explicitly* in the composition, that is, in its material appearance, programmatically and theoretically. Let me start by recalling a succinct observation of Derrida's that casts doubt on the signature.[5] In addition to replacing (taking the place of) the source—*its* source, the author—in the work (the statement), this symbolic presence, says Derrida, is also writing. Thus the signature constitutes a twofold relationship since it is simultaneously rooted in the present and in its source. With respect to the latter, there is the sense of its having been, once again, present in some manner. We know that as far as *Fountain* is concerned there is "really" no referent for the signature. R. Mutt does not exist outside the work; his existence is, rather, strictly limited to the work itself, where it functions as a sign or trace of the author—or, more precisely, as a representation of the idea of the author, of authorship. As for the signature's relationship to the present, it is confined to the strict sense of the writing's being present *here and now*. The question of the author, which is certainly of no mean importance, does not concern me at this point. Rather, I want to focus on the composition of the signature, considering it, like the urinal, to be a ready-made transformed in its very specificity by an act of writing. As we shall see, this is not the only, nor the most audacious or extravagant, of Duchamp's word games.[6]

Mott Work, the object worked upon in this case, was the name of the company that manufactured Duchamp's urinal.[7] R. Mutt was obtained in three operations. The first, a cut, consisted in excising the word *Work* from the name. Then an opening was made in *Mott*, that is, in what remained when *Work* was erased, when the "work" component was taken away.[8] More precisely, in this word taken simply as a word severed from its origin in industry, the O became a U, and a new field was opened up.[9] After this came the final operation, which essentially consisted of assemblage. To complete the effect of a signature, an R. was paired with *Mutt*. Note, however, that the given name, this unique, individualizing base of the already almost common and (to say the least) always ready-made patronym, was reduced almost to nothing [*à Rien*]. I propose now to read the resulting assemblage as follows: [R.M.] [utt]. In other words, as [Ready-Made] [+]: thus, the "already-there" *plus* something else, something that could tend towards degree zero but that would still be distinguishable as a supplement, a sign of difference. This something is "utt." Added to "R.M." at this point, in the very coming together of the signature, it is also the addition of the French verbal form *eût été*[10] to the word "ready-made."[11] Thus [R.M.] [+] or [R.M.] [utt] or [R.M.] [*eût été*]. In other terms, without the *plus*, without the transformation, there would have been only [R.M.]. Without the supplement, it would have been only a pure ready-made. [*Ce n'eût été qu'un pur ready-made.*] As a result, the transformation, the addition seems to exist solely to point to what was already there. Of no value in itself, it can therefore be something ordinary and insignificant. The supplement's familiarity works in its favour, since here it is merely a question of attending to what it is not, to what is around or in front of it, as when a urinal is placed on a pedestal in a museum. In *Fountain* the art institution, represented materially and rhetorically by the base that supports and presents the urinal as a work of art, is the thing designated as ready-made.

Thus the signature added to the urinal is more than a signature, more than an identification of or substitute for the author. For it takes the very process of the work that encompasses it and subjects that, as a process of writing, to a *mise en abîme*,[12] all the while echoing the work's aesthetic premise. It points to an *encounter* (or as Duchamp would say, a *rendez-vous*) between a signed object and the conditions governing its existence as a work of art. It seems to me that the entire meaning of *Fountain*, and to some degree its postmodern character, reside in this very encounter, this assemblage or installation of heterogeneous elements—in other words, in the interval [*entre-deux*], the dynamic of reciprocal relations between the components. It is an encounter in which the opposing elements possess an *indexical*, mutually signifying function. The radical or even brutal character of assemblage and confrontation in *Fountain* derives from the fact that it consists of an encounter between two ready-mades: the urinal (the sociological real) and the museum (the artistic real). Thus, with minimum but sufficient effort, *Fountain* manages to push back already established limits by inscribing within the museum, in the art institution, an object that takes this very system as its subject and, by reproducing its mechanisms, exposes the way they operate. Such an exacerbated state of affairs is typical of the postmodern work.[13]

Vancouver: The Sharawadgi Effect[14]

If others have written briefly on this work, it has been mainly to point out that it has borrowed from other pieces and to note its passing references to Joseph Beuys and others. I would like to look at it from another angle. *Vancouver* was an installation made up of some twenty elements arranged in twelve groupings in Room 422 of the Montréal Museum of Fine Arts. This room, which has doorways opening onto three others, is divided by an interior wall into two unequal parts, thus making it impossible to see the entire work from a single viewpoint. Thus there was no way that one photograph could reproduce the entire installation. By using successive shots to pick up where former photos left off, one ran the risk of only duplicating elements. This resistance to perfect reproduction, to a certain way of speaking (to recuperation by language, in this case photographic) was indicative of a characteristic feature of the work: the need for it *to be experienced*. Such a requirement also suggests that *Vancouver* was by no means a work in thrall to the power of the eye but one that drew upon the entire body. For this reason I would say that it was not, strictly speaking, a sculpture but an *installation* (even though an attempt has been made to expand the field of sculpture to encompass installations[15]). Sculpture would seem to perpetuate that face-to-face encounter in which the viewer, moving continually around the object, creates—if it is not already given by the composition—a focal point or centre where the formal dynamics converge, even if there is a countervailing desire for breakup and dispersion. Yet a work such as Carl Andre's *Spill (scattered pieces)* (1966) over-turns such attempts to place things in perspective because, to some degree, the viewer enters into it by walking among the pieces scattered on the floor. And Dennis Oppenheim's *Viewing Station* (1967), itself a highly ordered composition, switches the respective positions of viewing and van-ishing points. Reversing the meaning attached to things seen, the viewer from high up in his observation post becomes part of the spectacle for other visitors who feel that they, in turn, form the background of the work being observed.

Vancouver took up these two outlooks and modified them. The ele-ments of the installation were distributed more or less evenly throughout the room, in a predetermined order. They did, however, sufficiently allow for variations in the ways visitors meandered through them. *Vancouver* was a site. As Jacqueline Fry explained in the exhibition catalogue,[16] the work was a metaphorical installation of a city giving onto the ocean. Worked out in accordance with the topography of Vancouver, the composition implied that the twelve groupings—in relation, moreover, to another room—formed a whole.[17] The monochrome surfaces with their variations of grey, brown, and rust contributed to the sense of unity. The compo-nents did, however, lend themselves to a spot reading, to an elucidation of local effects—Fry was very attentive to them—in terms of the means of fabrication (often the pieces consisted of wood planks or laminated card-board blocks covered with encaustic or paint) or the iconography (abstract or figurative, depending on whether the "objects" were made from scratch or cobbled together from found objects). Yet an approach such as this, which focuses on connotative aspects of the work and identifies its influences (or its quotations, to put it more positively), makes it no less urgent to consider the installation as a totality. For within it there emerged brief series, the elements of which were not always contiguous: 3 small black masses, 3 small white masses, 3 wooden tubs, 3 large boxes/sarcophagi, 3 laminated cardboard blocks. ...[18] In order for these to remain associated, a certain amount of memorization was required of visi-tors as they strolled through the exhibition. Moreover, each discovery of a new element retroactively reduced the scope or semantic field of those already encountered. In other words, the sequence of elements and the linkages between them made it possible to construct a coherent whole that became the "landscape."[19] In this, each element assumed enough meaning to turn the assemblage (orientation) into a metaphorical narrative. Although they were originally collected fragments of studio works, once in the museum these pieces exhibited a specific blend of elements that in no way guaranteed a metaphorical reading.

The requirement of "adapting" to the "exhibition" site made it necessary for *Vancouver* to undergo a *transformation*, not in the number of its elements but in its mode of presentation. It was more concerned with creating an atmosphere than with literally or rhetorically describing a referent. In other words, the work was not only shown in a museum but had to come to terms with it. It was not a question of reproducing a blueprint but of making readjustments here or there, depending on the vicissitudes and potential of the place in question. From this angle, *Vancouver* mapped out the site. Consequently, the objects in this very specific arrangement were less signs than signals that pointed to one another and alluded to the room itself. *Vancouver* modified the space and was modified by it. The room was not a container, a void that accommodated objects indiscriminately, but part of a whole, a ready-made transformed by what the artist brought into it from her studio. In the ceiling of Room 422 there is a skylight of frosted glass; thus, until three o'clock each day *Vancouver* was awash in natural light. Artificial lighting took away from the relationship with the outside and between the objects and the space in the room. Positive and negative spaces articulated at floor level served as reminders that *Vancouver* developed beyond itself and that the spaces created an indivisible unity even as viewers strolled through the piece.

It is well known that the hanging of works in an exhibition is not an innocent act[20] but, rather, a narrative and often symbolic *mise en scène*. The museum is a narrative apparatus that writes history from a certain point of view, all the while conveying the impression that its role is not to comment but to simply represent. What do we make of installation, considering that it integrates the physical nature of the exhibition space as a component of the work? By using the museum in a different manner, installations such as *Vancouver* overturn its meaning, interfere with the fluid semiotics of the museographic machine. *Vancouver* was not a case of a museum exhibiting work but of a work showing that the museum is actually what enables works (of this kind) to exist (today). By focusing on the power of the museum, the installation revealed its specific temporality, a temporality constituted by the relationship between art works and the art institution, of which the museum is an emblem or, like the base of *Fountain*, a synecdoche. *Vancouver* was not an antinomy but a composition consisting of fragments (originating in the artist's studio) and the space of the museum. The work existed exclusively in the form of this encounter or relation which, while amicable, was nevertheless revealing. The lighting, for its part, only served to heighten the specificity of the relation.

Playing upon the phantasms of the scopic drive, the narrative apparatus of the museum catches (traps) viewers in the perspective of its *mise en scène* by having them observe from afar those images it presents (celebrates). Viewers' experience of *Vancouver* was not only visual, for they moved among objects that made the entire room resonate. Contact with the work was physical and, in some respects, affective—in the reactions to the colours, textures, volumes, allusions, connotations, lighting, arrangements of objects, as well as to the familiar and the foreign. Obliged by the bulk of the objects and the boundaries of the walls to stop and make detours, a stroller making her way through the work was invariably inscribed as part of it. But her mode of being within it was such that, for the others in the room, the viewer resembled the very objects among which she, in turn, placed them. In this manner, the mobility characterizing the installation was internalized, structured, and restructured through multiple changes of position. Life became inscribed in form, there to map out a rhizomatic itinerary. Thus the work was ultimately structured by the viewer's perception operating in the real time of vision[21] yet never completing the work, since this was never visible in its entirety. From this angle, the installation would more properly fall under the category of *Gestaltung* (as opposed to *Gestalt*). And its equilibrium would reside in movement in which its centre and foci change place continually, depending on the viewer.

If, metaphorically speaking, *Vancouver* was designed to be a redrawing of the city with its expansive vista on the sea, this was a fine pretext (pre-text) indeed because the construction was primarily meant to immerse viewers in the work.[22] And if visitors invariably plunged into *Vancouver*, it was because the presences haunting it were their very selves. As parasites on the work—isn't this the very label that certain people pin on those individuals who also happen to be art critics or theorists, that is, who use art as the basis of their work?—but as *necessary* parasites, as essential as the moss clinging to the rocks of Ryoan-Ji,[23] visitors functioned as grafts that gave new life to the installation, engaged with it and extended it into uncharted spaces. In their hesitant and errant progress, visitors affirmed the presence of objects yet eliminated any memory of them through the fullness of their own presence. Opening itself up to the actions of the viewer, the installation dismantled the symbolic apparatus of its components along with their signifying associations. The time, the theatrical time of the viewer (as in the theatre of Robert Wilson, that is) took shape, took shape along with its own signifying associations, condensed with every step the stroller took during this visit in which *Vancouver* figured as a *garden*—the comparison originates with Fry,[24] and comparisons are never innocent—as a garden existing for the sole purpose of receiving visitors, a garden of delights where time is dissolved in the intoxicated joy of vision and the awareness of vision. Like other installations, *Vancouver* incorporated viewers in order to move them. Translating emotion into ideas, they would later come to see the installation as a mechanism that shed light on the conditions of their subjectivity.

Passage in a Red Field: A Syncopated Promenade

This "construction" by Betty Goodwin was also made for walking, *wandering around in*. Unlike *Vancouver*, however, the promenade in question was not initially fully available to the gaze; in fact, its perspectival sweep was so reduced that the viewer was obliged to exhibit a certain degree of audacity. Actually, this sculpture/installation[25] was a form of "architecture" that, for those who engaged with it, underscored the reality of "entrances" or, more precisely, of the fact of "entering" (that is, the crossing of a threshold and the change of situation or state that this implies). What happened afterwards was in keeping with this initial experience. The whole was discovered piecemeal, explored by degrees in accordance with the extent of the viewer's own interest (or the work's persuasive power) in advancing the "investigation" of the sites. *Sites*, I say, for the plural is needed to indicate the parcelling out of the whole by the visitor's slow, exploratory meandering.[26] This breakdown of space, facilitated by the structure of the work, revealed the characteristic diversity of the sites composing *Passage in a Red Field*. Each moment of the journey was thereby marked off. And given that the construction was really an array of "rooms" and "corridors" that cut down on the number of variations in the itinerary, visitors' movements were less haphazard than in *Vancouver*. In short, one strolled through *Vancouver* whereas in *Passage in a Red Field* one could only halt. To me, this work was a reduction and abstraction of architecture to the *itineraries* it engenders.

We saw how, considered as a totality, *Vancouver* resisted complete reproduction. Photographic description failed even more dramatically with respect to *Passage in a Red Field*, which required a substantially greater number of exposures. However, since this work was an architectural construction, it is possible to come up with a plan for it.

Although one could use other means (elevations, isometric projections, etc.) to describe the architectural composition of *Passage in a Red Field*, such systems of what Peirce calls *interpretants*[27] would fail, regardless of their level of sophistication, to account for the elements that constituted the specific richness of the work. This said, we are constrained to resort to the plan for what it does show.

The room was completely reconstructed, the space reworked. Most of the right angles were eliminated, the height of the ceiling occasionally changed, part of the room was completely closed off in order to scale down the work, and a section of floor was covered with a steel plate. While *Vancouver* involved the arrangement of elements within a given place, *Passage in a Red Field* was, as we indicated above, a reconstruction of the site itself. Goodwin's way of delimiting space amounted to an appropriation or, indeed, a domestication of it insofar as her construction brought the dimensions of the room down to a more human scale and created a more intimate atmosphere. The work was not kind to crowds, generating palpable unease in cases where too many visitors tried to make their way through at the same time. It was as if every instance of sharing space automatically ended in pushing and shoving or, to say the least, impropriety. All haste was instantly regrettable.

Passage in a Red Field did not simply depict museums; rather, using strategies of integration and repositioning, it reproduced such essential components of the museum as walls, rooms, and corridors. However, the illogical nature of the pathways with their numerous dead-ends, the abnormality of the juxtaposed chambers, and the strange atmosphere all gave the impression that this reconstruction of museum space was designed to delay visitors on their way through and periodically elicit their regard. By *multiplying* the number of walls, the work literally used the museum as *material*: each wall became a painting, each space was sculpted by a play of light. This is why the way into the work was by paths that led nowhere,[28] although they were punctuated by numerous stops that organized the promenade *aesthetically*. In other words, moving from one place to another was not a goal-directed activity but a broken succession of moments in which strollers found themselves devoting excessive attention to detail. Such *exorbitant* attentiveness turned walkers into *viewers* and involved a concomitant demand from the gaze which sought a response in the singular, theatricalized space of the construction. Each time the pleasure of seeing became the sole activity, it disconnected the privileged details of architectural sequence and used fragmentation to highlight differences. From the artist's viewpoint, the architectural construction served to initiate the appropriation and domestication of museographic space. What viewers saw, what (for no particular reason) they adapted to successively, were the results of a marking operation that employed materials such as steel, wood, fine white fabric, magenta carbon powder, neon, graphite, and paraffin. Because the space here was marked off by unprogrammed markers or, at least, by markers that were not codified or meaningful (that is, not guaranteed to be fully recognizable[29]), because they were employed in novel ways, the construction placed viewers outside the known, the commonplace. Or one could say that the visitors' wandering brought out the place's unfamiliarity, and it was this that changed their perception of where they stood.

It would be futile to attempt to specify the precise point in space or time at which this transformation took place, where it *really* happened, because everything was a question of affect. In becoming aware of the effects of textures, lighting, and scale, viewers found that *their positions had changed;* yet their need to physically reach every element of the construction in no way lessened the visual impact of the work. For me, the interest of the piece resides in the paradox it engendered, which juxtaposed the necessity of walking (of time as an active constituent) with the temporal breakdown occasioned by the excessive attention devoted to certain features. A true description of this kind of installation would actually be a description of what happens in this process.

There is a tendency to consider this and other curious architectural constructions (those of Alice Aycock, for example) from a socio-anthropological point of view, to see them as mechanisms that involve visitors in a kind of rite of passage. To do this would be to reduce installations to the reconciliatory role of myths and symbolic forms and to overlook their founding paradox: a loss of meaning—not a symbolic displacement of it—orchestrated in aesthetic terms. If meaning is lost, it is because it is taken over by the *fact* of seeing. Such new forms are highly resistant to archaeological treatment because they are so difficult to reproduce. Of course there will always be people ready to provide us with the kind of diagrams and bird's-eye views one typically associates with labyrinths. However, while such strategies do disclose precise itineraries, they simultaneously cancel out the charms associated with wandering, secrecy, and surprise. *Passage in a Red Field* was a radical affirmation of these values. The construction "accidentally" and temporarily occupied the National Gallery room it was made for. It was unequivocally ephemeral. Yet it was just this that made it equivocal: while walking in the museum one forgot all about its existence. The multiple *itineraries* traced and experienced by visitors were all that remained.[30] Those who actually "visited" the installation were the only ones who could talk about it; and by talking about it, by trying to say what they saw there, they were really trying to say that they did indeed see. In this way, they implied that vision summons speech. In short, they *related* what they remembered of their journey within this construction, how they remembered it. It is easy to understand how their account could be of interest to us if, like a somewhat "crazy" Ariane in her labyrinth, they were seduced, lingered inside it, and tried to put off the moment when they would have to leave.

The foregoing explains why *Passage in a Red Field* has no reality or existence beyond the whole range of commentary it has generated.

Made to Measure: The Gaze Exposed

In my discussion of the two works above, I have focused on those aspects that revealed the impossibility of their ever being completely reproduced, namely, their rootedness in the context in which they were made and the sense of an itinerary that inscribed the mobility and temporality of the viewer in the work. Max Dean's installation gave concrete and, in a way, literal form to these same elements. Spanning two very different locations, a room at the National Gallery and the corner of Elgin and Albert Streets in Ottawa, the separate parts of the work eluded the kind of unity generally held forth by photography. Dean's description of his project will spare me the trouble of writing one of my own. While I cannot quote the complete description, I can, however, give the section that deals with the role viewers were to have in the piece.

> When a viewer enters the gallery, walks across the room in front of the Pintos and steps on the plywood platform inside the small space, an electric motor is activated and the Pintos within the room behind him advance. They will continue to move forward as long as the viewer remains on the plywood platform. Should he step off the platform, the cars will move back. This retreat can be interrupted by the viewer stepping onto the pad, at which time the cars will again advance. The cars will move forward to within 52 centimetres of the end wall and remain in that position until the viewer steps off the plywood platform; at that time they will begin to return to their resting position. While standing on the plywood platform the viewer will see the oncoming Albert Street traffic on the monitor in front of him. He will also see a video camera directed at him. Through the window the free-standing aluminium structure on the street below is visible. At this time, should a person on the sidewalk look at the two monitors in the exterior aluminium structure, he will see the oncoming Albert Street traffic on one monitor and the person within the small space in the Gallery on the other. If the sidewalk viewer moves close enough to the structure to break the electric eye beam, the camera mounted in the aluminium structure will turn on (as indicated by the red light on top of it). When this happens the image on the monitor upstairs in the small space in the Gallery switches from the traffic image to that of the person downstairs in the path of the electric eye beam. The two viewers, one

upstairs and one outside, then see each other, but to maintain this communication both viewers must remain in their positions, for if either moves away the light on the camera in the outside structure will go off and the upstairs monitor will return to the traffic image.[31]

The installation and the reversal it effected were inspired by the architecture of the National Gallery. There is, in the northwest corner of the room in question, a small door leading to a narrow corridor between the gallery wall proper and an outside glass wall. Part of this corridor was closed off by a sheet of Plexiglas, making a chamber just large enough to accommodate a plywood platform that, when stepped on, triggered the cars in the adjoining room to advance. Everything happened in this small space sandwiched between the activities going on in the street outside and those taking place in the museum. Pairs of viewers were brought face to face, bridging inside and out, when their respective positions accorded with certain parameters governing twin sets of cameras and monitors. In these portraits, this moment of the *captured and isolated gaze*, the gaze existing for itself alone, the work's full potential was realized. The identities of the "actors" performing within (or indeed *creating*) the work were really of little import. The important, the striking feature of the situation was the reciprocal mobilization of the gaze. At such moments, when surprise was not the least of the effects produced, each participant simultaneously occupied two positions since he both saw and was seen. In other words, because participants were at the same time observers and observed, their respective positions crossed over into confusion; sameness and difference were conflated by the dissolving of the gaze into its specular Other. Beyond this confrontation, there was only spectacle: the *mise en scène* of the traffic and the observation posts themselves.

Made to Measure was much more complex than our comments here could ever suggest; however, I do want to return to that culminating point that consisted in the encounter of the respective gazes. Via these dynamics, the viewer became the subject of the installation. When I say "viewer" I do not mean the individual, the singular subject contending with an apparatus intent on integrating his, but the person in his capacity as a viewer. In other words, the viewer as a character, the individual as a cultural object, as actant or function within the consumer system of art; or rather, within the socializing and socialized mechanism of approaches to art. I mean the viewer as conditioned by cultural demands that have been internalized, that are overwhelming for that very reason—individuals, then, confronted with the present of a work that involves them, with what is themselves yet more than themselves, with what constitutes them as *social* subjects, namely, the *rituals of image reception*. *Made to Measure* exhibited the act of looking itself, the *performative* aspect of the verb, the ensuing viewpoint, and in so doing denounced the power at work in works that unavowedly assign an observation point to each such act with a view to subjugating it. *Made to Measure* reversed the effect of this control of the gaze by making the gaze itself the object of the spectacle. Thus the violence of this installation would ultimately reside not in the threatening advance of the cars inside the museum, but in what it suddenly presented as *images* on television screens.

The Shock of the Cinema Effect

Without much further ado, I would now like to conclude by looking at two texts I consider relevant to the present discussion. They are Walter Benjamin's "The Work of Art in the Age of Mechanical Reproduction" and Martin Heidegger's "The Origin of the Work of Art,"[32] both of which appeared in 1936. Although they represent different philosophical outlooks, these texts are in agreement as to the effect of the work of art. Heidegger uses the word *Stoss* for the opposition between the "earth" and the "world" that is realized in the work. This shock, this clash in the work of art is due to the simple fact that the work *is*, that it exists at all. It is *there*, insistent; engendering the anxiety of uprootedness [*dépaysement*], it gives rise within the viewer to the uncanny (*Un-heimlichkeit*) sensation of "not being in the right place." A new perspective on the world, it has no other justification in meaning than the unconcealedness, the evidence, the openness of what is and what, as such, requires that a readjustment be made. The *Stoss* depends on the extent to which the work is capable of changing our view of historical existence, of modifying the *Weltanschauung*—to use a term popular in Heidegger's day—and, as a result, the course of history. The essential ambiguity of the work resides in the fact that it both makes and unmakes; according to Heidegger's own terminology, the work is the setting up (*Auf-stellung*) of a world and the setting forth (*Her-stellung*) of the earth. As established by the work, the world is the context of the meanings thereby instituted. The *Stoss* is produced because the work cannot be correlated with the totality of references, cannot form connections with already existing meaning or meanings. Here we would do well to go back to other texts in which Heidegger develops the concept of *framing (Ge-Stell)* along with the paradigm opened up by the act of *installing (Stellen)*. By looking at these observations in the light of what Benjamin has to say about the new status of the work of art, we will be able to specify the decisive change effected by the kind of work we have been speaking of here.

Benjamin's text is often quoted for his treatment of the notion of *aura*, that is, the cultural value that characterizes the contextualized work, and which is alienated by all forms of reproduction that displace it and cause it to lose its uniqueness. I, however, would like to focus on what he goes on to say about the cinema, which is: this most characteristic form of modern experience changes the essential nature of art. Benjamin begins with a reference to Dada which conceived of art as a projectile to be thrown in the face of the public, as an attack on its expectations and perceptual habits—in other words, on the *rituals of reception*. Cinema, which is in its own way a projection, produces a shock in viewers and demands sustained attention on their part. Each image projected at and received by the viewer is succeeded by another to which the eye must readapt.[33] The *encounter* between the viewer and the work is characterized by this uprootedness [*dépaysement*] which also colours the latter's effect on the former and provokes the anxiety (the experience of the absence of meaning, of disorientation) felt with respect to what must follow, to the course of events and their outcome [*déroulement, dénouement*]. Film viewers are obliged in one way or another to act; they are forced to readjust, to transform themselves, to install themselves in the world opened up by the work. With Heidegger as with Benjamin, the shock and uprootedness characteristic of aesthetic experience do not end in total familiarity. The world revealed in the work is always already marked by fluctuations between the familiar and the foreign. Like Heidegger's, this new outlook enables one to go beyond traditional aesthetics which, from Aristotle to Kant (and even to Hegel), have in various ways conceived of the art work as conciliatory and appeasing, as a kind of recovery of stability.

Of course Benjamin did not anticipate the history of cinema as the form of social alienation we know it to be today. He was sensitive to both the novel *form* exhibited by this product of industrial society and its impact on perceptual habits, but he predicted neither the content with which this form would be invested nor the controls it would be subjected to for the purpose of controlling viewers. In Benjamin's understanding of it, the cinema re-establishes neither the work's aura nor its fetishistic dimension (a mythic function restored, however, by certain contemporary anthropologically inspired interpretations) but points out the *hic et nunc* nature of its effects. I would like to point out that Benjamin's view implies attention to the material specificity of film and the serial nature of its projections (to time and the continuity marked by readjustments), increased recognition of the overall context (the work-viewer relationship), and emphasis on immediacy, plenitude, and the uneasiness engendered by uprootedness [*dépaysement*].

What I have called the *cinema effect* of *Vancouver, Passage in a Red Field*, and *Made to Measure* corresponds precisely to their critical use of the above-mentioned elements. The shock these works produce is bound up with the specific relation they maintain with these elements. It is not produced by the strangeness or diversity of the forms, since the entire twentieth century, and especially the last ten years, has accustomed us to renewed novelty and the increased heterogeneity of formal vocabulary. The critical scope of these works cannot be derived in a strictly formal manner. If it makes sense to describe them as *postmodern*, this is because they plainly go beyond the formalist perspective characteristic of modernism. They go beyond it because their problematic is no longer the work itself but the *analysis of institutions* it makes possible. It would be erroneous to suppose, as do certain critics and theorists nostalgic for humanism, that postmodernism signals a return to subjectivity. For Heidegger as well as Benjamin, the work is neither an ideal moment of stability nor the transcendence of some value, is not envisioned as an experience that would engage a subject along with an author or artist in some profound or authentic manner. For them, everything is looked at from the viewpoint of reception.

Because they were, in a way, devoid of all informational or expressive content, the installations we have seen became *works of art* by enacting the social conditions of their existence as art works. In forms of their own making, they exhibited the *ready-made* character of art institutions. The shock they produced derived from the fact that they did not merely reproduce institutional mechanisms but turned them against themselves by forcing them to work in a vacuum or by diverting them from their established functions. The shock came, again, from the excessive transparency of the mechanisms *set in motion* by the installations: the *narrative process* of framing, hanging, and arranging; the *historical* power of the museum, with its denials of the specific time of reception and the measured pace of the viewer; the *capture* of the gaze instituted by every mechanism of domination. Through dealing with these matters it becomes clear that, in the final analysis, the issue is really the status of the viewer.

The Challenge of What Remains

I have tried to show how installation places viewers within the work as *components*[34] of it, and how it eludes reproduction. I stressed the idea of walking, of wandering, that is, on the constant defocalization, the gaps and turmoil it institutes within the coherent construction of meaning. I made implicit and explicit use of the idea of the theatrical, so severely criticized by modernism's formalist aesthetics, in order to show that the theatricality of installations pertains to signals (the index and decoy) rather than to signs. In other words, installation is not representation but an interest in the mechanism of representation and its institutionalized forms. In light of these considerations, what are we to make of the "viewer" whose behaviour is radically changed, as opposed to directed, by installation? (What name can we attribute to him, if not that of *performer*?) The work becomes irreproducible, "non-repeatable" in proportion to the "viewer's" role as an active, necessary, and integral part of it. The work to be described will always include those who have experienced it, who *have made it what it is* and subsequently seek to describe it. The detachment required by description, as well as the minimum stability or *form* of the object to be described, will consequently be found wanting because the describer is the one for whom the work is intended, in addition to being an element of its form. To describe the work is necessarily to *speak about oneself.* Given that installation, the postmodern art work, is neither informative nor prescriptive, it presents "viewers" (even art critics and theorists are included) with a challenge. And the challenge is this: *to speak of* what remains, of the equivocality of the installation. Neither a discourse of knowledge nor a discourse of judgement, the discourse *engendered* here will, of necessity, be of the nature of commentary. It will constitute a *relay*, taking up and going beyond the work. And this is just another way of saying that installation will continue to require speculation.

Notes

The first epigraph is from Jean-François Lyotard, *Sur la construction du temps par la couleur dans les œuvres récentes d'Albert Ayme* (Paris: Éditions Traversières, 1980). Emphasis added. The second epigraph is from a conference-performance devoted to Filliou's work, which took place at the Art History Department of the Université de Montréal in 1979.

1.   René Payant, "Notes sur la performance," *Parachute*, no. 14 (Spring 1979): 13–15.

2.   The references in this text are to the particular way *Vancouver* was presented at the Montréal Museum of Fine Arts; however, the work was also shown in slightly modified versions at the Vancouver Art Gallery (January–February, 1980), the Winnipeg Art Gallery (June–July, 1980), and the Art Gallery of Hamilton (August–September, 1980).

3.   The jet of water issuing from the object (which sets up a relationship with the outside that is highly "abnormal" for a urinal) would shoot back on any user not satisfied with looking, with enacting the role that falls to him as a *viewer*,

that is, the task of creating the work.

4.　　　　Here I am thinking of the distinction that this enables us to draw between two kinds of relationships with the sociological real, namely, those represented by Jasper Johns's targets (*to look at*) and Dan Flavin's fluorescent tubes (*not to look at*).

5.　　　　Jacques Derrida, *Margins of Philisophy*, trans. Alan Bass (Chicago: University of Chicago, c1982).

6.　　　　For more on their complexity, see André Gervais, "Signed sign MD. Autobiographique portrait of an artist en rymes," *Parachute*, no. 11 (Summer 1978): 18–23. The article also appears in *Duchamp: Colloque de Cerisy* (Paris: Union générale d'éditions, 1979), 297–339.

7.　　　　See item number 110 in Jean Clair, *Marcel Duchamp* (Paris: Centre Georges Pompidou, 1977), 90.

8.　　　　Regarding the limited importance attributed to "work" in ready-mades and in Duchamp's aesthetics as a whole, see Gilbert Lascault, "Éloge du peu," in *Duchamp: Colloque de Cerisy*, 37–52.

9.　　　　The opening up of this field facilitates the interpenetration of internal and external spaces. In addition to the transgressions committed by ready-mades, we should also remember the *Large Glass*. [Note that *ouverture du champ* (opening up of the field) contains both a play on Duchamp's name and a reference to chess in the sense that one could take it as an abridged form of *ouverture à la Duchamp* i.e., an opening characteristic of Duchamp. The translator is indebted to Johanne Lamoureux for these readings.]

10.　　　[Now *eût été* translates as *would have been*; *eût* is phonetically the same as "utt," in French pronunciation of course.]

11.　　　Consider the alternate readings of *Mona Lisa, L.H.O.O.Q.*, 1919, private collection, Paris.

12.　　　[The term derives originally from heraldry, where it referred to the mirror effect created by surrounding the coat of arms with a border that reproduced the contours of the shield. It is used generally in semiotics to indicate the use of an element within a work to reproduce, in miniature, the overall or essential structure of the work in which it is found. Marc Angenot, *Glossaire pratique de la critique contemporaine* (Ville LaSalle: Hurtubise HMH 1979).]

13.　　　*Fountain* has other implications for the status of the postmodern author. Behind the pseudonym there is a subject who is made doubly absent by the signature, since the latter, in addition to being already a replacement, is also without a referent, is a sign whose referent is *unknown*. Consequently, the real role and status of the performer in the performance remain to be worked out.

14.　　　"The Chinese," said Sir William Temple, in his essay *Upon the Gardens of Epicurus* (1685), "are moved to sarcasm by European gardens in the symmetrical manner. … [They] scorn this way of Planting, and say that a Boy that can tell an Hundred, may plant Walks of Trees in strait Lines, and over-against one another, and to what Length and Extent he pleases." Not only that, but their sensibility was so far advanced, that they had a word for a phenomenon of which the very idea had hardly penetrated to Europe—the phenomenon of beauty occurring in the absence of discernable order or recurrent design. The word was "Sharawadgi." If they came upon a garden which struck the imagination with its unmathematical beauty, they would exclaim, 'The Sharawadgi is fine, or is admirable.'" Quoted in A.R. Humphreys, *William Shenstone: An Eighteenth Century Portrait* (Cambridge: Cambridge University Press, 1937), 40; also cited in Louis Marin, "L'effet Sharawadgi ou le jardin de Julie: notes sur un jardin et un texte (Lettre XI, 4e partie, La Nouvelle Héloïse)," *Traverses: Jardins*, no. 5/6 (October 1976): 114.

15.   As proposed by Rosalind Krauss in "Sculpture in the Expanded Field," *October*, no. 8 (Spring 1979): 31–44. However, this is merely a formal reading and represents a *formalist* perspective that ignores the presence and participation of the viewer.

16.   Jacqueline Fry, *Irène Whittome 1975–1980* (Montréal: Montréal Museum of Fine Arts, 1980), 14–21.

17.   With the oblique line traced by *Imprimerie*, a piece made up of forty-nine small, grey boxes laid side by side on the floor of the room devoted to Whittome's *Paperworks* (1978–1980).

18.   Fry, *Irène Whittome*, 16.

19.   Ibid., 15.

20.   Louis Marin, "La célébration des œuvres d'art: Notes de travail sur un catalogue d'une exposition," *Actes de la recherche en sciences sociales*, no. 5/6 (November 1975): 50–64.

21.   And neither the time of the museographic apparatus (which is denied) nor the symbolically infinite time of the objects exhibited.

22.   [The French text adds, *comme dans la mère* (as in the mother). Since this *jeux de mots* on *la mer / la mère* (the sea/the mother) does not work in English, it has been relegated to an endnote.]

23.   Daniel Charles, "Gloses sur le Ryoan-Ji," *Traverses: Jardins*, no. 5/6 (October 1976): 8–21.

24.   Fry, 20.

25.   The reader will understand how difficult naming becomes at this point. One casts about for compound neologisms to describe the hybrids such works generate.

26.   How many viewers never even made it to the end of the long white corridor, where they would have seen it shrewdly repeated in a mirror?

27.   The theory of the interpretant (involving operations of transfer and recodification, hence a reading of the sign) developed by Charles Saunders Peirce would be serviceable when it comes to specifying the untranslatable character of these installations.

28.   [Literally, *chemins qui ne mènent nulle part*, which also happens to be the French title of *Holzwege*, the volume in which Heidegger's essay, "The Origin of the Work of Art," originally appeared. Payant draws upon this essay further on.]

29.   If they were more readily recognizable they would signal their role as part of a system and would draw upon viewers' familiarity with certain areas.

30.   As well as a few photographs showing the installation empty and cut off, as it were, from one of its main elements.

31.   The description consists of almost four double-spaced typescript pages listing the materials and giving the dimensions of the components, as well as a highly detailed description of the inside and outside spaces and the relationship established between them by means of the closed circuit of television. I am not according special status to the author's description; rather, I am using it simply because it is convenient to do so. Published in French in *Parachute*, no. 20 (Fall 1980): 10–11.

32.   Walter Benjamin, "The Work of Art in the Age of Mechanical Reproduction," in *Illuminations*, ed. Hannah Arendt, trans. Harry Zohn (New York: Schocken Books, 1969), 217–252. Martin Heidegger, "The Origin of the Work of Art," in *Poetry, Language, Thought*, trans. Albert Hofstadter (New York: Harper & Row, 1971), 15–88.

33.   In a footnote to his discussion of this continuous adaptation, Benjamin makes a comparison with pedestrians in big cities who are compelled, for reasons of survival, to readjust their itineraries in order to avoid dense traffic and various other dangers. This example drawn from daily life illustrates the Heideggerian concept of angst (the being-unto-death that is an inalienable, integral character of human beings) which results from the shock produced by the work of art.

34.   Unlike spectacular apparatuses which, by regulating distance from the work and integration within it, produce an illusion of participation.

Translated from the French by Donald McGrath.

Walter Klepac

The Order of Words, the Order of Things: Deconstruction in Contemporary Art

I

When art enters into the world in the radically direct way it had in the period from the early 1960s to the mid 1970s, it calls into play the attitudes and the concepts that one normally draws upon in dealing with the world. It is not so much that one totally loses sight of the fact that one is dealing with a work of art as opposed to a real life situation; it is that the criteria for judging the appropriateness of our response to the work are to be found to a great extent in our everyday congress with the world. Twentieth-century modernist art has always been a self-conscious enterprise in one way or another. Within the decade of the 1960s alone, however, the focus of this self-consciousness shifted significantly: what was once a matter of questioning a given work's status as an art object turned into a question about its status as an object in the world. That is, the art of the "anxious" or the problematic art object gave way to an art in which the object was conceived of as a vehicle for investigating and revealing the fundamental *episteme* of the artist/viewer—the assumptions, cognitive habits, and network of associations upon which the artist's and viewer's conception of the world is based.

At roughly the same time, certain formal innovations appeared, particularly those initiated by major paradigms of conceptual art (throughout the last half of the 1960s), which effectively rendered the presence of the material object no longer necessary. However, in spite of this phenomenon, referred to in the literature of the day as the "dematerialization of art," much of the best conceptual art did continue to concern itself with and investigate fundamental aspects related to our condition in and knowledge of the world. It can be argued that it was the persistence of such concerns that gave underlying continuity to the move on the part of artists in the late 1960s and the 1970s to a diverse array of media and forms, such as text and language, performance, and mixed media installations. Furthermore, it was the move into these new, i.e., nontraditional, media and forms that provided artists with the tools and formal where-

This is an edited version of a text first published in *C Magazine*, no. 3 (1984).

withal to expand and extend their investigations into territories that otherwise would have remained inaccessible. This reciprocal stimulation between formal means and "content" characterizes the most resonant and at the same time most rigorous art of this period. On the one hand, a distinct content gave focus and purpose to the recently enlarged, formal means available to artists. On the other, the radical formal innovations gave form and coherence and enhanced modes of access to investigations of content (i.e., subject matter, the epistemic concerns). Together the two increased the scope and profoundly expanded the power of abstraction in contemporary art.

The radical innovations of the 1960s and the 1970s had in effect transformed modernism: they altered its terms, direction, and nature in a fundamental way, showing it to have evolved into something quite different than what it started as. So much so, that one could say the late modernist practice drastically exceeded the parameters of modernist theory. Indeed, there was considerable resistance on the part of most of the commonly accepted versions of modernism to absorb this new direction, or to accept or even to acknowledge its consequences. A good deal of this reluctance can be traced to the tendency within modernism to define art as an essentially self-reflexive concept or mode of discourse. That is to say, modernism was above all primarily concerned with the need to distinguish art from other forms of discourse and the "work of art" from ordinary "things." In his updating of modernism, Clement Greenberg insisted on interpreting the radical formal developments from Cézanne and Cubism onwards in terms of an attempt to purify art of all elements or references that were extraneous to what was essential to a work's being art. This interpretation was crucial to Greenberg's understanding of the idea of abstraction in modernist art. The formal breakthroughs from Jackson Pollock and David Smith to the postpainterly abstract painting and the sculpture of Anthony Caro, had reduced the traditional media of serious art, painting and sculpture, to their absolute and fundamental properties. However, once departed from the traditional modes of painting and sculpture, modernism was left with two general options—both of them based, in different ways, on the premise that art has to be about art. As advanced art moved into new media it became imperative that the work clearly demonstrate the specific nature of a chosen medium. Thus, by insisting that self-reflexiveness was to be understood as an end in itself, modernism could endorse works in video, texts, films, performance, and multidisciplinary installations, while at the same time it contained and limited them. The other option interpreted the mandate "to be about art" more or less anthropologically and consequently sought to locate the causes or sources of the phenomenon of art within a particular culture at a given time. Rather than indulge in metaphysical speculations about the ultimate nature of art, modernism instead seemed more interested in investigating the cultural institutions, the social and political systems, and the economic factors that made art possible and gave it its final character and shape. This option was Duchamp's legacy to modernism. Actually, the more *conservative* element within modernism tended to reduce this category of self-reflexiveness into a tautology: anything properly processed and endorsed by the dominant art institutions was by definition to be considered art. After all, these institutions ratified their choices by writing history and securing a place for these choices.

As it now stands, this conflict within modernism—in particular, its refusal to reformulate its basic theory in light of the implications of its radical formal innovations—remains unresolved. In fact, through the mid 1970s to mid 1980s there has been a pronounced tendency on the part of certain artists and critics to ignore the internal disparities, distinctions, and conflicts just mentioned and reduce them all to a set of manageable generalizations and attitudes which they then systematically reject. This is important to keep in mind when one attempts to understand clearly and critically the new art that has come to be known under the name postmodernism.

While this body of aesthetic and critical doctrine first gained prominence in the fields of literature and architecture, its prestige and influence in the area of contemporary visual art has become, since the mid 1970s, considerable and continues to grow. The concepts and key intellectual strategies that give postmodernism its strength and scope are rooted in the school of thought that has grown up around the writings of a group of predominantly French intellectuals referred to as the poststructuralists.[1] The connection between the two is so profound that postmodernism seems virtually inconceivable as well as inarticulate without poststructuralism in one form or another. While it is not at all uncommon in Western culture over the past two hundred years for a new art movement to bring with it new intellectual allegiances, postmodernism does not appear to be just another style or movement with its attendant new jargon; its affinities, fundamental attitudes, and habits of mind suggest a thoroughly new and different way of looking and thinking about art. By completely revising the conditions under which works achieve meaning in the existing cultural context, postmodernism has drastically altered the very conception of art. The present critical terrain has been transformed to the point where it is virtually unrecognizable from what it was in 1975. A large part of postmodernism's persuasiveness has been due to its apparent aptitude and applicability to the new art. Postmodernism readily claims under its banner, and validates representation for all media in recent contemporary art, figurative painting as well as all the various hybrid art forms unleashed by the radical formal innovations of the late 1960s and the 1970s. Postmodernism has not only submerged each of these new developments in its own vocabulary, assumptions, and overview but also reinterpreted the entire line of radical innovations that led up to and made possible most of the above-mentioned developments. The present essay will question the validity of postmodernism's account of the radical formal innovations (particularly those of minimal, postminimal, and conceptual art). It will also suggest an alternative account that emphasizes a continuity rather than a decisive break between those innovative paradigms and the art that followed them. Finally, it will initiate an attempt to separate postmodernist criticism from postmodernist art.

One of the most essential poststructuralist concepts in the postmodernist's arsenal is the notion, or should one say the project, of deconstruction. By itself deconstruction is an intellectually ambitious and audacious idea. Simply stated, the basic objective behind deconstruction is to destabilize accepted or traditional meaning. It directly challenges the assumption that language—taken in the broadest sense of the term—can adequately and objectively describe the world. It contends that meaning is not transparent, inherent, or "natural" but rather a product of an essentially arbitrary, historically relative system of signs. The postmodernist brand of deconstruction generally holds that the complex internal dynamics of such a system subverts the intention, reference, and meaning of even the most ostensibly unambiguous assertion or communication. The built-in disposition or biases of that system virtually predetermine the field of references and meanings. The postmodernist version of deconstruction attempts to reveal the biases and limitations of the system by jamming the gears of language and turning language in upon itself. Its main contention seems to be that thought is trapped within language, and if deconstruction does not show the way out of that trap at least it wants to make us sure of the trap's existence. In doing so, however, it imposes what many feel are its own biases and limitations with regard to the nature and function of language. For this reason the second section of this essay will present an alternative mode of deconstruction.

In his essay "Re: Post" Hal Foster argues that strategies of deconstructing established art conventions and practices are not the exclusive property of postmodernist art and criticism—as is widely believed today. He points out that:

Picasso, Pollock and Smithson all destructure modes of signification that they inherit. Magritte, Johns and Laurie Anderson all pose forms of rhetorical interference. They cannot all be recouped as postmodernist or proto-postmodernist. The strategy of appropriation, as seen in Duchamp and again in Rauschenberg, is modernist in origin, as is the deconstructive impulse. ...[2]

Foster concludes that deconstruction has been an integral part of modernism from the beginning, and what is perversely fascinating about so-called "postmodernism" is its attempts to see in recent artmaking the emergence of an entirely new set of premises and objectives. His critique of perhaps the most systematic postmodern visual art critics (Rosalind Krauss, Douglas Crimp, and Craig Owens) acknowledges the efforts of these writers to provide a coherent theoretical framework for the new art based on language and concepts borrowed from the poststructuralists. The value of Foster's essay is that its thoughtful examination of the logical structure of this framework enables us to discuss postmodernist deconstruction without becoming lost in its seductive and amorphous vocabulary. Furthermore, it allows us to see that the implications and import claimed for the new work by postmodernism are as much due to the particular theoretical orientation of the critics as to the nature of the work itself.

However, in order even to conceive of the possibility of an alternative mode of deconstruction that could effectively deal with the issues and themes currently monopolized by postmodernist criticism, one has to question seriously postmodernism's interpretation of the radical innovations introduced by late modernist art. This interpretation is crucial because with it the postmodernists are able to establish a clear point of departure for the new art they espouse and to convey a strong sense of its historical inevitability. While not all postmodernist critics select the same artists as examples for their particular views, there are a number of artists whose work figures centrally in the general postmodernist scheme of things. In particular, critics have claimed that the spatial sculpture of Robert Morris, Alice Aycock, George Trakas, as well as the video installations of, among others, Dan Graham, "decentre" the art object and expand the field of reference of sculpture. As a result, the long-standing assumption about the physical integrity (internal unity) and discreteness, the fundamental independence and autonomy of the work, is called into question. The point here is not that a work can no longer be located in or identified with a particular object but that it has no clear focus, something coherent and cohesive with which it can confidently be identified. Postmodernist critics point to this "decentring" phenomenon as evidence that a shift has occurred within the making of art: from a concern with an art work's syntax to a concern with its semantics.

For postmodernism, the concept of deconstruction is directed at what is thought to be the heart of modernism, i.e. the notion that a thing or an image is complete and knowable in itself or that an art work, regardless of its form or manifestation, is an ultimately unanalysable, irreducible, complex symbol. The postmodernists' attack on the integrity and autonomy of the concept of the work of art is, to my mind, the single most important issue broached by them. To think of decentring in terms of a strictly formal artmaking strategy is one thing; to extend it to cover the concept of the work of art as a whole is quite another. If the notion of decentring is taken to its logical conclusion, it is almost impossible to imagine how the concept of the work of art could remain tenable, theoretically, at least. Not even the postmodernists themselves could prevent complete closure of the concept.

Another point of general agreement among postmodernists is the view that the developments in sculpture and installation art from Serra and Smithson to Acconci and Oppenheim to Graham and Asher are, in effect, a direct assault on the supposed late modernist view that advanced contemporary art has to be medium-oriented. That is, postmodernism holds that this work actually undermines and refutes the idea that whatever medium is chosen as the vehicle for a work of art—whether it is sculpture (i.e., three-dimensional constructions of a specific material), painting, video, or photography—the work must reveal, by its appearance, the fundamental nature of that medium. Postmodernism is inclined on the whole to take this dictum at face value and then to foreclose on the entire enterprise.

But if medium-centredness in minimal and postminimal art had a point, it was not that the imperatives of medium or material were to be thought of as ends in themselves. It was rather that the medium or material was to be regarded as a touchstone of the work and, hence, inextricably involved in the statement made by the work. The viewer has to start with them in order to get to the work. The kinds of questions that occur to us spontaneously and naturally when we are confronted with some unfamiliar object in normal, everyday situations—questions such as, what material is it made of? how is it constructed or supported? what relations does it bear to its surroundings?—are the very questions that lead to a total engagement with the work. As attention shifts to the material or medium itself, a detached, highly critical self-awareness becomes imperative on the part of both artist and spectator. Faced with the stark, unembellished substance that is the work, the observer is thrown back upon himself, as it were. One is forced by the nature of the work to deal only with what is there, and yet, at the same time, one is drawn, inevitably, to relate this particular confrontation to one's experiences in the world in general.

Because of this the best work is able to probe insightfully into the structure of perception, thought, or psychic processes. (Ironically, it is this version of medium-centredness that one finds, more often that not, operating in much of the best radical sculpture and installation art of the 1970s, the same work that postmodernist critics claim had subverted the concept of medium-centredness!)

Postmodernism's treatment of medium-centredness is typical: it is a commonly accepted tactic of postmodernist criticism to bracket a particular work of art in terms of a given style and then to assert that that style, by definition, has only such and such a range of meaning or references. In other words, the viewer is required to relate to any work of art exclusively in terms of the predetermined and generalized conventions of some existing art form or art historical style. That is, individual art works are to be seen simply and primarily as examples of a particular art form or style.

Bracketing of this sort can, I think, be put off by considering the approach adopted by Arthur C. Danto in his *The Transfiguration of the Commonplace*.[3] Danto is attempting to formulate a conception of art that will successfully address the apparent tendency evident in early modern art, and dramatically accelerated in contemporary art, to eradicate the distinction between the objects, situations, and events denoted as art and their counterparts in real life. Danto insists that there is a difference and advances the view that art is a kind of free space where the culture allows for the artist and the spectator alike to confront and/or contemplate interests and concerns in a sustained and rigorously independent manner. An object's status as art seems, in this view, to guarantee that our attention will be focused intensely on that object of concern and will not be readily distracted by extraneous thoughts, associations, or practical motives. What makes the work of art art, and insures its integrity as art, has to do with the *form* of the work's engagement with some aspect of the world. The setting up of particular terms, and the creation of tensions or dialectics between these terms, are all ways in which *form* is manifested in works of art. It is clear that, in Danto's view, the work of art demands the full participation of the critical faculties, judgement, and the imagination from both the artist and the spectator. It is equally clear that Danto's view suggests a more open-ended conception of art than what is offered by postmodernism or by the way postmodernism defines modernism.

In order to properly understand the evolution of contemporary art forms, particularly the transition between minimal and postminimal sculpture and the various developments in avant-garde art from the mid 1960s on, it is essential to stress that where minimalism and often postminimalism employed solid physical materials, later works, such as conceptual art, installation, and performance, turned to film, video, photography, and texts. What complicates matters is that the majority of these media also serve as vehicles for communication and as modes of representation within the culture at large. Postmodernism has seized upon and exploited these complications, so much so that, as artists have become preoccupied with the representational aspect of these media in recent years, postmodernism has virtually monopolized critical discussion.

II

Perhaps one of the most impressive examples of the transition from material to medium in a manner that preserves the sense of the medium as material is to be found in Michael Snow's *Rameau's Nephew by Diderot (Thanx to Dennis Young) by Wilma Schoen* (1974). In a way, Snow's film can and has been seen as an almost encyclopaedic exercise in deconstruction. Snow's comprehensive and penetrating exploration of the inherent properties of the medium of film possesses a richness, flexibility, and complexity that turn out to be unexpectedly responsive to the artist's investigation of language as mediation between ourselves and the world.

The fact of the matter is that the mimetic or representational aspect in film is entirely dependent upon the nature of the medium itself. One can sense even in the case of commercial films the essential artificiality of the medium as a narrative mode. The element of time, for example, is an almost infinitely malleable variable and, with one important exception, not a constant. For the most part, however, past and present can be arranged and rearranged at will and can be run backwards, forwards, and simultaneously. Time can be speeded up, slowed down, made to unfold continuously, or served up in discrete fragments—in any order the artist chooses. The fundamental relationship between sound and image is also subjected to manipulation; basically, they can be presented in sync or out of sync. The expectation of consonance in this area in particular is extremely powerful, enough so that any tampering with it automatically puts the spectator on alert. A rationale is found within the structure of the work, or mechanical failure is blamed, and boredom soon sets in. In short, Snow transforms all the resources inherent in the film medium needed to create and to sustain illusion into distancing factors that virtually compel the spectator to hold the representation or narrative in suspension and to consider all that he sees and hears as open to a critical scrutiny. Snow is able to turn what could have been an exercise in medium self-reflexiveness into a brilliant, externally oriented critical investigation.

What distinguishes *Rameau's Nephew* from the postmodernist

deconstruction of language is that the latter, drawing heavily on the precedents of modern linguistic and recent literary theory, focuses on the notion of the work of art as text.[4] Given the nature of film itself, however, *Rameau's Nephew* is able to approach the concept, practice, and properties of language based on the model of speech, of interpersonal verbal discourse. Snow's film, in effect, naturalizes language. It gives us a fresh understanding of the nature of a host of fundamental contexts from which language takes its basic shape, and in so doing it redefines for us, by means of what one could almost call oblique reminders, the nature of the medium of language. Snow's film constructs basic situations that exemplify language as it is used or some particular aspect of its use (and then turns these situations on their head). The complex, accelerated fluidity of the sequences, their density and intensity, keeps the viewer constantly reexamining contexts and, in the process, continually questioning assumptions about how language works. Because *Rameau's Nephew* takes the phenomenon of everyday speech as its model, it directs our attention to specific situations and contexts and to the various possible interactions between speakers, rather than to a totally abstracted view of language in which all available meanings of all words used are present and potentially active.

Referentiality, in the strict sense, as used by postmodernist critics, requires a more stable, if not static, field in order to take effect properly. Such stability is needed before one can confidently ascribe particular meanings or clusters of meanings to the individual sign or image. In terms of the postmodernist's strategies of representation, however, a great deal of attention is paid to the matter of the reference of signs, that is, to those things denoted or depicted by those signs.[5] It is claimed that signs are a valid and even essential part of the culture and that, as such, the references they carry with them connect up to the objective, external world. The problem is that the web of references generated by such an approach exists outside (one is almost tempted to say above) the work itself. If one bars further justification in terms of the context of the work itself, one is forced to conclude that such references (i.e., the connections made between a sign and an object) are, in fact, subject to the personal interpretation of the individual spectator. In order to avoid this apparent regress into subjectivity, the postmodernist's move is to locate all signs and their references to an extant system of representation that is presently operative in the culture. But, because Snow's method of representation in *Rameau's Nephew* so thoroughly militates against isolating individual terms and prescribing particular references of meanings for these terms, it does not depend on positing any one given system of representation. To sum up,

Snow's method in *Rameau's Nephew* functions, by and large, in a heuristic, exploratory, and critical way rather than in the "archaeological" approach. If Snow's method of deconstruction is successful then it must be able to convince us, as I think it often does, that its probe of language has penetrated to the level of discourse prior to that upon which representation holds sway and effectively determines the context, structure, and meaning of our thought.

In the course of everyday events, as in the best contemporary art, our critical faculties and judgement are applied to our experiences in order to differentiate various kinds of things from one another, to compare the relations between things, to determine the nature of things as well as the limits of our ability to do so. In the case of *Rameau's Nephew*, however, the experience at hand is not, strictly speaking, our own. We watch, as we normally would in any film, something happen to somebody else. We are spectators to experiences, situations, and events. As a consequence, judgement seems to be exercised at one remove from our own immediate experience. It is the fact that the work makes us acutely aware of the manner in which these experiences are presented to us which, in the end, provides us with an opportunity to contemplate and analyse that experience.

Another way of making this point is to say that one of the fundamental conditions of the medium of film is that the spectator is rendered a passive observer. In film, as opposed to painting and sculpture, it is the artist who determines what the spectator sees, when he sees it, and for how long. The camera, in effect, does the walking around and the looking for the viewer. The only "real" time (time as a constant) involved in film is the time that the viewer spends watching the film unfold from beginning to end. While the viewer is being subjected to the extreme fluctuations of tempos and rhythms within the various sequences of *Rameau's Nephew*, a relentless and strictly literal order of time prevails and preempts everything else. This time is one of pure duration. In *Rameau's Nephew*, durational time is made palpable: no matter how repetitious and seemingly interminable a particular sequence may be, it does eventually end. (Obviously, for a film the length of *Rameau's Nephew*, roughly four and a half hours, duration becomes an abstraction; it cannot be comprehended except in terms of the film's individual sequences.) By differentiating the sequences as effectively as he does, Snow is able to enlist the property of duration in order to produce isolated segments of a kind of experience not available in any other medium. The discreteness, the particularities of its content, and the unique impression made upon the viewer are all expanded and intensified by strong contrast between a given sequence and those that preceed and follow it. Faced with the vast complexity and sheer density of

Rameau's Nephew, imagination and judgement can be exercised only in reflection and after repeated viewings. The shape and texture of the sequences and the particular kind of critical reflection they each elicit are all to be thought of as being part of the subject matter and ultimate statement of the film. It is this viewer's experience, demarcated and given form within durational time, rather than the second hand, depicted experience of the participants in the film, that provides judgement with its material.

There are at least two broad types of sequences in *Rameau's Nephew*, and each subjects the viewer to a distinct kind of experience. On the one hand, there are a number of sequences that are characterized by a manifest lack of comprehensibility. In this type, language is either reduced to the level of noise, unintelligible sound, or it is dubbed over totally unrelated visual images. The viewer is confronted with confusion and disorientation. Meaning and reference are not merely destabilized; they are entirely inundated by an opaque mass of seemingly random sensations. The viewer is shown a number of individuals within a single distinct setting: an empty nondescript room, someone's studio or apartment. The people seem to be engaged throughout the sequence in a basic repertory of actions or gestures. In the majority of these sequences, actions or gestures are articulated or developed up to a certain point, then abruptly repeated from the beginning. Each subsequent repetition is complicated by some variation on the original actions. While these repetitions or recurrences eventually build up a sense of expectation in the viewer, the overall effect is of being repeatedly battered. However, even in the cases where the viewer can clearly recognize the nature or object of the action or can begin to discern a coherent pattern of activity he is unable to match what he sees with what he hears. The densely layered sound track in these sequences piles up fragments of raw auditory information to the point where the viewer finds himself suspended in a medium of pure sensation. So dense and all enveloping is this medium that the viewer is no longer able to orientate himself by means of the faculty of hearing at all. His condition is close to that of anarthria for he virtually no longer seems to have the power to discriminate articulate speech. Words, phrases, and sentences have been effectively reduced to the level of sound. This type of sequence is Snow's metaphor for the noncognitive element in human experience. In these sequences, Snow deprives the viewer of his customary moorings and leaves him to deal with experience purely as a state of mind. What is so striking and poignant about these sequences is the desperate if necessarily fitful efforts on the part of the viewer to penetrate, to structure somehow, and to comprehend his surroundings in order, as it were, to get outside of his head and into the world. In his published notes on *Rameau's Nephew* Snow refers to speech as thought's body, and he remarks that speech and thought are not generally considered to be separate activities.[6] Snow has managed in these sequences to elicit from the viewer a self-conscious awareness of the operations of the mind deprived of language. It is extremely significant that Snow insists upon keeping the settings, incidents, and persona in his film ordinary and matter of fact; by rigorously eschewing any overtones or intimations of the mystical, psychedelic, and other-worldly, he has denied us any easy way out for the profound bewilderment he has forced us to confront in ourselves.

The other major sequence type is one in which the viewer is witness to a fairly coherent, more or less, straightforward presentation of an exchange between members of a small group of speakers. The group's activity is, for the most part, focused around the playing out of a simple but extended language game of one sort or another. These range from the prodigious and relentless torrent of puns aboard the otherwise empty jet-liner, to the tedium of teaching and learning the refrain of a Bob Dylan song by rote in a later sequence set in a large mansion. It does not take the viewer long before he begins to realize that the most rudimentary conventions of language are decomposing before his eyes and ears and within his mind. Such sequences reveal that when language is allowed to get caught up, as it were, in its own mechanics, the self-perpetuating abstract structures and inherent ambiguities within language take over, and meaning and reference, and indeed language's fundamental connection to the outer world and to the essential conceptual frameworks within a particular culture, are radically destabilized. The experience of the viewer in this second type of sequence is epitomized by a strong sense of detachment and distance. The viewer is a strictly disinterested, fully conscious, critical-minded observer to the various speech acts he is being shown. As a result, Snow's exuberant play with the film medium is now firmly set within a clearly comprehensible context. It is to be regarded as yet another relevant dimension of the topics under discussion by the characters in the film. That is, what is being done to the film medium *per se* is to be thought of as a comment on that subject or issue being raised. Medium reflexiveness is never more clear than at the end of the film in the "Hotel" sequence (the one made famous because it was censored by the Ontario Film Board). Here, for possibly the first time in the film, Snow gives his characters extended conversations on recognizable, nontrivial topics such as questions of how can we be sure of what we think we see and know, and the relation of fantasy and reality in the area of sexuality. The range of topics covered in this "Hotel" sequence is especially interesting because the topics are the same as those that now preoccupy postmodernist criticism. Considered from the prevailing climate of postmodernism, *Rameau's Nephew* is an astonishing anomaly. I would hasten to add that it is also a profoundly instructive one. Snow shows, again and again, in innumerable ways, that thought can operate in language *outside* or beneath the level of representation and does so in a manner that adds to our understanding of the world and of our place in it.

III

There is widespread consensus among postmodernist writers that late modernist art, particularly from minimalism on, is fundamentally self-reflexive or, more precisely, self-referential in character. Postmodernist theory seems to depend so heavily on this overextended, woolly-minded notion of self-reference that it has become virtually indispensable to the very definition of postmodernist art in general.[7] The fact of the matter is that the self-referentiality thesis not only profoundly obscures the actual achievement and full scope of (what purely for the sake of convenience we are calling) late modernist art but also provides a false and misleading foundation for postmodern art. Once this narrow interpretation of reference is questioned, it remains to be asked whether there is something about the nature of postmodernist art work that clearly distinguishes it from the late modern art work. In other words, does the postmodernist work in fact break new ground with regard to the making of art formally? Or does it simply depend on the predisposition of the viewer to interpret new art works in the particular way set out by postmodernist theory and criticism?

The answer to such questions will bring with it an understanding of another major misconception sanctioned by postmodernist criticism: that postmodernist art spearheaded the effort to return subject matter or content to advanced contemporary art and, furthermore, that these new territories of investigation (which include the cultural, political, and spiritual underpinnings of contemporary Western society) could be dealt with adequately only by postmodernist art and the critical assumptions under which it operates. It should be noted in passing that postmodernism would also lay claim to the host of formal properties that mark advanced contemporary art from the late 1960s on: "Appropriation, site-specificity, impermanence, accumulation, discursivity, hybridization—these diverse strategies characterize much of the art of the present and distinguish it from its modernist predecessors."[8]

In general, the issue of reference is central to the postmodernist position. For most modernist critics, as well as for the majority of poststructuralists, the concept of reference is absolutely indispensable to their views because it provides the theoretical mechanism by means of which the work of art (or any statement for that matter) is taken beyond itself and connected to things in the external world. Above all, postmodernism insists upon the distinctions between, and the irreconcilable separation of, the work of art and the world.[9]

Concern over referentiality reflects in an important way certain attitudes that not only underlie but also may motivate postmodernism. In short, reference becomes an overriding and central issue when you feel that you can no longer take the things you see and read at "face value," i.e., in and for themselves. The very idea that some particular object or image in the world has an intrinsic nature, meaning, or value no longer seems to be credible or valid. All this idea reflects is a highly developed and extremely self-conscious awareness of the fact that human knowledge and the language used to communicate it are, in the last analysis, artificial constructs, i.e., both are human-centred. The primary focus of intellectual and creative activity would, by this light, seem to be that of deciphering, decoding, or appropriating rather than discovering "the nature of things." For this reason, there seems to be a fundamentally anthropological orientation to postmodernism. As a consequence, there is a tendency to *bracket* any attempt to describe particular objects or conditions in the world and consider them, rather than to describe or investigate those things first hand. The question is not whether some particular statement is true, but why it is thought to be true by a particular culture at a particular time and what criteria confirmed this truth. Furthermore, postmodernism seems very much disposed towards viewing reference and meaning as profoundly influenced and even determined by the dominant ideological and cultural forces at all levels. Besides, language tends to preserve much of its basic vocabulary and grammar so that old words and constructions are constantly being given new uses and meanings. Hence, there is a conviction that language is not stable and that, in a word, words cannot be trusted to guarantee meaning or reference.

These attitudes are a stark contrast to the literalism that has characterized contemporary art since Pollock. This literalism and the rigorous formal impulse that provided its logic seemed to "reduce" art to the status of an object in real time and space. Throughout the 1950s, the 1960s, and long into the 1970s, advanced contemporary art maintained its adamantly literal-minded imperatives. In both painting and sculpture the natural behaviour or disposition of the materials used in a work had to be manifested directly and immediately, without attenuation or the least hint of artifice. Throughout this period, and especially in the case of minimal and postminimal sculpture in the 1960s and the early 1970s, this literalism often took on a pronounced philosophical resonance and, consequently, considerable intellectual and imaginative power. It was as if only by the direct encounter on the part of the spectator with actual materials of the everyday world displacing real space that the artist could quell and possibly subdue the nagging threats of scepticism and solipsism that disturbed the empirical convictions the artist shared with his peers at the time. Paint had to look and act like paint; constructions of steel, earth, and wood each had to reaffirm the properties of their very specific materials. The direct, unmediated experience and perception of the spectator were essential to the work's artistic truths and to the epistemological issues it addressed. To paraphrase Frank Stella's famous dictum, "what one saw was what there was." The artist's intention and the particular insights that his work shed on the nature of the external world were confirmed and validated by the observations of the spectator.

Gradually, however, the literal, along with the physically present (i.e., palpably real) and the directly perceivable, began to lose its authority once the deeply felt urgency over strictly empirical questions subsided. An increasing number of artists no longer felt internally compelled to raise, let alone answer, such questions in their work. Furthermore, the literal also seemed to lose its aesthetic interest. Even critics of the day eventually were to find the severe, uninflected form of minimal and postminimal sculpture insufficient in itself to sustain attention and curiosity. At one point in her *Passages in Modern Sculpture* Rosalind Krauss suggests that these forms were no longer enough to look at and to think about and that, as a result, serious advanced sculpture of the mid 1970s had to break out of the confines of the discrete object and disperse itself in pieces throughout the space it occupied.[10]

In effect, what has happened is that, even within the writing of the advocates of the minimal and postminimal movements, the literal was increasingly being equated with its surface appearances.[11] This attention to surface appearances represents a very serious turn for it seems to reduce the actual to the status and condition of an external image or sign. One is tempted to say that no room has been left for the object to take on the amplitude and complexity that it has even under normal conditions. Similarly the nature of the spectators' engagement with the work has, as a consequence, been radically constricted. The best minimal and postminimal sculpture, for example, has always set up an on-going critical dialectic between what appeared or what was assumed to be the case and what upon closer, more considered inspection was in fact there; this work illuminated and interrogated the interaction between the mind and the senses.

The activities of experience, judgement, reflection, and testing called forth by such works have been collapsed in favour of reading or deciphering a sign. The question of what a thing means or stands for has now, in effect, replaced the question of what that thing is and how we comprehend its nature. It is little wonder then that semiotics—the study of signs—has gained the central place it has for postmodernist thinking in general.

What "closes off" work of the minimalists and postminimalists and indeed all forms of modernism for the postmodernists is that it is impossible for the postmodernists to understand how an autonomous, self-contained work of art can relate to or implicate anything in or any part of the work outside of itself. Postmodernists believe that the only possible way that a work of art can connect to the world is, as we have said, by reference. For the postmodernists, the object taken in the public, i.e., the non-subjective sense, can be understood only at face value, in terms of its external appearance, such as a sign. They implicitly deny even the possibility that a work of art can function as analogue to things, circumstances, conditions, and events in the world at large.

Douglas Crimp's point about mediums and medium-centredness in his essay "Pictures" is aimed at demonstrating that the best of the new postmodernist art has clearly and simply nothing to do with "the integrity of the various mediums—those categories the exploration of whose essences and limits constituted the very project of modernism."[12] He insists that "the formal descriptions of modernist art ... were topographical, that they mapped the surfaces of art works in order to determine their structures,"[13] and were, consequently, not relevant to the formal structure of the new work nor to the way those works achieved meaning.

The hybrid installations and tableaux of postmodernist artists (Crimp mentions the work of Jack Goldstein, Troy Brauntuch, Robert Longo, and Cindy Sherman) virtually render the issue of medium incidental and of marginal interest. The concern of this work shifts instead to the image or picture presented by it. More importantly, one has the distinct impression that the image presented is somehow out of context and that what would, under normal circumstances, be regarded as familiar is being called into question. It is as if the image in the work, by virtue of simply being in the work, were being enclosed by quotation marks. The viewer is made conscious of the image as a kind of appropriation of sorts and of its being a part or a fragment of something like an existing code. One becomes aware of the image in terms of the particular way in which it organizes certain thoughts or feelings and presents them to us. One sees the image as being connected to particular unstated cultural assumptions or values in a way that seems to elicit a stock response from us. As Crimp puts it, "those processes of quotation, excerption, framing, and staging that constitute the strategies of postmodernist art necessitate uncovering strata of representation. Needless to say, we are not in search of sources or origins, but of structures of significance: underneath each picture there is always another picture."[14] In effect, and on a number of levels, the viewer is being drawn away from the idea of a work as an autonomous, internally coherent, structurally integrated, material whole. The largely rhetorical question that Crimp asks at the end of "Pictures" actually underscores the extremely problematic condition in which postmodernist art leaves the concept of the work of art: "And if it is impossible to locate the physical medium of the work, can we then locate the original art work?"

In "The Allegorical Impulse: Toward a Theory of Postmodernism," parts I and II, Owens has elaborated what is probably the most comprehensive theory of postmodernism to date. Not only does his exposition enumerate the largest number of distinct features of postmodernist art, but also it attempts to unify them within the terms of a single concept: allegory. In many ways and for an increasing number of writers, Owens's views have come to represent something of the standard overview for postmodernism in the area of contemporary visual arts; many of the moves and a good deal of the terminology are the same. Key concepts of thinkers such as Benjamin, Barthes, Derrida, and Lacan are deployed by Owens in a way that has become characteristic of and essential to postmodernist art criticism. It is for this reason that Owens's allegorical account of postmodernist art is of considerable importance. Criticisms of that account therefore can have far reaching implications for what are presently thought to be both the points of departure and the achievements of postmodernist art in general. To state the matter simply, I want to argue here that the individual parts of Owens's theory do not mesh into a uniform and consistent argument and that only some features described by it are valid or radically new. Furthermore, I think that the challenge of postmodernism to the autonomy and integrated wholeness of the work of art is serious, but ultimately flawed.

One of the hallmarks of postmodernist art is the degree to which the element of complicity on the part of the spectator is involved in the meaning and structure of the work. This work, in effect, forces one to complete it, that is, to locate and fix the meaning of its images and signs. In that art it no longer seems to be a simple matter of confirming one's initial impressions of the work by means of direct observation and critical analysis. Perhaps in large part because of the nature of its subject matter and its particular areas of interest, the literal (strictly material) aspect of postmodernist art seems instead to direct attention towards the possibility of a distinct and independent system of meanings beneath the surface of the work. That is, the work appears to deliberately set up a disjunction between its outward (literal) appearances and its implicit, rhetorical bias (what the former seems to have been programmed to say or to mean). The spectator, as a result, soon finds himself drawn into what amounts to a critique of values. The incompleteness of postmodernist work has to do with the need for the spectator to recognize and to acknowledge this disjunction and to commit himself tacitly to rejecting the two (literal and rhetorical) as equivalent.

That is, one is in effect asked by the work to see oneself as either the subject or the victim of an imposed system of representation that is so pervasive and so completely internalized as to be for the most part invisible, i.e., construed as natural and neutral, "objective," just the way things are. The object of much of this work seems to make the spectator see the rhetoric and the ideology behind the image in the work.

It is at this point that the element of tacit complicity enters into the postmodernist aesthetic. Postmodernist work and its explication in postmodernist critical writing demands to be read in terms relating to the dominant culture. The work is to be understood as a deconstruction of generally accepted "truisms" perpetuated by the ideology of that culture. It should be noted that no alternatives to the rhetoric and the values the work deconstructs are suggested or explored. The values questioned within and by the work are simply to be regarded as a bad thing, a false description, an imposed reality.

Most of the aspects of postmodern allegory outlined by Owens in "The Allegorical Impulse" are methods by artists to problematize images and texts, i.e., what has been seen as natural, transparent, readable. One of the most radical and most characteristic features of postmodernist art is that of *discursiveness*. It is almost an inevitable by-product of the postmodernist brand of deconstruction. Discursiveness takes on the form of a wide ranging commentary and allows for a freer play of meanings and associations than had been tolerated under the rigorous discipline and the highly focused organization of orthodox modernist art. By its very nature, it eschews even the possibility of the single truth or the single, all encompassing meaning that resolves all internal ambiguities and ties up all loose ends in a given work. Structurally, it enables work to change (its meaning) in and through time: it ensures an open-endedness to the work that permits the spectator continually to add something new or different to the work. The very notion of discursiveness implies that the spectator has, in effect, become a reader rather than a viewer and that art has become a text to be read rather than an object to be looked at or contemplated in the isolation of a museum or gallery space. The potentially profound ramifications of postmodernism on the traditional conception of the work of art (one that remained more or less intact throughout the reign of modernism) can, I think, begin to be appreciated only when one considers the importance assigned to the spectator's role as reader. (As reader, the spectator definitely does play a crucial role *in* postmodernist work.) The full import of discursivity is best summed up in the excerpt from Roland Barthes's essay "The Death of the Author" which is quoted in "The Allegorical Impulse" and throughout postmodernist art criticism:

> The reader is the space on which all the quotations that make up a writing are inscribed without any of them being lost; a text's unity lies not in its origin but in its destination. Yet this designation can no longer be personal: the reader is without history, biography, psychology; he is simply that someone who holds together in a single field all the traces by which the written text is constituted.[15]

In spite of the vast and complex critical apparatus that surrounds postmodernist art, including discursiveness and the transformation of viewer into reader, there are a number of instances (works) that, in and of themselves, can be seen as important extensions of the formal language of contemporary art. There is a quality of *ambivalence* in the works of Laurie Anderson and Robert Longo, to name two examples, that is new to contemporary art. The terms, images, or signs used in their work each carry conflicting or contradictory meanings. The meanings and resonances that are yoked together in these works often carry with them, and in them, powerful emotional charges. The simultaneous meanings never converge or even neatly reconfigure to form a clear paradox. Instead, they seem to cohabitate in a state of constant antagonism and antithesis. They are both permanently incompatible and irreconcilable. What makes this ambivalence and bipolarity so impressive and unnerving is that they call attention to the fact that language in general is the medium of our thoughts and feelings about our interactions with the world and with others. It is through that medium that we have knowledge of the world and others, and indeed, ourselves. It is thus imperative that we comprehend as accurately as possible the actual nature of this medium itself. This art depends completely on our immediate capacity to recognize the conflicting meanings inherent in certain signs and images as being incontestably part of the vernacular of everyday speech. They are further evidence that language is not a transparent window to the world. As Owens points out, "In a recent series of aluminium reliefs entitled *Boys Slow Dance* and based on film stills, Longo presents three images of men locked in ... deadly combat? amorous embrace? ... Suspended in a static image, a struggle to death is transformed into something that 'has all the elegance of dance.' Yet it is an aesthetic spectacle in photographs and films and on television."[16]

While Owens acknowledges Anderson's parables and Longo's images as "emblems of that blind confrontation of antithetical meanings" he goes on, to characterize both as "allegories of unreadability." Such a characterization, however, brings with it an inclination to destabilize meanings and to create opportunities for simultaneous, multiple readings by exaggerating the imprecision of the terms involved and by filling in the crevices and breaches with commentary. But it is evident from Owens's own remarks about the work of artists such as Anderson and Longo that the ambivalence that typifies their images and signs is something discrete, specific, and contained. Such images do not seem to offer an appropriate occasion for discursiveness.

There is also an immense difference between the phenomenon of *opacity* or what Barthes refers to as "obtuse meaning" found in postmodernist work and the function assigned to it by postmodernist allegorical theory. Although Walter Benjamin elaborated a concept of the opaque (or obtuse) within the context of his overall effort to rescue the allegorical mode from the oblivion to which it had been assigned by both romantic and modernist aesthetics, he does so in a way that emphasizes the density and intractability of the opaque. For Benjamin, the element of melancholy is paramount. If it is true, on the one hand, that the gaze of melancholy causes the life in an object to flow out of it and renders it "quite incapable of emanating any meaning or significance of its own" so that any significance it does possess "it acquires from the allegorist," it is true, on the other hand, that the allegorist does not have an entirely free hand in giving the object or sign any meaning he wishes. The disposition of the allegorist, especially the literary variety of the seventeenth century which Benjamin happens to be discussing, is all important:

> In allegory the observer is confronted with the *facies hippocratica* of history as a petrified, primordial landscape. Everything about history that, from the very beginning, had been untimely, sorrowful, unsuccessful, is expressed in a face—or rather in death's head. And although such a thing lacks all "symbolic" freedom of expression, all classical proportion, all humanity—nevertheless, this is the form in which man's subjection to nature is most obvious and it significantly gives rise not only to the enigmatic question of the nature of human existence as such, but also of the biographical historicity of the individual. This is the heart of the allegorical way of seeing. ...[17]

Above all, there seems to be a strong overtone of the *memento mori* in Benjamin's discussion of the opaque object. If the sign or image is unreadable it is because it is locked in a past that cannot possibly be retrieved or revived. Its essence as sign or image or object is its distance from us. It would seem that for Benjamin the task of the allegorist is to articulate or to interpret the human significance of that distance, that fundamental condition of distance and separation, the universal inevitability of entropy. The allegorist is not, by this interpretation, committed automatically to adopting a nihilistic attitude of "anything goes because it's all the same in the end anyway"; instead it is the lot of the allegorist, particularly if the allegorist is an artist, to acknowledge the effort to comprehend the human dimensions of that inevitability and to give that effort form.

Consider the approaches of two prominent postmodernist critics on the work of Troy Brauntuch. Both critics are attempting to explain how Brauntuch's enlargements of Hitler's drawings or photographs of concentration camp victims, exhibited without captions, become opaque:

> Every operation to which Brauntuch subjects these pictures represents the duration of a fascinated, perplexed gaze, whose desire is that they disclose their secrets; but the result is only to make the pictures all the more picture-like, to fix forever in an elegant object our distance from the history that produced these images. That distance is all these pictures signify.[18]

In the quote that follows from another critic the emphasis shifts from the prominence accorded to the fact of distance to that given to the need to "read into" or, in the author's words, to "decipher."

> Brauntuch's images simultaneously proffer and defer a promise of meaning; they both solicit and frustrate our desire that the image be directly transparent to its signification. As a result, they appear strangely incomplete—fragments or ruins which must be *deciphered*.[19]

Both the postmodern allegorist and a number of poststructuralists make use of the distinction and the relationship between the literal and the rhetorical. This basic formula pervades postmodernist thinking and its analysis of language in general. In ordinary discourse, as well as in nonallegorical literature, language is treated as if it were to be understood as being transparent; the literal and the rhetorical are assumed to go together. Opacity, Barthes's "obtuse meaning," is thought by postmodernists and certain structuralists to be a crucial if not indispensable instrument of this unhinging of the literal and the rhetorical. Opacity is regarded primarily in terms of the function it performs rather than as something significant in itself:

> The *absence* of obtuse meaning, is, in fact the very condition of communication and signification, but its presence works to problematize these activities. Since the obtuse meaning has no objective, indepen-

dent existence, it depends upon the literal and the rhetorical, which it nevertheless undoes. An unwelcome supplement, it exposes the literal level of the image to be a fiction, implicating it in the web of substitutions and reversals properly characteristic of the symbolic. The actor is revealed as the (metaphoric) substitute for character; his facial contortions, the emblem of grief not its direct expression. Hence every image that participates in what photography criticism calls the directional, as opposed to the documentary, mode is open to the intervention of obtuse meaning.[20]

By definition the meaning or reference of the literal is fixed at the level of its surface. The literal is the outer shell or husk of an image or sign. Its relation to meaning or reference is restricted by the theory and views under consideration to a very limited number of options: it can be transparent; it can be disjoined, i.e., no longer transparent because, for one reason or another, the meaning or reference has become dislodged from the literal, and the rhetoric that has supported this association has become increasingly conspicuous; or it can be empty, because the literal simply does not, or no longer has, any specific meaning or reference in the public mind. For the opaque or obtuse term to function in the way described by Owens it would have to be, in effect, empty. But the opaque is unreadable because we cannot decipher it; we are acutely aware of our inability to make out or determine its meaning or reference. The very density or resonance it still possesses for us is a signal that there is a meaning or reference that we cannot make out. If a term or image is empty, however, it is neutral, unoccupied, and completely ready to be reappropriated for general use. We simply fall into reading the empty and unused term once a meaning or reference were attributed to it, the way we read any term that is part of our "language" today. It would, in a manner of speaking, simply be reabsorbed into the "language." In other words, the opaque, unlike the empty term, cannot reasonably be considered a free floating signifier.

In conclusion, it can be seen in the examples chosen by the postmodernist critics themselves, namely the works of Anderson, Longo, and Brauntuch, that they are deconstructive and even "unreadable" in the postmodern allegorist sense of the word, just because they force the spectator to confront his ambivalences (precisely stated polarities) or opacity in a way that cannot be readily dismissed or equivocated. These works may elicit, as part of the spectator's or the critic's response to them, a kind of discursive commentary, but it should be clear that this commentary is not essential either to their substance or to their structure as works of art.

One final point: the strategy of appropriation common to a large number of postmodernist works may turn out to be a very important, but at the same time, very special case of what Owens has identified as the allegorical mode. One of the primary aims of this strategy seems to be that of opening up a fissure within the language at large in order to reveal a split between the outward signs or images used in everyday communication and the dominant rhetoric that in effect determines their meaning for us. It seems to presuppose that the function of postmodernist art is to engage in an analysis of what Owens, among others, calls the literal component (the signs and images) in terms of a particular rhetoric and the ideology behind that rhetoric. The object of works such as Cindy Sherman's film "stills" is therefore to make the spectator aware of the sign or image as an integral part of a given ideology's *representation* of the world.

Indeed, the strategy of appropriation best suits those familiar, public images that can be shown to exemplify fundamental social attitudes and the representational systems of a particular dominant ideology. Their very appearance, in what one has reason to believe is a sophisticated contemporary work of art, is enough of a tip-off that something beside the obvious is afoot and that one is in effect being asked by the artist and the work to reconsider what seems at first glance so obvious. Because of this and related reasons, the strategy of appropriation cannot be applied across the broad range of postmodernist works; it does not fit (i.e., satisfactorily account for) a number of key examples given by writers such as Owens or Crimp. It is simply that certain gestures, such as capacity in the work of Brauntuch or ambivalence in the works of Anderson and Longo, cannot be convincingly integrated into that strategy. At best, then, one can say with considerable justification that the strategy of appropriation is a subspecies (one of several) of the general allegorical methods outlined in Owens's pioneering essay. Furthermore, the clearly drawn connection between the literal and the rhetorical that the strategy of appropriation necessarily requires, and a theory like Owens's virtually demands, is not relevant to a number of postmodernist paradigms. In most cases either this connection would diminish the intensity or autonomy of the sign or image (the literal) in question or it would attempt to superimpose an otherwise gratuitous reading on it. It seems to me, therefore, that postmodernism's ostensible challenge to the fundamental nature of the work of art, which has been one of the chief and persistent concerns of the present essay, is not as radical or as wide-sweeping as some theorists have alleged. One is tempted to go even further and ask whether the strategy of appropriation by itself subverts in any serious way the traditional conception of the work of art as an autonomous, integrated whole. By and large, the strategy of appropriation operated within the parameters of a fairly determinate field or circumscribed frame of reference. Thus, the clarity of the intentions of a postmodernist work, as well as its reference to the external world and to the particular system of representation it seeks to exemplify, ensure that it will fit the traditional conception of a work of art, for if it does not, it cannot hope to succeed on its own self-defined terms and conditions. Rather than open up the work by destroying its boundaries and its autonomy, the strategy of appropriation needs a general complicity on the part of the spectator with regard to the ultimate meaning or interpretation of the work in question.

Notes

1.   Deconstruction is a major component of poststructuralism and so is the preoccupation with texts, writing, and the reader. Important versions of these and related concepts, as well as the relationship between structuralism and poststructuralism, are to be found in the writings of Jacques Derrida, Jacques Lacan, Roland Barthes, and Michel Foucault. John Sturrock's *Structuralism and Since* (Toronto: Oxford University Press, 1979) is a useful aid for keeping the leading figures and their respective views straight.

2.   Hal Foster, "Re: Post," *Parachute*, no. 26 (Spring 1982): 14.

3.   Arthur C. Danto, *The Transfiguration of the Commonplace* (Cambridge: Cambridge University Press, 1983).

4.   See Roland Barthes, "From Work to Text," *Image, Music, Text*, trans. Stephen Heath (New York: Hill and Wang, 1977).

5.   Poststructuralism has consistently taken serious issue with empiricists and others on the matter of reference. This disagreement, however, has tended to obscure certain fundamental similarities between the two positions. Most importantly, both poststructuralism and empiricism speak of the reference function in terms of, to put it roughly, a matching up of signs to specific objects and facts. What the poststructuralists object to is the claim made by empiricists that the reference of a sign, term, or statement can be independently confirmed by an observer and can, because of this confirmation, be regarded as an objective truth about the external world. Furthermore, poststructuralists are intent on denying the empiricist's view that language preserves this referential correspondence indefinitely. But where the empiricists would root referentiality in the objective, external world—subject to confirmation of the individual observer—the poststructuralist would locate it in a particular culture at a particular time in history. For the poststructuralists, reference is determinable but is not fixed, transparent, or permanent. Without reference, however, it appears that a sign or term could not have meaning.

6.   Michael Snow, "Notes for *Rameau's Nephew*," *October*, no. 4 (Fall 1977): 43–57.

7.   This tendency is cogently formulated by Craig Owens in "The Allegorical Impulse: Toward a Theory of Postmodernism," *Performance, Text(e)s and Documents*, ed. Chantal Pontbriand (Montréal: Éditions Parachute, 1981), 37–47. Also published as "The Allegorical Impulse, part II," *October*, no. 13 (Fall 1980): 37–47. "When the postmodernist work speaks of itself, it is ... to narrate its own contingency, insufficiency, lack of transcendence. ... Its deconstructive thrust is aimed not only against the contemporary myths that furnish its subject matter, but also against the symbolic, totalizing impulse which characterizes modernist art." (p. 47).

8.   Craig Owens, "The Allegorical Impulse: Toward a Theory of Postmodernism," *October*, no. 12 (Summer 1980): 75.

9.   By "problematizing" the reference of an image or a sign, the postmodernist work can show the external world to be other than the official culture assumes it to be and, consequently, can show how that art can subvert the normative, "objective" truths of that culture. But it is also for this reason that postmodernism rejects the romantic and the modernist conception of the work of art as something autonomous and self-contained in its meaning.

10.   Rosalind Krauss, *Passages in Modern Sculpture* (Cambridge: MIT Press, 1977).

11.   See Foster, "Re: Post," 11–15, and Walter Klepac, "Paradigms, Miscues and Continuities: The Formal Impulse," *Vanguard*, vol. 12, no. 3 (April 1983): 22–24.

12.   Douglas Crimp, "Pictures," *October*, no. 8 (Spring 1979): 76.

13.   Ibid., 87.

14.   Ibid.

15.   Roland Barthes, "The Death of the Author," in *Image, Music, Text*, 148.

16.   Owens, "The Allegorical Impulse, part II," 43.

17.   Walter Benjamin, *The Origin of German Tragic Drama*, trans. John Osborne (London: NLB, 1977), 166.

18.   Crimp, "Pictures," 85.

19.   Owens, "The Allegorical Impulse," 70.

20.   Owens, "The Allegorical Impulse, part II," 46.

A response to this text was written by Mark Lewis, "Concerning the Question of the Post-cultural," *C Magazine*, no. 8 (Winter 1985).

Philip Monk

Colony, Commodity and Copyright:
Reference and Self-Reference in Canadian Art

The history of art in Canada is short. That is to say, there is no history. Or there are many. This is one of them. I would like to think that this is more than one history of Canadian art; that this essay could trace a significant development in Canadian art. But given the geniality that has passed for criticism in this country, anything that is produced and written about is put into a history—a history of autonomous objects, of individualistic expression, etc. It is put into a history, not given a history. If it were given a history then we might learn of its conditions of production as well as the conditions of its reception of influences. The latter is a context of misunderstanding as well as understanding. Understood, this art is more likely to make its own authentic history not repeat one from elsewhere or consume it as a system of signs. This reception, moreover, is a response or a failure of response to its own context and history. Failure to respond is also a condition of its context.

The history I want to discuss, which may be *the* history of Canadian art, is a history of objects and subjects, where the objects have been replaced by subjects. Basically, it is a sculptural tradition, but sculpture that has been mediated by language, so that it might include installation, photo-textual work, video, or "pure" language works. What could be taken as a formal development in this work indicates another history. And it is what is most resistant to history and language: the presence of the work of art. Here I mean presence as the authenticity of art and hence its authority. What is presented to us in the work of art is an immediacy we experience in the work of our presence through it. What is presented to us is separate from the artist but "copyrighted," so to speak, under his name and image (under his authority), both of which are signatures. This presence can actually be registered moreover as an *index* of the artist. In the "examples" through which I trace this history, the artist is "there" in the work as an index, as a photographic index; indicated through the indexical process of the work; or as indicated by the enunciation of an "I." (An index need not resemble its object but must be modified by its object. It therefore has a physical or contingent relation to what it refers to or

This text was first published in *Vanguard* (Summer 1983).

signifies, such as a footprint in the sand or a photograph. Demonstratives such as "this" or "that" are indices, as are the personal pronouns "I" and "you.")

This presence is problematic; I do not accept its positive description above. It is problematic not because it has been put into doubt as one of the founding metaphors of Western metaphysics. It is problematic simply for being there. What absence does this presence indicate? Why has the artist or the index of the artist become the subject of this art, emblematic of a formalization of the processes of art? What does it displace? What reference does this self-reference replace? Why has the index of the artist become the object of the spectator's view? And why can we trace this through much of the most significant Canadian art?

This evidence is more than a theme within the history of one direction of Canadian art. More than a local version of a general indexical strategy, we could call it a theme if it did not express instead an absence of reality. The formal construction of this index as a presence or, as we shall see, a reference, is a conscious or unconscious response to that absence of reality. In making the index the formal identity of the work, a self-identity is asserted against that absence. If that absence defines our condition as Canadian, it helps explain why a history of art has been impossible. That is why above I called this work *the* history of Canadian art. This third history, now as an absence, has been recognized by this art somehow in its production but not by criticism.

The conditions of existence of contemporary Canadian art are complex. Not the least is the fact of having passed from premodernism to so-called postmodernism without a history of modernism. The work I discuss is situated in that conjuncture between the two. Our lack of a national art history is implicated perhaps in this absence of modernism as a failure of an industrial capitalist class to arise. Our continuing colonial dependency in the transition from mercantilism to corporate branch plant management is registered in some way on every level of culture as a lack of validity given to local production. This repeats both in institutions and individuals and in the relation of individual to institution, the structure of margin to centre of a hinterland to an imperial metropole. (In itself, this "I" is male and central Canadian.)

This work takes its place against the accumulation of absences that make our history. It attempts to suspend this history through an ontology; and it can escape its colonial nature by its acts; how and where it places itself; its recognition of the historical moment and its influences; the considered formality of its construction. In turn, however, each of these is a reaction to and product of a more consuming history than our colonialism, and that is the history of commodity relations based on the structure of the commodity.

"What is characteristic of the capitalist age," writes Marx, "is that in the eyes of the labourer himself labour-power assumes the form of a commodity belonging to him. On the other hand it is only at this moment the commodity form of the products of labour becomes general."[1] We presume the artist privileged to escape the commodity relationship in his work that maintains its organic process and immediacy in the unity of the product. But that privilege and unity is achieved at a price; it is predicated on turning the individual into a subject. It is not necessarily that the artist's labour is a commodity that belongs to him but that he becomes a *legal* subject. Copyright is the sign of this surrender. The index is its alibi. Copyright supports, the index confirms identity and presence. The absolute relation of immediacy of presence is secured by the index of the artist—the contingent evidence of his presence. This signature in turn assures the work's value. The museum is the work's (this presence) absolute validation, its signified. The gallery is its means of circulation—its signifier. The viewer is formally excluded; his or her function is to reassure this presence and authority by a consumption and confirmation.

The history of this art is not mere repetition. We find a general tendency from self-reference to reference. Reference and self-reference are opposed: in absolute terms, a work cannot refer to itself and outside itself at the same time. Any interrogation of the formal conditions of self-referentiality is bound to lead to the problems of referentiality in general (by which I mean, for example, the relation of a word to a thing or of an image to an object or event). The nature of an index is such that it can register a presence or indicate a reference and thus lends itself to both reference and self-reference.

Michael Snow's work has remained consistently self-referential. In many ways his photographic and sculptural work from the late 1960s set the terms for the serious, younger Canadian art that was to follow. The later work is a surfacing from Snow; it is also a move towards reference. Among the terms was the index. *Authorization* (1969) uses "photography in a very enclosed way so that there is nothing outside the work itself that is used in the photograph."[2] This work is a record of its process of making: it is an index of it. The set-up of a camera in front of a mirror ensures that the photograph will record nothing outside the work. The mirror indexes the photographer standing in front of it; the consequent photograph is an index of the reflection; and each photograph is a temporal index of the process of the work's construction. Since Michael Snow is the photographer, his image as well is integral to the piece.

The index of the artist presents itself naturally within the formalism of this piece: he was contingent to its construction. His image also appears "accidentally" in the photographic documentation of *Authorization* and *Scope* (1967). *Scope* absents the object of view in favour of the structure of viewing (it is a construction and frame for looking). The accident of Snow's appearance, however, is the *unconscious* of this work and all his other presentations. The index of the artist's presence, even when he does not figure in this phenomenological work, is the guarantee of our own. The name of the artist is never separate from this presence: Snow's film *Presents* (1981) is both "Michael Snow presents" and the present moments (presence) of its viewing.

The artist, Michael Snow—his image, his name, his history, and that of his work—becomes a formal constituent of his work. He "appears" through means of the photographic index in *Venetian Blind* (1970), *Two Sides to Every Story* (1974), and *Cover to Cover* (1975). Or he is referred to in his absence by his name, as in *So is This* (1982) or its variants, e.g., "Wilma Schoen" in *Rameau's Nephew by Diderot (Thanx to Dennis Young) by Wilma Schoen* (1972–1974). With Michael Snow, we have more of a self-given history, which does not mean self-expressive, more than that of any other artist in Canada. As such, his 1970 retrospective catalogue, *Michael Snow/A Survey*,[3] is a rich, social history of a *Canadian* artist as much as a document of a body of work, re-presented in the process of a bookwork. Perhaps we can look into that exemplary social document for the reasons why the social referent itself is missing from his work. This is part of our history, and history of art. The social is always returned to the formal when it becomes the index of the artist. What the index of the artist always guarantees is the formal autonomy of the work.

If Michael Snow mined his own proper name and biography as formal material for his art, General Idea appropriated the *fiction* of their own history. Their name already is a copyrightable corporate symbol. Now, rather than one artist to be indexed, three terms are put into play as a system. The lens and mirror of Michael Snow have become "mirrors mirroring mirrors" in General Idea: a mechanical mode of production has given way to the semiotic. The former one-to-one relation of object to index or index to referent—as part of the mechanical process grounded in the phenomenology of perception and the apparatus of the work's construction—has been elevated into a free-floating system of signs of absolute interchangeability and self-referentiality. Any referent is excluded from this system in order that it may function.

We all know the story of General Idea: "This is the story of General Idea and the story of what we wanted. We wanted to be famous, glamorous, and rich. That is to say we wanted to be artists, and we knew that if we were famous and glamorous we could say we were artists and we would be."[4] As the last statement indicates, this enunciation strategy is tautologous—a mirror image of itself, the mirage of a constitutive act. On the model of fashion, General Idea have done much to create a scene and a place for art in Toronto. Their work, however, is marked by the consequences of that necessity: it reflects the lack it signifies—the position of art in Canada. The necessity of making a scene, of creating their own institutions of support and distribution, have infiltrated their work at a metalevel. This metalevel is the form and content of the work; its enunciation is the simulation of its own effects. General Idea's resort to ambiguity, the multiplicity of meanings, an expanding system of verbal paradoxes, and their own self-referencing system has a tendency to raise the work in its entirety to a metalevel that is ideology itself.

The fetishistic, self-referential formality of this closed system has its consequences. In a system where signifiers exchange among themselves outside of any relation to a real or referent, no critique or reference can take place. The model of this system of value is based ultimately on capital. General Idea's strategies of metalanguage, appropriation, and artificiality, "borrowed" from Roland Barthes's essay "Myth Today,"[5] reproduce the effects of semiology itself: the tendency to distance itself from the real by instituting itself as a formal system of value (that it justifies all the same by reference to its "language-object" to which it stands as a metalanguage). *The 1984 Miss General Idea Pavilion*, as a third-order semiological system, is thus an expensive construction and luxury for us. Like myth, as a system of value, there is no adequation between it and the real; it is referentially self-sufficient, although ideological. It has no referent other than its own construction and past history, composed of a string of signifiers, a pure fabrication that does not need a referent. "We've tried to underline the fact that there is nothing behind it. No verso to speak of. The task of stringing together enough evidence to present the case is a labour of pure fabrication."[6] The referent is lost in favour of the system itself; its own history, and the story of General Idea, becomes the function of this system. As a recent statement on the *Pavilion*'s "room of the unknown function" (itself a statement emblematic of its own formality) puts it:

> The three artists of General Idea have reintroduced destruction into the architectural process. In their long-term project, the *1984 Miss General Idea Pavilion*, ruins are created as quickly as rooms are built. Accumulated layers of function and meaning slip in and out of focus, creating a shifting constellation of images which is the *Pavilion* itself.[7]

The system can accommodate destruction because it enters the system as its mirror image, as its absolute reversibility which is always already inscribed in the logic of the system.

Robin Collyer's sculptural ensemble *I'm Still a Young Man* (1973) was pivotal in the change from formal objecthood to referentiality. The personal pronoun "I" of the title referred to the proper name of the artist; but the title as a whole gave a sense to the work through its references in the work and their referents. But it is another work that uses an "I" less positively that is relevant here. In *Something Revolutionary* (1978), a text of six phrases accompanies six colour photographs—upside-down shots of a ceiling—the latter three through which a film reel spins. The text reads:

I am unimpressed by recent movements

I need a new direction

Something to believe in

To have faith in

An activity to turn to

Something revolutionary.

We are immediately disoriented by the photographs, an alienation that is furthered by the statements, which seem to talk down to us and which we have a hard time applying to the photographs. In spite of that disjunction we can cue the phrases to the photographs by applying the literal definitions of "movement," "direction," "turn to," and "revolutionary" to the progressive tilting of the photographs and to the turn of the film reel. In the context of the statements, however, these words have a metaphorical force, and they refer to values. The narrowing of semantic reference by the purely physical "interpretation" or illustration given by the photographs reinforces the impasse between content of expression and action. Action remains suspended, in the air. We cannot stand in this upside-down space nor act on these statements—make them performative. Even the implied continuity to the sequence, which is reinforced by the sequence of phrases, is denied, not only in the gap between the discontinuous spaces of the photographs in presentation, but also, as Philip Fry has pointed out, within the photographs in the implied narrative of the spinning reel. The sequence does not necessarily describe an event; it is a fictional construction more than the indexical process we find in Snow's *Authorization*.

If objects have moved towards language mediated by reference in Collyer's work, because they have become language in some cases does not mean that the work parallels and repeats the evolution of the commodity from object to sign system. Reference intervenes, as problematic as it was expressed in action in *Something Revolutionary,* to reduce the general commutability and nihilism of signs, products, and people that is our alienation in everyday life.

In 1978, Andy Patton started a series of language posters that were contingent to their sites. The first were descriptive, except the gap between description and site, between language and its referents, was intended to demonstrate the inadequacies of convention in general. The poster and site met in one word only with the repetition of an actual word in view in that location. It was as if that one word carried the whole weight of difference, as language strained at identity, as if the inadequacies of language in that site disputed the direct relation of work to spectator in the gallery. Instead the poster aimed for the audience of advertising—mass and accidental.

These posters appeared, disrupting the "naturality" of their industrial, urban settings; but they offered no message. They did not address us. An act put them into a site, but an intention or a voice behind this writing was absent. Patton's poster of November 1978, made for the Toronto civic elections and placed over mayoralty posters, directly addressed a viewer through an "I." Yet this "I" was tentative, unhappy with both the inexpressibility *and* objectivity of language. Against a form of political advertising that called for a referendum response on the part of the viewer/voter—a yes or a no to this face and name (the same stimulus-response of product advertising; the same face and name of the indexical art talked about here)—Patton inserted an individual voice. This insertion caused a wavering of advertising intent. It also pointed to questions of legitimacy, which ultimately are questions of property. The election posters were legal, Patton's "defacing," illegal. The poster directly confronted this apparatus of legitimacy rather than inhabiting its structure as a pseudo-advertisement. As uncertain as its message was, this direct, self-representational speech forced a halt to the equivalence and interchangeability of advertising and political messages that also speak with an "I" or address the viewer with a "you." Addressed as a "you" singly or collectively, our function is to buy the image; we are alienated from this political process while having a function within it and for it.

The direct speech of Patton's poster, however, is only the simulation of directness. It does not refer outside itself or lead pragmatically to action; that reference and reality is still problematic for it. It intervenes as an act by interfering with the structure of the political poster. But by situating itself in a place where it cannot act—in that political process; by accepting that "site" of the poster for its intervention; it expresses instead an inability to act (much as that inability expressed in *Something Revolutionary*). There is no longer a question of the inadequacy of language here: language is the only place for this subject to act.

The last posters (1980) retreat from this recognition. They take the attempt to blur the semantic markers of the conventional gallery context or sanction and to provoke a non-intentional response to its logical end with the reinsertion of the site in a site. These works were photographic reproductions of other postered sites; they indexed the nature of the poster, not its actual site; and they were grouped to make the appearance of an intention. The index here is as much a desire for absence as a desire for the utopia of pure process and presence. As I have written elsewhere, "this extreme of self-representational and self-referential act functioned through the delay of insertion and differential interruption. But it reflected a nostalgia for the site, a utopian desire for the surface of the world, for pure productivity in an urban capitalist reality."[8]

All of Tom Sherman's work is the presentation of an "I" and an image. But now this presentation is not positive or problematical: it is the subject of the work. The presence and authority of the individual voice of the artist's "I"—the artist who speaks truthfully or imaginatively as the guarantor of the presence, truth, and effectivity of the work—is undermined by another strategy that moves through the work constructing the work as a fiction and displaying it so. This becomes a model for every other presentation of information that speaks through an image as an "I" but not with an "I" and that composes facts in a fictional mode, as, for instance, news broadcasting. Here reality is constructed by the media; it is represented through the alliance of technical reproduction and codes of authenticity that operate through the simulation of reference.

Two works from 1977 and 1978 use the "same" text juxtaposed to two different images of the artist "Tom Sherman." In the first, a publication, a photograph of Tom Sherman with eyes closed and head tilted back is juxtaposed with a printed text. In the second, the videotape *Envisioner*, another image of Tom Sherman flashes between parts of a character-generated text that is excerpted from the soundtrack. The text is the same, "Tom Sherman" is the same, but now the artist looks straight towards us with eyes open. The two images oppose insight and authority; but as the text remains unchanged, the opposition breaks down as a vacillation of the same. We are made aware of the manipulation of the codes of realism in documentary and in "confessional," first-person texts, texts that operate on the basis of objectivity or sincerity established by reference to certain so-called referents of detail:

> To appear authentic in conversation or print I enrich each sentence I pronounce with a bit of general detail; perhaps I quote a number or tell a temperature or exaggerate the adversity of conditions affecting my body. For instance it burns my ass to hear people advertising their "1 of a kind" identities.[9]

In analysing all this work we do not have to accept traditional or critical categories that tend to autonomize the individual work of art. Instead, we can place these works in position against a referent and ask how each treats it. Do they reject, obscure, or direct us to it? For each of these cases we must go beyond the formal construction of the work—what is given and what is given institutional support. We must go beyond to understand what lack that reference or lack of referent is expressing.

For Michael Snow's self-referentiality, the referent never appears; it is not allowed in the concept. For General Idea, the referent is irremediably lost in a fetishized system of value; the "we" and the multiple images of the artists no longer even serve as indexes. The loss of the referent for them is no crisis as it is for Robin Collyer. He integrates the referent into sculptural work in the gallery in order to dispute the subjection over us outside the gallery of communications systems and representations. Andy Patton's subsequent work, which took over advertising formats, recognized that action, as constricted as it might be, can take place within convention. At least that is where it is directed against us. As for Tom Sherman, that referent must serve within a fictional enunciation for the purpose of communication and not for the dissemination of personality, as the death of the artist. For all, there are broader social and economic questions to ask about the loss of the referent and the struggle to regain it.

This analysis is not completely historical; it still refers to the present. Only the dynamics of the image have changed. The new painting or new expressionism restores this same subject to art. Its (coded) expressivity is a guarantee of the work's presence and immediacy; its gestures are the signature of the artist. But this painting restores itself and the subject at a more regressive level; objectivizing technique (the mechanical record of index) or the conventions of language have not intervened as in the work discussed above. These conditions alternately alienate the viewer from the work and refer him or her to something else. That is, they work for the viewer. Painting's expressivity, however, is completely institutionalized. It restores the most traditional image of the artist for the artist's and our consumption.

Notes

1.   Karl Marx, *Capital* (New York: International Publishers, 1967).

2.   Michael Snow quoted by Robert Fulford in Dennis Young, Robert Fulford, et al. *Michael Snow / A Survey* (Toronto: Art Gallery of Ontario, 1970).

3.   Ibid.

4.	General Idea, "Glamour Issue," *FILE*, vol. 3, no. 1 (Autumn 1975): 21.

5.	Roland Barthes, "Myth Today," *Mythologies*, trans. Annette Lavers (New York: Hill and Wang, 1972).

6.	General Idea, "1984, A Year in Pictures," *FILE*, vol. 4, no. 1 (Summer 1978): 38.

7.	General Idea, "Cornucopias" in Elke Town, *Fiction* (Toronto: Art Gallery of Ontario, 1982), n.p.

8.	Philip Monk, *Language and Representation* (Toronto: A Space, 1981), 12.

9.	Tom Sherman, from the videotape *Envisioner* (1978), *FILE*, vol. 3, no. 3 (Spring 1977): 54.

Johanne Lamoureux

Places and Commonplaces of the Picturesque

> Some naturalists suppose the act of ruminating, in animals, to be attended with more pleasure, than the act of grosser mastication. It may be so in travelling also. There may be more pleasure in recollecting, and recording, from a few transient lines, the scenes we have admired, than in the present enjoyment of them.
>
> William Gilpin

Phantoms

When I first began writing as a critic, it came back, all of it, streaming in from all directions—*representation, figuration, narration*. I could deal with these. Then *painting* and the *object*, and even the *tableau*, made their big return. I had read extensively on the topic of the *return*. I could see what a miraculous lifeline this "return" was that enabled a good many authors to keep writing while, at the same time, eluding not only questions about what actually resurfaced, but also and especially, other questions having to do with the modalities of such returns and their contingent character. Some authors panicked, said we had to put a stop to it; for them, it all came back as the Same. Others, and often the worst ones at that, were jubilant. They went so far as to claim that it had never really gone away or, paradoxically, in the same breath, that it was totally new, something completely unheard of. A few tried to pretend that it *really* had not come back at all; those were often the ones who had had the opportunity to initiate a different discourse just before that big return. They could just go on, outdoing themselves, spurred on in some way they didn't always acknowledge. I read what they had to say.

Recently, Thierry de Duve wrote this exacting yet consoling comment:

> It is one thing to go back over the past as an artist and a creator. It is yet another thing to go over it as an art historian. The second case demands an ethics. No more so than the artist is the art historian free of (or responsible for) the circumstances in which he finds himself. Should he decide that the art of his times is mediocre or decadent, he is at liberty to change professions, but not to condemn this art in the name of the past. History may not be progress, but it is irreversible;

This is a translation of a text first published in *Parachute*, no. 39 (1985).

failure to recognize this fact exposes one to all sorts of relapses. The art historian's responsibility is, then, to keep an eye on the work being done by artists around him. Such familiarity is necessary, just as it is necessary periodically to question it.[1]

Starting from this same familiarity which I find so problematic, I would like now to ask a somewhat dumb question. (Although it is a rhetorical question with a foregone conclusion, its repercussions are far-reaching.) Is painting now to be found uniquely and especially where we claim it has returned, where it is apostatized with such euphoria, that is, on the canvas, in a burgeoning, contagious iconography? For there is, after all, the current proliferation of painted objects, the whole crossover of disciplines. Theatrical, hybrid, multidisciplinary—there is no lack of predicates to apply to the situation. Yet when painting comes back as an actant within such strategies, can it still be isolated as painting? What would its ultimate reference point be? And would such referencing serve any purpose other than that of defending a plurality of disciplines, just as others serve to shore up an eclecticism of styles? In other words, how can we frame the question of the medium once it has been supposedly left behind? Is the question as irrelevant to postmodernism as some have claimed?[2]

I could also inscribe this set of questions within the context of my own theoretical interests, that is, relate it to assertions and concepts of late 1970s postmodern criticism, as they were formulated in conjunction with a new type of artistic production. I have in mind such texts as Rosalind Krauss's work on the photographic,[3] or on "sculpture in the expanded field." It is essential to ask at this point whether the strength of these texts, their relevance and effectiveness, are as incompatible as it seems with the so-called "return" of painting and the exhibitable object, with a resurgent interest in the realm of the iconic that is currently asserting itself in places where one had come to expect the indexical and the trace. Also, can we envisage such "returns" as occurring alongside, and independently of, any relation with these conceptual tools? Wouldn't it be just as simplistic to maintain this as to conceive their interrelations in terms of a cyclical reaction? The most dramatic aspect of this whole turn of events may well be the realization of the extent to which the old leitmotifs of art history have resurfaced in connection with such "returns." For again we are faced with the specificity of national styles, the sovereignty of heroic artists, the investigation of pictorial sources. ... We must not, however, conclude that this "defect" is inherent to the very practice of painting.

Should we not, instead, entertain the possibility that the return of painting may have also marked or reworked installation and its indexical character; that conceptual tools developed in connection with disciplines other than painting (in its hegemonic modernist phase) may now be pressed into service on its behalf; finally, that these tools, as well as our definition of painting, may have, in turn, been modified? How is it possible to respond to these questions without falling back on reductivist historicism or throwing up our hands before some supposed incommensurable novelty? I propose to negotiate between these extremes by returning to the picturesque, to what was originally intended by the term, to its aporias, its failures and changes of meaning; for certain of its shifts and setbacks are instrumental for an understanding of our own, insofar as the picturesque is already *painting working beyond itself.* Thus we shall have to study painting in its intersection with sites—that is, in installation—and see how this encounter brings about a grasp of installation after the "photographic." At the core of such a relationship there is already a "category" lying in wait for the theoretician, one which is, as it were, a model category (as well as being the category of the model). Here it is the picturesque, conceived as a site-compatible practice and understood, etymologically at least, as having a filiation with painting; yet within it can be found a tangle of other competing traditions which include architecture, landscape gardening, poetry, and sculpture. I would like to devote some time to this topic, taking upon myself those quandaries that arose immediately upon the term's formulation in the aesthetic theory of the eighteenth century and studying those operations by which contemporary critical discourse seems to portray the pictorial dimension of the picturesque as, once again, inadmissible, something to be sidestepped. At the end of our excursion I will gauge, albeit in too cursory a fashion, the picture effects produced by a number of installations visited in Montréal. To this end, a number of observations arising from our inquiry will be used to shed light on problematic aspects of the works in question.

Common/places of the Picturesque

Writing on the site-specific before the critical import of this concept was trivialized by certain art practices into just one more convention among others, Robert Smithson[4] brilliantly evoked the fate of the picturesque since the eighteenth century:

> A tree, for example, struck by lightning was something other than merely beautiful or sublime—it was "picturesque." This word in its own way has been struck by lightning over the centuries. Words, like trees, can be suddenly deformed or wrecked, but such deformation or wreckage cannot be dismissed by timid academics.[5]

Aside from the power of Smithson's imagery, his remark illustrates a logical operation that recurs in the discourse of the picturesque, one that heralds the term's fate as aporia:[6] the tree struck by lightning is picturesque, and the picturesque is a tree struck by lightning. Now Smithson is not content to reiterate the circularity that has plagued the picturesque from its very first formulation; rather, he implicitly connects this circularity with the fact that the picturesque constitutes something like an "other" category, a category for the other [*une catégorie "autre"*]. It would qualify, as will be seen, as a supplementary category; that is, it is a category *de trop* but, without it aesthetic experience would have remained, in a literal sense, unthinkable. It seems to me that the "wreckage" of this term was not at all the work of a thunderbolt; quite the contrary, it was partly a consequence of the term's failure to sustain a distinct meaning, and of its capacity to assume so many shades of meaning that its conceptual usefulness was undermined, and it inadvertently became something quite commonplace. Now this was a singularly ironic development since, in its heyday, the picturesque was defined as the opposite of "common." Once trivialized, however, it was bound to fall into disuse. Submerged in a theory of definitions, it lost whatever value it once had.

The picturesque emerged as a preoccupation in the aesthetic theory of the eighteenth century, a period that witnessed an inflation of the coefficient of values of painting in Great Britain. It is, then, inextricably linked to the notion of *painting as value(s)*, especially if *value* here retains its original pictorial connotations.[7] (This connection tends to be too readily forgotten whenever the picturesque is reformulated in light of the present critical juncture of postmodernism.) But as Marie-Madeleine Martinet aptly reminds us in her *Art et Nature en Grande Bretagne au XVIIIe siècle*:

> In order to suggest increasingly complex visual and imaginative experiences, principles of optics originally employed in painting were applied to landscape gardening. ... In addition to linear perspective, atmospheric perspective assumed ever greater importance.[8]

If it is now quite a common practice to recount the terminological crossovers[9] occasioned by inquiries into the origin of the word *picturesque*, one need only hear the term first in Italian to be convinced of its grounding relationship with colour, with colour as (back)ground [*ses rapports de fond avec la couleur, avec la couleur comme fond*]. The following passage, dated 1805, comes from Richard Payne Knight, who has given us the most concise and refined formulation of the picturesque:

> Such are the objects and compositions of objects, which we properly call picturesque; and we find that the style of painting, which distinguished them as such, was invented by Georgione about the beginning, and perfected by Titian about the middle of the sixteenth century;

soon after which the word made its first appearance in the Italian, and, I believe, in any language.[10]

Well before the English and French sought to carve out an aesthetic category from it, *pittoresco* in Italian meant "in the manner of a painter" *pittore*. Translated, it took on a host of often contradictory definitions, among which we find such nuances as "*painterly* effect" (the medium) and "*picture* effect" (the apparatus rather than the object *per se*). This plurality is important for an understanding of contemporary artistic production. Knight's historicist explanation evokes the Venetian school's way of blending and melting together ("massing") hair, leaves and stones, a practice that conferred upon them a "playful and airy kind of lightness, and a sort of loose and sketchy indistinctness not observable in reality, unless under peculiar circumstances and modifications of the atmosphere."[11] This improvement upon reality, achieved by the landscape painted behind the allegories and *storie*, is precisely what Nature, drawing upon theories such as that of the picturesque garden, sought to appropriate in order to commend itself to painting through the practised eye of the *traveller/connoisseur*. Thus at its very source the picturesque would be a supplementary or background effect, as well as an effect of distance that creeps up and seizes upon the whole countryside.

This said, the conception of the picturesque garden imposes problems of a scenographic nature.[12] In *An Essay on Landscape*,[13] the Marquis de Girardin, owner and designer of the Ermenonville Gardens, underscores the necessity of composing the garden on the basis of the site itself, of what it has to offer, instead of reducing it to the flat geometry of the French model. But respect for the nature of the site requires that the garden form a harmonious whole with the surrounding countryside, with the panorama extending beyond the grounds and walls. (Thus the ha-ha, a sort of negative fence sunk in a trench, or even just a trench by itself, would come to take the place of garden walls.) The vantage points from which the garden develops are also determined on the basis of the background, of what lies outside the garden proper, and the designer's skill consists entirely in correlating this background, this "backdrop," with the different parts of the garden via successive planes which Girardin calls "side scenes" [*coulisses*]. The model invoked here is Serlio's set design for the satiric theatre, the entire technical merit of which involved recreating a pictorial illusion by correlating a backdrop[14] with actual structures that receded in size and distance along an inclined plane.

A three-dimensional painting was constructed out from a backdrop. While the risk of destroying the illusion pushed the actor to the front edge of the stage and condemned Serlio's space to emptiness,[15] the picturesque garden was designed with a *flâneur* in mind. Now this conception was to have its share of problems since, although the garden ostensibly called for a stroller, it apparently also *still sought to produce the effect of "tableaux."*[16]

For Girardin, the site is a "canvas"[17] to be worked up from a sketch, resulting in a *tableau visitable* as opposed to a *tableau vivant.*[18] Ultimately, the stroller in a picturesque garden is neither "consumed" nor absorbed[19] by the painting, but makes his way from one of the many viewpoints to the next; it is exactly as if he were *in a museum*, but walking *behind the frames*. Girardin:

> Having now with our eyes travelled over the general design, let us walk over the detached parts. We must seek for them behind the frame of the great landscape; they are, as it were, little easel pictures in a gallery, which we are going to examine, after having for a long time considered the capital piece in the school.[20]

This takes us back to the conditions required for the formulation of the picturesque. If the word were originally meant to convey an effect of colour in painting (the role of intensity in the shimmering atmospherics of the Venetian school), the emergence of the picturesque as an aesthetic concept was bound up with a context (eighteenth-century Great Britain) in which an unprecedented value was attributed to painting. Its value at this juncture was, however, aesthetic (painting's unparalleled significance, its sudden status as an authoritative cultural referent) and consequently economic—"painting of value" implied the value of painting. (This conjunction of aesthetic promotion with the marketplace is a factor whose connection with the current "return" of painting cannot be denied.)

It goes without saying that this sudden delight in Nature and landscape through painting presumed growing familiarity on the part of an élite (or those who styled themselves as such) with certain kinds of pictorial production. For this, models were needed. As Elizabeth Manwaring[21] has shown, this familiarity was recent. It derived from artistic pilgrimages to Italy (to Rome initially, thence to Naples and the region's archaeological sites), from the trade in prints and engravings, and from the building up of private collections of paintings. Thus one could say that the picturesque establishes a practice of artistic and particularly pictorial recognition, that it sets in motion a complex set of relationships between the copy and the model.[22] With the picturesque, the experience of Nature—a Nature, however, "selected" and improved upon by the pictorial conventions of landscape painting—partakes of the domain of the aestheticizable. The finest sites are those where Nature surpasses herself and where, becoming more natural than Nature herself, she paradoxically enables viewers to recognize a Claude Lorrain, Salvator Rosa, or Nicolas Poussin—or, stranger still, an ineffable and inimitable amalgam of all three. These painters are in turn appreciated insofar as, in them, one recognizes an ennobled Nature *and inasmuch as they too (through their compositions, motifs, themes, etc.) are recognized as being both inimitable and reproducible.* It would be impossible to overstate the difficulties occasioned by the circularity of the picturesque and the contradictions bound up with it. Thus the picturesque can simultaneously designate what pertains to or reminds one of painting (Nature copies painting) as well as what is worthy of being painted (painting copies Nature)—on the basis, that is, of criteria made possible only by dissimulating the artifice existing on both sides. Likewise, the picturesque implies a singular character, an original, remarkable quality that, however striking, demands to be recalled and recognized. It is the nodal point of the original and the *déjà-vu*; what is more, it is the juncture that establishes their undecidable character, undermining the question of original and copy, rendering it moot. On the principle that one cannot assign an origin to a circle, the undecidable is more crucial here, given the circular operation of the picturesque, than it could ever be for photography (even today's photography) because the latter's reproducibility has little impact upon our referential prejudices. While it does not come right out and say that there is no such thing as an original, the picturesque attempts to apprehend the impossibility of having immediate and direct access to it, and it accomplishes this by interposing the relay of painting. (Rosalind Krauss has given us a penetrating analysis of this process in the work of Gilpin, leaving aside, however, the role and obvious contribution of painting to this state of affairs.) This situation sheds light on the contradictions of the Ermenonville Gardens, at whose entrance one could read: "Away with ye, exquisite sites, where all falls victim to art" [*Disparaissez, lieux superbes où tout est victime de l'art*].[23] Meanwhile, the proprietor of the gardens, the Marquis de Girardin, wrote in his treatise:

> … whilst poets and painters of every age have made the most touching pictures of nature, its beauty and simplicity, it is surprising that some one man of good understanding (for it is upon understanding that taste depends) should not have endeavoured to realize the descriptions and enchanting scenes which they all felt …[24]

To which he hastens to add (in the process reversing the order of priority governing models and copies) that his art of gardens "is to poetry and painting, what reality is to description, what the original is to the copy."[25]

In-citations

It may be that our postmodern "sensibility" is too easily seduced by such undecidability. Perhaps it would be better first to pinpoint the qualities and effects it has helped to produce, instead of going straight into raptures over how eloquent it is with respect to, or what it has in common with, our situation—even though this is the context in which it will invariably "speak" to us. For the picturesque does not give rise, in any true or essential manner, to citations of actual, specific pictures; only rarely is a known work taken up in its entirety. And, as far as we are concerned, the "realization" of pictures, in the sense in which Girardin used the word, is neither the most immediate nor the most notable consequence of the picturesque. Of course, in Girardin's *Tour of Ermenonville* one frequently comes across passages such as the following: "This snaking and sombre path leads to a site laid out in the Italian manner; it presents us with a painting composed exactly in the style of Robert."[26] (The reference is to Hubert Robert (1733–1808), a painter of ruins who drew his inspiration mainly from Roman Antiquity, and who collaborated with Girardin on the composition of the Ermenonville Gardens.) From this passage we can understand how the picturesque was able to function as a "label" that cut across genres, as a sort of *stylistic dispatcher* which made it possible to regulate aesthetic experience by classifying, on the basis of genre, scenes "selected" from Nature. Expressions such as "in the genre of" and "in the style of" convey the idea. But there was never any question of deception.[27] Rather, it was a matter of bolstering the new practice of discriminating on the basis of style, of reducing the artist's name to a given motif in which he could be recognized, of extending the scope of the motif to encompass everything (themes, palette, composition, etc.) susceptible of being recognized or transposed. Thus citing actual pictures would have been only a stratagem, a detour in what was really a vast endeavour to learn and to incite others to take up the discourse on art and painting—the latter understood both as a field and as individual objects. It is no coincidence that the practice of art criticism, as we know it, emerged at the same time as the picturesque. The picturesque is, therefore, historically speaking, one of those operators through which we have learned to speak of painting. In order to have a better understanding of what was at stake in this nascent terminology of art—art history as we know it today had not yet "taken place"—and to gauge more accurately the extent to which we are still in its power, we must try to determine the issues that shaped the early discourse of the picturesque.

Theories

To say that the picturesque is also important as an incitement to discourse is to bring about a shift in the "literary" role of the concept[28]—traditionally understood as the presence, within a site, of a programme of commemorative inscriptions, of compositional analogies following the rules of poetry. It is also to reveal the real interest and the *contemporary value* which was accrued to the term the moment it was formulated, to refuse to limit it to an obsession with the preservation of cultural memory. Everything would be much clearer if only we could strike an agreement about what this incitement to discourse really consisted of, what it produced. No sooner was the term formulated than it shifted meanings, and such shifts now stand in the way of our understanding. Let us hope that they also spur us on. The picturesque, it is said, was so long in attaining any stability that, by the time it did, it had already relinquished its use value and its distinction as one of the aesthetic terms of a particular period. Yet it will be understood how *this very time lag* could be efficacious—if one of the functions of the picturesque was as an operator of art discourse. However, this potential efficacy cannot be envisaged *in abstracto*; we must show how, and to what, the discourse was applied. The aesthetic discourse of the picturesque was largely the work of three authors: William Gilpin, Uvedale Price, and Richard Payne Knight. For lack of space, I will confine my attention to Gilpin and Knight, although Price's contribution represents a highly influential intermediate step.

Gilpin's texts, which kept coming back to the picturesque for nearly twenty-five years, positively ooze with good intentions. His project, with its considerable number of setbacks and contradictions, belongs to the increase in aesthetic commentary provoked by Burke's *A Philosophical Enquiry into the Origin of Our Ideas of the Sublime and Beautiful* (1757–1759). In his desire to supplement Burke's framework with the specific category of the picturesque, Gilpin soon realized that he needed to question the division into the Sublime and the Beautiful, to improve on it using a different category, a difficult and untenable one insofar as it was shaped by the constraint of having to follow in Burke's tracks and had, therefore, the task of *naming what was left over*. But what precisely did this quantity consist of? Was the picturesque to be a category covering what was neither Beautiful nor Sublime? Or was it not, rather, a "different" quality, another order, one that was *otherwise* worthy to represent "objects" already understood to be beautiful or sublime? For this reason we say, paraphrasing Smithson, that the ideal or "typical" figure of the picturesque is not the tree hit by lightning, but the ruins,[29] broken down architecture—or more precisely, the operation in which this "opening up," this loss of integrity of the fractured building is once more taken up in a recognizable and meaningful shape.

Of course the failure of Gilpin's formulation is due to his persistence in conceiving the picturesque as a quality of the object or scene, in proposing a workable (identifiable) inventory of objects and compositions deemed to be picturesque, that is, worthy, after considerable improvement, of being painted. The picturesque is, therefore, a code for the reproducible, a perpetually imperfect recipe for both painting and the discourse on painting. Its repertory would include ruins, waterfalls, fowl with ruffled plumage, shaggy animals, and sheer cliffs. The irony here is that this unassignable quality pertains to a characterization of limits. The picturesque object is rough and edgy. It has broken outlines and uneven surfaces that resist any effort to impose fixed boundaries. We have to wait for Knight's poem[30] in order to see the picturesque reformulated as a *mode of vision* severed from the contemplated object and reassigned to the eye blessed with the privilege of a culturally heightened gaze. At least this is what critics are now saying. But starting with Gilpin, this shift from the object to the subject is already programmed in advance. The roughness of the object—which is opposed to the smoothness and the conventional character of the Beautiful, to what Winckelmann would have called its insipidness—is only a pretext for foregrounding the execution. It directs the painter's touch and produces a roughness, a picturesque fashioning of the *surface* itself. The object *dictates* a "manner," naturalizes it, grounds it in nature. It acts in such a way that the effects produced by painting (what we have since called the "painterly") in no way opacify the referent but present it to us in its specific capacity as a picturesque object. The picturesque contains (and curbs) the germ of a discourse on the trace considered as antimannerist, on painterly rendering as it is rooted in the object instead of in artifices of style or the whims of the painter. The brushstrokes, the feverishness of the execution, are pledges of fidelity to the "great original" and lie at the heart of fantasies about the reconciliation of nature and artifice. In Gilpin we clearly witness the picturesque setting the stage for the Romantic shift from art as imitation to art as expression.[31] This implies that, from its inception, the picturesque confronts the subject and object with each other. (The subject here is still an author/subject, an enunciator, since Gilpin addresses himself to those who wish to recognize a scene in order to rework and transpose it.) The picturesque enables such a subject to leave marks as long as they attest to his own transparency as speaker and let themselves be interpreted as traces of some quality of the object.

When Knight relocates the seat of the picturesque in the subject, he sees the latter as enunciatee and makes reference to the context of reception instead of to that of emission. For him, the picturesque no longer alludes to what will be painted but to what is reminiscent of painting. He confirms the relevance of a repertory of picturesque objects, with the proviso that the *investment* of these objects with such a quality is owing to a series of cultural reflexes and assumptions originating with a subject/observer. Although it is generally considered *de rigueur* to recount this chapter in the life of the picturesque every time the concept comes up, the coincidence of this phase with the term's "decline," and especially with the issues that later strangled modernism, has not been fully understood. In *Art and Objecthood* [32] Michael Fried rejected minimalist sculpture because it postulated the work as a literal object, made it an element of the viewer's experience and contravened modernist conventions of artistic autonomy—understood ideally as pictorial. More recently, with respect to the period that concerns us here, he substituted Diderot for Greenberg as the champion of painting's incipient autonomy. Once again, this autonomy was deployed through a series of strategies that denied (devoured, absorbed) the viewer, who was considered to be an inadmissible subject. If more space were available here, we could look into how the picturesque essentially runs counter to this denial of the viewer and how it has been repressed for this by modernism. On this point, one could read the discerning analysis of Yve-Alain Bois. Still, it seems that, in speaking of Serra's work, Bois himself tries to suppress the pictorial dimension of the picturesque. But I would affirm that it is precisely this feature that is at work in contemporary installation, or at least in one of its paradigms.

Between Book and Mirror

In conjunction with the incipient pragmatism of Knight's book—a pragmatic view slated to be stifled—consideration must also be given to the way that the picturesque orchestrates a final shift between metonymic and metaphoric modes of experience. The location or detection by a "sensitive," "trained" eye of picture effects or a pictorial quality in Nature is a cultural habit which undoubtedly has its origins in the aspirations of a given class. By definition, this practice has recourse to a frame, requires the recognition of those vantage points on the basis of which one begins to detect the first faint outlines of a sort of virtual frame or border around the site. It is akin to the practice of taking samples. From the very beginning, the experience of the picturesque has echoed its metonymic origins in that precious instrument, the "Claude glass."

No one knows exactly how this mirror was used, since its use was bound up with the picturesque as an experience, and with that experience as it offered painting the literal embodiment it sought [*et de l'expérience comme ce en quoi la peinture essaie de prendre (le) corps, faire corps avec l'espace*]. We know that several types of these mirrors existed. Ever alert to the contingencies of the weather, Gilpin recommends two mirrors, one on a dark foil for sunny days and another on a silvered foil for when it was overcast. Thus one had the pleasure not only of isolating a fragment of nature, but also of enjoying its soft tones, its pictorial quality and colour modulations—in short, those supplemental painterly effects the mirror conferred on the scene, especially on elements such as foliage. Carried in a small case which, sigificantly, opened like a pocketbook, the Claude glass was used for selecting the best views of Nature. Elizabeth Manwaring[33] tells of a gentleman who, having fallen with his glass in his hands, is delighted to find his precious visual prosthesis still intact and himself with only a few broken knuckles! This anecdote is undeniably a good illustration of the importance attributed to this specular device in the experience of the picturesque; yet I, for my part, am struck by the way the fall of this noble personage (aside from being the acme of picturesqueness) embodies the implications of this practice. Fascinated by the glass, by its portable frame and range of soft tones, the picturesque *flâneur* can no longer see where he is going. Oblivious to those very irregularities [*accidents*] of terrain that go to make up the picturesque, he loses sight of the site and can only manage to enjoy the view within the closed circuit of his precious bookish gadget.

One must therefore understand that the aestheticization of Nature had a twofold and paradoxical effect: it simultaneously *extolled* and *negated* the site on behalf of what served to mediatize it, in the process using the apparatus proper to painting. By the same token, however, this recourse to the Claude glass, with all that this implies in the way of references ranging from Brunelleschi's *tavoletta* to the *camera lucida*, accentuates the indexical structure that lies at the core of the picturesque—and perhaps of painting itself, according to what Philippe Dubois has written about its origin.[34] But then this whole facet of the picturesque falls under the category of metonymy. Knight, for his part, thrusts the experience of the picturesque into the realm of metaphor when he anchors it in the viewer. For him, Nature recognized as painting is but a step that serves to kindle the imagination. The value of the picturesque experience resides in the fact that it stirs up "trains of conceptions" which it then reworks, modifies, and reorganizes. In contemporary terms, the picturesque experience is not very literary for Knight; it makes the stroller think, recount, and feel, and it produces something akin to what René Payant shrewdly refers to as the *narration effect*.[35]

Hung Up

But how does all this relate to what we see around us today? Does it simply imply that no real change has occurred; must we fall back on an old historicist reflex, try to show that recent installations reflect the same thought processes as the gardens of bygone years? I certainly hope not. But let us backtrack a bit. More so than the category which I seem to have presented it as—in the process echoing the vocabulary of the eighteenth century—the picturesque appears to have functioned as an operator that was under the sway of the pictorial ("a sort of loose and sketchy indistinctness not observable in … reality") but which, nonetheless, made the foregrounding of the photographic and the indexical qualities of painting the condition of access to this supplementary effect [*effet-en-plus*]. In terms reminiscent of Smithson, it will be said that the concept of the picturesque, like this "quality" it originally sought to name, has always tended to be thought of as superfluous. In each phase of its development, from its formulation to its failure, it has only had the *appearance* of a pivotal concept. In the final analysis, it adds to issues without necessarily clarifying them, satisfied, as it were, with simply redistributing them or stringing them together in new ways. Thus it aspires to superimpose itself on the Sublime and the Beautiful in order, finally, to transcend them; it makes it increasingly difficult for us to decide which comes first, copy or model; it institutes a shift from the plane of imitation to that of expression; it glides from pictorial citation to an incitement to discourse; it diverts a praxis of the metonymic gaze towards a reactivation of metaphoric processes (Knight's "trains of conceptions"). Finally, it makes room for a pragmatic dimension within aesthetics.

Not only does the picturesque operate via this superfluity effect, but it can also be thought of in terms of a background effect. Paradoxically, it is as a "site-compatible practice"[36] that the picturesque is most intimately bound up with painting, dependent on painting's *mobility* and potential for displacement. Mobility here exists on two levels. First, it pertains to what can be found in paintings, to such features as Poussin's style, Lorrain's seaports, or the bandits of Salvator Rosa. Already, objects, motifs, and styles are thrown together and levelled in the picturesque's shift from art to Nature. But the most decisive mobility, the one most likely to be found behind pictorial citations, is that which belongs strictly to painting, to individual pictures with their frames and the wires strung across the back of the stretchers. This too belongs among the picturesque's citations; for the latter include not only what we find *in* paintings, but also the picture as an apparatus, a "mode of presentation" that binds things in a whole. The picturesque is a matter of pictorial liaison; better still, it is the cohesiveness of elements with a background and among themselves. That is why the picturesque, as Girardin's title suggests, cannot dodge the question of composition. And this is all the more problematic, as are the dominant characteristics of the picturesque, according to Uvedale Price. One must acknowledge this specific dimension in order to hear Girardin's French expression of *tableau pittoresque*, as something other than a mere pleonasm. For in *one* of its pictorial modes the picturesque strives to compose *tableaux* independently of what is cited, and the ambition of the picturesque garden is ideally to hold these separate pictures together. In this project the picturesque, as a site-compatible practice, is articulated on the picturesque as a mode of vision. Thus we come to sense the importance, as well as the acutely problematic nature, of the *flâneur* or stroller. For to this figure falls the task of crystallizing or dissolving *tableaux*; moreover, by his meandering he plots the difficult question of their relationships, their chains, and arabesques, what Hubert Damisch[37] would call the "system between pictures." Given the current crisis of forceful, individualistic systems, of "master narratives" and clear-cut categories, it should come as no surprise that the picturesque is still highly relevant today.

Just as painting cites motifs and styles, installation today would cite painting, that is, cite it insofar as it offers, by virtue of its interpictoriality, an apparatus that quotes and, by virtue of its *faire tableau*, a mode of organization. But what works are we talking about here? What do I have in mind when I talk about picturesque work at the heart of current practice? The "repertory," it seems, would be vast and not necessarily homogeneous. I will deal with it only briefly for the time being. I believe that the expression was initially suggested to me by "hangings" rather than by works, especially insofar as the picturesque implies a composition, an ensemble, a desire to arrange works in *tableaux* [*faire tableau avec des œuvres*], to have them work with or against each other instead of leaving them to be individual, irreducible pieces. To my mind, the best example of this was *Hypothétiques confluences* (Montréal, 1983), while the worst was *Von Hier Aus* (Düsseldorf, 1984). From the outset, the question of the picturesque was bound up with the question of a design (as both pattern and intention). In the first instance, the hanging generated meaning by reiterating a series of hypothetical, unverified propositions; in the second, it masked an inability to harbour any kind of *design* whatsoever, and strove to attain cohesiveness by means of the décor. Intermediate to these,

Montréal tout-terrain (1984) deserves special status since, on this occasion, the artists themselves chose spaces which they were relatively free to treat as they saw fit. The way space was broken down often seemed to reflect an interest in whatever anecdotal value it might have, or else it displayed a curious indifference to the context. These, we would say, represent the two poles of picturesque installation, a continuum that it would be more advisable to modulate than to oppose.

To fully grasp the possibility of picturesque installations, we must briefly take into account the site-specific relationships recently developed by painting itself. (However, the works that concern me here are those that show installation inflected by painting and the picturesque, displaying a certain mode of inscription within the site, with the place as background, with its specific architecture.) In the first case, we would have to consider the *immobility* of painted works owing to: (a) their fragility (due to the medium or shape) or the contingencies of presentation; (b) their use of the wall as an interval instead of a background, as the connective principle for disparate elements held together only by their joint display; (c) most radical of all, their claim to space in its entirety, a claim grounded in the relationship established between the placement of a painted object and what it represents. As examples of such contextualization we may take Joseph Branco's *Natures mortes* (Motivation V, 1984) and Galerie Jolliet, 1985) and the work of Sylvie Bouchard (Powerhouse, 1983). This pictorial work summons up and conquers space, reifies it, as it were; via this seizure, it intrudes upon our status as *flâneurs* and obliges us to cast about for some kind of re/pose. (A more in-depth analysis of this type of work would in turn require that it be situated with respect to the modes of presentation of what have recently come to be designated "unassimilatable" objects.[38]

No more so than these site-specific paintings does picturesque installation, as I would define it, constitute a cluster of homogeneous works; rather, I would reserve the name only for works that use certain features of the site. Before all else, however, picturesque installation seems to me to originate at that point where "obligatory" interest in the extramuseological site becomes quite commonplace, prompting artists to exploit it in new and inventive ways. Remember that installation, at least the kind that followed minimalism, was originally the flip side of an "incurable" (i.e., "not amenable to museological conservation") desire.[39] Consequently, its taking into account of the site implied a refusal to be *transplanted.* In its resistance to institutional space, installation—like Girardin's picturesque garden, that "gallery of little easel pictures"—took it upon itself to be both work and context. Whence the habit of inscribing a site with a whole series of contingent and indexical marks, using, for the purpose, strategies associated with the work of the trace which Rosalind Krauss has labelled as the "photographic."

Darkrooms, Rooms for Rent

In the text that accompanied her *Golden Gates* exhibition in March 1984, Eva Brandl clearly expressed her relative indifference to the site. The work, she said, could just as well have been elsewhere. But the luxury of debate was denied,[40] as the installation was visible only after nightfall when the site vanished, as it were, into darkness. This installation, whose themes of travel, departure, and "gateways" were so resonant, was transportable, "detachable." Yet the night's obliteration of the context alone made this point obvious. What was really behind this secreting away [*mise au secret*] of the site? How did the "blackout" in the installation function? Anyone who visited *Golden Gates* would have a hard time reducing the role of the darkness to a pure and simple negation of the site—unless, of course, what they saw there was a positive negation, a denegation, an exacerbated refusal in which could be heard the admission, the unconscious acknowledgement, of resistance. While it is clear that the installation did not directly orchestrate the marking or display of the site, it did order an ensemble in which the site *revealed* more than it hid—just as a black background is said to project images forward and bestow greater visual acuity on objects. But the comparison lacks precision. The blackness in question was also a "hazy" one that was initially disorienting and confusing. As Chantal Boulanger pertinently observed,[41] by paring each element away from its context the darkness made it imperative (and difficult) to grasp the relationships of the elements among themselves. These relationships could very well have been rooted in the iconic since the strangeness of the installation stemmed from velleities of *figuration within the space* and not from any inscription or inflection of the site. On the plastic level, the fragmentary elements of the piece all shared a concern with various states of light and reflection, a concern that linked them to the condition of visibility of the site: shimmering, nebulous material, projections, luminous objects radiating or temporarily catching light, each island emerging from the darkness with a distinct quotient of intelligibility and legibility, indissociable from the site despite the latter's "depersonalization" by the blackout. ("Emerging" here means *still in the dark*, not standing out against it.) On the one hand, the black we have here is *connective*, atmospherical, a sort of chiaroscuro, capturing and binding the "constellation" of objects together. On the other hand, it is *connected* inasmuch as, *like the objects* in the installation, its dark quality embodies a modality or state of the absence of light [*(non)-lumière*]. This complex use of black functions not only as a (photographic) capture of each element *but also* as a reification of space, of space as an object among the others it connects. These functions may go unnoticed due to the pragmatic consequences the blackout has for our visit of the site. The darkness privatizes one's path through the work and extols that quality some would call oneiric but which we here consider metaphorical. In other words, association[42] provides the key to it insofar as each element, because of its connotations as a fragment, exemplifies the gaps in the installation's narrative rather than its cumulative "exposé."

I believe that the first "black" ever to pose a problem for me was one I experienced at Lyne Lapointe's *Caserne #14* in January 1983. At the outset, nothing in this near-heroic installation was more natural than its obligatory darkness—the city of Montréal had temporarily relinquished this abandoned fire station to the artist on condition that it remain without electricity. More than just one aspect of the site, this feature dovetailed with one of the challenges animating the project's socio-political programme, namely, its rejection of cultural institutions. Upon entering the station, visitors were informed by the artist that they could have a guided tour if they wished. Although I am not particularly fond of package tours, I went along with the idea. I didn't see a thing; the stairs were treacherous, and it was freezing. Lapointe had a lot to say, so much in fact that I was surprised an installation could require so much narration. In the shower stalls on the second floor, there was soot on the walls. Lapointe explained that this commemorated the return to the station, and the subsequent ablutions, of firemen blackened by smoke. She had *put the soot back* herself. At the time it occurred to me that this both was and was not a trace—call it a false trace (just as, in the eighteenth century, one might speak of false ruins). It was, then, a figurative trace, an *icon of an index.* The indexical inscription of the site was either an illusion—I could very well have taken it for the "real" thing and not noticed it, not retained it as a significant characteristic of the installation—or it required interpretive decoding. Thus the index had been reinvested, if not with pathos, then at least with *affect.* And this kind of interest in the "affective depreciation" [*désaffection*] of a site, the loss of attachment to it, betrays the resurgence of the picturesque.[43] The significance of the trace resided not so much in its contiguity with the *corpus delicti*, nor in its actualization of the site; rather, it lay in the chain of associations generated in the observer, who would then use this chain to reinvest the trace with an affective dimension. Thus the soot ultimately referred neither to smoke nor to firemen's bodies, but to the poor, courageous, and heroic fireman. The trace led us towards its possible connotations, instead of to what it denoted.

Since that time, the works of Lyne Lapointe (*Musée des Sciences,* 1984, with Martha Fleming and Monique Jean) have made us aware of the symbolic nature of their relationships with the site, however closely bound up with the indexical their strategies and images may be. When they appropriated a former post office as an exhibition site, they diverted the building's original functions of categorizing and distributing mail in order to symbolize the same operations within repressive medical discourse. This way of drawing upon the specificity of an appropriated site, of using features other than the properly architectural, takes us beyond the purely indexical. It begins by situating the *power* of the place (and of the installation) outside relations of contiguity with the material conditions of the site; taking another route, it foregrounds physical features which need not have anything to do with the original function behind the key metaphor. Thus the particular arrangements the artists carried out in the corridor or in certain closet spaces of this installation, as well as the presence of darkrooms, had nothing to do with the fact that the building was formerly a post office—although several of the interventions did eloquently appropriate the building's architectural potential for the overall project.

The site's original function was more obviously determining for the work in *Caserne #14,* where it provided a narrative framework for the whole. The appropriation of space and distribution of interventions, as well as the selection and presentation of actual working procedures, were all determined by the partitioning of the station into dormitory, showers, kitchen, captain's quarters, etc. The layout prompted Lyne Lapointe to follow the existing syntagmatic breakdown—useful for domesticating the disarming obscurity—with its attendant connotations of nostalgia in the dormitories, heroism in the showers, and disapproval in the kitchen (a pinup inside a cupboard door) or in the more comfortable captain's quarters. The given breakdown of rooms structured *Caserne #14* like a series of *tableaux* that were apparent through their emergence (as rooms "framed" and often poorly illuminated by makeshift means) and were latent with meaning—that content the "guide" made up for by translating architectural structure into a narrative structure, inserting a "Claude glass" into a "pocketbook," and metonymy into metaphor. A parting peek under the hood of the *camera obscura* downstairs provided ample justification for seeing it not only as an instrument for sampling or carving up the Real but also as an image of the role of architectural partitioning in the apprehension and capture of the site, as well as in its insertion in discourse. Inside this black box, this metaphor of the supposedly metonymic character of installation, the photographic, as a mode of appropriation of the Real and as a postmodern label for the index, revealed itself as *also* an object, a figurative object translated into narrative.

In recent Montréal installations, rooms seem to function on two levels. On the one hand, they serve to scan or to fragment an itinerary, "fixing" various of its points in successive *tableaux* made inevitable by spatial constraints and arbitrary by adherence to existing layouts. Used in this way, rooms reveal a shift in interest away from vast anonymous fields towards places of greater intimacy, places whose appeal outstrips the functions of articulating (dismembering the viewer's totalizing perceptual apparatus, composing and complexifying the experience of the itinerary) and being articulated. In the installation that Pierre Dorion and Claude Simard executed on Clark Street in the winter of 1983, the layout of rooms "scanned" the relationship between painting and architecture, a relationship that, through this encounter, seemed to reiterate the question of figure and ground originally raised in their strictly pictorial work. The proliferation of figurative imagery in this exhibition led to questions regarding the background it hid. Did this ground consist of the paper sheets, or the wall next to them? Did the proliferation of figures succeed in making us forget the paper only insofar as the paper enabled it to underscore how its exuberant play submitted to those very architectural constraints it was meant to accentuate? For these "propagating" figures were entirely dependent for their organization on the architecture they invaded; once marketed, they could be bought by the metre. But what could possibly induce one to buy them? Could one do so without exposing the contradiction involved in producing work that, at one and the same time, exhibits some quotable motifs and an all-over lay-out. By definition, the act of recognition and the emergence of specific motifs run counter to the abolition of the figure/ground distinction and the principle of nonhierarchical composition, both underpinnings of the all-over. Are we to understand that the concept of all-over was cited here in the same way as Matisse or Gauguin, i.e., as something "in the style of"? The apparent all-over treatment—reduced and transposed, paradoxically, into a figure—would thus also be part of the quotable content and would not function as a principle of composition; or rather, it would do so only as a dominant figure against an architectural ground (constituted by the breakdown of rooms) which organized and compartmentalized the overall piece. While rooms cannot be reduced to the order of the quotable [*l'ordre de la citation*], they possess a similar mediating function. They orient us in our exploration of sites, by the measured temporality they bring to the itinerary and by the hold they exercise on the viewer through their relative closure; for, faced with an onslaught of images, a room will maintain, indeed impose, its own character. And again this is bound up with the room's original role within the series of domestic functions one finds in a standard apartment of this kind. This role (or value) will be discernible in variations of scale and types of annexes (cupboards, etc.), as well as in a certain *decorum* conveyed by means of the linoleum motifs and the resistant quality of certain household objects such as bathtubs.

Because of these marks, the rooms fall back on their internal structures rather than set themselves up as series of paintings. Indeed, the anecdotal character of such marks is what enables rooms to take on a certain narrative quality and a range of familiar and, in this case, familial connotations. Here the painter's task is to make the most of all the domestic accidents of architecture, to devour them through painting. Thus assimilated, these elements would appear to run counter to the process of articulating rooms; no longer underlying or composing fields for painting, they would tend, rather, to superimpose themselves on it. Painting would then appear to be caught between two ways of using the site, between structure and ornament; it would also seem to signify itself as undistinguishable from the site it has just fully reinvaded, while abandoning the purely indexical fashion of doing so.

Mottled Space

René Payant suggested that the interest in architecture in painting stems from the former's ability to embody the idea of *construction*. By quoting architectural motifs, paintings would foreground the fact of their own construction.[44] My own view constitutes a pendant to this assertion. For it seems to me that the kind of relationship to the site found in installation is different from what it often was during the 1970s; the distinguishing feature is to be found in the current recourse to the picture-effect potential [*pouvoir faire-tableau*] of the site's architectural constraints. This is one aspect of what, to me, seems to be the picturesque face of installation; that is, a way of integrating the site within a work through picture-effects— *insofar as these effects are, in turn, modified by being transplanted onto a site.* Not only is there the picture-effect of the room but, as well, a chiaroscuro effect and a narrative effect stemming from architectural irregularities [*accidents*], various motifs, or even accompanying texts. The list could be extended by drawing upon all those features of eighteenth-century gardens that have undergone modification in installations (or more precisely, using what this art of gardening now enables us to see at work in installation).

It remains to be seen how, used in this way to reinvest the index (even when it is false) or, to manage a proliferating space, or a pliable, unruly, or strict interpictoriality, the site becomes indistinguishable from what is found there only insofar as it assumes a shape, reifies itself, and, in turn, appears not only *with* but ultimately *similar to* those objects whose connective principle it is. Thus the return of the object would have, as it were, contaminated space (somewhat in the way that Gilpin saw the properties of the picturesque referent[45] spreading even to the pictorial surface). Through this operation, space, as both a structure and a figure, reverses the notion of *camouflage* as defined by Jacques Lacan. "The effect of mimicry is camouflage, in the strictly technical sense. It is not a question of harmonizing with the background but, against a mottled background, of becoming mottled."[46] Lacan, following Caillois, distinguishes three dimensions of mimicry: travesty, camouflage, and intimidation. Instead of disguising itself in the manner of travesty, the site, as it appears in recent installation, works to dismantle itself as background by making itself into a thing among other things, by becoming mottled, crystallizing into *tableaux*. It is somewhat as if a leaf, stealing the initiative of a well-known strategy, were to outdo the chameleon at its own game. So this picture-effect [*faire-tableau*] has at least a twofold effect; for here, to paint is also to faint [*faire la toile*]. In other words, the site as support disintegrates before it crystallizes into a potential mobility that conceals it and it is also that mobility through which the installation is articulated. This apparent iterability of the picture-effect confronts us with our own mobility through the parcelling up of the site: in particular, it forces us to think about the relationships and organization of things and places, something that is, overall, a difficult question in today's critical climate.

This said, we have come to the difficult question of the itinerary, of movement in a picture-like space[47]; in other words, we have to consider the pragmatic level of the picturesque. This would be the rallying point for the "museological" (to use Girardin's expression) dimension of the picturesque. (You may have noticed how, in recent years, an increasing (and symptomatic) degree of terminological confusion has crept into the distinction between extra- or paramuseological exhibitions and installations proper.) In any case, here, there is absolutely no question of reducing the picture-effects of the installation space to the distancing, frontal viewpoint of traditional perspective. In fact, regarding this issue, the picturesque allows us to understand how the life-size realization and experimentation of pictures in Nature can be thought of as a welcoming matrix for the body in motion. And this is why it is also important to point out how vain it is to persist in considering the picturesque apart from painting or even painting apart from its own interdisciplinary nomadic tradition—as we have here defined the picturesque.

Notes

The epigraph is from William Gilpin, *Essays on the Picturesque* (London: R. Blamire, 1794; reprint, Westmead: Gregg International Publishers Limited, 1970).

1. Thierry de Duve, *Nominalisme pictural: Marcel Duchamp, la peinture et la modernité* (Paris: Éditions de Minuit, 1984), 274–275. [English translation: *Pictorial Nominalism,* trans. Dona Polan (Minneapolis: University of Minnesota Press, 1991).]

2. Rosalind Krauss, "Sculpture in the Expanded Field," *October,* no. 8 (Spring 1979): 31–44. This essay has been reprinted in *The Anti-Aesthetic,* ed. Hal Foster (Seattle: Bay Press, 1983), 41. "[W]ithin the situation of postmodernism, practice is not defined in relation to a given medium—sculpture—but rather in relation to the logical operations on a set of cultural terms, for which any medium … might be used."

3. Rosalind Krauss, "Notes on the Index: Part 2," *The Originality of the Avant-Garde and Other Modernist Myths* (Cambridge: MIT Press, 1986), 210–220.

4. As quoted by Yve-Alain Bois, "Promenade pittoresque autour de Clara-Clara," *Serra* (Paris: Centre Georges Pompidou, 1983), 11–27.

5. Robert Smithson, "F.L. Omstead and the Dialectical Landscape," in *The Writings of Robert Smithson,* ed. Nancy Holt (New York: New York University Press, 1979), 118–119.

6. Note that the term "aporia" made its appearance in French in 1807 (*Lexis*), that is, roughly about the same time as the picturesque became an object of scorn due to the contradictions contained in the term—this despite the sophisticated theoretical treatment it received from the pen of Richard Payne Knight (1805). In this connection, see Elisabeth W. Manwaring, *Italian Landscape in Eighteenth-Century England* (London: Frank Cass & Co., 1965), particularly chapter 7.

7. We should point out that "value," in the sense attributed to the term by the colourist terminology of the "fine arts," is an anachronism here; it was to take on this meaning only in the nineteenth century (or in the eighteenth, according to *Lexis*).

8. Marie-Madeleine Martinet, *Art et Nature en Grande-Bretagne au XVIIIe siècle* (Paris: Éditions Aubier-Montaigne, 1980), 10.

9. On page 120 of a postscript to the French translation of Gilpin's *Essays on the Picturesque,* Michel Conan writes: "Christopher Hussey, echoing Elisabeth Wheeler Manwaring, quotes a judgement pronounced by Stendhal in his *Mémoires d'un touriste*: 'The picturesque comes to us by way of England: fine landscapes are as important a part of an Englishman's religion as they are of his aristocratic nature; for him, they are an object of true feeling.' It is equally curious to find Pope taking the opposite view; in 1712 he wrote that the word *picturesque* was

of French origin." See *Trois essais sur le beau pittoresque*, trans. Baron de Blumenstein (Paris: Éditions du Moniteur, 1982).

10. Richard Payne Knight, *An Analytical Inquiry into the Principles of Taste*, 4th ed. (London: T. Payne and J. White, 1808; reprint, Westmead: Gregg International Publishers Limited, 1972), 150–151.

11. Ibid.

12. Even these considerations took account of colour harmonies: buildings were introduced because they enabled one to fix a point of view or make a foreground stand out in some specific way. But if ruins were exemplary among buildings, this was because their patina contributed to a *unity* of tone that did not threaten the integrity of the scene/painting. See René-Louis de Girardin, *An Essay on Landscape*, trans. Daniel Malthus (London: J. Dodsley, 1783; reprint, ed. John Dixon Hunt, London: Garland Publishing, 1982). The arrangement of trees was likewise designed to resolve problems associated with perspective, yet the types of trees employed depended on their distance from the viewer and had to be consistent with the principles of atmospheric perspective. See also William Mason, *The English Garden*, Book I (Dublin: n.p., 1772). The relevant passage is also given in English in Martinet, *Art et Nature,* 200–202.

13. Girardin, *An Essay on Landscape.*

14. Robert Klein and Henri Zerner, "Vitruve et le théâtre de la Renaissance italienne," *La Forme et l'intelligible* (Paris: Gallimard, 1970), 300.

15. On the problem of the pictorial transposition of a theatrical model which was itself influenced by painting, allow me to refer the reader to chapter 3 of my thesis, "Le théâtre comme métaphore dans quelques discours sur l'œuvre d'art" (M.A. Thesis, Université de Montréal, 1983).

16. Girardin's attachment to the pictorial model invariably crops up in commentaries. In his postscript to the 1979 reprint of the original edition of Girardin's *An Essay on Landscape*, Michel Conan takes the opposite view and attributes Girardin's success among his contemporaries to his antipictorialism. Now the autonomy that Girardin claims to find in the art of gardens inevitably derives from the recourse to painting as a method that provides a principle of cohesion ("the unity of the whole, and the connection of the parts") as opposed to a model to be imitated. More recently, Yve-Alain Bois stopped short of accusing Girardin of being "stuck on a pictorial composition of the picturesque," a conception in which the picture-effect [*le faire-tableau*] of the picturesque hinges on discussions of composition and figure and ground. Yet it may be time to acknowledge that this attachment, because it literalizes painting, changes the very Western definition of the pictorial.

17. Girardin, *An Essay on Landscape*, 9. "… irregularity and caprice can [no] more compose a fine landscape with the real objects, than it can upon canvas." [The choice of "real objects" for *terrain* in Daniel Malthus's translation of Girardin hardly makes it easier to grasp the present author's point, which hinges

on the analogy in the original French between the "site" and the canvas. Girardin's original reads: "... *le désordre et le caprice ne sont pas plus suffisants pour composer un beau tableau sur le terrain que sur la toile.*" The analogy of *tableau* and *toile* keeps coming up in the text.]

18.   Which by definition presupposes the immobility of the scene and the exclusion—indeed the negation—of the viewer. We might do well to take over Pope's expression, *moving picture*, which he employed when speaking of his grotto. See Alexander Pope, "Letter to Edward Blount, 2 June 1725," *Works*, vol. 6 (London: n.p., 1739), 69. Michael Fried rightly remarks on the degree to which the *tableau*, as the concept was reformulated in eighteenth-century France, remained undiscussed in art history. See Michael Fried, *Absorption and Theatricality* (Berkeley: University of California Press, 1980), 89–90.

19.   Fried, *Absorption and Theatricality*. For Fried, absorption has two levels. It is first and foremost that of the subject represented, who makes use of it to negate the presence of the viewer. Yet it can also be the absorption of the actual viewer who imaginatively enters into the painting and, in it, loses the sense of himself as a viewer. This latter dimension is studied by Fried in connection with the critical strategies adopted by Diderot. Absorption is therefore conceived as the swallowing up of the viewer by the painting; unlike the case of the picturesque garden, neither the viewer nor his exploration of the site is taken into account.

20.   Girardin, *An Essay on Landscape*, 51.

21.   Manwaring, *Italian Landscape*. See especially chapter 2.

22.   In this connection, see Rosalind Krauss, "The Originality of the Avant-Garde: a Post-Modernist Repetition," *October*, no. 18 (Fall 1981): 47–66. By 1712 Joseph Addison had finally grasped the indeterminate nature of this relationship as it was articulated by the picturesque: "[Y]et we find the works of nature still more pleasant, the more they resemble those of art: for in this case our pleasure rises from a double principle; from the agreeableness of the objects to the eye, and from their similitude to other objects: we are pleased as well with comparing their beauties, as with surveying them, and can represent them to our minds, *either as copies or originals*." (no. 414, Wednesday, 25 June 1712; emphasis added.) See Joseph Addison, "The Spectator," *Works*, vol. 3 (London: n.p., 1721).

23.   See page 128 in René-Louis de Girardin, *Promenade ou itinéraire des Jardins d'Ermenonville*.

24.   Girardin, *An Essay on Landscape*, 4–5.

25.   Ibid., 5.

26.   Girardin, *Promenade*, 137.

27.   Even though, after answering a string of questions in a manner that leaves him feeling dissatisfied, Gilpin writes: "Shall we then take an opposite ground, and just say the reverse ... that painting is *not* an art *strictly imitative*, but rather *deceptive*—that by an assemblage of colours, and a peculiar art in spreading

them, the painter gives a semblance of nature at a proper distance; which at hand, is quite another thing ..." Gilpin, *Essays on the Picturesque*, 29.

28.   In his analysis of the work of Serra, Yve-Alain Bois opposes the Sublime picturesque to the Beautiful picturesque, the latter being for him essentially narrative and pictorial. Bois recalls how Capability Brown, the first great master of the "picturesque garden," used to compare his art to literary composition. For him, the series of small *tableaux* constitutes a narrative conception of discontinuity. See Bois, "Promenade pittoresque," 22–23.

29.   Luigi Salerno, "Picturesque," in *Encyclopedia of World Art*, vol. 11 (Toronto: McGraw-Hill, 1959-c.1983), 339–342.

30.   Richard Payne Knight, *Principles of Taste*. See also Jean-Jacques Mayoux, *Richard Payne Knight et le pittoresque* (Paris: University of Paris, 1932).

31.   See Philippe Lacoue-Labarthe and Jean-Luc Nancy, *L'Absolu littéraire* (Paris: Éditions du Seuil, 1978). I regret that I cannot treat the articulation of the picturesque within Romanticism at this point; it is just as revealing as the relationships of the picturesque with the Sublime and the Beautiful.

32.   Michael Fried, "Art and Objecthood," in *Minimal Art*, ed. Gregory Battcock (New York: Dutton, 1968), 116–147. Also see Fried's *Absorption and Theatricality*.

33.   Manwaring, *Italian Landscape*, 182.

34.   Philippe Dubois, "L'Ombre, le miroir, l'index: à l'origine de la peinture, la photo, la vidéo," *Parachute*, no. 26 (Spring 1982): 16–28.

35.   René Payant, "Travestissements architecturaux," *Parachute*, no. 36 (Fall 1984): 16–23. Or in the catalogue, *Hypothétiques confluences* (Montréal: Galerie Jolliet, 1983).

36.   Christopher Hussey, *The Picturesque: Studies in a Point of View* (London: G.P. Putnam's Sons, 1927).

37.   Hubert Damisch, *Les Normes du tableau* (Paris: École des Hautes Études en Sciences sociales, 1984–1985).

38.   Patrick Javault, "Les états du lieu: Klingel, Höller, Luy, Mucha, Schütte," *Artpress*, no. 90 (March 1985): 37–41.

39.   Smithson, *Writings*, 132–133. "Works of art seen in such spaces [museums, galleries] seem to be going through a kind of aesthetic convalescence. They are looked upon as so many inanimate invalids, waiting for critics to pronounce them curable or incurable."

40.   It is interesting to consider such outright indifference in connection with the fact that the space in question is actually the artist's studio.

41.   Chantal Boulanger, "Eva Brandl," *Parachute*, no. 36 (Fall 1984): 50–51.

42.	At this point we may recall Gilpin's metaphor in which he says that "the imagination becomes a camera obscura." See Gilpin, *Essays on the Picturesque*, 52.

43.	Martinet, 246 and following. [If English readers are referred to a French source, it is because Martinet's book has compiled the relevant English sections for quick perusal.] Already for Uvedale Price, the picturesque is essentially linked to the pathos of human traces or ruins, to what Martinet refers to as "the introduction of a melancholic reality into art."

44.	Payant, *Travestissements architecturaux*.

45.	Gilpin, *An Essay on Landscape*, 29–30.

46.	Jacques Lacan, *The Four Fundamental Concepts of Psychoanalysis*, trans. Alan Sheridan (New York: Norton, 1981), 99.

47.	Let us not forget that Lacan takes up the subject of camouflage in the chapter dealing with the insertion of the subject and his self-orientation *vis-à-vis* paintings.

Translated from the French by Donald McGrath.

Bruce Grenville

Mapping the Surface:
The Process of Recent Toronto Sculpture[1]

The history of recent Toronto sculpture constitutes a rising to the surface and an acknowledgement of that surface as the locus of meaning. This rising to the surface takes many forms, but in general we can see it in the work of those artists who seek to decentre their subject either formally or conceptually, or both. The five artists discussed in this article [Renée Van Halm, Bernie Miller, Louise Noguchi, Brian Boigon, David Clarkson] are, like many of their peers,[2] united by a desire to break with that field or territory we traditionally call sculpture. This unity, however, is not to be located on a table of resemblance, either in formal or conceptual terms, but is instead to be found on a map of difference. They have chosen to open up the term sculpture, to work at its periphery, bringing in strategies and ideas from other fields. In a very immediate way we can see evidence of this practice in the use of techniques borrowed from film, painting, photography, theatre, and printmaking. In part, this process, which we can call (after Deleuze) deterritorialization, is formulated in reaction to the modernist notion of purity and self-criticism, but it is also part of a larger attempt to break down the logic of representation.

Within the production of contemporary sculpture, the process of deterritorialization holds many implications, but perhaps the most important for our purposes is the realization that the primacy of the sculptural object as an adequate representation of a thing or idea can be maintained only as long as its territory is not breached. Whereas territorialization requires a unity of intent, an axis of representation (i.e., a good or bad copy), and a denial of process, deterritorialization shatters the category, splits the axis of representation, and returns a sense of process and temporality to us.

The five artists discussed in this article come together at a site that I will call "mapping." Ironically they are here unified by a process that seeks to deny unity and congruency. As we will see, however, theirs is a unity of disparity and a repetition of difference.

This text was first published in *Parachute*, no. 47 (1987).

Towards a Theory of Mapping

In using the term mapping, I am proposing a form of analysis that will acknowledge both the incorporeal status of the work of art and the complex strategies of its production. However, before setting out the terms of such a theory, it is worth briefly addressing the question of why such a theory is necessary or applicable to the analysis of sculpture. That is to say, why should a theory that gives primacy to the notion of incorporeality be used to discuss an art form that traditionally gives primacy to the corporeal? The answer to this question lies in an understanding of the development of recent Toronto sculpture.

Over the past fifteen years we have seen a consistent movement from "object to reference,"[3] that is, from the production of self-contained, unified objects to a form of artmaking that is intended to refer to an event or a proposition outside the physical presence of the object.[4] This reference is formally achieved by recourse to the use of other media, e.g., photography, video, text, language, film, painting, printmaking, and the like. On a very simple level, this use of multiple media within sculptural practice breaks down the traditional notion of sculpture as a self-determined and self-contained activity. Furthermore, we see an increased use of nontraditional materials, such as plastic, plywood, and Styrofoam. These are materials that not only expand our notion of the construction of the sculptural object but also, by their very nature, throw the work's continuing physical existence into question. These formal shifts both accompany and echo a conceptual shift within the field of contemporary sculpture.

The conceptual shift is most readily visible in the general critique of the notion of full presence, that is, a critique of the founding metaphor of Western metaphysics that equates *being* with *presence.* This desire for full presence, which pervades all aspects of our lives, is historically acknowledged as a fundamental factor in the development and production of the art of the Western world. The quest for full presence in the history of art takes on a variety of forms ranging from the development of single point perspective in the Renaissance to Clement Greenberg's notion of the production of a self-critical art object. In recent Toronto sculpture, we have seen a critique of the notion of full presence, first by formal means and then through a process of reference, which places less emphasis on a phenomenological interaction with the sculptural object and more emphasis on the interpretation of the subject of that reference. More often than not, the subject itself also speaks of the impossibility of full presence within contemporary society, all the while recognizing the pervasiveness of the desire for presence. The move from object to reference is a movement from the realm of the corporeal to the incorporeal, and it is this movement that I seek to document by way of the term mapping.

Mapping

The term mapping is intended to evoke, within the reader, a multitude of ideas and associations. Generally, maps are understood as objects used by individuals or groups to situate themselves within a given physical environment. In this instance, the map is analogous to the environment that it maps or represents. This interpretation proposes both an understanding of the map as a simple tracing of an environment and the acknowledgement of an equivalence between the site and its representation.

While I would like to hang onto the notion of the map as a two-dimensional representation, I will propose discarding the Cartesian grid and the necessity of an actual physical object or map. In the place of the grid and discrete object, we will substitute a concept of the map as an open and flexible mode of cognition. Following the suggestion of Edward C. Tolman, we can call this process a form of "cognitive mapping."[5] According to Tolman, the production of a cognitive map allows for the development of a flexible structure that enables the individual to produce hypothetical observations about a given situation. Equally important is the ability of the individual to test the validity of these hypotheses. Tolman's notion of cognitive mapping proposes three basic postulates:

> First, all organisms, including humans, are characterized by the propensity to pursue goals in whatever environment they happen to be placed; second, these goals can only be attained insofar as the organism has succeeded in synthesizing a functional subjective representation of that environment from the fragmentary bits of information received through previous contacts with the object world; and third, general knowledge is therefore neither inherent in the organism nor statically present in the environment, but rather a result of the organism's highly selective construction of such representations in an ongoing, dialectical interchange between itself and the environment.[6]

Again there are two elements in this description that are useful in our attempt to construct a theory of mapping. The first is that mapping is achieved through a synthesizing process that is created in the gap between the environment and its apprehension, and the second is that this synthesizing process emerges from an ongoing dialectical interchange rather than as the result of a static or closed act.

To reiterate briefly then, mapping is an ongoing, cognitive process that exists at the level of the surface. This process emerges as the result of a

dialectical interchange between the map maker and the environment/
object. Furthermore, if we accept the possibility of an analogy between
mapping and artmaking, then we might be able to make the following
observations. First, in removing mapping from the realm of tracing or
copying, it is proposed that artmaking no longer will be considered a
question of competence, i.e., defined by a degree of likeness to the original
or the model, but rather will be defined as a question of performance (and
process). Whereas tracing always draws us to an axis of right or wrong,
mapping defines artmaking as an engaged process. Second, in defining
mapping as an ongoing process, we acknowledge the map/art object as a
plateau[7] or point of intensity within the process. Third, artmaking, as
mapping, proposes a process open to single and/or multiple participation
and constant modification through reversal, montage, perversion, rupture,
and flight. So too, the art object must be understood as being open,
mobile, discursive, allegorical, and decentred, both in form and meaning.

Finally, I would like to push this concept of artmaking as mapping
to its logical conclusion, thereby linking it to the title of the article. An
understanding of artmaking as mapping acknowledges that art and its production belong to the realm of the incorporeal. This incorporeal realm
may be identified as a surface that flows over and above the object/envi-
ronment in question. Thus, we cannot say that art *represents* the
object/environment because that would presuppose art as a form of tracing, but rather that it *topologizes* the object/environment, creating a shifting and fluctuating surface.

The Process of Recent Toronto Sculpture

If, as I proposed earlier, the history of recent Toronto sculpture constitutes a rising to the surface and an acknowledgement of that surface as the
locus of meaning, then we must now look to that work and examine the
terms and conditions of its production.

In the work entitled *Escaping History (Parts 1 and 2)* (1986), Renée
Van Halm provides an excellent introduction to the formal strategy of
decentring and to the process of mapping in general. Formally we can
look to the disjunctive structure of the piece as an attempt on Van Halm's
part to throw into question the work's presence as a unified object. This
disjunction is achieved by literally breaking the piece into various planes
and sections as well as by mixing painterly images with sculptural/archi-
tectural objects. Furthermore, if we adopt the traditional strategy of walking around the sculpture (an attempt to unify it under our own presence),
we come to realize that it is built like a stage set. This reference demands

that we acknowledge the work as a fabrication, a product of the incorporeal world of the surface. Clearly then, we are intended to read the work as a
compilation of images and surfaces. In this way Van Halm frees these
images from their traditional use in depth (and depth models) and opens
the way to the surface.

It is upon this surface that Van Halm proposes to map a critique of
the ideal. Through the formal structure, we are invited to play the images
off against each other, thereby building relationships within a model of a
pavilion for the 1939 New York World's Fair (a utopian vision of an ideal
building); the image of the atom (an image of the ideal proposed as a discourse of the real); the hypereroticized image of a woman (an ideal state of
being as determined by advertising); the model/sign of a Classical porch
(the ideal of Classical architecture); and the collapse of an apartment
building (the collapse of the modernist ideal). All these images in turn
pivot around an image of nature, our culture's ultimate image of the ideal.

If one keeps the title of the work in mind, it would appear that the
history that Van Halm proposes to escape is, in fact, that history imposed
upon us by our allegiance to the ideal. The history of the ideal is *the* history of the modern Western world, for it is the history that supports the one
and the same. It is a history that defines the real as a category of the ideal
and invites us to order all things on that axis.

In mapping an allegory of the ideal, Van Halm seeks to return a
sense of temporality and process to what we call history. If history is to be
useful, it must be freed from the axis of the ideal and the same and
mapped across a surface of difference. Here the categories and systems that
traditionally define history will be dispersed, and history will come to be
recognized in the absence of the same.

In a work such as Bernie Miller's *Future Use* (1985), the formal critique of presence is to be found not only in the physical disjunction of the
object but also by way of an oblique reference to language—specifically, to
the breakdown of syntax. What, for example, are we to make of the camera-like object that stands before the wall? I have called it "camera-like"
because it is mounted on a tripod and calls to mind the early cinema camera. Yet the "camera," or what should be the camera, looks like a theatrical
spotlight, and the shape that emerges from it looks like a cross between a
light ray and a bridge trestle. In this description I think it is evident that
we cannot clearly identify the object but rather come to an awareness of a
loss of syntax and a rising to the surface. Miller proposes to break down
the signifying chain, to deny the traditional unity of the signifier and the
signified, and thereby to throw the logic of signification into question.

Throughout the work, we witness a similar rising to the surface.

The monumental wall, for example, appears to be made out of concrete or sandstone, yet, as we move around the corner of the wall, we realize its artifice. It is an artifice, similar to that seen in Van Halm's piece, that is literally linked to a loss of depth. Likewise the projector behind the wall does not project into the depths of darkness but rather reduces the city to a shadowy surface cast upon a movie screen. In fact, the whole grouping of objects behind the wall—the radio, the slide tray, the tape deck, the fluorescent tube, the screen, the shadow, etc.—seems to offer a series of puns and plays on the notion of incorporeality and the surface.

In titling the piece *Future Use*, Miller appears to be making some sort of reference to Utopian or future thinking, i.e., a method of speculating or projecting another state of being. But like the projector that does project, the future of Miller's *Future Use* is not intended as a projection into time. It is instead a projection into the incorporeal space of the present. The estrangement that we experience in *Future Use*—the collapsing of depths, the broken syntax, the fractured gaze, the sliding surfaces—is what is created in the rising of the phantasm.[8] Future thinking creates a phantasm that rises from the incorporeal surface, descending only to retopologize the body in question.

In their work Van Halm and Miller seek to create a sense of disjunction principally through a formal strategy of disruption and juxtaposition. In the work of the following three artists we can see a tendency to internalize this disjunctive process so that a process of deterritorialization comes to us by way of the realization of an increased emphasis on the manipulation of the subject of their reference.

In her recent work Louise Noguchi seeks to map the place of the subject as it is intersected by belief and desire. She achieves this by creating a web of reference among the elements of her installation. Photograph, text, sculptural object, and image—each demands a different strategy of reading; each opens the work up to further reading; each undermines the presence of the other, and, ultimately, the notion of presence itself.

Noguchi's *Fruits of Belief: The Grand Landscape* (1986) consists of three principal elements, a wooden cornucopia-like object, a distorted painting, and a life-sized head with the brain exposed. The sense of ambiguity that we experience in our identification and interpretation of the cornucopia stands as a paradigm reading of the work as a whole. Traditionally, the cornucopia is understood as a symbol of plenty, but this one is empty, and so we are left wondering whether it is to be understood as a symbol of plenty or of loss. Likewise, there is some ambiguity as to whether the painting and the head are to be understood as fruits of the cornucopia, or whether the cornucopia is a vortex into which they are being dragged. Within this field of ambiguity, we come to realize that the cornucopia is not so much a symbol of loss or of plenty but rather a symbol of the presence of belief and desire. Similarly the landscape painting (derived from a painting by the eighteenth-century British painter Thomas Gainsborough) is intended to act as a reference to the presence of the ideal—for this landscape is based not on the observation of nature but rather on the late eighteenth-century concept of an ideal landscape. Furthermore, because the painting carries the compressed shape of an object emerging from the cornucopia, we are invited to suppose that the ideal is in fact one of the "fruits of belief." This reading is in turn echoed and multiplied by the references to the brain/head, and by a related "brain" drawing entitled *Deliverance* (1986), which proposes an ironic reading of the brain as the source of being and deliverance.

Finally by way of a rather oblique reference to photography, Noguchi allows us to map her observations on the seventeenth- and eighteenth-century belief systems onto the space of the present. I am referring to the fact that Noguchi's painting is traced over a distorted photograph of the original Gainsborough painting. Here the very presence of the photograph invites us to question its position in the creation of a new ideal for the twentieth century. The new ideal that photography proposes is the ideal of objectivity or the belief that the photograph offers a true and accurate transcription of a given event. Noguchi reveals this belief (which includes a general belief in all objective forms of knowledge) to be yet another instance of the desire for the ideal.

In Noguchi's work we gain a profound sense of the complexity and range of critique available through the process of mapping. Here we can sense its potential for rupture, sudden reversal, and decentring.

In his recent work Brian Boigon seems to have taken the notion of the denial of a sculptural presence to its furthest possible extreme. In doing so Boigon acknowledges that sculpture need not be determined by an adherence to a specific medium but rather is a mode of discourse. Through his use (and misuse) of the print medium, Boigon seeks to question the role of presence, authenticity, and authority in the creation of a meaning for the art object. In his repetition of the printed image, we come to realize that our history is the history of the same and that the production of art is concerned not necessarily with the creation of subjective experience but rather with an adherence to the narrative of the same. In a number of previous installations, Boigon addressed the role of the master narrative in the production of modern art and ideology. Here he continues to develop this critique, while at the same time building a critique of his own participation in the narrative of the history of sculpture and installation art. It is within this web of reference and self-reference that we begin to experience a rising to the surface.

The installation that I am referring to is entitled *Nausea* (1986). In its most recent form it consisted of nine, repeated images which varied only in their titling and framing. That is to say, the position of the red, yellow, blue, and white elements of the frame changed from work to work; the title indicated an alphabetical ordering of the prints. The print itself consists of two principal images. The larger is a photo-engraving of the Northland Shopping Mall in Detroit; in the lower left corner is a picture of two children looking up at the vast array of objects and cryptic signs which seem to float across the surface of the shopping centre. Beneath is a smaller photograph of an artist (Emily Warren) restoring a painting. Like the larger image, this smaller one too has been partially obliterated by a web of objects and signs etched across its surface. Within this web of repetition, reference, interference, and deterritorialization, we begin to sense a loss of depth. This is expressed in a variety of ways: for example, through a critique of the modernist architectural project, a reference to Mondrian's desire for a universal spirituality, and the master narrative of the museum. Perhaps it is most eloquently visible in the reference to Emily Warren. Here she is depicted restoring some paintings she had done as a Canadian war artist. Within the repetition of the image we recognize the sad irony of this artist restoring history. For this is the same history that continues to deny her contribution and the contribution of other women artists. There is no room for a different voice within the narrative of the museum or the narrative of the history of art. History is the voice of the one and the same.

Within the structure of repetition we come to recognize the necessity of difference. This perhaps is the nausea referred to in the title of the series. It is a nausea akin to that described by Jean-Paul Sartre, in that, through an understanding of the predominance of the same, we experience a rising to the surface and a falling away of the reassuring narrative of depth.

David Clarkson's "sculptural paintings" offer a final instance of the process of deterritorialization and mapping. In these works, Clarkson draws us to the surface by shattering the traditional categories of sculpture and painting, splitting the axis of good and bad representation, and forcing us to question the traditional processes of making and reading art.

In the work entitled *A Liar's Pleasure* (1986), we are invited to draw an equation between the notion of an incorporeal surface and our understanding of the surface of a mirror. Looking into the mirror we gain an illusion of depth, but, in proposing that the mirror reflection offers a true depth, we confuse depth with limitlessness. A mirror reflection offers only a limitless *surface*, a perversely accurate vision of the incorporeal.

We gain a similar sense of the difference between depth and limitlessness in Clarkson's *Surface and the Deep* (1986). Initially we are struck by the muteness of these objects and by our inability to read them as images. We realize our dependence on seeing images in depth, that is, contextualizing them with the logic of representation and the order of the same. The only image we can readily recognize here is the sign of the registered trademark, a sign that is rendered meaningless without some image to name or register. Thus, we understand naming to be a product of representation and categorization in which naming acknowledges the primacy of the same. In the "painting" on the left, we may wonder if we are looking at a map or a skull; while in the "painting" on the right, it seems impossible to recognize anything but the Ben Day dots, which are signs of the presence of representation and repetition. In fact, we can recognize these images as an image of a steak and an image of water, respectively, only if we acknowledge representation as a form of distortion. Here then, the axis of good and bad representation is split by the notion of a persuasive and unavoidable distortion.

We can encounter a similar sense of distortion throughout Clarkson's recent work. From the process of the work's construction to the mechanics of its reception, this distortion blocks our desire for a passage into depth and in its place maps a surface of resistance.

Within the work of these five artists we can clearly see a desire to shatter the traditional presence given to the object/subject and to cast it into the space of the incorporeal. By seeking to locate the meaning at the level of the incorporeal surface, we witness a critique of those depth models and other similar structures, such as representation and narrative, that give a primacy to hidden or latent meaning. The depth model ultimately proposes a unified presence at the core of an object or event from which meaning is generated and to which meaning attaches itself. The pervasiveness of our culture's understanding of the depth model as the site or locus of meaning is easily visible in an enumeration of the structure of contemporary philosophy, theory, literature, or science. In virtually every instance, it is proposed that the true meaning of an object or event is to be located somewhere in depth, hidden away from the eyes and mind of the average observer. Yet such a belief system can only keep us from acknowledging our own role in the shaping of an event. In rising to the surface, we gain an awareness of the world events around us and our role in the shaping of those events.

In this article I have attempted to set the basic parameters of a contemporary theory of mapping. It must be stressed, however, that this description is far from complete because its principal function is to assist in the interpretation of the work discussed here rather than to present a closed theory of mapping. If such a theory is to remain valid, it must continuously shift and reformulate itself in reaction to what I have termed "recent Toronto sculpture." But even in the naming of that plateau, the reader will sense it slipping away as each description opens up new terms and fields of inquiry.

Notes

1.　　　*Mapping the Surface: The Process of Recent Toronto Sculpture* was the title of an exhibition I organized for the Mendel Art Gallery, Saskatoon, in October–November 1986. The following article constitutes a reworking of the original catalogue essay for that exhibition.

2.　　　The choice of the artists discussed in this article was, in part, determined by the original parameters of the exhibition. Under different circumstances this article would also have to include the work of other Toronto artists such as Liz Magor, Robin Collyer, Ian Carr-Harris, Lee Dickson, Brian Groombridge, Bob McNealy, and others.

3.　　　The reference here is to an exhibition organized by Philip Monk and entitled *From Object to Reference* (shown at the Carmen Lamanna Gallery, Toronto, June 3–30, 1983); and to an installation of the permanent collection at the Art Gallery of Ontario, Toronto, in 1985, entitled *Object and Reference*.

4.　　　For an in-depth analysis of this process in Canadian sculpture since the 1970s see Philip Monk, "Colony, Commodity, and Copyright: Reference and Self-Reference in Canadian Art," *Vanguard*, vol. 12, no. 5/6 (Summer 1983): 14–17 [reprinted in this anthology]; Bruce Grenville, "The New City of Sculpture," *C Magazine*, no. 3 (Fall 1984): 76–114; or Bruce Grenville, *Territories* (Toronto: YYZ Artist's Outlet, 1985).

5.　　　Cognitive mapping is a term developed in the late 1940s by the psychologist Edward C. Tolman in an effort to describe a subjective process developed by rats which enables them to orient themselves spatially in maze-like situations; see Edward C. Tolman, "Cognitive Maps in Rats and Men," *The Psychological Review*, no. 55 (July 1948): 189–208.

6.　　　Richard Bjornson, "Cognitive Mapping and the Understanding of Literature," *Substance*, no. 30 (1981): 51–62.

7.　　　The term plateau as it is used here was developed by Gilles Deleuze and Félix Guattari. See "Rhizome," *On the Line*, trans. John Johnston (New York: Semiotext(e), 1983).

8.　　　　"Phantasms must be allowed to function at the limit of bodies, because they stick to bodies and protrude from them, but also because they touch them, cut them, break them into sections, regionalize them, and multiply their surfaces. … Phantasms do not extend organisms into an imaginary domain; they topologize the material of the body." Michel Foucault, "Theatrum Philosophicum," trans. Donald F. Bouchard and Sherry Simon, in *Language, Counter-Memory, Practice*, ed. Donald F. Bouchard (Ithaca: Cornell University Press, 1977), 169–170.

Jeanne Randolph

The Amenable Object

It feels like the mental equivalent of contorsionism to attempt to write about art, having set two conditions—that the writing be subjective and be founded upon psychoanalytic theory. Just as the soles of the feet curve gently upon the contours of the brow, the intellect must be limbered until it can reach around to meet heart, gut, and spleen. And how pliant can psychoanalytic theory be? There must be a way for it to reach into art and yet avoid pulling an art work apart so extremely that the next step can only be psychonecropsy. And maybe that way is to think about art backwards from what is usually assumed. Instead of viewing art as a subcategory of psychological activity and, as such, determined partially, if not completely, by psychical needs and processes, one can see psychological theories of behaviour as subcategories of artistic creation. What is meant by this statement is the following: if ideas or theory were a form of creative production—not fact but a more plastic approximation awaiting adaptation or even distortion for unforeseen or new situations—then, as is true for the audience of other art forms, the audience for psychoanalytic theory would be free to contribute from its experience and imagination in assimilating the theory. What follows here, from this reversal, is a reflection upon some aspects of Freudian theory, in the context of the ideas of D.W. Winnicott whose contributions to psychoanalysis were written in such a way as to invite being toyed with. Winnicott did not avoid classically Freudian concepts in order to make his observations about culture, though Winnicott's work developed from the "object relations" branch of psychoanalysis rather than the "id psychology" of Freud.

It was Freud after all who invented psychoanalysis, so it is impossible to organize one's perceptions and reactions in psychoanalytic terms without confronting Freud's assumptions. In order to explore how Winnicott's discoveries contribute to the pleasures and headaches of writing about art, however, the Freudian conceptual model for how an art object is interpretable should first be examined, for within the Freudian conceptualization, which can be summarized as an "art-as-neurosis" paradigm, there is a fundamental assumption about the function or nature of art, what Freud described as "primary process."

If one looks to Freud's theories of psychopathology, there seems to

This text was first published in *Vanguard* (Summer 1983).

be no way to avoid conceptualizing art as neurosis. When one conceptualizes the art object as an interpretable communication, the construct on which a critical interpretation is based must be the schema or construct Freud invented for describing neurosis. The *form* of this construct must remain intact, although the art critic need not necessarily agree to the *content* of this construct of neurosis, the content being that neurosis—and therefore in some way art—is something in need of a cure.

Neurosis, to a logical, practical person, is a symptom that appears to be meaningless. But Freud proposed that the neurotic symptom, for example, hysterical paralysis of the arm, is not meaningless but is disguised communication. The hypotheses about the underlying mechanism of that communication may be applied to acts and objects other than neurosis, but such an interpretative process must be based on characteristics that the analysable act or object appear to have in common with neurosis.

How can an art object be like a symptom of neurosis? First, the generative source of the art work, like that of the neurotic symptom, would be the artist's subconscious, from which the work would originate as private, intrapsychic experience first, before it became anything else. Secondly, like the hysterical paralysis, the art work would be a disguise of the intrapsychic experience, externalizing that experience in conformity with traditional or socially acceptable endeavours, such as the techniques of sculpture or of painting. Like the cryptic neurotic symptom, the art work would employ imagery determined in the unconscious by primary process. Primary process would have determined the underlying content of the art work, as it does the form and imagery of the neurotic symptom. The underlying content, therefore, of the work of art, as in neurosis, is the artist's sexual and aggressive drives in constellations and conflicts, shaped by events in the artist's infancy as he or she developed psychosexually, events reawakened, aroused once again in the artist's present predicament.

This is the model of a mechanism by which art expresses psyche to a real world external to the psyche. Art criticism based upon this model of the art object must address the consequence of such a model, that is, the basis of the aesthetic response is the recognition of (and therefore unconscious participation in) the relief of libidinal excitation through forming symbols rather than taking action. What a challenge to anyone who wants to identify the ways in which a particular work seems authentic in its embodiment of interior, psychological experience. If psychoanalytic theory has any insight into the artist's subjectivity as revealed in his or her art, then it would seem that the viewer's and/or the artist's unconscious gratification must become accessible to exploration and articulation. It would be gripping indeed to read a critical review in which the writer is able to reveal in what way certain of his or her very own most hidden libidinal longings are linked to the quality of a particular art work.

The other way to acknowledge that gratification is at the centre of the work's psychological authenticity is for the writer-as-viewer to claim objectivity and to reveal instead the most hidden of the artist's libidinal longings. But this always ends up revealing more about art-as-neurosis than art.

Without the art-as-neurosis model is there a psychoanalytic framework for perceiving the relationship of art and psyche? The concepts out of which art-as-neurosis were created cannot be slung around simply as slang. Maybe "primary process" really does account for an actual mental mode. It would be impossible to write about art from a psychoanalytic perspective without deciding whether primary process is involved in artmaking. And if it is, is it any more active in the formation of the art object than in any other human production?

Having asked these questions, a carefully considered, two-part definition of primary process will be offered: there is first of all what primary process does and secondly why it does it. What primary process does is to operate by way of disregarding logic, disregarding reason, disregarding practicality, ignoring the physical and political restraints of day-to-day action, interchanging basic intrinsic qualities of things, and rearranging and regrouping qualities of things, parts of things, and whole images of things to condense them into symbols. Secondly, why it does this, is that the sole aim of primary process is the discharge of any accumulated erotic or aggressive arousal. Through displacement, symbols become the means by which this excitation is relieved. When intrapsychic quiescence has been re-established that is, by definition, pleasure, the pleasure that is intrinsic to the unconscious.

If in some way primary process can be said to be visible in a work, and even if it cannot, what aspects of primary process form the basis of an analysis of the work and its effects on the viewer? One way to puzzle over this question is to see whether there is first of all a subjective answer to it, and, then, maybe it is possible to relate this subjective answer to the answer provided by psychoanalytic theory. Subjectively, the most nettlesome aspect of primary process is that its aim is to establish quiescence, to undo disequilibrium, to calm excitation. Its aim is, in short, the inevitability of the intrapsychic status quo. Therefore, from what psychoanalytic perspective could one address primary process in a work and still cling to the particular prejudice that artmaking is intrinsically revolutionizing and anti–status quo? It is an agonizing proposition to confront that, from a Freudian perspective, primary process is intrinsically reactionary; that resorting to symbol for wish fulfilment is the antithesis of taking action; and that, regardless of what the work looks like, the psychic impulse from which it arises is the need to conserve the intrapsychic status quo.

If one returns to the first part of the definition given above of primary process, however, the antilogical, rearranging aspect of it, the opposite seems to be taking place. Change in perception, change in values or priorities is possible only when convention, definitions, and precedents are denounced, their boundaries distorted, or their validity suspended. Primary process is without convention, definitions, or precedent. It distorts the boundaries of convention, suspending the validity of definitions, ignoring precedent in the form and function of things.

Which is central to primary process, wish fulfilment, or this unhindered restructuring? Which is central to artmaking? Are these questions to be answered by philosophers, scientists, therapists, or artists? Is the question answered within the art work? It is certainly already answered in the strictly Freudian definition of primary process. The choice then for the writer is to avoid mentioning that artmaking is essentially, through primary process, "regressive and infantile," or to persevere humbly and rigorously in spite of this unfortunate truth, or to find a way to address the possibility that artmaking is not the efflorescent of an inherently reactionary impulse.

The psychoanalytic work of D.W. Winnicott, particularly as expressed in his book *Playing and Reality*,[1] raises the possibility that in art it is the ambiguity between the objective and the subjective that gives art works a unique psychological validity. Through Winnicott's observations and speculations, the model of the art object is of an object amenable to an interaction with the viewer, reflecting the hypothesis that in some way the materials and methods with which it was made have been rendered by the artist into something amenable to his or her subjective interventions— a subjectivity very like primary process yet exploratory, not reactionary. Winnicott invokes the writer's imagination rather than forcing the individual writer to ask what is proved or unproven about the creative process as an object of study. The discoveries of Winnicott, unlike art-as-neurosis, impose no obstacle to the possibility that art criticism can be the articulation of an experience, with no denial of the validity of the writer's aim to interact with a work.

"Object Relations" is interaction, and Winnicott added to the understanding of the interplay of an essentially inseparable couple, infant and mother. He began to speculate upon the origins of cultural experience when he realized the ramifications of the discovery he termed "the transitional object." It must have been his curiosity about the origins and uses of symbols that led him to notice this phenomenon, which is the floppy, semishapeless thing that a little kid carries around—Winnie-the-Pooh, Linus's blanket. Winnicott observed and contemplated the fate of these objects at the hands of their owners, two-year-old toddlers.

There are two main aspects of Winnicott's work: the clinical observations and their relevance to psychoanalytic theory. For the sake of clarity, however, as these two aspects of the transitional object are summarized, mention will be made of only those observations and ideas that seem most adaptable as a model of the "art object."

In observations about transitional objects, it was noticed that these objects appear in the child's life for the first time at age six months, and the child becomes even more intensely attached to an object as he or she reaches the age of two years or so. Mothers reported that, from the many things they would provide, the infant would choose what was to become his or her own object. As an infant and two-year-old, the child would give the most active attention to it when the mother was at a distance or away altogether. At that older age this object would be stretched, pummelled, squeezed, squealed at, etc., along with the usual cuddling, cooing, and clinging; in other words, the child had begun to play.

Winnicott was interested in how the transitional object served the child in his or her attempt to become a body and self distinct from the mother's body and self. And this is the reason for the term "transitional," referring to the developmental phases in which an infant is in between, in between experiencing the mother as an extension of itself and experiencing the mother as separate from itself. But when we begin to wonder whether any of this has an application to a theory of art objects, what aspects of this phenomenon are relevant?

The transitional object, which is physically malleable and whose shape responds to manipulation, does not have a utilitarian function dominating its form. But still it is a palpable, physical thing that obviously has perceivable, tangible properties. A child will interact with it as if it were experiencing life along with him or her. Winnicott called it "the first 'not me' possession," and he believed that, when a child begins to play, this is in fact "neither a matter of inner psychic reality nor a matter of external reality." The transitional object is neither inner nor outer, but rather partakes of both.

What follows from Winnicott's concept of this phenomenon that is in between fantasy and reality, partaking of both, is that it is necessary "for the initiation of a relationship between the child and the world." The child has chosen some thing that can accompany him or her in the external world. Winnicott considered this to be the first use of a symbol and the first instance of using an illusion to aid in experiencing what is real. But this object is not a symbol that replaces the mother, not an ersatz mother. It is a symbol of experience, the experience of being in union with the mother; it is an illusion of a responsive being, an illusion that enhances the child's capacity to explore. It is an instance of what Winnicott identified as "a symbol of body experience," rather than the Freudian symbol derived from body function. Winnicott thought that the creative impulse, in this context the impulse to turn a soft, floppy thing into a responsive enhancement of perceptual experience, that this creative impulse should be looked upon as a thing in itself. The capacity to use objects as a temporary, illusory definition of the boundary between the subjective and the objective is dependent on the creative impulse. Winnicott did not see how there could be something objectively experienced without some aspect of it having already been anticipated by creative subjectivity. As he said "to some extent, objectivity is a relative term because what is objectively perceived is by definition to some extent already subjectively conceived of."

Winnicott had observed that "maximally intense experiences are in the potential space between me-extension and the not-me." In later life the emotional, perceptual, even philosophical, or political experience of the potential space between subjectivity and objectivity can be no less intense or crucial. Winnicott would see the creation of art works, in this context, like play, where subjectivity and objectivity overlap, not as regression to the toddler's level but instead as an adaptive relationship with the mysterious world. It is not that the adult artist reverts to a baby-like state when he or she is artistically inventive; it is as though to play were one of the first adult modes that the child acquires.

Winnicott's hypotheses, as a viewpoint from which to write about art, seem to invite certain distortions that I have perpetrated in my conceptualization of an art work as "the amenable object." Such an adaptation involves using discoveries as if they were a floppy, semishapeless, transitional object, allowing exploration without disrupting subjectivity. Reshaping Winnicott's theory to the aims of art criticism allows a way to interact with the art work as an intentional revelation of the artist's version of experience, intentionality that need not be explicit or disguised. Unlike art-as-neurosis, this model is not a theoretical model of the art work from the purportedly objective view of someone who wants to study how the artist creates it. This is a view of the art object once the artist has left it in public.

The characteristics of the amenable object began as and would have remained merely an expression of contrariness against the art-as-neurosis schema, if it were not for Winnicott's theory. Contrariness found Winnicott's theory; the idea of the amenable object arose from their interplay, but there were also four particular art works exhibited in Toronto over the course of the past year that enlivened my reflections upon this particular psychoanalytic figment.

When Winnicott stated that "it is not possible to be original except on the basis of tradition," it seemed as if tradition were a repository of man-made things waiting to be found again. Already public, like any other "found object," whatever is already known becomes a wonder when it is reused in a subjective way. It is in this sense that one characteristic of the amenable object is that it is both a found object and a symbol of the artist's subjective experience. It partakes of both, and the ambiguity that is revealed about the familiar object (or idea or image) cannot ever quite be distinguished from the artist's idiosyncratic perception of the object.

One of Lorne Wagman's small sculptures, *The Beast of Leaside* (1981), for example, is literally a found object, a root or a branch that was not allowed to keep its definition but was adorned with gems and semi-precious stones at every point where some quadruped might have an anatomical or spiritual feature. *The Beast* is both a wretched root and a bejewelled being, both objectively perceived and subjectively conceived of. Another characteristic seen in this *Beast*, a tomfool thing, is that it is (although as unruly as anything rearranged by primary process) no disavowal of the real world but belongs, as Winnicott said of play, "to the experience of relating" to it.

Shelagh Alexander's compilation photographs, which have an extremely elaborate but instantly discernible underlying order, seem to give validity to the phrase "primary process made visible." Her assembled images defy perspective and scale and thereby metaphorically defy gravity, time, thermodynamics, probability. The perceptual plasticity manifest in Alexander's work is the embodiment of a third characteristic of the amenable object. It is the antilogical, rearranging aspect of primary process that gives the amenable object the potential to extend perceptual capacities, to skip precedent for the sake of more intense or extensive perception, or to envision other potential realities. The viewer, seeing this revolutionizing of perception, recognized there is no need to translate the work literally into a verbally logical message. Within the amenable object there is the intrinsic meaning that a change in perception can initiate a future reality.

Another characteristic, that can only be subjectively known, is the capacity to sustain a response that is unsettling or thrilling. It is the absence of a solution, the absence of resolution that is significant. The viewer realizes there is no interpretation that will validate retreat into quiescence, no reassurance. Instead there is the uneasy recognition of the artist's insistence that he or she can contribute to the store of potential public realities. Andy Fabo's *Laocoön* (1981) has this demanding quality. It crams a tragic mythological moment into a cocky cartoon style. *Laocoön's* bygone green and blue agony is dumped into the present, the paradox of contemporary nobility in the form of venerable vulgarity. There is every reason in the world to feel this remarkable painting is preposterous, but all of the reasons attest to the painting's insight.

A final characteristic of the amenable object, that it is in some sense incomplete, means that it retains ambiguous elements that allow leeway for the viewer's impulse to play with the illusion that has been created. The viewer's own creative impulse, in Winnicott's sense of that phrase, is not irrelevant. The viewer's subjective notions can find in this object an external form through which to elaborate their own existence. Elizabeth MacKenzie's work exemplifies this potential. In her paintings and drawings the images will absorb any story, including the next story that contradicts it. Mutually exclusive choices are all possible, and none are confirmable. No interpretation can ever come to rest in the viewer's mind, and it remains inconclusive where MacKenzie's narrative leaves off and the viewer's narrative begins.

These then are the attributes of the amenable object, the idea of which is an abstraction that creates a context for me to write about art with a kind of systematic subjectivity. If there is to be any validity in such a search for the psychological dimension of a work, it must not be at the expense of the work's potential to change the conditions into which it has been received. To have searched at all means only that there is still a possibility that psychoanalytic ideas can extend into a realm not where they are used to reduce art works to a psychological derivative but rather where creative production suggests new forms for psychoanalytic ideas.

Notes

1.   D.W. Winnicott, *Playing and Reality* (London: Tavistock, 1971).

William Wood

The Difference of Times

The analysis of the archive, then, involves a privileged region: at once close to us, and different from our present existence, it is the border of time that surrounds our presence, which overhangs it, and which indicates it in its otherness; it is that which outside ourselves, delimits us. The description of the archive deploys its possibilities (and the mastery of its possibilities) on the basis of the very discourses that have just ceased to be ours. ... In this sense, the diagnosis does not establish the fact of our identity by the play of distinctions. It establishes that we are difference, that our reason is the difference of discourses, our history the difference of times, ourselves the difference of masks. That difference, far from being the forgotten and recovered origin, is this dispersion that we are and make.

Here Michel Foucault redefines the term archive; from a collection of public records and documents he extends its regime to encompass "the general system of the formation and transformation of statements."[1] His philological elegance disrupts the archive, making it become active as a series of traces still to be acknowledged and followed, changing its functions to becoming a participant in the power relations of the present. To that extent, this passage describes the practical conditions of the archival works of Roy Arden—they issue from archival records and constitute reformations of historical imagery with attention to the relations that form and contain the potential to transform imagery. Each of Foucault's adumbrations leads to Arden's series—the notion of an historical belatedness that insists upon our difference; the recognition of ourselves as based on an ideologically maintained otherness; the sense of falling away from what can no longer be said.

Instead of finding identity with the past, Arden encounters its representations via an ambivalent vocabulary of elegiac differentiation. We see it in some of the titles of his works—*Rupture* (1985), *Abjection* (1985), *Mission* (1986)—as each term implies forces ripping, throwing, or sending the subject away from the position it once held. The events displayed and the forms the works take entail further repositioning for the historical subject and the spectator. The multiple panels and various additions engage questions of the attitude we assume before recorded events, of the allegorical possibilities of representing such material, and they insist on the fabrication of the work as a labour removed from the event and its recording.

This text was first published in *West: Roy Arden* (Vancouver: Artspeak Gallery, 1988).

329

In the most overt gesture in this direction, Arden produces the works in diptychal formats, always presenting an accompaniment to the imagery—an other within which we may metaphorically visit alternate positions and emblematic associations with the recollected past. Through cropping, rephotographing, and the addition of accompaniments, these works place us in a realm of partial presences, neither opposed nor consuming, but effected by our recognizance and their established finality—and by their forced departure from the surveilling construction of news journalism and documentary photography. The entire project serves an unwieldy project of desiring to activate selected scenes amid a decisive refusal to proscribe or mask their meaning.

Addition, reproduction, and otherness take central importance as figures in Arden's work. Each term is marked by a logic of recuperation and repetition and carries along the serial processes of shock, stutter, incomprehensibility, and ambivalence which characterize attempts to approach and entail historical material. Arden denies the institutional authority of the archive, preferring to disperse its contents. Yet this dispersion is not a matter of releasing images from the constraints of history. Rather, they require reproving, and, for the archive selected, they need a burden placed upon them.

Picturing the history of one of the newest parts of the New World—British Columbia—the images used are characteristically novel and unstable because they are virtually unseen. Marginality and periodization have kept them and the events they describe under the wrappings of peripheral vision, within the idiosyncrasies of the local. Extending just into the last century, they barely participate in the accredited history of North America. Portraying a nascent culture estranged from power centres, they display how it drew on colonial tactics just when that ideology was becoming decrepit and being superseded by corporate capitalism. They thus discomfort, for they possess the compressed aberrance of a roughly dealt suppression of difference in a social formation that was based in subduing the other—whether that took the form of excising immigrant, dissident, or aboriginal populations, or taking advantage of the lavish *availability* of natural resources. Given this mandate to overwhelm and subjugate, the imagery was produced under the aegis of forgetfulness; infected with drives to assimilate, it back-handedly condemns the processes of regulated identity that consecrate the institutions of modernity.

The subject matter composes this aberrance within Arden's formation of the elegy as a matter of allegorical division. While unemployed workers receive punishment for their rioting in the nine panels of *Rupture*, above each image is the repeated photograph of a featureless passage of blue sky. This is both register of the indomitable persistence of class struggle and a near-traumatized fixing of memory on some sanguine potential for reckoning with its determination. The imagery of "social distress," unmistakable evidence of state brutality, has almost disappeared from North America's postindustrial landscape and image-repertoire, even as the social facts of economic privation and disparity have remained a key foundation for late capitalism. The sunny sky may not exactly figure this exacerbated condition, but its aesthetic division is a conflicted emblem of the abstraction of the social in the discourse of the contemporary.

Following a similar format, *Abjection* shows Japanese-Canadians facing the confiscation of their property, and subsequent internment, posed beneath equal-sized black exposures of photographic paper. If here the accompanying panels suggest utter bleakness, they are approached as a blow-like refusal to picture more than the unassimilable actuality of the scenes below. The division into image and erasure (or "image and alter-image," as Ian Wallace has written[2]) partakes of the psychic and social economy where the division of Orient and Occident, self and other, citizen and dissident are constituted—both representation and effacement in turn conjure repressed drives to account for the organized irrationality of economic dispossession and racist manipulation. Underlining this, the monochromatic abstraction takes form through the instruments that preserved the pictorial records; the exposed film is hypostatic, at once mask for the event and fundamental to present recognition of the masking performed. As well, in the unconscionable, *retardataire* politics of today, these works recall the open sore of class relations in the (failed) social politics of the Solidarity coalition in B.C. and the drawn-out federal negotiations for redress to Japanese-Canadian internees. The integral components of the pieces irrupt the composure of social memory to render that memory as something discombobulated, undifferentiated—precisely diseased.

Three works issue from *Rupture: Black Sun* (1986), *The New Objectivity* (1986), and *Polis* (1986); all portray the events of the "Bloody Sunday" riots of 1938. If, in discussing the foundational piece above, I failed to locate the "Bloody Sunday" events specifically, it is in the way of the work. Arden includes no captioning or contextual information— *Rupture* and *Abjection* articulate their division alone. The three following works reform the previous archival transformation through different types of contextualization and accompaniment. *Black Sun* is composed of prints from microfilm of pages of the 1938 *Vancouver Sun*, including reports and images of the riots; centred atop the prints are plates of flowers from a book on botanical reproduction. The bursting buds are contesting allegories of the historic events—but not those of the local riots alone. The pages detail the context of the social disturbances: the late thirties with its emergent culture of the spectacle—advertisements for therapies ("Don't Operate for Enlarged Prostate Gland") and sports reporting (a story on the Max Schmeling/Joe Louis fight presages the Second World War in its text of a black American "beating" the "Aryan" German) occupy positions next to local colour, simple anecdotes of robbery and fires and garden hints. The multiplied relations of events prevent us from viewing the flowers alone as emblems of social space "ruptured" by the rioting. They are conditioned by more than the regulated sources of historical record, and Arden pictures this excess with the flowery fructifying made parodic under the heliotropically negative *Black Sun*. To those fond of melancholy, Arden sarcastically related the Eliotic "Bloody Sunday" to "Breeding lilacs out of the dead land" without succumbing to a naturalized mythology of social relations. The link of event to flower is allegorical convention and aesthetic dispersion and directs attention towards global conditions of discontent.

The New Objectivity and *Polis* concern a less energetic aspect of the event: the rioters took possession of the main post office and federal offices in downtown Vancouver and also occupied the old Vancouver Art Gallery. In *The New Objectivity*, a work executed for strategic placement in the new Vancouver Art Gallery,[3] images of the rubble and debris left by the occupants in the gallery are placed above two Marcel Breuer chairs of the kind currently used in the gallery. The aesthetic and political orientation of the German *Neue Sachlichkeit* and subsequent formalist/functionalist movements—the universalized "new objectivity"—is made historically problematic by being placed against the most fervent cooptation of its principles in postwar North America. This imported aesthetic of total design represents, Arden intimates, a spoil of war brought in to veil prewar social disruption. But the reception of the aesthetic is not simply "objectified"—there is the implicit request that spectators take the chair and realize their complicity in possessing an historical position supported by and continuing the consequences of forgetting.

Polis imposes the same condition through diptychal divisions of two types of images: depopulated visions of the street rubble left by the riots above images of the construction of the late-deco Vancouver City Hall. With this, the architectural forms of the ruinated pseudo-Georgian Federal Building and those of the already belated, weirdly fascistic pseudomodernism of City Hall perform as emblems of the passage from colonial to corporate consciousness. Against the rough granite blocks in the old structure, the strewn glass and litter left from the street battle index social violence as event and process, while the rise of the smooth, hierarchical blocks of City Hall marks the beginning of the loss of colonial memory. The lack of human figuration in both sets of images is virtually complete, suggesting the voided subjectivity of postindustrialism but for the remnant of the past in a commemorative sculpture before City Hall—a figure surrounded by scaffolding and dwarfed by the façade of mutant modernist decorative grillwork.

These works all take the coming of the Second World War as a pivot for social relations in the province and continent—soon the unemployed will be working for the war effort or occupying the fishing fleet of the interned Japanese-Canadians. The war, with its (now fulfilled) promise of corporate hegemony, is dispersed into a field of loss, wherein its means of construction becomes clear as an eradication of the other through a dual-sided homogenization of social discourse. The Occident regroups around the ideal of saving the Old World of Europe—deferring its divisions in class and race in a spurious end-run around colonial/capitalist injustice that involves a reassertion of racist "rights" in devising the duplicitous bogy of Oriental spies. By including traces of his own protomodernist aesthetic within the works, Arden expands upon the question of the residual and encumbering legacy of these events by invoking the aesthetic as diversion and also replacing avant-garde criticality in the formation of complex statements. The complexity involved here is that of belatedness. Unable to account or speak for the past or in its diction, the imagery and accompaniments render aesthetic recuperation as at once suspect and incomplete but ultimately necessary in order to figure the shock of realizing the potential damage of forgetting.

In another work, most clearly related to the new piece *West* (1988), Arden moves farther back in time and engages another, related conflict of historical complexity. In *Mission*, against a wall painted the colour of dried blood, six panels show a group of Natives watching the ritual performance of live actors re-enacting the Crucifixion. The panels take two closely related views of the event and split them each into three—interrupting both the clear passage of time and the passage of pictorial sense. Yet this is a minor disruption, a "double take" that uses repetition to indict the apparent benignity of the event. The audience passivity, the stiff banality of the actors, the palpable absence of conflict each engenders a level of unknowing, of incomprehension in *Mission*. That this "quiet" effect is the formula for the ideological dissemination and erasure of Native culture and society is exactly what the documentation cannot admit into its careful set-up. The first assimilation needed to establish this place was the subjection of the Natives, and Arden's title resonates—the "mission" as the institution sponsoring the performance (St. Mary's Mission, at what is now Mission, B.C.) and the overall ideological move of collapsing difference to form a colonial node in the province. Christ's role as image of suffering plays ironically here, for the message is not one of the revival of meaning or the transcendence of history but remains transposed as a warning of pervasive suffering, of the unrecuperable obliteration of meanings once in place for a culture formed in different guises than the West. In the iconographically stable bloody wall, the "delimiting" after-effects of the assimilation become clear. We can no longer view this as a patrimonial mandate—our place is indentured and reliant upon an historically suspect privileging of hegemonic oblivion.

Notes

The epigraph is from Michel Foucault, *The Archaeology of Knowledge* (New York: Pantheon, 1982), 130–131.

1.   Foucault, *The Archaeology of Knowledge*, 130.

2.   Ian Wallace, "Image and Alter-Image II: Roy Arden," *Vanguard*, vol. 16, no. 1 (February/March 1987): 24–27.

3.   The work was installed as part of *The Broken Muse* exhibition, curated by Helga Pakasaar and Keith Wallace for the Vancouver Artists' League, at the Vancouver Art Gallery, November 28, 1986 to January 18, 1987.

William Wood

Facing West

Gifts must affect the receiver to the point of shock.

Walter Benjamin

I

The West Hotel on Carall is built just on the east side of this city's mangled grid. Its eight storeys are normal for the area; its clientele, only slightly more congenial—they'll sit down and order a round before beginning to rag you. The machines for gambling on trifles are out of shape, and the wood panelling has been kicked out in a couple of places, but the West has more about it than expected. Pictures from the archives show trestles with steam locomotives crossing, work crews easing the trains along their way—the scratches and flaws of the negatives blown up to scar-like proportions across a burned-out tonal abomination marking the sky. The age of the pictures is about double that of the average inhabitant, and they decorate an oddly emblematic locale.

Placed between Hastings and Pender, the West Hotel can be sited along a line terminating in no man's land. An original Skid Row, the region is populated by those to whom the railway brought mixed blessings—the Whites to live, the Chinese to work, the Natives to displace. The bars on Hastings are some of the more derelict in this city; opening at nine, they collect those refused business elsewhere—the chronics, the Natives, the nearly passed-out, the time-worn street walkers. On Pender you're in Chinatown, where gentrification has hit the banks and the bakeries—squeezing out some curio shops and putting pedestrian crossings with newly laid tiles and brass, bilingual street names set in the roadway. It is all Hong Kong money you will hear, here and in prestigious residential areas to the southwest, as if we Whites had made a bad investment in importing the Chinese in the first place. But on the West wall the refaced brick bears graffiti as follows: "West is Racis," the last letter never executed.

This libel is undocumented, and, while some of the neighbouring establishments have been taken to court for letting employees beat on Natives, the West possesses no record. The past is always there in the archival blow-ups and the brick facing as the mixed crowd of Native and Whites go on drinking beneath signs of their difference. Even so, time's

This text was first published in *West: Roy Arden* (Vancouver: Artspeak Gallery, 1988).

past erupts occasionally in other ways. Last year someone spotted a Native man in the alley behind the West, his pants down at noon, perched over a Coca Cola bottle and moving down either to shit in the opening or to admit its tender spout into his butt.

II

There were never enough White settlers in the northwest, not enough willing to build the railway and do the gardening. So the Chinese and East Indians were brought in, and the Natives, if they didn't congregate around the canneries, were left to missionaries and poverty. The fur trade dropped off; settler demands reduced the size of the reserves in pursuit of gold and grazing land; Confederation was mandated and the CPR came in taking right of way without Native assent or compensation to the bands. The Native population declined until the 1930s. It is still below precontact estimates as land claims are refused recognition and Meech Lake continues the xenophobic exclusion of Native voices in decision-making.

An irony here is that initial contact brought about "increased artistic and ceremonial life and led to a golden age of northwest coast Indian development."[1] Many of the great totems, boxes, and masks in Western museums were carved with chisels brought by itinerant British and New England vessels. They came for sea otter pelts to trade in China for, at first, fantastic sums. The coppers of the "potlatch" were executed with imported materials traded for furs, and the Hudson's Bay blanket, its industrial aura a pastiche of the handwoven cedar article, was the major currency for Natives along the coast for much of the nineteenth century. The sea captains and company traders found the coastal tribes to be canny at trade, and, while the otter was quickly hunted into virtual extinction, the profit margin was as swiftly eroded by the demands of the trade.

It is an old story of promises of wealth bringing less than expected, but loss is very much to the point here. The copper you see in the top panels of *West* harkens to the demands of trade. The twelve-sided penny and the Kwakiutl copper index wealth, but they do so in radically differing ways. Pennies multiply into the dollars of abstract worth, incrementally accumulating in a sliding scale of exchangeable returns that remain in the vaults and equity of capital. The copper was an entity unto itself; it changed hands not with an assumed wealth of demonstrable investment but with a heritage of previously traded values and always something more—more blankets or more *oulichan* grease on the fire, *more glory for him that gives it away*. Where the penny is good currency anywhere, the copper was bad to the bone: it demanded more, always more, and carried its own name and identity. Franz

Boas translated and listed copper names of estimable threat: "All Other Coppers are Ashamed to Look at It"; "Making the House Empty of Blankets"; "About Whose Possession All are Quarrelling."[2]

Hardly something worth spending a penny on.

The offering of a copper meant that the wealth "given" in return was further subject to circulation and expense. An investment of spiralling return with no equity—no base in the sameness of currency—the "potlatch" was viewed by Whites as a heathen practice encouraging the elaborate accumulation and eradication of property that could have been put to "industrious" purposes. Colonial administrators balked at such a system of loss and rapid expense, reacting by banning the "potlatch" (though it continues in variant forms today). Anthropologists explained the phenomenon in ingenious, ethnocentric ways, devising a most detailed literature of speculation. Some said it was a "primitive" economy out of control, a savage display of wanton waste; others wrote of it as a means of social ranking and peacekeeping for a warlike people. None could explain why it was that no one seemed to come out on top.[3]

III

The giving, the source of the Chinook jargon word "potlatch," was the thing. Promising allegiance to the gods through mimicry of their powers of endowment and destruction, as well as symbolically replenishing sea and land creatures and spirits by assuming their form in dance ceremonies, the Kwakiutl celebrated rites of passage through expenditure. The god of greatest import for giving was the Man Eater (*Baxbakualanuxsiwae*), a ghoul covered in mouths to devour the dead, a force of resurrection whose initiates ate human flesh and threw it back up in imitation of his prowess—in order to tame his appetite.

Attesting to ambivalent relations between cultural, natural, and supernatural realms, the Kwakiutl represented death and rebirth as a continual inhabitation of past and future solace and menace. The excess of giving was edged with the knowledge that power ties the subject to itself and to the group—producing the dual being that in giving at once vomits forth and devours the substance of the world. Giving and destroying served mechanisms of social control, ritual appeasement, and exaltation—to interpolate repeatedly the figure of transformation into ritual life and to obligate rival and spectator to participate in a circulation of identities and objects.

Made of Man Eater sun-like substance, coppers were traded for thousands of blankets and bunches of slaves, canoes, furs, and bracelets. They were broken, thrown into fires, drowned in the sea, and put back together again. Their value increased with their history of offering and expense as tribute to the psychic and social investment in the network of intertribal relations. Yet it was not a harmonious totality of cheques and balances. As its excess would suggest, what the distant Georges Bataille would call a "deliriously formed ritualized poker"[4] was critically constituted around the dread of static power, the perversity of capital.

IV

We could say that the copper finds a parodic form in *West*. Coppers are divided into two sections split by ridges half-way down: a lead-coated top displays the familiar creature of the ancestor to whom the copper is dedicated; the bottom is an otherwise unadorned copper sheet of the top half and breakable panels. *West* divides itself into the copper sheet of the top half and archival images of derailed trains on the bottom—multiplying this scheme in diptychal frames across six panels. A viridian tint lends the photos the submarine green of oxidized copper, while the top, sure to decay, now performs as an imperfect mirror—potentially imaging the spectator regarding the work and the gallery extending beyond.

The front face of a copper dipped into the sea signifies the coming of darkness; the dipping of the back, the return of light. *West*, aligned vertically even as it is metaphorically "wet" on its face, contrives to accommodate these appearances. In one aspect, the resemblance to the copper has been upset, for the Whites' ancestral familiar of the train appears in the bottom half, and it appears in the guise of disaster—off the rails Enlightenment—reversed like a Tarot card or heraldic emblem under effacement. Though the images are face-up, the trains are overturned, dysfunctional: a scattering of machines and glass, incidents of unwilled destruction. The engines and cars are pathetic monsters transformed to flaccid stillness, ciphers of agonistic expense that has no social or ritual importance in a culture recognizing acquisition and expansion.

The floating sheet of the photograph returns the dark to light but also arrests it. Placing the spectator in a relation of distance to what is given, and thus neither endowing nor destroying the perceptible item, the trains remain fixated on ambitions undone. Lost face, pictures of the end of the line, copper pipe cooling after bursting open in collision. Conversely, the reflection of my image in the copper sheet arrests the loss of history in a distorted face—an elegiac recruitment of self-image to represent an ambiguous gift of presence before work attesting to vanishing modes of subjection—"harmonized" into postindustrial miasma.

Between the *hamatsa* cannibal dancer and the Western property manager, there comes the fall of being subject to imitating a god to tame his destruction and taming a god to destroy other people. While the Kwakiutl mimic and eat to vomit forth excess flesh, late-Christians ingest and become lord over the heathen, acquisitors of the West—transubstantiating their prowess through coercion and administration. Hence the loss comes not in the way of a gift but in the establishment of the banished, the occluded, and the now obsolete. A wiping out or defacement that hopes to eliminate rather than transform.

As proof of oblivion, what is left to face but the need for destruction in devising the present? History unwritten in a play of investments. And further, stupid questions: What disturbed patient was visited in the night by the national dream? Which undead arose pierced by the golden pin of the last spike?

V

Certain other information should appear. The "potlatch" has a history without an origin for the West; the coppers made with traded goods are registers of posthistory, as declines in Native population were already evident by the time Franz Boas paddled into Fort Rupert to do his famed fieldwork. The Kwakiutl giving, despite its legendary status, was on the wane, and it decomposed under Western eyes. Precious little is known of the rituals before contact, but the available information suggests, as Lewis Hyde describes:

> As first studied, the potlatch was the progeny of a European capitalism mated to an aboriginal gift economy, and with freakish results: sewing machines thrown into the sea, people embarrassed into sitting in houses set afire with fish oil, Indians dancing with silk parasols or stooped under layer after layer of cheap wool blankets, and as the sun set the Canadian Royal Mounted Police [sic] riding off with coppers and ritual property to suppress the potlatch.[5]

Opposing the "potlatch" to the West is then not so easy. The excesses apparent to the administrators and anthropologists were already contaminated by the contact that mandated their attention. It is tempting to imagine the situation as a fun house mirror where the "potlatch" becomes a carnivalesque dispersion of property, infuriating the colonials as it acted out the worst repressions of their psyche. This helps explain the suppression of the practice and is carried through Bataille's use of "potlatch" as a model of glorious spectacle for social unity-in-inequality contrasting to the banal nonreturns of bourgeois accumulation. But demands for more always entail this subject, and the idea of the Kwakiutl reacting with deri-

FRANZ BOAS
PRINCE RUPERT

sive waste posits the other as an amorphous mass that only reflects the dominant. What comes through in the literature is the attempt to project onto the other—accounts of usury and negotiation, of diplomacy and spiritual difference—with little if any attempt to imagine an endowment that has an uncanny persistence without proprietal identity.

Whether aided by Western goods into deformity or attenuated to achieve a massive burnout, the ritual of giving circumscribes the limits of the West. It is not stock market crash, nor anarchic expense, nor conspicuous consumption, but it was perniciously influenced by those who came to remove wealth and enforce industry in the name of a political economy producing such ends. The observers may well have seen reflections of their degradation in voluminous destruction, but they made sure its traces would never return.

A man follows me out of the West Hotel. Weaving slightly, he gets on the bus, and we head to the rear. I notice that, at this hour, we're the only Whites, and the bus is headed east. He picks the last row in the corner, just behind me, and, as the trolley gains speed, he reaches up to open a window above my head. Asks my permission for this with an unpleasant undertone and then adds: "Its not that I mind the smell of people. I only want the gift of fresh air." He moves across and starts bugging an Oriental kid carrying hockey gear.

V I

Place a penny on the track, and a train passes by. The tarnished face is obliterated to reveal a warm, unformed metal spilling out. Ruined but satisfied, a hotter thing goes back into your pocket. There is more copper in the miles of telephone lines, plumbing, and circuitry than estimates say is lying in the ground. It is metal of little consequence due to abundance, but it conducts heat and electricity well, is malleable for sheathing and tubing, not to mention its quack medicinal value. Dubious, tart-smelling mineral, third-class to gold and silver, copper is weak compared to iron, progressively going green as if it should never have seen the light of day. For the West it is a material of transmission and dross, radiant but lacking in lasting value—except as a link to the energies of fiscal, vocal, electric, and hydro power. Transforming nothing for us, but taking its toll as entropic resistor, toxic deposit, and institutional face, copper remains invisible to us—an infrastructure of conduits and passages that we placidly disavow.

The nomination of Vancouver as "Terminal City" is of course double-edged: the end of the line, the point of no return, but also the link to power, the place to where things come. We may forget how eager this

West Coast was to be joined up and removed from maritime isolation: the railway gang coolies built eastward, heading into the canyons and mountains towards the straight-line rails of the Prairies. This place was constructed in the image or in the pursuit of an unspecified elsewhere, only finding broken reflections in its productions as a result. But that elsewhere, that bent allegorical pole has never been stable, so that modernity here leaks incontinently into colonial occupation, and communication slips into anxiety about who's listening. Most of the past gets swallowed up in the process, shunted off as yet another lost identification superseded by assimilation. Facing West, no one wants to look over their shoulder.

West is a gift and a mirror of the endowment of this place: its occupation made silent, detumescent trains, its frustration made horrid by taking in your face. The railway moves stray goods now, the telephone line transmutes into the transparency of glass fibre. We are "progressively" circulating an identity by laying waste on the pile of Post-it notes (postindustry, postmodernity, postideology), forgetting that our racism is built on assuming that we own while they waste.

Notes

The epigraph is from Walter Benjamin, "One Way Street," *One Way Street and Other Writings*, trans. Edmund Jephcott and Kingsley Shorter (London: Verso, 1985), 70.

1.   Robin Fisher, *Contact and Conflict: Indian-European Relations in British Columbia, 1774–1890* (Vancouver: University of British Columbia Press, 1977), 21.

2.   Franz Boas, *Kwakiutl Ethnography*, ed. Helen Codere (Chicago: University of Chicago Press, 1966), 84.

3.   A novice in this area, I have consulted the following texts: Helen Codere, "Fighting with Property," *Monographs of the American Ethnological Society*, no. 18 (New York, 1950); Phillip Drucker and Robert F. Heizer, *To Make My Name Good* (Berkeley: University of California Press, 1967); Irving Goodman, *The Mouth of Heaven* (New York: John Wiley & Sons, 1975); and, the foundation for all these studies, the fieldwork of Franz Boas as found in the edition cited above.

4.   Georges Bataille, "The Notion of Expenditure," *Visions of Excess: Selected Writings, 1927–1939*, trans. Allan Stoekl, with C.R. Lovitt and D.M. Leslie (Minneapolis: University of Minnesota Press, 1985), 122.

5.   Lewis Hyde, *The Gift: Imagination and the Erotic Life of Property* (New York: Vintage, 1983), 30. Unfortunately Hyde's error in identifying the RCMP makes his statement useful if erroneous. The agents suppressing the "potlatch" usually acted after the fact from reports from Native collaborators.

Elke Town

Prince Charming and the Associated Press: The Needlepoint Work of Colette Whiten

This essay is an analysis of the relationship between Colette Whiten's past and present work. It traces the common ground and the differences between the past and present work to suggest a coherent order where there appears to be disjunction and contrast. This essay also positions Whiten's work in a specific relationship to feminist art practice thereby suggesting that Whiten's practice as an artist may be a way of looking at art in general and women's work in particular.

When Sleeping Beauty pricks her finger on a sharp needle she falls into a deep, dreamless sleep from which she is awakened one hundred years later. In some versions of the tale all that is needed to release her from slumber is a single kiss from Prince Charming. In other versions, Charming's gaze suffices. Despite the passing of an entire century, nothing in the world around Beauty has changed. Love, marriage, baby carriage, and they live happily ever after. For interpreters like Bruno Bettelheim, who stress emotional and sexual development within the social order without actually questioning the nature of the social order, Beauty's pricked finger signals the onset of menstruation, and Charming's kiss, or gaze, is Beauty's full-fledged awakening into the sexual order. The one hundred years of sleep is, he claims, a convenient metaphor for permissible passivity, a lethargic surrender to biology. What Bettelheim does not suggest is that Beauty's initiation-into-the-sexual-order-through-sleep keeps her pure by keeping her stupid. It guards her from the complexities of sexual knowledge and returns her, like a perfectly baked bun, to a never changing world order in which Charming calls the shots and assures that there will be no change in the status quo.

At the opening of Colette Whiten's exhibition at the Carmen Lamanna Gallery in the late winter of 1987, I turned around to hear ample evidence that Charming plans to live happily ever after in more than children's fairy tales. "This," Charming triumphantly declared surveying the exhibition, "is the kind of work she should have been doing all along."

The objects of Charming's attention were a series of unpainted plywood structures snugly fitted against the gallery walls and lining the

This text was first published in *Descant*, no. 59 (1987).

gallery-like lecterns or display stands. Each stand had a groove cut into its surface and into each groove were fitted two pieces of tightly sandwiched-together glass, angled slightly against the gallery wall. The glass in turn held in place a white piece of cloth in the centre of which was stitched a small, black-and-white needlepoint picture. Strange, tiny pictures recognizably extracted from newspapers, pictures of political figures and events, of sporting events and tragic events that shape the news, make history, and linger in memory. The men: Brian Mulroney, Grant Devine, Kurt Waldheim, Oliver North, Mikhaïl Gorbachev and Wojciech Jaruzelski. The events: a boxing match, a bombing in Beirut, a search for a missing person. Images to be remembered for only a short time; others, much longer. All transformed by needlepoint from the least labour-intensive image to the most labour-intensive image as though the poignancy of the events could be returned to the image by the sheer intensity of labour involved in fabrication.

It is the inclusion of needlepoint in these sculptures, however, that specifically caught Charming's attention. In fact, he barely saw the bare wood, table-like, supporting structures. Nor did he notice the reading room effect created by their installation. Stripped to the bare minimum of material necessity, the support structures were sufficiently predetermined in their careful design and precise, albeit simple, construction that they could be read as discreet, demonstrative elements in the work. Whiten had, after all, chosen not to frame the works simply as domestic samplers to line the gallery like so many pictures on a wall. The structures provided a sharp contrast to the highly articulated, almost overdetermined appearance of the needlepoint pictures.

"This is the kind of work she should have been doing all along." Words of praise or disdain? In fairy tales, these words are Charming's kiss of approval. But Whiten is no princess, and, if she has had an awakening, it is to the character of her own activity, her practice as an artist, which is independent of Charming's critical judgement. In the gallery setting, however, Charming's ambiguous words also convey his relief that Whiten has given up her old, more masculine, ways of working and also conveys his disdain of the properly feminine medium she has chosen to replace the unwieldy process and cumbersome product of her past work.

This anecdotal vision of Charming at a Saturday afternoon gallery opening is included here not because Whiten's needlepoint works have any reference to fairy tale sexuality but because lurking behind Charming's cunningly ambiguous comments are two questions, only one of which has anything to do with Charming's sexism. First, what are the similarities and differences between past and present work? What comprises and describes these differences, and how may the thread of similarity link past to present work? And second, is there something inherently *different* in women's work? Even more, can this difference constitute a legitimate art practice?

The first question is really a series of questions provoked when an artist with an established career and "trademark" work exhibits new pieces that reveal a very dramatic shift in materials, method of working, and subject matter. Is the new work simply a novel variation on the older work? Does it shed light on or obfuscate the previous work? Or, has the artist radically changed her aesthetic and political criteria for producing work?

The subject is complicated by critical and public expectations of the continuum of an artist's work and of what constitutes engaging, timely work. If, as in the case of Whiten, the change in the work gives it a new currency, then it is the viewer expectations and attitudes that are seen as limited, stagnant, and outmoded. Whiten has, after all, become well-known for her life-size body castings and has made a career out of recording the mutability of the body through the many nuances and variations the casting medium and the body permitted. Now, as a by-product of not doing what is expected of her, Whiten has challenged the notion that an artist must refine her ideas by mastering a single medium. She has also challenged the viewer's notions of what constitutes a continuous body of work. Yet, even more importantly, she has raised the question of what constitutes the span of time during which an artist's work can be of interest and of when it becomes passé. Whiten's new work is certainly not a gratuitous bow to any current interest in the appropriation and recycling of mass media images, nor has she intentionally shifted practice to produce culturally meaningful work with a poetically articulated Marxist-humanist twist. Yet the continuum through her art practice is much harder to perceive than the readily evident differences between different phases of her career.

Undoubtedly, the Prince Charming of our story was remembering the structures in Whiten's past work, particularly the huge, indelicate appliances for constraint, built to contain and cast the body, life-size: large-timbered structures like medieval instruments of torture, so contradictory and alien to the suppleness of flesh, to the sense of self in the body. Structures fitted with metal restraining braces, ropes, and rubber thongs—all parts necessary to support the body, to render it weightless, to show no articulation of muscle, no strain or effort. This was the body in bondage, in the service of its own passing history. All records of what was, of a presence now absent. These were structures to which Whiten had subjected many more male than female bodies.

Connie Hitzenroth, who was both witness to and participant in the making of an untitled December 1972 work, described the process as follows:

> At 8:30 on a Saturday morning all arrived. The men undressed and each stood in front of the casting space while the women (myself and three of Colette's other friends), each with a bowl of warm water, razor, shaving cream, and towel shaved the legs, arms and armpits of the men to prevent the molds from adhering ... the men were placed with arms outstretched and fingertips overlapping in the structure, according to the spaces designed for them. The helpers worked clay between the legs and wood to provide a separating surface for the two halves of the mold. ... Several helpers were constantly mixing plaster. After the leg molds were set and removed, the arms were placed in wooden forms which could contain the plaster ... during this time, the assistants gave the men drinks of water and cigarettes. ... After the arm molds were completed and removed (it was then five o'clock) the men showered, dressed, and returned to watch the final positioning and recording of the empty spaces.[1]

Theirs must surely have been a fascination to see a likeness of themselves in a way that no other method offers. The mirror image proves intangible; a photograph is distant and immaterial; a painted portrait projects the painter's subjective involvement with the medium and the subject; a sculpture likewise reveals both the inherent characteristics of materials and the individual artist's skill at life-like representation. Intimately direct about the real physicality of the body, casting accurately records every hair and pore, every crease and fold, thereby giving a substantive, and absolute, materiality to the body.

But to return to the first question posed by Charming: the differences between the needlepoint works and the life-size castings. In the circumstances of production alone, the difference is dramatic. Apart from the physical amount of space required in the casting works, there is the need for people, real bodies from which to shape the casts. There is the quantity and kinds of materials; the tools for building the massive body-support structures; the mess of so much water and plaster, the need for assistants to work quickly and efficiently, all merely to leave a negative imprint.

There is a great contrast between the fragility and accuracy of reproduction of the cast and the unwieldy cumbersomeness of the structures themselves with their primitive appearance, the rough-hewn timbers, metal restraining braces, and rubber thongs. That these indelicate appliances for constraint could connote intimacy points only to the susceptibility of the body to either pain or sexual arousal. The structures were not built to inflict pain or create states of extreme discomfort. Along with their suggestion of torture and brutality is conveyed a suggestion of innocence, free of psychological implication. The apparatuses look frightening, but what they can do is relatively simple. They provide a site against which the viewer can judge the space of his or of her own body.

In contrast, the material demands of needlepoint are minimal: a box of newspaper clippings; some tracing paper and graph paper to pattern the image; pieces of evenly-woven needlepoint cloth in the smallest weave available; a selection of coloured thread; a hoop to hold the cloth stiffly in place; needles; and, finally, magnifying glasses to enlarge the cloth's fine weave so that it can be worked. These materials and this work take up little space. It is work produced in solitude and silence. No retinue of dutiful assistants, nor groupings of friends and models enliven the production process. Unlike the cast works, the completed needlepoints do not offer the viewer a site for self-referential physical comparison. What is offered for consideration is a three-dimensional object which, because of its obvious reference to a photographic image, appears as only a two-dimensional image. The fact that the needlepoints have depth, a real, raised surface, is disguised by the fact that they are so easily read as photographs. The manner of their display, however, directs the viewer to a more sculptural interpretation. Yet it is only by seeing the back of the cloth, where threads are tied off and the image has lost its readability as a photographic image, that we can finally be assured that this work, like the castings, is genuinely sculptural. In fleshing out the ephemeral photographic image—essentially in using it as raw, sculptural material—Whiten has given it a physical dimensionality that inevitably will alter its meaning.

Apart from medium, scale, and process, the subjects of Whiten's needlepoint works are also radically different from her previous work. The subjects of her large cast sculptures were primarily family and friends; those of the needlepoints are all strangers, men lifted from the pages of newspapers. It is highly unlikely that Brian Mulroney, so expressive in the tiny needlepoints, would be available to cast. Would he stand in his underwear or in the nude? Would he be shaved of all body hair, would he willingly be cut out of his clothes simply to have a cast of his body on display in a gallery? Surely a simple picture in the paper better suits his needs and those of his party. It is understandable that friends might merit an intense degree of labour, but what warrants such an output of labour for photographs of strangers? The gesture of the cast works is elaborate, even grand, extending the full reach of the body; of the needlepoints, it is close to the body, no longer than a length of thread.

Despite their differences, however, the casting structures and photography have something crucial in common. Both are apparatuses that record how something or someone looked at a specific moment in time. Although this moment can never be recreated, both casting and photography allow for multiple reproduction. In comparison to the camera's instant *taking* of a picture, casting is of course a more archaic way of *making* an exact likeness. Early cameras which extracted from sitters a fortitude and patience—perhaps not unlike that required of Whiten's models—have something more in common with the casting apparatuses than today's motor driven models.

The casting works and the needlepoint works have in common a concern for ways of creating human likeness and for the value of labour. Yet what a difference there is between the castings and photographic images. The bodies in Whiten's castings are tangibly authentic while the bodies depicted in photographic images, like the photographs themselves, are insubstantial, mere traces on paper. They have no substance, no height nor direct weight, no measure unless it is described in an accompanying text. Yet, like the sculptures, the photographs are a record of the impermanence of the body, a reminder of a life past and, as Roland Barthes has described in *Camera Lucida*,[2] a premonition of death to come. Each photograph or cast is a one-time-only event, and each retains a memory of what it once was. In time, the casting model's body will change and not fit like skin in the cast made from it. Similarly, the subject of a photographic portrait will never again take the same picture.

There is no clear answer to the second question raised by Charming's comment. Any work that makes reference to or, more specifically, uses media, methods, and techniques historically associated with women's work immediately enters the discourse about women's work. It is impossible to look at needlework without thinking it is work that would only be done by a woman. Needlework *is* woman's work. The term alone conjures visions of intricately detailed, decorative embroidery or more homely, stitched samplers enhanced with domestic mottos such as "God Bless This Home" or codes of behaviour as quoted by Rozsika Parker in *The Subversive Stitch:*

> Seek to be good but aim not to be great,
> A woman's noblest station is retreat
> Her fairest virtues fly from public sight
> Domestic worth still shuns too strong a light.[3]

Legitimizing needlework—or any other "craft" historically practised primarily by women—within the wider canon of contemporary art practice is a battle that has been fought with no winner. The incorporation of needlepoint into Whiten's work, therefore, unavoidably makes reference to its exclusion and general devaluation as a significant medium for artistic practice. But exclusion, and its abreactive companion ghettoization, are no strangers to women.

Some feminist work has taken up the issue of difference as it is described in all textual and visual representations of woman in art, politics, psychoanalysis, and the theoretical constructs that emerge from them. To highlight this difference, many feminists have insisted on differentiating between sex, a biological given, and gender, a social construct. But feminism is not a single, seamless ideology, and therefore different positions for contending with the assumed givens within society have emerged. Out of these positions some specific strategies for producing art have emerged. Many of these strategies are based on: retrieving art forms and practices traditionally described as feminine; interrupting the dominant discourse of art by altering its content, context, and method of presentation; rewriting traditional histories and reworking conventional forms; and inserting the specifics of personal experience and observation into existing theoretical frameworks.

American artist Sherrie Levine has attempted a critique of authorship and the notion of a single, creative genius by blatantly rephotographing "old masters" work and also by producing generic work. Her rephotographing of Walker Evans's well-known photographs of migrant workers serves as a prime example. Levine questions not only the value placed on original photographs (which, in fact, are endlessly reproducible through a variety of techniques) but also the dominance of the fine art photography tradition that affirms the value of the individual print over the multiple copy. Levine asserts that the right to copy an image that has already been copied a million times over is hers. Her copy is as much an original. In a very different way, New York artist Barbara Kruger, by using the graphic punch of advertising and linguistic imperatives, has both inhabited and analysed these forms of address to unsettle the viewer's response. Commands and accusations such as "We won't play nature to your culture," "You invest in the divinity of masterpieces," "You destroy what you think is difference," and "Your manias become science" combine with images that suggest conflict and ambiguity. Other artists have questioned and exposed how media formats prescribe and limit the representation of women; while still others have written texts that specifically refuse to locate the *she* in the work by obscuring either the language or visual representation in such a way that normal narrative closure is denied.

A feminist rewriting of fairy tales such as *Sleeping Beauty*, for instance, would use the elements of fantasy and romance specific to the genre, while at the same time reworking the narrative to permit an order that presents a subversion of the status quo to emerge. In Angela Carter's short story *The Bloody Chamber*—a generic, sexual awakening fairy tale— Beauty does not fall asleep at the onset of menstruation. Instead, she packs her bags, checks the time on her train ticket, kisses her mother goodbye, and sets forth to meet her husband, a wealthy, sadistic Marquis for whom she is the fourth in a series of wives who have included a countess, an artist's model, and an opera singer.

> Now and then a starburst of lights spattered the drawn blinds as if the railway company had lit up all the stations through which we passed in celebration of the bride. My satin nightdress had just been shaken from its wrappings; it had slipped over my young girl's pointed breasts and shoulders, supple as a garment of heavy water, and now teasingly caressed me, egregious, insinuating, nudging between my thighs as I shifted restlessly in my narrow berth. His kiss, his kiss with tongue and teeth in it and a rasp of beard, had hinted to me, though with the same exquisite tact as this nightdress he'd given me, of the wedding night, which would be voluptuously deferred until we lay in his great ancestral bed in the sea-girt, pinnacled domain that lay, still, beyond the grasp of my imagination.[4]

Once ensconced in the Marquis's castle, however, our heroine discovers her husband's treacherous past and a split second before she too is to join the ranks of women mutilated in the Marquis's bloody chamber of torture, she is rescued by her mother who has galloped miles to her aid. The Marquis is dispatched to his death, his wealth is divided among the townsfolk, and our heroine settles into a life of bliss with her mother and her blind piano tuner who is also her lover.

Whiten's reworking of the subject matter of needlepoint and its traditional place and method of presentation is a similar disruption of convention to that presented in Carter's short story. Like Carter, Whiten has, through her choice of subject matter and her display method, altered the script in such a way that the ideological biases of the original become evident. Whiten has not, however, simply appropriated the craft of needlepoint solely as an historical text for reinstatement within a dominant art system that has historically excluded needlecraft, as well as other kinds of craft work. Strategies such as reclaiming lost or debased art forms and returning them to the realm of mainstream art are now an accepted part of feminist art history. In and of themselves, without mediation, these strategies are viewed as redundant and reductive. While Whiten did not conceive of her work with a *return* strategy in mind, such a reference is, by inevitable association of Whiten's needlework with all other needlework, a built-in given. As a *sotto voce*, reference evokes both a memory of when that strategy was fresh and a discomfort at being in the presence of such a reminder.

Needlework was seen at one time to depict the essence of femininity. It was considered a suitable pastime for nineteenth- century bourgeois women, one to which women were by nature, by the very fact of being women, suited. Roszika Parker points out, in *The Subversive Stitch*, that as a signifier of the social and economic status of women, needlework was also a site of contradiction, of subjugation and subservience on the one hand and idealized refinement and self-containment on the other. Apart from being a genteel preoccupation for women, however, needlework is physically demanding, labour-intensive activity. It is a medium in which a great deal of labour goes into the production of something of little significance or value. In the service of deluxe ornamentation and luxury goods, it is also the site of sweatshops, weakened eyes, sore backs, and low wages.

By the time Sigmund Freud made the following observation, needlework was firmly inscribed in the social order as a primary signifier of feminine diversion. Needlework had obviously debilitated both body and mind, however refined and genteel its practice might have seemed.

> We have nothing new to say on the question of the origin of these dis-
> positional hypnoid states. They often, it would seem, grow out of the
> day-dreams which are so common even in healthy people and to which
> needlework and similar occupations render women especially prone.[5]

As a site of both action (labour) and passivity (silence and introspective thought), of hysteria and simple day-dreaming, needlework is thus seen as labour wasted and thought distracted. If this is indeed the case, any contemporary woman cognizant of this condition stitches more into a needlework than simply an image. Every stitch also rerecords the history of women, and every work constitutes as much an attack as a reaffirmation. The images in Whiten's needlepoints are immediately recognizable as being photographically-based and even more specifically as having newspapers as their source. The *news* filled with pictures streams through daily life, and it has altered definitions of self in complex ways that are contested, questioned, and challenged. There are few ways of revenging the news and no way to shut it up. Every day fresh news arrives with morning coffee and is the nightcap before sleep. Here is another meeting of world figures, another riot, another sports victory, yet one more violent incident on a picket line, in a war, or on the street, and one more search for a missing child. Very little news occurs on our own block and even less in our house. Yet in some places in the world, the news is happening all the time.

Most of the people in the news are people you will never see. If you see pictures of these people frequently enough, however, the pictures become a believable and acceptable substitute for the person. In other words, you know these people.

The news is made not so much by the people and events that appear in the news but by the very apparatus of the news itself, by people we don't see and an apparatus that remains hidden. *Making* the news is being taken literally by politicians whose most important ally may be a good ad agency and a retinue of professionals. Appearances must be groomed, suitable backdrops chosen, facial and body gesture rehearsed. A good drama coach is an asset; a new hairdresser can rework a tired look; and a smartly tailored Armani suit can add a touch of class to an otherwise drab-looking politician.

The fact that Whiten's images are immediately recognizable as being photographically-based, speaks of the authority of photography, of a persistence of vision, a habitual seeing in pictures. The strength of the photographic image—even when *degraded* as it has been in Whiten's needlepoints—is unquestionable. Waldheim, Mulroney, North, Gorbachev, Jaruzelski, boxers, a bombing, and a search. Important people and events recorded in an unimportant medium. Needlepoint interrupts the seamlessness of the photographic image, as does isolating the images themselves from their original, contextualizing front-page format. They are rendered non-iconic by being stitched in needlepoint, less important, de-signified while at the same time being given permanence which matches their continual presence.

In the process of converting the images to needlepoint, Whiten has simplified and reduced them to the point at which they can't be made any smaller without being lost entirely. In this way, they have much in common with miniature objects and, like all miniaturizations, they demand a closer look and incite wonder. They are fascinating for their relationship to the real as well as for the labour required to produce them. Being on the brink of visual dissolution gives Whiten's needlepoints both their delicacy *and* their urgency. Each stitch in time disrupts the seamless flow of events just long enough for a look.

One of the earliest extant needleworks is *The Bayeux Tapestry* (c. 1080). It is 270 feet long and documents the exploits of William the Conqueror from the accession of Edward the Confessor to the defeat of Harold at Hastings. The tapestry was thought to have been produced by Queen Mathilda, William's wife, who laboured on it—while William was away in battle—not for her own glory but for the confirmation of William's. The elaborate needlework is now believed to have been commissioned from a workshop rather than being the singular object of labour by queenly hands.

Like many old tapestries that are a record of the exploits of men at war, Colette Whiten's needlepoints also record the exploits of men. Many of Whiten's contemporary heroes and villains are not, however, literally away at war, and their histories are seldom written in handmade pictures imbued with personal reverence. Whiten's heroes and villains fight in a more public arena where the camera is a constant presence, ceaselessly recording events. Under such a level of scrutiny, it is not surprising that it often appears that events do not simply happen but are in fact staged for the media. Whiten's heroes and villains fight for space on the news front, a modern kind of battlefield on which ideological warfare is waged for public consumption. The men and events that have captured Whiten's attention have done so neither for the kindness nor for the treacherousness of their deeds. Their existence in a well-shot image within the constantly-changing flow of events is itself sufficient to merit attention.

In choosing her images so dispassionately, Whiten re-presents the news photos in much the same way that she re-presented cast impressions of the body, or the casting structure itself, in earlier work. By so clearly emphasizing concept and process, Whiten provides the viewer with a theoretical apparatus for understanding the work and for creating a bridge between past and present work. Whiten's lack of a specific, politically-based criticality or an obviously-stated advocacy position differentiates her work from that of many artists who have a direct political agenda and work with media-based images in order to question the content and use of those images.

The very idea, however, of turning newspaper images into needlepoint is an act of subversion. Whiten directs the intensely private, close to the body, labour of needlepoint against its stereotypical conventions, as well as against the medium that lacks authority (needlepoint) with one that signals it (news photography). The resulting clash in media proposes a criticality that acknowledges feminist strategies for artmaking while at the same time conveying an understanding of current issues in art. By freeing needlework from its traditional subject matter, place, and method of display and by removing news photography from its dependency on columns of explanatory text, and combining them in a sculptural format, Whiten permits each medium an altered illustrative potential, outside the history of its individual discourse.

In keeping with the practice of much contemporary media-based work, Whiten converts a widely-proliferated, disposable image into a unique object. As objects, Whiten's tiny needlepoints have an aggressive substantiality that matches the constant branding of media images on the mind. Stitch by sharp stitch, each of Whiten's images is given its due on the small battlefield of the needlepoint frame. Each image is built from repeated attacks by a sharp needle that do not stop until the image is completed.

This is the history of women, of Whiten herself, in art.

Notes

1. Connie Hitzenroth, *artscanada*, no. 178/179 (May 1973): 46.

2. Roland Barthes, *Camera Lucida*, trans. Richard Howard (New York: Hill and Wang, 1981).

3. Rozsika Parker, *The Subversive Stitch* (London: The Women's Press, 1984), 165.

4. Angela Carter, "The Bloody Chamber," *The Bloody Chamber and Other Stories* (Harmondsworth: Penguin Books, 1981), 8.

5. Sigmund Freud, *Studies in Hysteria*, trans. A. A. Bill (Boston: Beacon Press, 1950), 150.

Carol Laing

How Can We Speak To Painting?

How Can *We* Speak To Painting? The very title of this text masks an earlier effort, "How Does One Speak To Painting?", a title I had already
cribbed, and changed, from Julia Kristeva and her 1971 *Tel Quel* essay
that "reviewed"—her word—the work of Roland Barthes. That text,
"How Does One Speak To Literature?"[1] went on to save the literary
avant-garde project in general and to promote the writing of Roland
Barthes in particular; its terminology, eighteen years down the road,
names a litany that is by now familiar: the Subject, the text, the shattering
of meaning in language, difference, the Other, Desire, heterogeneity,
metalanguage. It all hinges, finally, on a preposition: on changing "about"
to "to," for, in speaking "to" literature and not "about" it, Barthes—
according to Kristeva—positions himself outside both scholarly discourse
and science, in a theoretical territory that searches for the laws of its
desires. A critical discourse whose language, as jargon, Barthes defends for
jargon is "a product of imagination" and "the language of the other, what
is not self"; it inserts "within society a practice that it censors; to communicate what it cannot understand or hear." This reading of jargon is at one
with the avant-garde project and shares its intention to "shock"; in
Barthes's hands, it promises a knowing subject's constant questioning of
the relationship between the symbolic and its subject, which in this case is
the same as saying the relationship between language and its user. In this
projected "laboratory of new discourse and new subject," we can expect,
Kristeva says, a "positive subversion of the old universe" whose own new
discourse will be neither stagnant, nor eclectically academic; instead, the
new knowledge will be "original, mobile, and transformative."

Certainly, so far, feminism has everything to hope for from such a
critical project even though Kristeva's self-deprecation on the text's second
page—"How could *I* match [Barthes's] talents as a writer?"—is unnerving,
reinstating as it does the familiar master/student hierarchy, and though
the subject the essay describes is still an ungendered one, like the impersonal "One" of its title, "How Does *One* Speak to Literature?"

My own "How Does One Speak to Painting?" repeats that imper-
sonality and formality. It is as disinterested in gender as Kristeva. But we
need to place those choices within the conditions that decided them for I

This text was first published in *C Magazine*, no. 25 (1990).

can still remember very consciously choosing in 1984, in my Modern Critical Methods and Theories class that year, the only writer on our reading list of fifteen titles who was female. Perhaps Kristeva's description of motherhood, as an experience in the world, might be continuous with my own, I thought, even if her reference was to "Motherhood According To Giovanni Bellini," Bellini who never experienced it at all.

What I was looking for was some acknowledgement not only that Desire might be gendered—Freud and Lacan gave me that—but also for a gendered Desire that might better fit both my needs and my life experience; unfortunately, it is still too true that education, here and elsewhere, throws so few crumbs to its women students. Kristeva, predictably, turned out not to be the Mother of us all; with hindsight, it was a monstrous hope, as swollen as my choices were meagre; and hadn't she won by acclamation, after all? To be fair to her—and it is important to be fair to her— she had never offered herself as such.

Anyway, my "How Does One Speak To Painting?" was not concerned with motherhood. It was concerned instead with at least the possibility of pleasure, a pleasure tied to colour, as the "mechanism" (Kristeva's term) of a certain eroticism, that is, *jouissance.* In short, I *was* a painter. And what I was not learning in studios as a student was a language that was helpful. At this time, I still believed in the possibility of "a new language"; I was even hoping that painting might be that language. Kristeva, and Barthes before her, had played with this idea. In 1969, Barthes posed the question in a text whose title is the question: "Is Painting A Language?"[2] Till then, he said, he'd had no answer: no one had been able to establish either painting's lexicon or its general grammar; nor could semiology, as a science of signs, make inroads on art for the image is not the expression of a code; pictures were not systems. Instead, they generate systems. So, according to Barthes, the practice of pictures generates its own theories—which, luckily, and even conveniently, gives the writer who transcribes pictures' systems a job.

Not that this writer is just a writer talking *about* painting. No. This writer is the *grammatographer:* the one who writes the picture's writing. No wonder painters frequently loathe, fear, and even envy, so-called *grammatographers* whose work, after all, often seems intent on displacing their own. Here is Barthes's description, written in 1973, as *grammatographer*, about painting as a project, by way of a dead artist who is, among other things, one who can't talk back. This artist becomes the emblem of Barthes's writing, the artist/"savage" Barthes calls a "Redskin" who is also conflated with all painters. So far, Barthes's penchant for stereotypes is clear, as is his racism. Gender bias follows when he goes on to characterize what painting is: it is, he says, like disgust:

> ... a panic erection: it is the entire body-as-phallus which swells, hardens, and collapses. This is what constitutes painting: it gets a hard-on.[3]

(And in this writing, I can almost *see* Barthes hastily pushing, or pumping, his penis-pen, as he collapses painting into writing.) Then he continues to totalize painting by quoting the artist Requichot's remarks on his attitude to his work:

> I am talking about that simple rhythm which for me makes a canvas start up slowly, then gradually becoming more involving, and by thrilling crescendo leads me to an effervescence on the order of orgasm. This paroxysm is followed by a great disappointment.[4]

Which Barthes calls *détumescence.*

I think it is important to make clear, with my critique of Barthes's reading of painting, that I am not at all opposed to the sexualizing of the painting project; what I am objecting to, and strenuously, is the substitution of a specifically *male* desire for all Desire, especially in an area where such readings have long become clichés: this is patently not "a new discourse"; it's the same old discourse, not one that is deserving of the description "transformative." At the end of Barthes's more ludicrous than seminal writing on painting, I am, like the painter Requichot, disappointed. But it is a *different* disappointment. It's clear, isn't it, how little this gives women painters to go on.

Kristeva, too, asks whether painting is a language, but she takes the question elsewhere: for her colour problematizes the language analogy:

> "Color" is difficult to *situate* both within the *formal system* of painting and within painting considered as a *practice*—therefore, in relation to the painter. Although semiological approaches consider painting as a language, they do not allow an equivalent for color within the element of language identified by linguistics. ... If it ever was fruitful [Kristeva decides] the language/painting analogy, when faced with the problem of color, becomes untenable.[5]

Perhaps, I thought, a painter's theorizing might be more helpful. So I turned to Gisela Breitling, a free-lance artist and writer, living in Berlin.[6] Breitling makes no attempt to align painting and language, but she does see a crucial link between them in the growing taboo—developing from the early 1970s forward—that increasingly confronts women artists who would be painters. And this is a different problem from the one that was also there in those years for virtually any artist who wanted to be a painter. This latter situation had more to do with the exhaustion and commodification of late modernist (i.e., Greenbergian) formalisms and Pop Art, the rise of conceptual art, and the arrival of new time-based video and performance work; the situation Breitling describes has more to do with the task (one that is still there for women in art discourse) of breaking a silence that is thousands of years old. It is time to say that the truth of this "silenced silence" is not a truth women can (or should) deliver, any more than male artists have been able to deliver the "truth" about painting, despite Derrida's quotation of Cézanne's promise to deliver it, in language. An answer would continue to keep female speech in a separate category, ensuring, Breitling says, that, like most female speech, it would not be listened to. Women artists who are interested in painting now are not interested in being *paintresses*—which is not the same as saying that they aren't interested in painting as women.

Difference need not mean separation; in fact, it is separation, all along, that has been harmful. It is the separating out of women from men that has allowed men to construct the universals whose assumptions are that so-called common, human experience is as the masculine describes it. It is this falsification in all our descriptive systems that has, effectively, kept women's experience from registering. It is this falsification that, on the simplest levels of grammar, still continues in the media, daily newspapers, and in schools with use of the generic "he," or the formal and neutral "one," for what needs to be much more specific in regard to gender, and especially when generalizations are at stake. For women and for men— though it may be less clear to men—the bad fit of language to experience begins here for it is here that the specificities of gendered experience are not acknowledged. And this is why I no longer believe that "a new language" will arrive, even if its imagining is sometimes a useful and necessary utopian project for, in the realer world, it is already a task larger than us all to change the existing language. The language that is not going to go away. I now believe that women artists need "a new language" much less than we need access to the existing language whose speech and writing taboos already enforce enough prohibitions on perception and reception. This language that is power is also what can make invisibles visible; or as women well know, visibles, invisible—an invisibility that is not utterly different from the invisibility visual artists often experience when their work disappears under someone else's language.

But I want to return to the early 1970s rejection of painting and to the work that displaced it, for work that grew out of painting's rejection, even painting's necessary temporary rejection, has come to dominate feminist production in the 1980s. It is important to return to the terms of painting's rejection, for, first, as we all know now, painting did not die. In fact, like the repressed, it was already returning with a vengeance by the end of the decade and, in many quarters (not least of which, the market), it was heartily welcomed back. That work was, as paintings go, big, brash, full of self-importance, often verging on the sexist and even the fascist. So it is not surprising that this particular return was quite consistently read as one face of the Janus-faced postmodern, the reactionary and neo-conservative face that looked back. The face that looked forward was considered both progressive and even radical, and this work—critical, fragmented, often intentionally anti-aesthetic—was the image-text work that has come to be designated the scripto-visual. And surely what was wrong with such a reading was the simplistic splitting of art work on the grounds of its materials, a split that, projected forward from modes of production, would divide opposing political territories, that would predictably clash over the new issue of theory.

In this configuration, painting was cast as incapable of political effectivity despite evidence to the contrary in the history of painting in the work of, say, a Courbet or a Goya, and even while Courbet's value as a political painter was being substantially revised upwards. But painting, it was said, was too contaminated and still too much at one with its patriarchal, high art history to be a viable medium, especially for women. Too bad, in retrospect, that its history became confused with its nature, as a medium. Too bad that just when women finally had access to painting and were even beginning to construct a history, albeit an incomplete one, painting suddenly dried up as a possibility for practice. Not viable, then, because it had such a history. Not changeable because there were virtually no women painting teachers, few art historians who had anything other than a sexist perspective on gender, few curators—women or men—who might have constructed other readings. So painting became, quite simply, politically incorrect: a chauvinist theatre intolerant of women who could not identify with Renoir's conflation of painting tools with his own sexual organ in his much-quoted statement that he painted with his prick. This didn't mean then, and it doesn't mean now, that there are not other ways to paint.

Still, it is true that at that time, other modes of production seemed to promise women more; modes that, it was said, had less problematic histories; modes that, increasingly—if not quite able to generate languages of their own—were comfortable and confident in adopting what they needed in language from other disciplines: from sociology and psychoanalysis; from literature and philosophy; from film and critical theory. There was the hope then that image-text work, and/or installation, would be exempt from commodification, a hope that now looks unrealistic, and something that could have been learned even then from the commodification of conceptual work and the earlier oppositional work of the historical avant-gardes. What has become clearer with that work now is the essentialism (a charge always quickly directed at other forms of art production) of some of its own readings: in psychoanalysis, for instance, where Woman, as a socially constructed category, remains either a fiction, a fragment, a stereotype, or a lack. If a decade of work on *the Body* has not been able to deliver a consensus on the role of the body in art, it certainly has opened up *the Category of the Body*. But, predictably, interest in *the Body* remains high (not only to image-text work), not least because we all have, and are, bodies, with all that that means.

But I want to return to the scripto-visual case against painting.

In Britain—where scripto-visual work is strongly positioned—a discourse has been building that intends to revise the prospects for women and painting. Katy Deepwell, in her essay called "In Defence of the Indefensible"[7] describes the split territories referred to above and goes on to critique Sandy Flitterman and Judith Barry's influential 1980 text "Textual Strategies: The Politics of Artmaking"[8] which describes four possible avenues open to women artists, only to close, subsequently and immediately, three of them down. The three rejected categories include:

1. Work that glorifies an essential female art power
2. Women's art that is in a form of subcultural resistance (e.g., the valourisation of craft)
3. Work that is produced from either separatist or nonfeminist perspectives.

The fourth (approved) category is closely tied to certain kinds of theory that construct a notion of art work "in which the social construction of meaning and the functioning of discourses in shaping social reality" are clear. Martha Rosler, Deepwell says, will soon go on, in this redefinition of the personal/political, to insist "that the naming and representation of the personal constitutes a feminist practice *only* when inserted within political discourse." What Deepwell is strongly objecting to are the severe restrictions being placed here on women's art choices. She is not convinced that the political aspect of the work must be clearly visible in the work as part of its intertextual component. Aren't the politics of art works also read in their reception? And why can't painting and drawing, too, be considered components of intertextual practices? Certainly, here in Canada, a strong case can be made that they can in the work of artists like Shonagh Adelman, Buseje Bailey, Rebecca Belmore, Cathy Daley, Lynn Fernie, Janice Gurney, Jamelie Hassan, Nancy Johnson, Nicole Jolicœur, Elizabeth MacKenzie, Lani Maestro, Mary Scott, and Joanne Tod where political references, in drawing and in painting, are highly visible. Deepwell is appalled to think that feminist theoretical positions could—or should—be so prescriptive; their being proposed as such, on the grounds of politics alone, dismantles the possibility for a collective feminist art activism grounded in, and respectful of, difference(s).

The British artist/writer Angela Partington, in her text "Conditions of a Feminist Art Practice,"[9] begins by arguing with the expectation that feminist art should formulate "a new language." Instead, she is in favour of decolonizing existing imagery by investing it with feminist values. She rejects the formalism of scripto-visual work and its deconstructive strategies based on the flawed language metaphor that an art work is (only) a text. And she reads deconstruction backwards as the already familiar—and privileged—strategy of historical avant-gardes within modernism. She rejects, as well, interpretations of *the feminine* that insist on reading Woman/women as irrecoverably immersed in flux, and language-less, especially since this does nothing to dislodge *the masculine* from the fixity and homogeneity that allows it to go on reinscribing the authority, unity, and certainty that characterize patriarchal culture.

Against the limiting of feminist practices, Partington proposes strategies of celebration and negation that insist on the understanding that knowledge, and so, art production, is gender-based. So she is for the return of the vaginal, the mythic, the bodily, and the domestic—all forms of feminist production which surfaced in the early 1970s and were quickly repressed—and *against* the types of feminist theorizing that she feels, ultimately, betray a shame of women's culture. All of these positions lead her to revise the possibilities of painting for women on the grounds that women ought not to exclude themselves from traditional forms of production: any medium, and any image, she insists, can become the site of struggle. Finally, Partington revalourizes consumption which she says is women's work: the pleasures of form should not be placed above the pleasures of use.

So painting is regaining practitioners among women artists, and an article by John Roberts called "Painting and Sexual Difference" speaks to, what he feels, are the issues. He, also, splits painting from theory and says that "the question of painting *for* women today is how do women represent sexual difference across the spaces of the social without essentializing difference, without turning the pursuit of a female 'visual economy' into the language of the Other."[10]

Once again, we are offered the old chestnut that somehow it is *only women* who are different. As it is *only painting* that is riddled with ambiguities. As if language, or photographs, weren't. Once again, we follow Roberts's theorizing of painting and object-making as masculine territories, initially moving women—it is in our interests, of course—towards photography, film, and video because, he says, only these media are *out-side* the dominant nexus of institutional arrangements and official art history. And it is hard to believe that anyone in contemporary culture who has eyes could write that the recent histories of photography, as in advertising, of film, as in Hollywood, and of video, as in mainstream television, have not both oppressed and marginalized women. Painting is not, *pace* Roberts, the only place where masculine pleasures have consistently been on voyeuristic display. Roberts then goes on to charge Mary Kelly's Lacanianism with having placed an ideological "embargo" on painting, a charge he can level with impunity since he has learned—from a post-Lacanian move—that painting, *per se*, does not in fact carry a sexist bias. Happily, he reads the psychoanalytic register more correctly: Lacan's political extinction of Woman, Kristeva's confinement of her to the pre-Oedipal *sémiotique*, and Irigaray's "female imaginary" which insists on keeping woman "outside" language—all leave dominant circuits of exchanges in place, precisely because they refuse to participate in them.

Ultimately, Roberts is convinced that painting as a practice can find its conditions of criticality, but his qualification is that painting must also be the same for women and men. Sexual difference cannot be founded on the sexes' different experiences of the world because they do not inhabit different worlds. And to insist that they do, Roberts says, is absurd. Who, among women painters, could be surprised that, once again, our ticket of admission to the same (old) world—however newly described—is our invisibility?

I want to end not on Roberts's spurious last move, which wants to erase sexual difference, but with history which Roberts himself maintains is the only (real) space, and to end with history is to end with language, history's medium. I want to end with an excerpt from a text called "A Letter" by the East German writer Christa Wolf, "A Letter, about Unequivocal and Ambiguous Meaning, Definiteness and Indefiniteness; about Ancient Conditions and New Viewscopes; about Objectivity."[11] I ask readers to understand the writing woman as a metaphor for the painting woman, on the grounds of a continuous and shared experience of the world. In this way we can at least bring the painting woman inside language.

> We see a landscape generations wide where the writing woman still tends to get lost: lost in the man, the male institutions, federations, churches, parties, states. We have eyewitness and earwitness documents of how men and women talk to each other. Let's take the things the man Elnis says to the woman Ebba—"A woman who loves a man can do anything." "I am so tender inside." "My sufferings are your sufferings. We are one body and one flesh." "You shall have no will.

You shall no longer be there. I want to absorb you." "You must become my slave, and I must become completely your slave." "I have seized on you the way a male animal corners his mate. I defend my prey. I will think about you so rigorously that it will keep you at my side spellbound." "You must trust in me blindly. Naturally I cannot have someone near me who doubts." "Put an end to yourself if you feel sorry for yourself. Hang yourself, walk into the water! Then there'll be one less woman." "I will make a human being out of you yet."[12]

And what does the woman say in this forlorn landscape? What can she reply to this man who is diseased in himself? She says things like this:

"I cannot see my way in my life anymore. Am I not a human being who feels things?" "You will not be a slave, not you." "It is terrible." "You would not ill-treat people if you were not handsome." "Mine is a nature that sees ahead. I can renounce things." "I am always forced to see the abyss. I could scratch the eyes out of my head." "I want to become different."[13]

Wolf continues:

… you know as well as I do that you cannot argue against such sentences, using other sentences that begin, shall we say, with "But." I claim that every woman in this century and in our cultural sphere who has ventured into male-dominated institutions—"literature" and "aesthetics" are such institutions [and I would add, "painting"]—must have experienced the desire for self-destruction. In her novel *Malina*, Ingeborg Bachmann has the woman disappear inside the wall at the end, and the man Malina, who is a part of her, serenely states the case: "There is no woman here."[14]

But, of course, there are women here. And we, women, will go on being here. So, "How Can We—Women—Speak To Painting?" With all the means at our disposal. And with language. Against our long history of an enforced silence, in order, out of *difference*, to make a difference. To make painting different. Because what we don't need any more is more of the Same.

Notes

1.   Julia Kristeva, *Desire in Language,* ed. Leon S. Roudiez, trans. Thomas Gora, Alice Jardine, and Leon S. Roudiez (New York: Columbia University Press, 1980), 92–123.

2.   Roland Barthes, *The Responsibility of Forms,* trans. Richard Howard (New York: Hill and Wang, 1985), 149–152.

3.   Barthes, "Requichot and His Body," in *The Responsibility of Forms,* 212.

4.   Ibid.

5.   Kristeva, "Giotto's Joy," in *Desire in Language,* 216.

6.   Gisela Breitling, "Speed, Silence and the Discourse of Art," trans. Harriet Anderson, in *Feminist Aesthetics,* ed. Gisela Ecker (London: The Women's Press, 1985), 162–174.

7.   Katy Deepwell, "In Defence of the Indefensible," *FAN,* vol. 2, no. 4 (1987): 9–12.

8.   Judith Barry and Sandy Flitterman, "Textual Strategies: The Politics of Artmaking," *Screen,* vol. 21, no. 2 (Summer 1980): 35–48. Republished in *Visibly Female,* ed. Hilary Robinson (London: Camden Press, 1987) and in *Framing Feminism,* ed. Rozsika Parker and Griselda Pollock (London: Pandora Press, 1987).

9.   Angela Partington, "Conditions of a Feminist Art Practice," *FAN,* vol. 2, no. 4 (1987): 13–15.

10.   John Roberts, "Painting and Sexual Difference," *Parachute,* no. 55 (July/August/September 1989): 25–31.

11.   Christa Wolf, "A Letter," in *Feminist Aesthetics,* 95–107.

12.   Ibid., 104–105.

13.   Ibid., 105.

14.   Ibid.

A response to this text was written by Sheila Butler, "More Thoughts on Painting," *C Magazine,* no. 28 (Winter 1991).

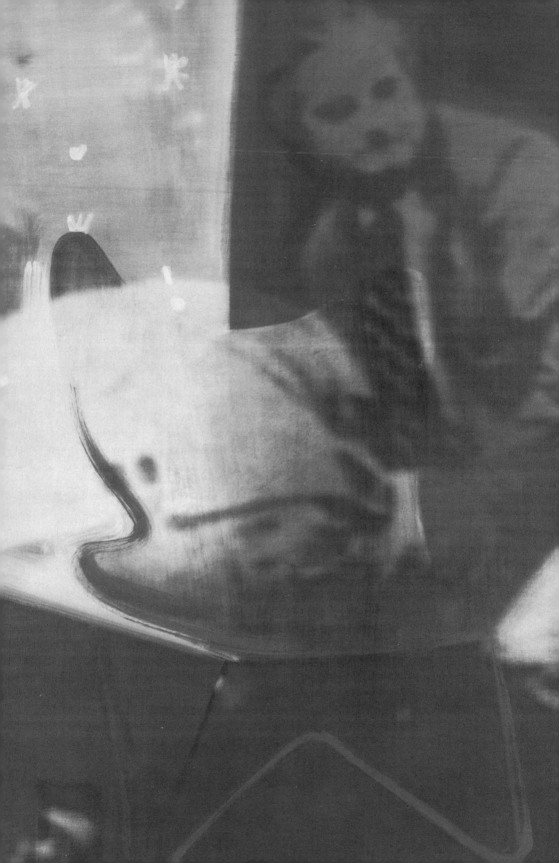

transitions and transgressions

Varda Burstyn

Art and Censorship

All societies have rules about what their members can and cannot do. Indeed, what defines human society is the human capacity to generate a set of agreed upon customs that regulate at the most minimal level elementary aspects of the taking of life and its opposite, the begetting and nurturing of children. Because what we say and what we make are part of what we do, all societies have ways of regulating the expression of their members as well. In simple societies, that regulation is constantly created and recreated as the older generations pass on to the younger the customs that are special to them, and which give shape and meaning to their lives. Taboos against what can be said, made, and done do not take the form of state censorship—a form of regulation imposed, as it were, from outside and above the majority of people. Rather the rules operate through a process of social consensus with two complementary facets. On the one hand, taboos are internalized and expressed in commonly held notions of good and bad, permissible or forbidden. They work both consciously and unconsciously, and in the latter sense they lend the psychoanalytic concept of censorship its meaning. On the other hand, taboos are expressed in a set of sanctions that are taken by the natal group when the bad and the forbidden happen, as they inevitably do from time to time.

Elementary morality, embodied in this system of customs, is a necessary, defining condition of human society. If we attempt to derive universal tenets of morality from those rules and customs common to all human groups, we find that basic rules prohibiting murder (killing of kin) and incest (sleeping with too many of them, especially mother) provide the basic social structure that enables humans to cooperate with one another to create social life. Strong feelings about violence and sex are connected to sanctions and rules that are fundamental to our psychosexual history as a species, and they carry with them the weight and power certainly of hundreds of thousands, possibly of millions, of years of species existence.

States, by contrast, are a relatively new creation in terms of our species history, dating back a mere five to seven thousand years. State structures are not universal to human culture, and they represent important changes in social organization. States are manifestations of stratified,

This text was first published in *Fuse* (September/October 1983).

hierarchalized societies in which there are some people with wealth, military, and religious (later secular) ideological power, and others who lack these privileges, but whose productive labour sustains those at the top. This is not an ideological point, but a factual one. History reveals that unless there are contradictions of power and privilege in society, humans do not seem to need or to create politico-military structures that are alienated from but that control the mass and expand in the name of "god" or "king" or "country." Contradictions in society mediated by state formations are colloquially expressed in sayings like "one law for the rich, another for the poor," or in the codification of the double standard of sexual behaviour in patriarchal law since prebiblical times. The existence of state in any given society expresses a series of contradictions between universal laws that enable humans to regulate their behaviour in the name of egalitarian cooperation and those that work to sustain the power and privilege of those strata who are on top in society.

However, power and privilege do not flourish in conditions of instability, regardless of what dominant class form organizes a given society (slave, feudal, capitalist, or so-called existing socialist). All states have had to contend with this fact, and in it lies the most compelling reason for the personnel of state formations to try to reconcile the advancement of ruling-strata interests with at least some degree of "satisfaction" of the needs of the labouring classes. Specific relations between the state and the nonprivileged mass do differ in important ways, however in different political and social systems, so that once the general point is made, discussion can proceed only if we focus on the system in question.

The System in Question

The debates we are having about state censorship today are unfolding in the context of a liberal parliamentary democracy, the political form associated with mature capitalism in the metropolitan centres of the industrialized world. Liberal democracy is predicated upon a real measure of popular support for given governmental teams that can be elected or thrown out of office by an electorate now based on universal suffrage of the national citizenry. The right of "free speech" or "freedom of expression" represents in the first instance the need felt by the different political representatives of the privileged strata to protect themselves from overly harsh persecution from one another, to allow for the give and take of the electoral game. In the second instance, it represents a much more fragile and tentative gain: the right of the underprivileged and oppressed to speak in their own voice about what goes down in society. To understand the difference between these two levels in Canada, for example, one need only look at how often members of the Conservative, Liberal, or Social Credit parties have been harassed, jailed, and/or banned, and compare that with the experiences of people and parties active in the left and the labour movement during this century. To understand the fragility of the latter gain, one need only remember the War Measures Act in 1970 in Québec and the internment of Japanese-Canadians during the Second World War; and also the complicity of successive Canadian governments in most undemocratic undertakings in the Caribbean, Latin America, and elsewhere.

The fact that our memories of 1970 and 1942 are not sharp and clear; that many of us are not aware of the harsh repression of socialists and labour activists in the past as well as in the present; that most of us never think about the conundrum of Third World dictatorships when we think about "democracy" on Parliament Hill indicates that to those who control information in our society it is important that we believe that we live in the best of all possible worlds in the best of all possible times. This belief sustains the possibility for popular support of nonpopular governments.

Liberal democratic states like ours grant great importance to the functions of ideological legitimation at various levels. Budgets and departments and programmes within departments are dedicated to the careful cultivation of the kind of social and cultural activity that encourages people to think of state bodies and norms as genuinely "public authorities," bodies and laws that represent everyone's interests more or less equally, aiding pluralistic expression and even advancing progressive social change. A thought to various forms of social service and a quick glance at a number of really admirable projects sponsored by the Canada Council verifies the rosy impression.

But what is missing and needs to be brought into the picture are the projects that do not get funded, the larger (so *much* larger) budgetary allocations of "aid to the private sector," the activities of the RCMP, civilian "security" forces and armies, the offices of the attorneys-general, the function of the courts and the ultimate, precise logic behind the seemingly random and endless snafu of government bureaucracies.

In any case, it is important to the existence of liberal democracy that people see the state as a voice and an instrument of the "whole society" and not of any given, privileged sector. Consequently, any act of state censorship is inherently a rather tricky operation, for it can potentially expose the fact that a state body is acting arbitrarily against members of a given community or society, therefore imperilling the appearance of neutrality and justice. State censorship is not the favoured but the last resort of an intelligent government body, but it is also a necessary resort in instances where the state feels itself or the larger social order threatened. The nature of the threat may differ. It may be effective political criticism, orthodoxly defined, which has somehow managed to escape its usual confinement in small, fringe media. It may be material that defies important rules about gender relations in sexually explicit terms—material that is also political, as I will explain shortly. It may be material that breaks a combination of class and sex taboos. Or it may be people who have openly flaunted the *authority* of the state itself, or questioned too loudly the state's right to decide what may or may not be expressed, and need to be brought to heel.

Decamouflaging the Contradictions

State censorship is a potentially dangerous act of ideological coercion that can easily appear to contradict the right of freedom of expression, unless the contradiction is camouflaged by popular support. Because all of us share, to a greater or lesser extent, certain values, ideas, and feelings, the state can appeal to us ideologically in its moves for legitimation. These values, ideas, and feelings are embedded and expressed in a system of sanctions that take psychological, interpersonal, and economic forms, as well as the directly political form of state censorship. (The state needs to censor only that stuff that has escaped self-censorship, family and peer group censorship, and economic censorship, as in "there's no market for *that*.")

The ideology that informs these sanctions is an insidious admixture in which the rules all people need to survive are co-opted and skewed in the service of the rules that maintain the privilege of the dominant strata in our society—capitalist, white, and male—in their overwhelming majority. In the name of "social responsibility" and "community standards" and "national security" the patriarchal capitalist state appeals to important communal values concerning the abuse of violence and sexuality, while in reality it works to strengthen a social system based on the right to private exploitation not only of the environment and human labour but of sexuality itself.

No wonder the strictly civil-libertarian anticensorship strategy that evades or belittles issues of morality and social responsibility is so inadequate to the tasks at hand. Most people are neither artists nor actors in the political arena, more's the pity. The call to defend "freedom of expression" does not resonate with the same force as the call to reject murder and sexual abuse. For most people the right of free speech is important only in very abstract terms of democracy ("it's better here than in Russia"). In daily life it is almost meaningless given the domination of information and expression by the huge corporations and government, and the material they deem suitable for dissemination. Opposition to state censorship, if it is to be effective, must grapple with the kinds of feelings that incline people to support the Mary Browns ([then] Chief Censor of the Ontario Board of Censors) of the world. Such an opposition must demonstrate that it is part of a movement that is constructing a different kind of society than the one mediated by the censors. I shall return to this point at the end of this article, but, for the time being, I want to move on to consider one particular strategy that has been advanced as a possibility for dealing with state censorship in the arts community.

A Privileged Status For Art?

How should artists situate themselves philosophically and strategically in relation to state censorship? One direction that has been explored is the demand for a special status and exemption for art from the jurisdiction of the state censors. I disagree with this direction, for several reasons.

If the definition of state censorship is clear—an ideological intervention backed by coercive means to support the status quo and strengthen the authority of the state—the definition of art is not. Beyond saying that art is a form of symbolic production, there are no firm criteria by which we can all agree on or objectively measure what art is. If, for example, we try to define art in terms of its conditions of production, distribution, and exchange—we might say that art is produced by artisanal labour and consumed within relations and spaces that are outside of those of the mass media—we immediately see that material produced within such relations is constantly being incorporated by the mass media, and it is not at all clear when or whether that material ceases to be "art." Likewise we all know the futility of setting purely aesthetic criteria. One person's or one period's beauty or enlightenment is another's kitschy or ugly nightmare. If we set moral values on art, we find one person's nightmare is another's dream. Though we might like to call art that which expresses resistance and opposition, we would be hard put to account for the mountains of stuff that support the dominant or even fascist ideology. And if we set attitudinal values as our yardstick—art encourages people to think, question, evaluate, whereas other forms of representation encourage people to accept, accommodate, nod out—that won't do either because a lot of what some people consider art measured this way, others think to be pablum or social anaesthesia.

My personal definition of art would be made up of a number of these criteria, but I am opposed to demanding a *legally formalized set of norms* by which art may be set off from other forms of ideological production, because I fear (among other things) nasty state policies about what art can or cannot be, like the infamous socialist realism of the Soviet state, or the reinforcement of the less systematically ideologized censorship of capitalist states. Both of these are odious forms of the subordination of art to politics, which I abhor.

I also think the demand of a special status for art is strategically wrong because its rationale misreads the central reason for censorship in the first place. The state reaches out to suppress artists in the same spirit that it reaches out for other kinds of "agitators" and social "criminals." State censorship is not simply a function of offices like Mary Brown's, after all. Decisions to prosecute relentlessly publications like the *Body Politic* or to go after Canadian Images Film Festival or Glad Day Books to the point of threatening their survival are decisions taken or reviewed at the Cabinet level. Art is not censored because of epistemological, phenomenological, or existential qualities that inhere in its "artistic" nature. Art is censored because of what it is saying about, and to, the larger web of social relations of which it is an integral part.

For both these reasons I think it is misguided and dangerous to demand privileged treatment for art. I think that this position simultaneously divides us from potential allies and reinforces the censor—the voice of the dominant ideology—in our own heads. If art wants special status it should forge it out of a special willingness to challenge the *status quo*, to take on what the state represents, and to defy its censorship of what needs to be said. Art should criticize, illuminate, agitate, foment, meditate, prefigure, remember, invent anew, and transcend; it should give the state the metaphorical finger, and then it should form alliances with other people who have embarked on the same enterprise in their own ways. Art should work in the service of, but never subordinated to, social change: engaged art, an alternative culture in the best sense of the term. But these are just *my* preferences—art can be whatever it wants to be so long as it doesn't paint itself into a corner and cut itself off from allies by abandoning them to repression. Ultimately, this would suffocate art itself.

The Feminist Critique

If prior censorship is not the route nor a special status for art, what is left is to build an alliance against state intervention with other forces who oppose the weight of the dominant ideology and what it represents in our culture as a whole. One would think a natural ally in this undertaking would be the women's movement, the most dynamic social actor of the 1970s and, along with the environmental/antinuclear movement, one of the two progressive social forces now able to mobilize energy and vision. But the artist-feminist alliance these days is in trouble.

In a series of public actions and campaigns, the women's movement has animated an extensive critique of much mass produced and distributed explicit sexual material—or pornography as it is commonly called. Some part, although by no means all parts, of the women's movement have come out in favour of state censorship of some of this material, and almost all feminists favour some forms of regulation of the material—both at the production and at the distribution ends. On the other hand, a number of artists and arts organizations have rejected that critique and/or declared that it works as a direct invitation and sanction to state censorship. Because so much censorship has targeted sexual representation, many artists are fearful of and predisposed against the feminist critique. Not surprisingly, relations are strained at best between the extreme poles of the arts community and the women's movement and are still very shaky in the middle ground where these two communities intertwine and overlap. I want to look very briefly at the reasons for that tension and to draw a few strategic points at the end.

The central subject of contention is how to look at, and what to do about, explicit sexual representation in the mass market—whether through photography, film, video, print, or live performance—and its relation to artistic representation and censorship. Feminists have pointed out that the vast majority of readily available porn, soft- and hard-core, is rife with sexist values. Feminists have argued that this material is an important *agent* of these values, not simply a passive carrier, and that, far from being part of an oppositional current in culture, this material is reactionary. Feminists do not think that this kind of judgement comes out of puritanism. They are concerned that at a time when women are seeking a fundamental renegotiation of the relation between the sexes, a renegotiation that requires the winning of strength and social power for women, our environment has become saturated with images that constitute a direct intervention at the psycho-sexual core of our mass psychology: a clear sub- and countertext, in directly sexual terms, to what the women's movement is trying to achieve in economic and political terms.

Questions of Interpretation

I know many artists, mostly but not only men, reject this reading of the proliferation of porn, but I have never heard a good argument against it, motivated in terms of a rigorous textual analysis of that material. It amazes me that artists and critics who are capable of the most sophisticated "readings" of many other kinds of artefacts and discourses, who are able to discern all the signatures and signposts of the dominant ideology at a glance in any other form of mass media, can turn into symbolic illiterates when confronted with just your normal, everyday, soft-porn display at the corner store.

To the vast majority of feminists questions of reproductive rights and erotic pleasure—that is questions of sexual freedom—are fundamental parts of the larger feminist programme and vision. They are not objecting to the sex in porn but to the sexism. They have not lost sight of the fact, however, that, through sex, the sexism carries a very, very powerful wallop.

In order to deal with strategic issues like state censorship, we must be able to hammer out at least some questions of interpretation. In order to do that we have to find a shared vocabulary for reading the symbols in front of us, otherwise we will be talking at cross purposes and continue to grow farther apart. There are standard systems and methods of interpretation we can use, critical interpretive tools that make our analysis accessible and potentially shared. Of these I think the most useful are semiology, psychoanalysis, Marxism, and feminism, and obviously these need to be employed with a sense of historical precedent and context, both socially and in terms of the received conventions of the discourse at hand. Semiology is a method devised to identify and decode signs—to understand what meanings are attached commonly and differentially to certain kinds of representations; psychoanalysis is a method that encourages one to search for a symbolic and unconscious dimension to artefacts and representation, and to look for connections between sex and power; Marxism predisposes one to look for particular arrangements of power as it works between men in different social classes, nations, and even races at its best; feminism alerts one to power relations between men and women, as they are played out between people of all classes.

Proper interpretive use of these theories demands an understanding of the social relations in which and by which artefacts are produced, distributed, and consumed. And so, in discussing questions like "meaning" and "social impact," we must look at artefacts as part of the field of reality from which they came and in which they intervene.

When feminists look at much of what passes for erotica these days (at mass produced and distributed pornography) they are concerned with all of these dimensions, not just with one or two. To me, and to a large number of feminists, it is the increasing commodification of sexuality that is most troubling, for its dynamics combine together some of the ugliest aspects of capitalism and patriarchy. We are concerned that in the world of public heterosexual sex it is primarily women whose sexuality is bought and sold and primarily men who do the purchasing. Large numbers of women are becoming sex workers out of necessity.

Fantasy and Reality

The problem is that what appears as "fantasy" in masturbatory representations for men is not a fantasy to the women whose bodies are used to make the representations. Here lies a crucial distinction between drawings and literary texts, which are unmediated expressions of the producer's imagination, and material in which the producer's imagination is mediated through the real actions of real people within a network of unequal economic power relations. (This point assumes that there is at least the freedom involved in selling sex for a wage. Such a situation does not obtain for truly enslaved women, a point I will take up at the end of this article.) So we worry about the means and relations of pornographic production.

But we also worry about the means and relations of pornographic distribution and consumption, about the fact that, as porn pervades all the places around us, the community milk stores and video outlets, the television stations available at the flick of a switch, all of us—men, women, and children—are being bombarded with "soft-core" images of women which display the following signs:

1. *Youth and slenderness*: feminists have talked at length about the demoralization women experience as a result of sexual stereotyping, and that is indeed unfortunate. Regardless of the stereotype, we simply do not all have similar bodies. But what is far more damaging is the latent content of the stereotype so dominant in porn today. Most human beings grow larger with age, gain some weight, and acquire wrinkled skin and greying hair. Women, even more than men, tend to accumulate fat—it is part of our genetic programming. These characteristics (large size, silver hair, the lines of experience) are still signs of power when associated with men and are not split off from men's sexuality.

Images of women, on the contrary, constantly split these characteristics off from women as sexual beings, working to diminish the sexuality of older women, and the potential for power of younger ones. We have arrived at the point where the idea of a heavy older woman in postures of sexual abandon is considered ugly (a change even from the pornography of Victorian times, which worked off the premise that everyone did have, underneath, a sexuality that was hidden as a result of the prevailing puritanism). Linking women's sexuality only to adolescent bodies is a socially meaningful phenomenon having to do with the control of women's power. It is least of all an issue of aesthetics.

2. *Accessibility, sustenance, and submission*: there are many of these signs, and we can read them well with a little help from social anthropology as well as the other systems I have cited. Three central examples: (a) the ubiquitous smile or coy pout signal nonthreatening, cooperative assent to the wishes of the absent masculine voyeur; (b) bared breasts, often uncovered in a motion of the girl's hand, give the appearance of offering up sexual (and underneath, associated with that, maternal) sustenance; (c) posterior and/or vagina, covered or bare, in what is called presenting posture, which is the submissive invitation to aggressive mounting behaviour, a sign read universally and even across mammalian species as one of accessibility, submission, and acknowledgement of superior power.

3. *Props of bondage*: (here I am referring to the so-called vanilla porn, not the S&M material) high heel shoes, a form of hobbling akin to footbinding, lace corsets for artificial control of stubborn body contours, and, along with heels and tight skirts, impediments for free movement and locomotion; make-up, complete body make-up for that matter, not as an expression of theatrical *joie de vivre* or even a mating ritual but as a mask to hide individuality; and of course the complete absence of body hair (except for the well-trimmed pubis), the presence of which is associated in all cultures with adulthood, and in Western culture with masculinity, sexuality, and power.

4. *Absent signs*: the insignia of social power. Where are the last names, the professional statuses, the big cars, the executive suites, the prowess in sports, manual labour, or military activities? All these have been regularly found to accompany men's images in *Playgirl* and the few other "women's magazines" that have and still do exist, as well as characterizing a lot of gay male porn. Where is the strong, challenging, unsmiling, full-frontal gaze found in male gay porn? Where is the sweating, determined, instrumental masturbatory posture? Where are the signifiers of powerful, aggressive, and independent desire? Indeed, where are all the men? Above all, in terms of missing signs, where is the penis?

The penis is absent as the signifier for male power, while a series of its symbolic stand-ins abound: swords, guns, cars, tools, towers. This absence requires some explanation, since the vulva and vagina are now regularly exposed to any Tom, Dick, or Harry who wants to flip through the magazine rack. I think the absence of penis, especially the erect penis, is explained by the rules of our social order that declare that we must not take this particular sign in vain. We must not objectify and trivialize it by allowing it to stick up and out so vulnerably and even ludicrously in public places, the way we have done with women's breasts and genitals. It would lose too much of its mystique, and god knows it can't really afford to lose any more. It has already lost all its magic and retains social power only through its association with big money and armed might. Indeed, I think we need to be clear about this: today's distinction between hard and soft porn (even the words give it away), is not as arbitrary as it seems at first. Since women's sexual apparatus has been fully exposed for a long time now, it is a distinction that aims at maintaining some degree of phallic mystification (e.g., in Ontario intercourse is forbidden, in Québec, ejaculation). Insofar as some non- and antifeminist men struggle against the legalization of hard-core porn, they are struggling against the banalization of the phallus by its inclusion in the world of everyday life. They are not struggling to protect women.

If all these signs are the standard basic vocabulary of soft-core pornography, if in certain respects they are continuous with the presentation of women in advertising, television, and cinema (which they are), it would be a mistake to think that most hard-core porn is in some sense "better" because it makes erect penises visible and shows women who are active. Most of what I have been able to see of this stuff in New York (magazines, video, and film) compensates for the visibility of the penis by stances and actions of sexual service by women for men—always ready to accommodate, even worship the great god unveiled. (Again, I want specifically to address questions of real sadism and bondage a bit later on.) There is no automatic improvement in porn by virtue of its being hard-core, no more "realism" or "honesty." For the most part, that porn is just a further extension of the sexist wish fulfilment of soft-core and, insofar as it is a model for behaviour, penetrates, so to speak, to an even more intimate and precise place than soft-core porn. But, as I stated before, hard or soft is not the issue. I have seen a little bit of hard-core material and the occasional soft-core spread which, if taken out of their sexist context, could be considered reasonably benign in terms of their messages about gender and sex. I have also seen a lot of erotic representation by Western artists and those from other cultures which is explicit in the extreme and which I found not only benign but also positive from that point of view.

Distinguishing Sex from Sexism

Perhaps the distinction between sex and sexism can be made a little more concrete by comparing the vocabulary of mass hetero-porn to Barbara Hammer's short experimental film *Multiple Orgasms* (1977). Much of this film is taken up by a juxtaposition of the following imagery: a full-screen, unretouched shot of an open, moist vulva and vagina and a hand working towards and achieving eight orgasms; a range of massive, bare granite rocks; and a strong, lined women's face, eyes open or closed, but at all times taken up with internal and alternating processes of effort and ecstasy. This film breaks a lot of the patriarchal rules. It shows an older women, without make-up or smile or concern for the male gaze. It shows an active vagina and vulva in instrumental sexuality, and it associates that sexuality with the strength, eternality, and superb indifference of a range of primeval rock. I'm sure Mrs. Brown would not find this film acceptable. And although I do not think she would be able to articulate it, the Ontario censor would also probably find this film objectionable because it breaks a lot of capitalist rules. It was made for next to nothing, it is only a few minutes long, and it refuses the usual forms of ideological seduction that virtually define the capitalist media. It defies incorporation and co-option within a large-scale profit system, and, unlike *Playboy* or *Penthouse* or any number of porn videos and films made in any number of southern condos, it sells no commodities or life-styles. All it does is challenge these, by the implication of criticism and opposition suggested in the broken conventions that lie shattered around it.

Hammer's erotic representation is political in the sense that it exposes the conventions, and by implication the rules, of a complicated set of power relations that grow out of two distinct but intertwined systems of social inequality. Patriarchy, the system of masculine privilege embodied in social, economic, sexual, and state relations, is an older system than capitalism. While it has structured capitalism in very important ways— unequal pay access for women and men in the paid work force, and unpaid female work force in privatized units for reproductive labour—the two systems also conflict, and this tends to weaken them. For example, capitalism erodes really central bases of patriarchal power relations because it needs a smaller work force than an agrarian economy, less physical strength, cheap labour pools, and an ever expanding market for its commodities. (This last factor is responsible for the mass generalization of commodities as different as contraception and video porn.)

All these factors combined both compel and encourage women to take greater control of their reproductive capacities. This development strikes at the fundamental premise of patriarchy—masculine control over women's reproductive and, necessarily, erotic activities. Patriarchy's weakening does not in any simple way strengthen capitalism, however. On the contrary, the experience of the women's movement at both ends of this century has amply demonstrated that when women start to seize control of their sexuality, they tend to become less docile on the job, and they start to question other aspects of economic and social inequality. The growth of working class feminism is a very ominous development from the point of view of a system that is in a continuous state of cyclical crisis, and therefore congenitally incapable of resolving either gender or class contradictions.

Tensions notwithstanding, capitalism cannot simply displace patriarchy. For all of their conflicts, the two systems are now fused into symbiotic relationships, and their tensions must be resolved in such ways as to preserve the general structures of the power characteristics of each. The state is the central site for the mediation of contradictions that cannot be resolved without recourse to public debate and action, not only between dominant strata and the nonprivileged but also between different factions, opinions, and interests within the dominant strata. Censorship and the debates about it are part of these activities, and they are focusing on sexual matters at this stage for at least two important reasons.

First, as women gain greater control over their economic and procreational activity, masculine control can no longer be exercised through reproductive control; it thus tends to move over the field of erotic pleasure. Material independence can be subverted by ideological subservience, and the vernacular of porn is ubiquitous propaganda for that subservience, cloaked in the emperor's clothes of the sexual revolution. The reason that women can be so affected by sexual material—be it in advertising, television, soft- or hard-core pornography—is the same reason men are so touched by it. Sexual material has a special charge because it affects us not only sexually but also more generally, as it intervenes at pre- and unconscious levels of the psyche where sexuality is connected to other capacities, values, and ideas about individual and social behaviour. Censorship of sexual discourse is thus more clearly a political act than it is usually thought to be, and sexual practice is a more political terrain. For the state, sexual material that undermines the capitalist mobilization of patriarchy (or vice versa) is by the same logic politically subversive and must be brought into line if it gets out of hand.

If it seems that a disproportionate amount of censorship comes down on the arts community, perhaps it is because artists, who are self-consciously removed from the immediate dictates of the mass entertainment markets and who are self-consciously dedicated to *expressing* something about their own (and society's) sexuality, find themselves breaking the rules much more often than the people whose material gets churned out for profit in the male market. If the material that gets produced within the artistic milieu is intended as, and constructed to be, a dialogue, no matter its marginal situation, whereas mass produced porn is a broken, refracted mirror of men's unease about their sexuality and social status, maybe it is easier to understand why art suffers so much more than commercial sexual representation. But as pointed out earlier, art is suffering because it is breaking that same set of rules that nonartistic endeavours break, not because of some existentially given "artistic" quality *per se*.

Strategy and Morality

In light of all these considerations it seems to me that artists have a twofold responsibility, having to do with artistic productions on the one hand and political struggle on the other. In terms of artistic production, I would call for more works of an erotic nature that continue to explore and push further the barriers to gender equality and sexual ecstasy. We need works that not only arouse but also enlighten, encouraging us to understand our own eroticism in a whole number of ways. We need art that can serve as a living, breathing alternative to pornography: art that encourages people to pleasure themselves and each other; to assert their physical, emotional, and social needs and to reflect on those needs at the same time; and to understand how these needs have been shaped by the biographical as well as the historical details of our lives.

This process simply cannot get very far unless more women make sexual representations that are then seen and discussed by women and men. But the sanctions against women producing this kind of material are in fact quite heavy: lack of economic resources, pressure from peers, and even the threat of sexual harassment and violence are all difficulties to be faced, quite aside from the almost inevitable consequence of state censorship. It is thus all the more vital that men, too, make a commitment to support women's efforts and to deconstruct analytically their own pleasure and unpleasure, just as women have been doing within discussions in the women's movement for the last ten years. Men need also to try to understand and make clear to others how gender inequality and capitalist sexploitation operate in our most intimate lives. They need to criticize the values and methods of the capitalist sex media as ruthlessly and intelligently as they do the values and methods of the other mass media. In plainer language, this means that men will have to stop defending most pornography ("if I get off on it, there can't be anything really wrong with it") and freaking out when women criticize it. Men, as well, need to help people understand and overcome erotic alienation.

I say "people" because men are suffering from the porn proliferation as well and indeed, I believe, just as seriously as women in a number of crucial respects. For men as well as for women what is prescriptive is also restrictive ("what kind of man reads *Playboy*?") and generates anxiety about sexual performance when men's bodies, sexual organs, feelings, and desires don't correspond with those depicted in porn today. Porn sets up expectations of female behaviour in response to brittle, stupid notions of "masculinity" which creates distress when not met, causing anxiety and, often, serious hostility (rape, rape, rape, rape) on men's part. The manipulation of sexuality to invest commodities with prestige and glamour and to sever relations of solidarity between people are both enormous problems for men, as I have discussed at greater lengths elsewhere.[1] Although women have raised the first organized voice in protest over the content of pornography, progressive, psychoanalytically-informed social theorists have long argued its debilitating effects. It is not uniquely a "women's" issue. It is a human issue.

Which brings me finally to political strategies with respect to art, sex, and censorship. I will focus on issues regarding sexuality because so far no debate has occurred about whether or even how to defend artists whose work is censored for more orthodoxly defined "political" reasons. But sex is political, too. If it weren't, there would be no need for its political regulation. We must make some choices in terms of appropriate measures to deal with matters of art and politics which do not reinforce already dangerous powers. We need measures that will, on the contrary, undermine the economic and social relations in which the exploitation of labour and sexuality create such regressive gender propaganda.

My recommendations would include: (1) The regulating of working conditions within the sex industry, that is, the conditions under which people sell *their own* sexuality or have it otherwise alienated from them. This would include the regulation of the conditions under which profit is realized from this commodification, including its distribution and exchange, covering both private and public sectors of the economy and infrastructure; (2) Retraining, a living wage, and protection from harassment to all women who are sex workers so that no woman ever has to sell her sexuality out of necessity. But as long as women do, we can support the demand for decriminalizing—not legalizing—prostitution and other aspects of the sex trade to stop the victimization of women; (3) Heavy taxes applied to the porn industry; and (4) Regulating the places where porn appears. This respects the rights of those who don't wish to look at porn without infringing on the rights of any adult who wishes to obtain it. For example, porn should never be permitted in workplaces because the vast majority of working women experience it as a major form of sexual harassment. And before accusations of "prior censorship" get hurled at feminists by civil libertarians, let's remember that porn can be easily, cheaply obtained almost anywhere, in video, film, or magazine form. It's not as if it's hard to get.

The most difficult part comes when we are up against that two or five or ten per cent, some say more, of porn that would be classified as pure hate literature if Blacks or Jews or political prisoners were its subjects. This is the stuff made with enslaved women, women who are not "freely," so to speak, exchanging their sexuality for a wage, but rather kidnapped, imprisoned, tortured, mutilated, and sometimes even killed. This material has lost even the most tenuous connection to "fantasy" embodied in a women's exchange of her body for money. This material is the visual record of acts of pure brutalization, and as such it has lost its claim to be protected by the law that claims to protect the freedom of expression. Here there is no "theatricality," no element of "performance," no "exchange of ideas." Just as we have begun to describe rape as assault, not as sex, we must call this assault, not pornography.

We should forbid all sales of material made from the exploitation of children and enslaved women. We should prosecute those who produce this material with heavy penalties, and we should contextualize exhibitions within educational and community institutions to enable people to understand what this material is and what it represents: the very opposite of freedom of expression, the product of terror and sickness.

Developing a Vision for the Future

But none of these regulations will mean anything unless we collectively raise children who will be able to live lives of greater freedom than ourselves. And that in turn depends on the presence not only of good erotic art but also of good sex education for them, and for us.

The long term solution to sexual problems at individual and social levels cannot possibly lie in returning to the puritanical and repressive norms out of which we have been emerging in the last few decades. Prostitution and pornography are products—the dialectical companions—of that sort of repression. But neither must we mistake the dominant forms of sexualization of our environment as the doors to liberation. As adults we need to learn more about sexuality, how it works, how ours works, how to help our children move beyond some of the scars we have accumulated as a result of our lives and generational experiences.

We need to take appropriate measures to find nonauthoritarian ways to regulate sexuality in a public space shared by people of all ages and from many different cultures, respecting our collective needs for existence and our individual or generational needs for autonomy. Because the state is not an instrument that will in its existing form act as an instrument of these needs, we need to be very careful about how we use it and what we call on it to do. We must regulate our public life, but we must find the ways to do it that empower large numbers of people to think and act for themselves, and not encourage an alien structure to decide what is or what is not acceptable. For this reason I think militant informational pickets outside porn outlets or strip joints are fine because pickets are an expression of feminist opposition to sexual commodification and part of the free flow of ideas. But I do not agree with allowing bodies like the Ontario Censor Board the powers to say what will and will not be seen or said by us.

There are many contradictions and no ideal solutions. But we can move towards better solutions through the creation of an alternative erotic culture and through strategies and demands that move us towards a society where women and men and children live together without exploitation and domination.

Notes

1.　　　Varda Burstyn, "Freedom, Sex and Power," interviewed by Lisa Steele, *Fuse*, vol. 7, no. 5 (February 1983): 251–254.

Guy Sioui Durand

Quiet Censorship

Must today's artists meet certain conditions before they can work in Québec and Canada? A first glance tells us that censorship and repression remain exceptional and rare forms of proscription here at home, where they are inevitably met with cries of protest from the intelligentsia, cries that are sometimes seconded by the general public.

The situation is quite different in countries under the yoke of military dictatorships like Argentina's,[1] in totalitarian states such as the Soviet Union,[2] or wherever there is obscurantism associated with the kind of fanatacism we see in Iran. In this connection, we may read the following comment from the *Association internationale de défense des artistes victimes de la répression dans le monde* (AIDA):

> For having recounted true events, artists—be they writers, filmmakers, musicians, or painters—are intimidated, censored, proscribed, incarcerated, tortured, and murdered in a growing number of countries. Reasons of state, which serve as arguments in the absence of proof, forbid all criticism and individual freedom of expression or opinion, particularly where artists are concerned.[3]

The intolerance our state apparatus shows towards certain groups or individuals does not rely on denunciations carried out in a climate of fear and systematic violence. Rather, a pluralistic array of ways of thinking and acting only camouflages quieter and more subtle, but no less effective, forms of censorship. In the words of Ignacio Colombres, "self-censorship begins where censorship leaves off, and what happens then is sadder and more sordid."[4] In place of fear, one has strategies designed to transform citizens into "harmless and docile subjects."

It is important to keep in mind that any criticism by artists of those accommodating or validating functions the powers that be would have them perform is met with either censorship or self-censorship, regardless of whether we are dealing with television, radio, newspapers, books, music, visual arts, or education. This political relationship will always be marked by failure, for contemporary art turns all forms of censorship into a loss of institutional control despite the fact that, in its quest for control, the existing ideological apparatus has a powerful trinity to deal with every imaginable form of dissent.

This is a translation of a text first published in *Intervention*, no. 14 (1982).

First among these are government regulations, whether national or municipal. In the form of laws and standards, these regulations define and sanction socially acceptable forms of behaviour. In them we find, under the sign of violence or the sacred, coercion as the foundation of social life. Historically, good and evil, normal and abnormal, healthy and pathological, legal and criminal have been filtered through a variety of controlling agents ranging from the priest to the soldier and including the judge, psychiatrist, technocrat, and educator. Everything begins and ends with rules. In art it was the Academies which, as arms of the state, sought to regulate and standardize artistic creation; in this endeavour, they have dwelt less on actual works and more on the very imaginations that produce them.[5]

In the second place we have propaganda which makes use of an official style in totalitarian countries and a pluralist permissiveness in liberal regimes. In both cases, however, the function is the same: to make cultural production conform to the norms of economic and political consumption. At this juncture the state institutes, under the cover of progressive reforms—insofar as social struggle and change can modify existing policies —a real and increasingly sophisticated process of recuperation that systematically forestalls the subversive impact of even the slightest deviation from the norm. The demand that the "techno-bureaucratic society of controlled consumption"[6] makes on artists and citizens is quite simple: accept the limits set by the system. In Argentina, for example, the junta requires that artists abstain from all social criticism, every form of abstract or politically committed art, and all denunciations of militarism—actions the authorities consider "inimical to national traditions."[7] In Canada and Québec, political polemics and artistic experimentation are permitted, but in low-impact "parallel" venues and among experts of the art élite.

The third controlling force consists of a brutal restoration of order involving punitive repression or the destruction of works deemed to have transgressed accepted limits. This is the stage in which censorship assumes dramatic features.

Repression, censorship, and self-censorship form the very core of class society, regardless of whether it is capitalist or socialist. Every time the authorities resort to such means, the set-back is felt along two fronts: the shock to the system is as great as the rebuke experienced by the rebellious. Every act of repression only draws the noose tighter around those forces that keep the élite, with its codes of good conduct, in power.

The Game Plan

Every society argues for a sense of identity (e.g., nationalism) commensurate with a specific cultural development and economic system. In this quest, the fine arts have always been entrusted with the task of establishing a system of rules that reflect the homogeneity and tradition of power. Today, the aims of cultural policy (even when it is progressive) and those of art converge in an apparently harmonious manner to meet the objectives of the dominant class through works that glorify the values and prestige of those who have been successful; or, failing this, art serves as a neutral witness to reality, to what justifies this "success."

In Québec society, there is no doubt that the art market has subjected artmaking to the laws of commerce. Despite this subjection, however, cultural policy has certainly been advantageous to contemporary art. The emergence of numerous public programmes funded by Québec's ministère des Affaires culturelles and the Canada Council have opened up new options to artists.

This new "social" contract has, as it were, given a breathing space to a number of art projects that are incompatible with the servility demanded by both private sponsors and the world of business.

But let us not deceive ourselves. This organized system of art is shrewdly intended to create the kind of "funded" mentality associated with regular monetary support from cultural programmes. Acquired outside the art market, such permissiveness is enshrined in rules of operation and a specific type of venue, the universe of "parallel" art spaces.

At this stage it is more appropriate to talk in terms not of censorship but of recuperation via self-censorship. The impact of political denunciations of power in galleries serving a small, informed clientele is inevitably negligible. Intended from the outset to be cunning, the trap combines a "funded" mentality with little-known and poorly frequented outlets designed for siphoning off those "issue-driven" energies whose message is condemned to be understood only by those in possession of the proper codes. This is one of the political dimensions of Explorations and other programmes, such as the Ose-Art grants made to community groups.

Is this the "liberal" solution to the control of art? Obviously not, because this willingness to support whatever happens to favour the system of power—the money doled out to official art institutions is many times what artists receive in grants—and its control of anything likely to contest it, necessitates censorship.

This situation can be explained as follows. The new options open to artists have placed renewed emphasis on a certain level of social commitment, a development that can be observed in a number of practices confined to the "avant-garde," notably, criticism of art institutions and the dematerialization of the art object.[8] Often, strategies such as these clearly do not fit into the official mould.

Recipes for artistic production (training in art departments, exhibitions in private galleries or state museums, academic art history) that were meant to tie professional success to economic status have been less effective than anticipated.

Weaknesses of the Defensive Stance

Official art discourse rarely mentions such dysfunctional episodes as the iconoclastic destruction of works or images, or the highbrow pillaging of popular culture in the industrial, urban age. With sponsors, publics, institutions, artists, and works all in the fray, obvious distortions keep creeping into the picture. An artist transgresses the limits set by a client, a work or an artist is rejected by the sponsor or public, institutions ignore certain works, succumb to in-fighting—the censorship one observes in each instance points to a disruption of the established order.[9]

If certain art practices inevitably draw censure upon themselves, this is not (says Hervé Fischer) owing to any quality, intention, or subversive militancy attributable to the artist, but simply because the system reacts negatively to questioning.[10] Censure is heaped upon the arts every time they (in however marginal a way) say something that is not in the official discourse. Yet an artist who shakes up the social scene neither necessarily nor deliberately attacks the authorities—except (and this is fundamental) insofar as he or she draws attention to the conditions that initially prompted him or her to act.

The threat to society comes not from art works but from the social conditions that so often prompt artists to act. The most vehement exhibitions or calls to revolution are weak compared with the brutality of daily life, with its regular diet of violence, injustice, and hypocrisy.[11]

We can safely say, without any risk of error, that the social role of contemporary artists hardly justifies the extent of the repression they feel world-wide. Yet the authorities obviously take the opposite view. In their estimation, the degree to which docile art glorifies them signifies the potentially corrosive power it can acquire once it becomes confrontational. The tables can easily turn; all it takes is an accusing finger levelled at the authorities, or some action or work that discloses the aspects of reality slated to be suppressed. Moreover, censorship reappears the minute politicized artists adopt institutional means of production to denounce social injustice.

The Long View

Recent events confirm that "unofficial" art milieux bear within themselves the first faint stirrings of socially oriented communication aimed at a concerned and nonélitist public, impulses that eventually find an outlet in the public forums of the streets and mass media. For example, during the 1976 Olympic Games in Montréal, artists made use of large-scale events such as *Corridart* to get their message across.

There is no way that art works and practices that take place in the public sphere (as opposed to within the confines of the avant-garde) can avoid censorship. Nothing unforeseen or planned must be allowed to stand. Fly the flag at half-mast! In a pluralistic society, such institutional attempts to censor are publicized and denounced, in the process generating debates that occasionally even make it to the courts.

Every act of repression, whether it takes place in the courts (the liberation of Paul Rose), the theatre (the fate of the play *Les fées ont soif*), or the visual arts (Jordi Bonnet's mural at the Grand Théâtre in Québec, *Corridart* in Montréal) exposes the nature of the dominant ideology. It becomes easier at such moments to see the relationship between the values those in power truly espouse and the means they are ready to use to co-opt and repress every trace of opposition.

Debates engendered by acts of repression or censorship also throw light on the collusion that exists between the various agencies controlled by the establishment—for example, the news media, the judicial and legislative apparatuses. Two cases will illustrate my point. The first involves the dispute kindled by the message that artists Peloquin and Bonnet inscribed on the mural of the Grand Théâtre in 1971. It read: "Aren't you sick of dying, you bunch of suckers! Enough is enough." At that time, private televison stations in Québec were unstinting in the airtime they made available to Roger Lemelin, then spokesman for the ruffled bourgeoisie and subsequently president of the newspaper *La Presse*. Likewise, in a judgement handed down in 1981, a certain Judge Deslauriers concurred with the view that art should promote such élitist values as complacency and honour. He gave institutional, legal, and moral sanction to the dismantling of *Corridart*, a decision taken unilaterally by the Mayor of Montréal.

While such events do disclose certain forms of repression, we should not forget other more sophisticated forms that are just as real.

Budget cutbacks and administrative wrangling ostensibly justified by financial restraints weigh heavily on most of those cultural and artistic groups who depend on grants for survival. In this, censorship and self-censorship reign freely. In 1975, for example, Québec City's Galerie Comme lost its Canada Council funding just as its members decided to adopt a political approach to artmaking. And in 1980, Montréal's Articule received no financial backing for an event that supported Amnesty International by showing artists' solidarity with political prisoners around the world. Surely these are vexing coincidences!

Such conditions of repression and censorship, here as elsewhere, confront contemporary art strategists with a political choice: either conform willingly to the laws of the art market and grant-application criteria and produce charming but silent art, that is, make art for art's sake; or opt for a course of action which, while acknowledging the limited usefulness of existing cultural structures, takes every opportunity to force institutions to break their silence and speak out on the conditions affecting artists in particular and citizens in general.

I have already put forward the idea of cultural guerrilla warfare as a form of opposition to permanent careers within institutions.[12] In other words, one should create works, events, and other forms of intervention that not only flout the sophisticated mechanisms of prohibition but also show solidarity with cultural workers. In this connection, AIDA's position on the fate of persecuted artists is worth reading:

> It is imperative that artists the world over now join together in order to collect and distribute information, record testimonies and make the name of the most humble of the oppressed, whether interred in some dungeon of Buenos Aires or sequestered in an insane asylum in Moscow, known throughout the world. Artists must no longer be satisfied with signing petitions, but must take to the streets and display their solidarity instead of providing security for those in power. They must ask questions and make their own governments accountable, something which the latter tend to resist. Finally, they must fight alongside those who have already fought to secure a basic respect for human rights.[13]

Of course this type of committed action is in conflict with the established order and makes no concessions to servility. Yet censorship by itself tends more and more to signal an admission of failure insofar as it leads to the denunciation of the commodities sought by those in power.

In opposition to repressive mechanisms, contemporary art must promote the challenge of social change. "Mercantile art, which depends on a score of merchants or functionaries, 'is, in the eyes of some, a dead end.'" Thus we must, as Fischer so aptly put it, "relinquish the symbols of social standing and the elements of aesthetic decoration"[14] in favour of the lucidity that comes with being an artist. He breathes new life into those art practices that probe beneath the surface of social reality.

Notes

1.   AIDA, *Argentine: Une culture interdite. Pièces à conviction 1976–1981* (n.p.: Petite collection maspéro 258, n.d.). This report on cultural repression in Argentina is composed of press clippings from government-controlled newspapers and of statements from exiled Argentinian artists and intellectuals. Ignacio Colombres's article, "Les arts plastiques domestiqués" (141–150), portrays the cruel fate of the country's artists.

2.   The many excesses Russian totalitarianism has committed in cultural matters are being denounced with greater frequency. To take another case of censorship and intolerance, Agence France Presse reported in September 1981 that the official press launched a savage campaign against art critic Vadim Gaevski's *Divertissements*, a book that criticized the conservativism of the Bolshoi Ballet and its director Yuri Grigorovitch. The attack focused mainly on Gaevski's preference for the Western ballet whose attributes—it is said to be "formalist, erotic, mystical and subjective"—are all considered crimes against a social realism viewed as being not in the least traditional nor supportive of the status quo. As a result, Gaevski's book was withdrawn from circulation, and he was blacklisted by Soviet publishing houses—with the exception, that is, of IssKoustvo, the offending publisher whose director, M. Nicouline, was dismissed. Also, the tradition of the Bolshoi was reaffirmed. John Berger, for his part, cites the case of sculptor Ernst Neizvestny in a book that not only examines the conditions of artists hampered by severe bureaucratic restrictions on culture but also investigates the foundations and evolution of Russian art and the consequences of Russian cultural policy since Stalin. "Revolutionary art," as it is often called, and the political consciousness of artists, appear in a new light. See John Berger, *Art and Revolution: Ernst Neizvestny and the Role of the Artist in the USSR* (n.p.: Writers and Readers Publishing Cooperative, 1969).

3.   AIDA, "Pourquoi l'AIDA?", in *Argentine: Une culture interdite*, 203. Established in Paris in 1979, the *Association internationale de défense des Artistes victimes de la répression dans le monde* has devoted itself to breaking the silence that surrounds political repression by defending artists' right to work and express themselves throughout the world. With offices in five countries (France, Germany, Belgium, Switzerland, Holland), AIDA has worked on behalf of at least six persecuted artists: Vaclav Havel in Czechoslovakia, Ené Rammeld in Estonia, Alba Gonzalez Souza in Uruguay, Liber Forti in Bolivia, Breyten Breytenbach in South Africa, and Wei-Jingsheng in China.

4.   Colombres, "Les arts plastiques domestiqués," 150.

5.   Berger, *Art and Revolution*, 23.

6.   Henri Lefebvre, *La vie quotidienne dans le monde moderne* (Paris: Gallimard, 1968). See especially "Comment nommer la société actuelle," (90–131) and "La société bureaucratique de consommation dirigée," (133–209).

7.   Colombres, "Les arts plastiques domestiqués," 141.

8.   Richard Martel, "Vers l'art contextuel: La critique institutionnelle," *Réflexion sur l'art conceptuel* (M.A. thesis, Université Laval, Québec, 1979), 89–99.

9.   Enrico Castelnuovo, "L'histoire sociale de l'art: Un bilan provisoire," *Actes de la recherche en sciences sociales*, vol. 6 (Paris: Maison des sciences de l'homme et de l'École des hautes études en sciences sociales, 1976), 75.

10.   Hervé Fischer, "Le statut social de l'artiste," in *Penser l'art contemporain: Rapport et documents* (Paris: Office Franco-allemand pour la Jeunesse, 1980), 116. Conference proceedings of the 1980 OFAJ Paris Biennial.

11.   Stefan Morawski, "L'art et la politique," *Revue internationale de recherche et de synthèse sociologiques*, no. 26 (Paris: Éditions Anthropos, 1972), 156. This special issue is entitled *L'Homme et la société*.

12.   Guy Durand, "De la guérilla culturelle aux actions de guérilla artistique," *Intervention*, no. 12 (June 1981), 4.

13.   AIDA, "Pourquoi l'AIDA?," 203.

14.   Fischer, "Le statut social de l'artiste," 117.

Translated from the French by Donald McGrath.

Dot Tuer

Video in Drag: Trans-sexing the Feminine

A few weeks ago I was glancing through a Toronto newspaper when a reproduction of the Mona Lisa caught my eye. Her famous Renaissance smile, however, was askew, distorted by a self-portrait of Leonardo da Vinci superimposed over one half of her face. A computer, the accompanying article informed us, had compared both portraits and irrevocably concluded that the enigma of Mona Lisa's smile was not a feminine one but in fact Leonardo's own features painted as a woman. Technology had conspired to transform the painting into the premise of a transsexual[1] self-portrait. The claim that the Mona Lisa is not the quintessential representation of femininity but da Vinci in drag tells us less about Leonardo than about contemporary fetishizations towards technology and sexuality. The Mona Lisa becomes a modernist obsession, not with the mysterious but with the identification/construction of the image and sexuality. "She" provides an odd slip, a strange misnomer in a contemporary world subsumed by gender definitions, where sexual difference is played out to maintain a status quo system of binary oppositions and hierarchical construction. In this consideration of the construction of the feminine as it emerges from the intersection of feminist theory and mass media in video art, the Mona Lisa as drag queen plays a bit part in the text. But, as an aside to the text, beside feminine sexuality, she becomes Eris, the spirit of strife, who, as an uninvited guest at a party, threw an apple of discord to create a fight between the three Greek goddesses.

Like the three goddesses fighting over the golden apple of discord, the debates around gender, sexuality, and representation in feminism have often been a site of conflict and contradiction. But in the last few years, three major positions have emerged, each maintaining a discreet rather than heated distance from the others. Gender-role theory, which frames the construction of women's sexuality within narrative and historical parameters, focuses on the issue of conditioning in the construction of female/male divisions. Primarily an American canon, gender as patriarchical construction is a widely disseminated position, used by advocacy feminists to wring political and legislative concessions from the state. Analysis is rooted in empirical and behaviouralist models, where society, not anatomy, produces sexual difference. Research rather than fiction, experience

This text was first published in *Parallelogramme* (February/March 1987).

rather than abstraction, statistics rather than speculation are privileged. Desire becomes an issue of sexual data to be compiled and classified, while oppression is located in a heterosexual configuration of gender roles and the family. Normative patterns in patriarchy are of a primary concern, with radical feminists calling for a cessation of sexual relations between men and women, while an emphasis on child-sharing practices and state regulation of sexism dominates a populist platform. In comparison, "French feminism" appears like an inverse mirror of "American feminism," where psychical explorations collide with the psychology of gender construction.

Rising from the ashes of master narratives in philosophy, and rebelling against the psychoanalytical mastery of Jacques Lacan, French feminism has emphasized the reconstruction of femininity rather than the dismantling of gender. Theoretical, utopian, and literary, the French feminism identified with the work of Luce Irigaray, Hélène Cixous, and Michèle Montrelay seeks to create an-other language for women, beyond the binary syntax of linguistics and located in the metaphors of feminine sexuality and woman's body. Reacting against the heterosexism of Lacanian theory, which locates sexual difference in the triad of an Œdipal structure, castration, and the child's irrevocable entry into a hierarchical symbolic where language privileges the masculine or phallic term, French feminists have sought locate a feminine sexuality in a pre-Œdipal stage of development. In this imaginary location, the mother/daughter are fluid, all and not one; the phallus cannot penetrate; and sexuality is polymorphous and liquid. Intertwining this imaginary with the oppression of the symbolic, themes of excess or *jouissance*,[2] the inscription of the body as language, the primacy of touch, masquerade, a fascination with mirrors/doubling, and a privileging of lesbianism and bisexuality emerge in the focus of a revolutionary femininity that will subvert patriarchy.

But, while French feminism seeks to displace feminist representation from the sociological to the utopian, it has also been interpreted as a densely veiled essentialism. This third position within feminist theory takes up the body, and genital difference, as the primary site of sexuality. Anatomy becomes a revolutionary destiny, where a woman's body and the unique qualities flowing from this source are feared by men for their superiority and thus repressed/oppressed by the patriarchy. Rather than an analytical or deconstructive platform, the essentialists invert hierarchy to reclaim the privileged term. Imagery alluding to woman as nature, mother-earth, goddess; formalist explorations of female genitalia; the reification of matriarchy; and womb envy and religious revisionism, particularly pagan, to privilege woman's spirituality, are associated with essentialist representation. A gloriously unambiguous declaration of women's sexual energy and creativity, essentialism has been strongly criticized as an ontology that does not account for the socio-economic and political oppression of women within patriarchy. By grounding women's sexuality in the biological rather than the social, the flip side of essentialism is a patriarchy that appropriates this specificity to reinforce the oppression of women as a genetic inferior and an idealized Other.

Within contemporary art, with its recurring theme of representation and sexuality, influences emerging from these theories can be identified. In some instances, feminist work clearly owes its allegiance to the enunciation of one particular position; in others, the visual is located as a site where contradiction between theory and practice is played out. Recent video art in Toronto, in evidence at the *New Work Show* in October 1986, proved particularly slippery in its positioning of female sexuality. In proposing a strategy for imaging women's sexuality, video art must account for the cross-pollination of a medium where consumer technology meets high modernism, where feminisms must battle the powerful narratives of mass media. Within the representational empires of the media, feminine sexuality becomes the property of the reproducible image and the subject of narrative repetition. Generic heterosexuality and androgynous clones pose from billboards and wiggle their disco hips in seven-minute intervals of airspace. Narratives tend towards the ideologically sublime. Librarians take off glasses to transfix the unsuspecting hero. Muscle-bound creatures roam the earth with submachine guns. Vacuous teenage stereotypes engage in even more vacuous entanglements with a heterosexual coming of age. Harlequin romances and serial sex murders offer up extremes of masculinity.

Video art, however, with its argued distance from the capitalist infrastructure and its reputation as an alternative/marginal practice, has been seen as a critical and "cool" medium: of the media but not subsumed by its commodification. But it is not as simple as challenging the moronic spores unleashed by a blender concoction of patriarchically mediated sexism. Video art has also to contend with the politburo of the critical canon; for in the climate of 'post'-modernism, sexual imagery has become deluged by the strictures of theoretical zealots. Heralded as the "post"feminist era, historical objectivity is discredited, but subjectivity is consigned to the laundry basket of romantic individualism. Sexual difference becomes fodder for the subscribers to the Book-of-the-Month Club while Lacan, rather than his feminist rebels, is cited as the last word on the construction of the feminine/oppression of the Other. Essentialism becomes perverse idealism, and bad taste to boot. Prescriptions for gender migraines include banishing images of women altogether. The theoretical terrain of sexual imagery has become a labyrinth.

In negotiating at this bargaining table array of feminisms, postmodernisms, mass media, and formalism, a twist to the proceedings could be observed at the *New Work Show*. In the tapes that took female representation or characterization as their overt subject matter, there was a fascination with the construction of the feminine. Men in drag became exaggerated women. Women occupied a site of cultural disassociations, of masculine stereotypes. Voice-overs displaced the visual signification of sexuality. The positioning of the camera and disjunctures in narrative expectations confused the point of view (traditionally masculine). Characters inhabited melodramatic spaces with disruptive habits. Gender blurred. Slippage from heterosexuality to lesbianism, from sexuality to sensuality, was played out. The feminine became masculine fetishization. The masculine became feminized. Within all of this, its seems that a transsexual strategy emerged as the odd bedfellow of subversion. By positioning the exploration of female sexuality and identity within transsexual constellations, the tapes seemed to seek a construction of the feminine that could sidestep the implication of the hetero-male spectator and sneak past the straitjacket of sexual difference. The problem of subjectivity being linked to objectification of the Other was tackled by occupying the position of the Other.

The Mona Lisa, wrote Walter Pater in 1895, is "older than the rocks among which she sits; like the vampire, she has been dead many times, and learned the secrets of the grave."[3] The transsexual, writes Angela Douglas over a century later, is "free from the chains of menstruation and child-bearing ... transsexual women are obviously far superior to Gennys in many ways. ... Genetic women are becoming obsolete."[4] Woman as Madonna, as Whore, as Witch: idealized, feared, fetishized, raped, and revered, but above all distinct from man. As the stronger sex, the better half, man could oppress woman, imitate her, represent her, but he could not become her, until, in the late twentieth century, medical science and social psychiatry decided that "gender dysphoria" could be cured on an operating table. And, in this meeting of the idealized woman and the constructed female, anatomy is not destiny but a destination in gendered society where the word made flesh by religion becomes flesh made gender by science. Transsexualism becomes a contradictory site where desire and sexuality is conflated. A woman trapped in a man's body completely disrupts the constructions of difference. As a man sleeping with men, "she" is a homosexual but craves heterosexuality. Inversely, she, as a he who desires women, must play out lesbian desire within a heterosexual economy of binaries. Difference is not signified by the Other but by being caught in a mirror reflection where the Other is the same. This is a no man's land, where desire and gender clash, where desire and technology meet.

In feminist theory, of woman born, the transsexual brings not masculinity but femininity into question. For the essentialists, the transsexed female would discredit their celebration of biological difference, forcing them into the shady terrain of genetic configurations. Thus, desire is discounted for the sake of science, and she remains forever a he. French feminism, with its continental upbringing, leaves biology to the Americans, but their emphasis on pre-Oedipal bonding would bar the transsexual latecomer from a feminine *jouissance*, locating "her" desire as the ultimate castration. And for feminists who locate oppression in gender construction transsexualism becomes a transgression of women. In the case of Janice Raymond's *The Transsexual Empire*,[5] political outrage is vented against transsexual heterosexuals for their adoption of a conservative stereotypical femininity, while her moral outrage is saved for those transsexuals who claim a feminist-lesbian position and thus are able to infiltrate women's communities with the body of a woman and the conditioning of a man. Thus to identify within artists' video a transsexualist strategy is to identify a strategy where the issues of sexual difference become an issue of sexual politics, where the question of desire plays tricks on representation. And transsexualism, not as a medical disorder, but as the site of feminine desires, suggests a space outside gender but within culture, where theory and practice meet. As a point of reference, a signification, it offers the promise of a space where men can presume to construct the feminine from the desire for the other, rather than of the Other.

The most obvious *representations* of transsexualism occur in drag. Drag, as exemplified in Shakespearian theatre, developed into a comic device popular in music hall and vaudeville productions. This burlesque use of drag, where sexuality becomes second fiddle to gags, is employed by Sky Gilbert in *Marie Antoinette* (1983) by Byron Ayanoglu and Ric Amis. In this tape, disguised gender does not comment upon contemporary sexuality but is used to create a one-liner comic effect: Marie Antoinette acting even sillier and more self-centred as a drag queen than one could imagine her as a woman framed by historical context. In comparison, both Shalhevet Goldhar's and David MacLean's tapes make use of David MacLean's characterization of women replete with wigs and stereotypical mannerisms to comment on modern perceptions of sexuality and gender. In Goldhar's *Bleachables* (1986), MacLean portrays identical blond-haired sisters who switch roles, exchanging security as a well cared for housewife for the sexually "liberated" life of the single, working woman and vice versa. The punch-line comes when the audience discovers that the house-wife was murdered during the switch-over by a dubious lover, and her sister decides to continue the charade indefinitely. In a speech which crosses Hamlet with a David Letterman talk show, she informs the audience that women's "lib" is a sham, with its precarious economics and unstable lovers. She prefers the "other" life, where one can revel in the secure boredom and faithful attention of a husband in the suburbs.

With MacLean's portraiture of the sisters assuming spectacularly camp proportions, the tape piles fantasies upon caricature as it examines the flip sides of modern woman's stereotyping. But, in presenting the "myths" of the sexual revolution and Prince Charming through the device of transsexual drag, any sense of a feminist dismantling of stereotypes dissipates. Women are, in effect, absent from the tape, and, in their stead, a male imitation/connotation of their representation and gender roles remains as residue. Both sisters, played by a man in drag, are male-identified. Disrobe the parody, and the identity of women vanishes. Instead, superficiality becomes a parody of itself, and desire flattens to a comic book lie of the feminine in the guise of a Bramalea housewife drag queen.

In David MacLean's own tape *Bon Voyage My Love* (1986), transvestism plays itself out as a critique rather than a parody of gender strait-jacketing. Becoming his own alter-ego, MacLean portrays a black-haired, sultry melo-dame waiting for her sailor-lover. But she is really a he (also MacLean) who cruises the backways of Union Station, wanting to fuck the pretty boy in the sailor blue. Here, he as a she uses drag to call into question the narratives available to gay men in a gender-defined culture. Homosexuals, the tape implies, take up a media-constructed position of the feminine in order to live out a fantasy denied them as media-constructed men. But, in representing transsexualism as a stereotyped feminine, neither video is able to construct an alternative to a dominant definition of difference which designates "woman" as the Other and homosexuality as deviance. Mass media gender roles assume the significance of a master narrative, where sexual identity becomes trapped in a revolving door; where drag is not a signification of feminine construction but an outfit one wears to a fancy dress ball where no one can tell the difference; and where homosexual and feminine narratives are subsumed by, rather than dissent from, a dominant culture.

Drag, however, does not need to be gender specific, although traditionally it has been considered either a male dressing as a woman (rarely seen in mainstream narrative) or a woman dressed as a man (appropriated by mainstream narrative to signify male expectations of a lesbian). Tanya Mars in *Pure Virtue* (1985) is definitely a first-class drag act. As a woman playing the Queen, in this case Elizabeth I, drag becomes a means to contextualize sexuality historically and politically rather than to exploit the inane antics of an in-bred royalty. She constructs a feminine that is neither dependent on a binary masculine, nor an essentialist vision of women's superiority. Rather, she has street smarts, a transsexual not of gender but of power relations. Her Lords are literally cardboard figures, and her lover must, unfortunately, lose his head. Gender roles are clearly a construction. Nevertheless, she will not relinquish her desire as a woman but rather warns of its narratives and its pitfalls. If virginity is an accompaniment to femininity, then, the Queen advises, avail yourself of remedies to disguise its absence, to construct a false identity. And, she warns, in between a juggling act and barbell exercises, that "freedom in a woman breeds not love but suspicion." The feminine, nevertheless, is not to be discarded but reconstructed to account for the differences of history, the inequities of power, the oppression of sex.

Hygiene (1985), by Andy Paterson/Jorge Lozano, and *No Voice Over* (1986), by Colin Campbell, on the other hand, propose a transsexualism in the convention of the narrative rather than image. In *Hygiene*, a melodramatic story unfolds around the life and loves of a character named Rachel. But rather than present a "straight" alternative, where melodrama becomes a formal device to frame a dissenting narrative, the characters occupy a space between gender reversal and gendered parodies. Rachel's unrequited love is projected onto a villainous pastiche of masculinity, asserting his virility by eating crackers, and meeting a messy death more in keeping with the suffering heroine than the calculating womanizer. As the jilted woman, Rachel shifts between hysteric femininity, roaming her apartment in despair, and drunken masculinity, drowning his sorrows at the bar. The handsome man who rescues our ailing heroine from a self-destructive disintegration is not a man but a lesbian. However, a lesbian love affair is not a possibility, since all around her the plot unfolds in a mock-up fashion where heterosexuality is not only an assumption but also a melodramatic construction. Reading *Of Woman Born* by Adrienne Rich on the beach, Rachel is interrupted by the obligatory male who walks into the frame. He usurps the narrative by being a "nice" guy who makes Rachel "happy" but very restless, and probably bored. The climax comes, not in orgasm, but after sex. Turning on the television news, she hears that the lesbian who had befriended her was killed in a fire-bombing of the Women's Book Store. Rushing, not to the scene of the accident, but to a women's bar, she stands outside while a drunk rhapsodizes a religious apocalypse, and she realizes that true love, of course, comes too late.

By using filmic conventions to reconstruct the feminine as active, and by mixing up gender and convention, Paterson and Lozano create the possibility for a transsexual position in the spectator. The conventions of melodrama call for a point of view that will project the identity of the viewer as male. However, the blurring of feminine/masculine roles, where Rachel constructs the plot, but not her "femininity," disrupts the assumption of the narrative and the expectations of the viewer. Slipping in and out of a binary representation of heterosexuality, the video demands that the viewer, through narrative disjunctions, reconstruct another story than sexual difference. Confronted with males who are wimps, a together lesbian who declines to offer the viewer a voyeur construction of the Other, and a heroine whose Prince Charming is a convenience—a clear convention—the spectator's position falls to pieces. If men want to identify rather than objectify, then they must desire to become the women in the narrative. Conversely, women, in a position where transference to a male character is no longer demanded, can participate in the construction of the feminine.

In comparison to *Hygiene*, which plays dismantled sexual difference through the perversion of heterosexual convention, Colin Campbell chooses to construct the feminine by banishing the masculine. *No Voice Over* intertwines the stories of three M&M women: Mocha, Miranda, and Marcella. A patron, Dix-Ten, is the absent father and, in effect, the voice-over. The women, whose postcards and tapes to each other tell their stories, construct a feminine where adventure, intrigue, glamour, art careers, and mother/daughter relations figure. Close friendship, desire, premonitions, and speculation create a narrative of bonding to which Dix-Ten has no access. His links are economic and benevolent; he coordinates their movements, he admires their feminism, but he is outside their construction of the feminine. Dix-Ten, as the interventionist who fails to colonize, in some way represents the desire to become the feminine. He becomes the closet transsexual, a woman trapped in a man's body, speaking from a male position. He becomes, in effect, a stand-in for the video medium, which is trapped by conventions of narrative and media signification that construct the feminine as the property of a masculine point of view. And, in the search for an alternative language within the video medium, there emerges the desire to trans-sex the feminine: to explore the representation of desire as it is constructed between women and outside of sexual difference.

Transsexualism and feminism may appear as strange bedfellows, but their meeting suggests the possibility within contemporary video to offer the viewer an-other means by which to conceptualize gender, sexuality, and desire. Using difference as a rigid barometer of masculine/feminine construction not only leaves the video artist tied to dominant narratives of sexuality, but also enforces the masculine position of the spectator. The difficulties of exploring the boundaries of feminine constructions from this model of sexual difference are amplified in Rodney Werden's tape *Money Talks, Bullshit Walks* (1986). In this tape, Werden hires prostitutes off the street in order to interview them about their work and the ways in which men relate to them as objects of exchange. Werden, like Dix-Ten, is absent from the camera: a voice-over who pries information from his subjects from an observer's position. But, unlike Dix-Ten, Werden gives the women no possibility of expressing their own sexuality.

The camera functions as a voyeur, the women are framed by a map of the world, and the questions they are asked pertain to a male's curiosity about women rather than a desire to be a woman. As the "john" who must hire prostitutes to talk rather than fuck, Werden becomes the signification of failed masculinity. As the "pimp" who controls the position of the camera and the direction of the questions, he becomes the privileged term, the phallus, in a sexual hierarchy. Women are visible, naked icons of sexuality, but they are absent as a construction outside the male point of view. Thus, as a viewer, also taking up a position of looking from behind the camera, the audience must either accept a hierarchical model of sexual difference or conclude that raw documentary is, in this case, the fiction of male fantasy.

In many ways, *Hygiene* and *No Voice Over* are also the fictions of male fantasy, but, in their constructions of narrative, there is a possibility for the imagination of what it means to be a woman rather than a man looking at women. It is in this possibility, where transsexualism rather than difference becomes a site of sexual politics, that boundaries between the masculine/feminine begin to break down. Transsexualism may be for many an uncomfortable strategy, for it calls into question not only masculine stereotypes but also the security of feminist analyses. However, in so doing, it offers a conceptual position from which to challenge hierarchy, morality, and dominant media constructions in sexuality. Sexual difference, Julia Kristeva suggests, will only cease to be an oppressive site of gender when it is reconceived as a metaphysical rather than socio-political signification.[6] Strategies of transsexualism in imagery, narrative, and spectator position begin to question the site of sexual difference as an absolute site of sexual construction. And by posing questions, rather than providing answers, these strategies are beginning a long and convoluted process towards a metaphysics of sexuality. Transsexualism offers a framework that challenges the claims of transgression. Popularized by male artists in the 1970s, transgression framed sexuality in exploitative extremes, where the feminine disappeared under the turgid weight of the voyeur's insistent look. Better the confusion and questions raised by transsexualism than the adherence to a model that believes an extreme framing of exploitation will explode domination, or the belief in the safety of an essentialism that precludes contradictions. To be a man trapped in a woman's body and a woman trapped in a man's world makes the construction of the feminine through images and narratives a paradoxical desire; but it is preferable to explore the parameters of this paradox than to resolve confusion through posing the video camera as the pimp, and the feminine as its prostitute.

Notes

1.   Transsexualism refers to the medical process of anatomical sex conversion which reached public awareness in the documentation of the Christine Jorgensen case in 1953. With the establishment of the Johns Hopkins Gender Identity Clinic in 1967, it became a select but established medical procedure to "cure" gender dysfunctions. The process begins with hormone treatments and progresses to intense gender therapy focusing upon the establishment of "normative" gender characteristics. Patients must live as the opposite sex for two years before going through operations that medically reconstruct gender. For the purposes of this article, I am referring to male-to-female transsexuals although there is also a smaller percentage of female-to-male transsexuals. And in the context of this article, transsexualism is being considered for its conceptual, political, and social ramifications as a sexual practice rather than as a strictly medical phenomenon.

2.   *Jouissance* literally translates as orgasm. Total sexual ecstasy is its most common connotation, but, in contemporary French philosophical, psychoanalytic, and political usage, it does not stop there. It is a word with simultaneously sexual, political, and economic overtones. Total access, total participation, as well as total ecstasy are implied. Transsexualism and feminism may make strange bedfellows, but their potential to explore difference without hierarchy is a preferable alternative to straight pimping.

3.   Walter Pater, *The Renaissance: Studies in Art and Poetry* (London: MacMillan and Company, 1910), 125.

4.   Angela Douglas, as quoted in Janice G. Raymond *The Transsexual Empire: The Making of the She-Male* (Boston: Beacon Press, 1979), 117.

5.   Janice G. Raymond, *The Transsexual Empire.*

6.   Julia Kristeva, "Women's Time," *Signs,* vol. 7, no. 1 (Autumn 1981): 13–35.

Monika Kin Gagnon

Al Fannanah 'l Rassamah: Jamelie Hassan

> The effort to invite a persistent displacement of the bewildering contradiction between life and art relates to the displacement of the bewildering contradiction between the conditions of life and the professions of our profession.
>
> Gayatri Chakravorty Spivak

> They put me in a hotel in the UN district where UN soldiers hustled airline stewardesses while eating fresh shrimp cocktails and drinking Dubonnet. When the staccato of machine-gun fire went off, the maître d' didn't flinch as he joked about the night show free of charge.
>
> Jamelie Hassan

"Without the reading of the world as a book," Gayatri Spivak writes, "there is no prediction, no planning, no taxes, no laws, no welfare, no war."[1] The imperative undertaken in Jamelie Hassan's work is to intervene in some of the representations by which the world is dominantly "read" and comprehended, to reveal the social and political underpinnings of those representations, and to inspire a different knowledge. From the lucid simplicity of a destroyed gallery wall coupled with black-and-white photographs of Beirut souks in *"Is War Art?" (Beyrouth)* (1980), to the dozens of object-fragments, texts, and photographs in her installation *The Mukhabarat State or Zenobia's Wall* (1986–1987), Hassan addresses the separation between living in a world of "massive brutality, exploitation, and sexual oppression"[2] and the conditions of her own production as an artist working in London, Ontario.

Propelled by highly-charged social and political subjects, Hassan's works eschew simple description, exposition, presentation, or analysis. Instead, autobiography and factual (historical, social, geographical) information are combined in constantly different forms with an array of materials and an expansive range of subjects derived from Hassan's extensive travels through Central and South America, Europe, and the Middle East. The resulting transhistoric, cross-cultural mêlée of traditional and contemporary aesthetic forms reveals influences as far-ranging as Islamic pottery, Mexican folk arts, and popular mural forms, blending with contemporary media such as photography and video. In all of Hassan's works—from the floating historical documents in *Water Margin*'s (1984) massive water

---

This text was first published in *Vanguard* (November 1988).

pond, to the powerful oscillations of meanings produced by double-exposed images in *vitrine 448* (1988)—the viewer is repeatedly situated in imaginary spaces that irresolutely move through shifting personal, geographical, social, and political expanses.

The regenerative qualities of this fifteen-year span of production of some twenty installations are very clearly discernible in two works produced in the early 1980s: *Desaparecidos* (1983) and *Slave Letter* (1983). Both hold to optimistic possibilities for alternative modes of representation by exploring culturally distinct forms of resistance and protest. *Desaparecidos*, or the "disappeared ones," derives from a ritual of collective, silent demonstration performed by an Argentinian association of female relatives of "disappeared" civilians. *Slave Letter* incorporates an allegorical language of transmitted common objects sent by incarcerated slaves to their families. Significantly, both works adapt rather than directly appropriate or document these "languages," revealing Hassan's interest in not only conveying factual and historical information but also incorporating and evolving the radical implications of alternative representation as part of her own practice.

Desaparecidos adopts elements from weekly public demonstrations by members of *Madres de la Plaza de Mayo* during the brutal 1976–1983 military dictatorship of the Argentinian Generals Videla, Viola, and Galtieri. These women donned white headscarves proclaiming the names of their "missing" relatives in a series of silent, collective demonstrations held in a Buenos Aires city square, Plaza de Mayo. Hassan's installation comprises sixty-four porcelain pieces shaped like scarves, each painted white and inscribed in blue with the name and disappearance date of a "missing" Argentinian. Accompanying the porcelain scarves, which are interspersed across the gallery floor, is a photocopied dossier of files compiled by the *desaparecidos* relatives and presented to the Argentinian government to protest the lack of investigation into cases of "missing" individuals.[3] Hassan's uncompromised transmission of knowledge about the "disappeared" and her mediation of the ritual scarves as constructed porcelain objects (rather than the scarves themselves, or photographic documentation), broaches the impossible reconciliation between empathetic affinity with the *desaparecidos* or their relatives and the horrific political realities of Argentina's torture camps. Moving through the grave-like memorial fragments of *Desaparecidos*, reading the vital statistics filed on standardized forms, viewing photocopied photographs of "disappeared" individuals, we do not merely encounter a summary of information. Rather, we become witness to tangible testimony to the fragility and power of the individual and collective calling to be heard when confronted with the oppressive violence of political dictatorship.

Like the sensations evoked in *Desaparecidos, Slave Letter* relies on a meditative process of quiet discovery, provoked by Hassan's self-reflexive recovery and fabrication of tactile objects. A black cloth remnant tied into a pouch sits on the gallery floor surrounded by four clay tablets inscribed with short texts. On the wall, a watercolour replicates the label of a popular Middle-Eastern perfume, *Bint el Sudan* (in Arabic, "young girl," or "accessible" woman, from Sudan). This peculiar but delicate composition of objects requires the viewer to approach and open the black pouch, upon which four objects are disclosed: a stone, a piece of charcoal, a dried red pepper, and kernels of corn, all of which resonate with texts inscribed in the clay tablets. Such "letters" from enslaved, captive correspondents— composed merely of actual bits of rock, cloth, vegetables, grain—would hold immediate allegorical significance for their receiver: "As grain is shrivelled, so gaunt will my body become through its suffering," translates one tablet; "As the pepper is hot, so too is my spirit aroused," reads another.

Although presumed illiteracy amongst slaves precluded the possibility of conventional letters, *Slave Letter* attests to the possibility of overcoming the silencing power of repression by recourse to alternative channels of communication. In both works, factual details are elusive, fragmentary, rather than explicit or definitive, provoking an extended process of speculation and curiosity about the subjects in ways that are intimate to each viewer. The watercolour elliptically elaborates the cultural references of these "letters" to other disjointed but related images and motifs: the Sudan with its long history of high traffic in slaves; girls and women as sexual slaves, but, also, subject to female circumcision (still practised in Sudan); and the perfume. The scent—an olfactory luxury that, like the adorned girl in the watercolour, sharply contrasts the evocations of violence and incarceration—has historical origins tracing it to Lebanon, to Hassan's family roots, and the exportation of the *cedrus libani* to Egypt over 4,000 years ago.

The expansive, socio-political range of subjects addressed within these works might simply, but misleadingly, elicit the label of political art, *point final*. However, that category, devised to contain and manage work with extra-aesthetic agendas, cannot fully account for these works. While Hassan's practice is political, it forcefully questions many of the conventions and assumptions of so-called political art—particularly political documentary. The provocation towards investigation and reverie distinguished her work from the informational, frequently didactic tendencies of much documentary-based practice that upholds the transparency of the medium and an alleged objectivity on the part of the artist. Hassan's choice of materials (ceramics and watercolour in *Desaparecidos* and *Slave Letter*, for instance) asserts her presence in production. Even when using photography or video (with the indexical favouring of so-called objective reality in documentary practice), Hassan foregrounds the impossibility of neutral representation. Yet this rejection of documentary does not, alternately, privilege a subjective knowledge. Simultaneously aligned with the aims of documentary practice in presenting factual information, Hassan's viewer and Hassan herself are placed in fluctuating positions of knowledge that are in continual processes of construction and reconstruction rather than being fixed or stable.

Her work is concerned (to employ a familiar chiasmus) with a politics of representation rather than a mere representation of politics. Crucially, this is a consideration of representation that, in recent works, is increasingly refracted through an analysis and critique of orientalism, the discursive body of knowledge and associated stereotypes created about the Orient, whose implications have far-reaching effects. Edward Said has observed that this critique is taking place "across planes and axes of different fields," rather than emerging within one disciplinary topography.[4] And, perhaps, it is within this expanded terrain and its complex concerns that Hassan's practice is most accurately contextualized.

While *Desaparecidos* and *Slave Letter* attend to problems of documentary and direct cultural appropriation, *The Hong Kong, for Dave and Lucy* (1983) recounts Hassan's witnessing of racism within her own community. Several photographs of a barricaded restaurant are dispersed around two text plaques, all "framed" by an architectural detail and a dominant wooden sign carrying the name of a restaurant, "The Hong Kong," in Chinese characters. In addition, a small marble fragment from the restaurant's façade sits on the floor. Although initially localized and personal in its lamentation for the owners of a vandalized Chinese restaurant in London, the first-person voice of the texts intimates a problem of racism in a greatly expanded sphere. The owners, Dave and Lucy, become "a way of getting close to things Chinese," writes Hassan, who befriended them and frequented the restaurant when there were occasions to celebrate. The violation of what Hassan describes as a cultural presence is a culmination of racist aggression—"racist words smeared in excrement on the walls of the dining rooms"—motivated when a thief failed to locate any money on the premises. Despite massive property damage and the subsequent closing of this small business, "these words," concludes Hassan, "hurt Lucy most."

The Hong Kong reveals some of the strains of relaying factual information while simultaneously attempting to complicate the underpinning conventions and assumptions that traditionally make the representation of specific information possible. Despite a lack of ambiguity here (exactly what gives other installations their poignancy), *The Hong Kong* nonetheless introduces themes that figure in effectively complex ways in later works: Hassan's use of subjective voice; questions of racism and the implication of colonialism, orientalism; the relation of images to power; and the possibilities for alternative cultural and aesthetic representations already developed in *Desaparecidos* and *Slave Letter*.

Meeting Nasser (1985) comprises Hassan's only work conceived as a video installation, and it is characterized by an aesthetic reference to "amateur" documentary usage.[5] A ceremonial airport scene depicts the rear view of a young girl presenting flowers to Egyptian President Nasser, the latter typically surrounded by several dignitaries and official personnel. The black-and-white photograph is enlarged and flanked by three details (a close-up of Nasser, an accompanying guard, and the girl), all suspended on the wall above the video monitor, along with a blown-up family snapshot of a young Hassan affectionately holding her baby sister (she wears a ponytail virtually identical to that of the girl in the airport photograph). The airport scene is presented again as an almost full-frame backdrop in the video, in which (another?) young girl (donning a similar ponytail), reads excerpts from a book by Naguib Mahfouz on the interrogation of Egyptian writers and artists under Nasser's rule. As she reads, she intermittently moves back towards the airport scene backdrop, blocking the girl in the photograph, in order that she herself may present flowers to Nasser's static image.

The confusion of these two girls and Hassan's identities, their similar appearances and possible relations, is increased by an ominous layering of motifs alluding to power and manipulation. As William Wood has suggested, the girl in the airport photograph is "presumably chosen as an 'innocent,' chosen to thank the leader for his presence."[6] As "innocent" (a position that the young actress in the video repeatedly occupies as she moves to offer her bouquet), she amplifies the power of the six men towering over her and their presence within the male-dominated arena of world politics. In the video, the young girl reacts to the adult voices directing her from off-screen. She reads from a text she could not possibly comprehend, a text that we, as viewers, can discern only with some difficulty, given the disjunction between her "innocence," her obedient behaviour, and the powerful, cryptic words she recites of "indoctrination" and how knowledge of brutality came when "locked hearts opened to me explaining the

mysterious events." The striking resemblance between the two girls conta-
minates the familial purity of the third image of Hassan's youth. It is
Hassan's tenuous recognition of the airport girl's ponytail as her own
(could she be Hassan?)—dissonantly tainted by the young actor's oblivious recitation of Nasser's government policies suppressing dissent—that
propels this fantasy of meeting Nasser into ambivalence. Nasser's dominating centrality in the installation, the liberating presence of his Arab
nationalism in Hassan's youth, is disturbed by layered conflicts of meaning: the innocence of the young girls, the evocations of brutality in the
young actor's reading, and the highly manipulated nature of her performance. This insistent emphasis on staging, and on video's materiality (the
rough editing, the pounding rain on the soundtrack, the child's distracted
reaction to off-screen direction), in turn degrades the composure of the
airport scene and foregrounds its artificiality, calling forth the contradictions between this public, ceremonial display of power against attestations
of the institutionalized, clandestine violence harboured behind this façade.

> History, politics, and economics do not matter. Islam is Islam, the
> Orient is the Orient, and please take all your ideas about a left and a
> right wing, revolutions and change back to Disneyland.[7]

In her insistence on complicating the extant separation between subjectivity, culture, politics, and art, Hassan forges an implicit alliance with recent
critical strategies in cultural and feminist practices that have attempted to
question and challenge the supposed neutrality of representation. In order
to fracture the monolithic "imaginative geography" of orientalism (a
Disney-like construction, as Said facetiously remarks), it is necessary to
subvert the dependence on reductive representations that the notion of the
"Orient" presupposes. And it is perhaps this imperative that is the key to
understanding the cross-disciplinary, mixed media range of Hassan's
installations. The absence of clearly defined topical or formal parameters
and the insistent refusal to remain faithful to any one medium force us to
recognize the profound effects of "Oriental" stereotypes in generalized and
repetitive imagery. As Said has remarked, the United States' "recent
Japanese, Korean, and Indo-Chinese adventures ought now to be creating
a more sober, more realistic 'Oriental' awareness," although the Near East
(the Middle East), continues to be rigidly typecast in order to legitimate
current political and economic interests of Western governments within
that region.[8]

A general alignment can be made between a critique of orientalism
as an analysis of the effects of dominant representations of the Eastern
world in Western culture and the aims, very generally, of feminist art
practice, as the conscious production of art within a field that has histori-

cally and discursively marginalized women. In a 1984 essay on Hassan's work, Christopher Dewdney effectively introduces biographical and personal information in his discussion of Hassan's installations (in great part acceptable because of his close friendship with Hassan since childhood, and because of the nostalgic, personal tone of his essay).[9] It is important to recognize, however, that, historically, reference to the private, domestic sphere in relation to (women's) artistic production has frequently had a detrimental effect, trivializing women's work and restricting it to the margins of art history and criticism. The use of the first-person voice has subsequently become a particularly ambivalent (and self-conscious) strategy for women artists.[10] Hassan herself seemed aware of this potential difficulty when, in 1983, she wrote:

> The general lack of dialogue about this work and the repeated suggestion that *"Is War Art?" (Beyrouth)* answered only a *personal therapeutic* need for me continues to persist. The work is generally not seen to be a *legitimate* response to experiences which I had.[11]

In fact, *"Is War Art?"* does not represent one of Hassan's more personal works. Yet, her continued attempt to integrate subjectivity as an unstable but constant space within the artwork constitutes a provocative thematic continuum. This insistence that the personal is political (to reiterate another well-worn feminist phrase) serves not to claim subjectivity (or, more significantly, a heroicized *artistic* subjectivity) as a definitive source of truth but rather to suspend both artist and viewer within a highly complex social space, as *Meeting Nasser* effectively does.

In *The Mukhabarat State or Zenobia's Wall* and *vitrine 448* (1988), Hassan complicated the institutionalized discourses of anthropology, fragmenting the generalizing effects of ethnological museum exhibitions in the former, and mimicking, but simultaneously disrupting, the obsessive, classificatory system of Claude Lévi-Strauss's 1938 fieldwork on Brazil's Caduveo Indians in the latter. These works introduce complexities into the supposed neutral investigations of anthropological practices, underlining their emergence within, and service as a discipline to, the colonialist will to power.

The public postures that camouflage abuses of government power are again the subject in *The Mukhabarat State*. As Hassan underscores the repetitive rhetorics of war in the work *Primer for War* (1985),[12] or the repressive activities of the Argentinian and Egyptian government military, she enlarges her scope to encompass similar practices in President Asad's Syria. Drawing on travel notes and dozens of archaeological-like fragments, photographs, panoramic watercolours, and historical and personal texts (gathered and produced during three visits to the Middle East over the last two decades), *The Mukhabarat State* loosely takes the form of an ethnological museum display, although with considerably different effects. Mounted on a highlighted rectangular surface on the wall, these various objects elliptically illustrate and narrate Hassan's encounters with the Syrian secret police—the *mukhabarat*. The paranoia of surveillance and the threat of bodily harm is evoked by Hassan's travelogue and by the shrapnel-like pieces of stone, pottery, and tiles surrounding these hand-written texts. Although the work is formally reminiscent of an ethnological display, the latter's apolitical nature—its function in gathering objects and data on various people and cultures, without developing the socio-political actualities of such contexts—is subverted and permeated instead with the violent realities of constant monitoring and brutality by the *mukhabarat*.

The book *vitrine 448* employs a similar travelogue-style of text and replicates Levi-Strauss's format of classification in the anthropological archives of the Musée de l'homme in Paris. Hassan appropriates nine of his file cards (composed of a photograph of Caduveo women, geographical information, and excerpts from his *Tristes Tropiques*) and intersperses them with a reconstruction, contained on identically styled panels, of her visits and research in Paris on Lévi-Strauss. As an installation, the cards from the book are hung in sequence on the gallery wall, with a small wooden table and chair placed by them. Several of Lévi-Strauss's photographs are enlarged, along with a poster advertising an exhibition at the Musée, and surround the sequence of cards from the book on the gallery walls. Circular forms appearing on the girls' painted faces are doubled in wooden architectural details surrounding the images.

Notwithstanding the precise organization of materials in *vitrine 448* (the obsessive attention to detailed classification, the standardized format, the clandestine nature of accompanying numbers), the nineteen panels finally undermine the apparent authority of Lévi-Strauss's discourse, spec-ulating instead on the problematic way in which his object of research, the Caduveo, were constituted. Hassan draws three seemingly disparate sub-jects into a revealing and disturbing communion: the Caduveo girls' and women's painted faces and bodies are highlighted as sites of a literal and permanent cultural inscription; their subjection as object of Lévi-Strauss's research doubly articulates this cultural writing on their bodies; and Lévi-Strauss and the Caduveo both become objects of *vitrine 448*'s own reflection.

The source of Hassan's contentions with Lévi-Strauss's research can be illuminated by his statements in a 1967 interview. Lévi-Strauss com-mented:

> My political attitude has not really been modified by the fact that I am
> an anthropologist: it remains outside, and almost impervious to my
> professional thinking and so I must admit that it is an essentially emo-
> tional attitude. This is all the more true in that it is very difficult to
> bridge the gap between the *objective attitude one strives to maintain*
> *when considering other communities from the outside and the situation in*
> *which one finds oneself, willy-nilly, inside one's own society.*[13]

Lévi-Strauss's failure to acknowledge that anthropology (and field research
in particular) is in itself an historically, politically aligned activity is
implicitly disclosed by *vitrine 448*. The painted faces of the Caduveo in
Lévi-Strauss's photographic research, of which seven appear in *vitrine 448*,
are allegedly meant to function as mere documentation. The seeming
innocence of this photographic activity, however, is questioned when
Hassan, in one of her file cards, reveals that in spite of Lévi-Strauss's
unquestioned access to his subjects (in the name of anthropology), she was
prohibited from photographing the display cases at the Musée for her own
research.

Hassan overcomes this prohibition in a presumably illicit act of
photographing *vitrine 448*, the last of five double-exposed images presented on her own cards. The pottery vases contained within the glass casing
echo an earlier quote by Lévi-Strauss, who revealingly remarks on the similarities between the Caduveo designs on the necks of vases and those on
the faces and bodies of the girls and women. Hassan's image of *vitrine
448* is doubled by a shadowy head and shoulders, a silhouette that immediately recalls the anthropological photographs in preceeding panels. This
eerie image, an entangled visual space repeated in Hassan's other photographs, creates a virtual vertigo of images and texts, as Lévi-Strauss's
invasive trace imposes itself across all of *vitrine 448*. Hassan's own data is
structured after his, and the images of Paris and the Musée have accidently
permeated all her family snapshots in London. As a result, Lévi-Strauss's
supposed neutrality as field researcher becomes equally pervaded by his
subjective presence. Being framed by the Musée, hunted down, "discovered," classified, and encased becomes a threatening fantasy in *vitrine
448*—this hallucination resonates within every picture and every text.

Lévi-Strauss's inability to recognize anthropology's implicit political
justification of colonialist practices ("from religious indoctrination to labor
laws and the granting of basic political rights"), as well as his reluctance to
admit "the role of subjectivity in both culture and knowledge about culture," are issues precisely reinscribed by *vitrine 448*.[14] As Spivak has con-
tended, all interpretive activities are permeated by politics, in spite of
claims to their absence. Hassan's works repeatedly and poignantly remind

us of this in their poetic attempt to relocate the bewildering contradictions of an increasingly antiseptic and homogenizing image world. As one of Hassan's texts speculates on behalf of the police in *The Mukhabarat State:* "Why did I spend hours in the same spot painting? Why did we sit around in the evenings drinking tea and looking at the desert sky? Why did we gather rubble from the streets of Palmyra?" Hassan evokes the fragility of the body—the evidence of the body's relations to the powerful institutions of oppression is to be located and struggled with, not only in the realm of the "purely political" but also in the aesthetic markings that are the signs of an everyday humanity that must also live and breathe that very oppression.

Notes

The epigraphs are from Gayatri Chakravorty Spivak, *In Other Worlds: Essays in Cultural Politics* (New York: Methuen, 1987), 95, and from Jamelie Hassan, "Is War Art?," *Incite*, vol. 1, no. 1 (July 1983). *Al Fannanah 'l Rassamah* is a classic Arabic phrase translated as "artist/painter" (feminine).

1.   Spivak, *In Other Worlds*, 95.

2.   Ibid.

3.   This document was delivered to a London church by three travelling members of the Grandmothers of the Plaza de Mayo (an offshoot of the mothers' group concerned particularly with "disappeared" pregnant women's children who were born in captivity).

4.   Edward Said, "Orientalism Reconsidered," *Cultural Critique*, no. 1 (Fall 1985): 105–6.

5.   Hassan's performance work *The Oblivion Seekers* was recorded on video and exhibited in 1986. See Judith Doyle's interview with Hassan, *In a Different Voice* (Toronto: The Funnel and YYZ, 1986).

6.   William Wood, "Skinjobs," *C Magazine*, no. 11 (Autumn 1986): 81.

7.   Edward Said, *Orientalism* (New York: Random House, 1979), 107.

8.   Ibid., 2.

9.   Christopher Dewdney, *Jamelie Hassan, Material Knowledge: A Moral Art of Crisis* (London: London Regional Art Gallery, 1984).

10.   And a powerfully distinctive strategy as well. Mary Kelly and Barbara Kruger, for example, have insistently conceptualized this subjective positioning as an integral part of their works. Hassan's works, too, insist on the significance of this space in constructing meaning.

11.   Hasssan, "Is War Art?." Emphasis added.

12.   In her artist's statement, Hassan writes that *Primer for War* attempts to "point to the absurd and irrational nature of the motivating principles of war, whether at the beginning or the end of the century: the rhetoric remains the same." *Primer for War* (Halifax: Mount St. Vincent Art Gallery, 1985).

13.   *Conversations with Claude Lévi-Strauss*, ed. G. Charbonnier, trans. John and Doreen Weightman (London: Jonathan Cape, 1969), 13. Emphasis added.

14.   Both quotes are from Johannes Fabian, *Time and the Other: How Anthropology Makes Its Object* (New York: Columbia University Press, 1983), 63, 69.

Loretta Todd

Notes on Appropriation

While making a presentation on cultural autonomy and appropriation at the Independent Film and Video Alliance meeting in Halifax in June 1989, I quoted Walter Benjamin. Someone challenged my use of Benjamin as an appropriation of Western culture. My response was that, as I am a part of Western as well as Native culture, Benjamin is of my culture. "Aha," say the appropriators, "then our use of Native images and stories is analogous to your use of Benjamin, since Native images and stories have become part of contemporary culture." Was this clever reasoning or just specious argument? What was this cultural crossover of which they spoke?

For me, the definition of appropriation originates in its inversion, cultural autonomy. Cultural autonomy signifies a right to cultural specificity, a right to one's origins and histories as told from within the culture and not as mediated from without. Appropriation occurs when someone else speaks for, tells, defines, describes, represents, uses, or recruits the images, stories, experiences, dreams of others for their own. Appropriation occurs also when someone else becomes the expert on your experience, and they are deemed more knowledgeable about who you are than yourself.

The concepts of cultural autonomy and appropriation evolved for me as part of my political education and awareness: the basis of cultural autonomy is contained within the concept of Aboriginal Title and Rights. Aboriginal Title has been described as a concept of jurisprudence that articulates a relationship of a people to their traditional lands. Traditional lands are defined by traditional use and occupancy; from Aboriginal Title flows Aboriginal Rights.

A second definition, a more subjective one, describes Aboriginal Title as a sacred trust with the land, a religion as some have said, a belief system that establishes our relationship with the land and reminds the world that we were here first. As part of the negotiations over Aboriginal Title, First Nations' representatives developed a list that outlined the jurisdiction over which Aboriginal Rights preside: land, resources, and environment; collective self-determination of self-government; citizenship/membership in Aboriginal nations/communities; economic development

This text was first published in *Parallelogramme* (Summer 1990).

and training; hunting, trapping, fishing, harvesting, and gathering; customary law and enforcement; language, culture, and religion; education; health; and fiscal relations.

In my presentation on cultural autonomy I attempted to understand why artists, filmmakers, videomakers, dancers, and writers who purport to be on the side of progressive change would appropriate Native culture in their practices and their theory, particularly when appropriation is so obviously an agent of colonialism and patriarchy. I wondered when this appropriation might be thought of as an effort to understand and to champion our cause (as paternalistic as that might be), and when it was simply personal aggrandizement, a sure grant application, or an absence of an artist's own ideas or images. Is there a difference? Is there a point of convergence where the work seeks to "imagine the Other" or dream of a "classless, aesthetic" society?

The current flurry about the appropriation of Native culture is not new. It may be newsworthy for *The Globe and Mail* or *Maclean's*, where recent attention has been paid to the film *Where the Spirit Lives* and the work of W.P. Kinsella, for instance. But the issue of cultural appropriation, and awareness of this by First Nations, began when the first European arrived. For they perceived the land—those who inhabited the land, the resources the land held, and the means by which others expressed their relationship to the land—as their property, to be conquered or subdued and finally possessed.

Our concept of ownership evolved independently of European concepts of ownership, and it persists today. Without the sense of private property that ascended with European culture, we evolved concepts of property that recognized the interdependence of communities, families, and nations and that favoured the guardianship of the earth as opposed to its conquest. There was a sense of ownership but not one that pre-empted the rights and privileges of others, nor the rights of the earth and the life that it sustained. By respecting the rights and privileges of others one gained honour and prestige.

Capitalist patriarchy was not pre-eminent; therefore the question of the father's property, as well as his jurisdiction over the family, was not paramount. Lineage was important, as was kinship, since we were not ignorant of science. But lineage was not necessarily bound to property as much as it was related to powers and territory. (There is a difference between the two, if you read territory as something earned rather than bought.)

Ownership was bound up with history. Without a written language, we nonetheless recorded history and knowledge. Communities, families, individuals, and nations created songs, dances, rituals, objects, and stories that were considered to be property but not property as understood by the Europeans. Material wealth was redistributed, but history and stories belonged to the originator and could be given or shared with others as a way of preserving, extending and witnessing history, and expressing one's world view. Contained within our concepts of ownership was the respect for different world views, stories, and histories.

When the Europeans arrived, there inevitably was a conflict with our concepts of property and cultural values. Appropriation of land, resources, and wealth was initiated with a vengeance, as Europeans carried out what they perceived to be their right to conquest. I do not intend to recount those conflicts, but instead I will focus on the conflict over cultural expression.

In the appropriation of Native cultural expression and images, the issue begins with origins and who has the right to name whom. Non-Natives may feel that the traditional structures of our cultures no longer exist, that we are no longer essentially oral cultures, and therefore our authority over our cultural expression no longer exists either, or is no longer relevant. As well, many feel that because they reject Western culture, they can adopt another. Others may feel that they have a right to whatever is before them. Even other reasons are cited for acts of appropriation, but, whatever this reason, a conflict ensues. In fact, there is seeming surprise at our anger when we resist appropriation.

Like Aboriginal elders, leaders, lawyers, researchers, historians, and others who participate in the struggle to exercise and assert Aboriginal Title of land and resources, artists similarly exercise Aboriginal Title over cultural expression and language.

In court, the issue of Aboriginal Title versus colonial ownership often comes down to naming. The colonizers named the land Canada, British Columbia, Vancouver and in naming the land justified the theft. Yet, there were names before those names, and in court the evidence often involves Aboriginal Nations stating those names of mountains, rivers, lakes, plains; in signifying use, occupancy and jurisdiction are thus signified.

For the First Nations artist, there is no courtroom, *per se*, although copyright issues involving intellectual property are making their way to the courts. Instead, our struggle is played out in other institutions: the galleries, museums, academies, cinemas, theatres, and the libraries and schools, as well as the marketplace. Here, the appropriation is performed in the guise of multiculturalism, so-called cross-cultural understanding, and good old-fashioned artistic licence, as well as, should I add, profit and career enhancement.

In contemporary "alternative" art, dominant culture is deconstructed in order to reveal and dismantle its workings within the marketplace. Questions of the Other and of fetishism are often included in theoretical discourses and practices. The process of renaming and reclaiming exists around class and gender. So why is it that appropriation persists even here?

In an *Art in America* issue on globalism,[1] Martha Rosler suggests that "the culture of peripheral areas is increasingly valorized," and she questions the fate of difference within this valorization. Rosler cites cultural theorist Stuart Hall and suggests that progressive forces should take advantage of a "new, global postmodern village culture," one "far less firmly rooted in nation states and national cultural traditions." Rosler also cites the work of marketing professor Theodore Levitt and his concepts of a world united into a "few markets (or taste cultures)." For Levitt, "regional tastes must fall before this world culture and the task of advertisers is to develop universal images" that will destroy the "vestiges of the hardened, inherited past."

At first glance, the premises forwarded by Hall seem positive, a sincere effort to avoid cultural conflict and "recognize difference." But ultimately, the valorization of peripheral cultures is frequently undertaken through acts of cultural appropriation. In an extension of the concept of property and colonial conquest, the artist does not value or respect cultural difference but instead seeks to own difference and with this ownership to increase one's worth. They become image barons, story conquistadors, and merchants of the exotic. This process of creating a postmodern village, which involves cultural appropriation, consequently levels difference in paving the way for Levitt's future of a world culture organized by "a few markets." The United Colours of Benetton advertising campaign, with its billboards and ads that mix images of racial harmony with fashion, is a virtual merging of Levitt's and Hall's theories. It is a denial of difference and of conflict in the service of capital. The "hardened, inherited past" is glossed over and made invisible. As Trinh T. Minh-ha has written, "What I resent most, however, is not his inheritance of a power he so often disclaims, disengaging himself from a system he carries with him, but his ear, eye, and pen, which record in his language while pretending to speak through mine, on my behalf."[2]

If there is to be a "new, global postmodern village culture," one organized around the recognition of difference and the acceptance of its "opaqueness," it cannot include appropriation. The artist must be aware of the specificity of culture, or the artist will give way to the Benetton myth, of recording in "his language while pretending to speak through mine." The artist must be wary of the use of "universal images" that will serve capital's drive towards a "few taste cultures."

Examples of appropriation abound, some more dangerous than others. When W.P. Kinsella writes about Hobbema, it is unlikely that he is thinking of a global village culture but rather of a conceptual antecedent, the universal man. He levels the humour of the Cree to that of slapstick. And while there is an element of slapstick in most cultures' humour, the healing, the revitalizing nature of humour as often used in Aboriginal cultures is not revealed. If he seeks to make the "universal man" laugh, then why must Native culture be the tool, the mechanism?

Anne Cameron seeks another version of the postmodern village culture. In her work, Native culture is healing and provides a break from patriarchy. She excludes the male from Aboriginal stories and wonders why there is anger. She persists in using the experience and knowledge of Aboriginal women as a source for her own healing, yet she does not heed their requests to stop. How can anyone heal if they won't respect or honour another's autonomy and self-determination?

What is most revealing is that, in the appropriation and naming of Native as healer, as storyteller, as humourist, the appropriators name themselves. We become the object against which the threat of difference is disavowed. Our difference is covered over by becoming a symbol, a fetish.

By being fetishized, we become mere objects of consumption, which initiates a production of desire: we become style, fashion, commodity; a source of script material, of choreographic inspiration, of literary realism. Our land taken, attention is then turned to the imagination, the interior realm of our territories and powers.

Fetishism disavows racism since, after all, if you include our images and use our stories, how could you be considered racist? It disavows history, even when the topic is historical, since it retains the authority of appropriation, of colonialism and dominance. And it denies our place as exercisers of Aboriginal Title and of self-determining collectives and individuals. When the federal government is reluctant to negotiate with our nations, or when those negotiations are based on a request that Aboriginal Title be surrendered, or narrowly defined, the politicians and artists have played a role. The artist sends a message that there is no Aboriginal Title, that the dominance of colonialism and postcolonialism rules.

As fetish and as Other, Native people are reduced to being one concept, one name given to us by the artist and spectator. They say as artists/spectators that we are beautiful, we are poor, we are mystical, we are radical, we are drunken. These are the names given to us, transfiguring us and not allowing us our own voices and names. We become generic images, names, histories, and stories. Traditional oral history accommodated difference, ritualizing the telling of histories and stories through the act of witnessing. There was not one story, or one song, or one dance.

Is there a point of convergence? Is it possible to "imagine the Other," to "dream of a classless, aesthetic society"? Are there instances of appropriation that are inadvertent? Are there times when the artist's work seeks to reveal and implicate dominant culture? Artists who feel the need to show the pervasiveness of dominance and therefore the many cultures and people who have been marginalized and exploited?

It would appear that when an artist is producing work that sets forth to reclaim a history of a community, for instance, or perhaps other aspects of contemporary life from which Native people were excluded, should they again be excluded in order not to be appropriated? After all, Native people have also been engaged by issues of gender and class in contemporary society. We worked as nurses in hospitals, fought in wars, and died in industrial accidents. Yet, when one speaks to the older people who fought in those wars, they will tell you how they were treated differently from other soldiers because they were Native. In this instance, it is up to each artist to ask each person or community involved. Their absence without their consent would be just as disrespectful as their inclusion without their authority. Native people are capable of making such decisions themselves.

Perhaps there is a point of unity in the face of increasing homogeneity that threatens to remove all difference. For me that place begins with the recognition of Aboriginal Title and cultural autonomy. Aboriginal Title is a powerful force against homogeneity, which, when strengthened, strengthens all quests for self-determination.

When negotiations over land resources are undertaken, there is room for sharing once Aboriginal Title is acknowledged and established. I was taught that Aboriginal Title should never be surrendered and that coexistence comes only when Aboriginal Title is law and the basis from which negotiations begin. This is not simply seeking refuge in a new class power, or even the advocacy of an essential "nativeness." Instead, it is the place that recognizes that Aboriginal Title is the term under which we negotiate with the colonizers, and, more importantly, it is a place that asserts a reality that existed without European mediation, before Native peoples were positioned as Others.

Our cultures, our cultural expression, and our political will and institutions have always directly confronted colonial rule and authority as they do today within postcolonialism. Artists who are committed to resisting dominant culture must acknowledge our authority, not merely our so-called "wisdom." Failure to do so will only further a hegemonic aesthetic which will become commodified within consumer society. And our difference will be reduced to style in the production of universal images intended to serve the making of a "few taste cultures."

Notes

1.　　　Martha Rosler, "The Global Issue: A Symposium," *Art in America*, vol. 77, no. 7 (July 1989): 86, 151.

2.　　　Trinh T. Minh-ha, *Woman, Native, Other: Writing Postcoloniality and Feminism* (Bloomington: Indiana University Press, 1989), 48.

BIBLIOGRAPHY

A general bibliography of feature articles, books, and exhibition catalogues on art in Canada through the 1980s.

Articles

An asterisk (*) at the end of an entry indicates that a translated version of the text is published in the same issue.

Ames, Michael. "Is the McDonald Hamburger a Work of Art?" *Parachute*, no. 49 (December/January/February 1987–1988).

Arbour, Rose-Marie. "Les arts ont-ils un sexe?" *Intervention*, no. 12 (June 1981).

Arts Magazine. Special issue on Canada, vol. 65, no. 6 (February 1991).

Balkind, Alvin. "The Long Rhythms." *Vanguard*, vol. 10, no. 1 (October 1981).

Barber, Bruce. "Appropriation/Expropriation: Convention or Intervention?" *Parachute*, no. 33 (December/January/February 1983–1984).

————. "Architectural References: Post-modernism, Primitivism and Parody in the Architectural Image." *Parachute*, no. 21 (Winter 1980).

————. "A Subjective Appreciation." *Parallelogramme*, vol. 14, no. 2 (Fall 1988). *

Bociurkiw, Marusia. "Women, Culture and Inaudibility." *Fuse*, vol. 8, no. 1/2 (Summer 1984).

Boulanger, Chantal. "L'installation: au-delà de l'in-situ; Jocelyne Alloucherie, Mario Bouchard, Louise Viger." *Parachute*, no. 42 (March/April/May 1986).

Burnett, David. "Looking For the Work of Art: A Stand on Current Art Criticism." *artscanada*, no. 234/235 (April/May 1980).

Burstyn, Varda. "Porn Again: Feeling the Heart of Censorship." *Fuse*, vol. 10, no. 6 (Spring 1987).

Butler, Sheila. "More Thoughts on Painting." *C Magazine*, no. 28 (Winter 1991).

Canadian Curator. Special Issue of *Provincial Essays*, no. 3 (1986).

Cariani, Marie. "Sémiotique de la photographie post-moderne." *Protée*, vol. 18, no. 3 (Fall 1990).

Cardinal-Shubert, Joanne. "In the Red." *Fuse*, vol. 12, no. 1/2 (Fall 1989).

Carr-Harris, Ian. "Standing on the Mezzanine: Ewen, Wiitasalo, Monk and the AGO." *Vanguard*, vol. 17, no. 6 (December 1988/January 1989).

Crean, Susan. "The Declaration of Independants." *Canadian Art*, vol. 3, no. 4 (Winter 1986).

——————. "Circling the C." *Fuse*, vol. 12, no. 3 (November/December 1988).

Dault, Gary-Michael. "Up from Irony." *Vanguard*, vol. 11, no. 4 (May 1982).

Denis, Jean-Pierre. "Fiction, vérité et invraissemblance." *Parallelogramme*, vol. 15, no. 4 (Spring 1990). *

Dewdney, Christopher. "Oregionalism: Geocentrism and the Notion of Originality." *Provincial Essays*, vol. 1, no. 1 (1984).

Diamond, Sara. "Of Cabbages and Kinks: Reality and Representation in Pornography." *Parallelogramme*, vol. 8, no. 5 (June/July/August 1983).

Durand, Guy. "La critique d'art au Québec." *Protée*, vol. 9, no. 1 (Spring 1981).

——————. "L'ère des signaux faibles." *Inter*, no. 36 (Summer 1987).

——————. "Les réseaux d'art: alternative au centralisme." *Intervention*, no. 19 (June 1983).

Elder, Bruce. "Redefining Experimental Film: Postmodernist Practice in Canada." *Parachute*, no. 27 (Summer 1982).

Finn, Geraldine. "Against Sexual Imagery." *Parallelogramme*, vol. 12, no. 1 (Fall 1986).

Folland, Tom. "Uneasy History." *C Magazine*, no. 29 (Spring 1991).

Fournier, Marcel. "Art et régionalisme(s) au Québec." *Protée*, (Spring 1983).

Frenkel, Vera. "Discontinuous Notes On and After a Meeting of Critics by One of the Artists Present." *artscanada*, no. 240/241 (March/April 1981).

Gale, Peggy. "Colour Video/Vulgar Potential." *Parachute*, no. 29 (December/January/February 1982–1983).

Gallagher, Bob. "The Political Importance of Sexual Images." *Parallelogramme*, vol. 12, no. 1 (Fall 1986).

Greenberg, Reesa. "Unframing the Canadian Frame." *Vanguard*, vol. 13, no. 1 (February 1984).

Grenville, Bruce. "The New City of Sculpture." *C Magazine*, no. 3 (Fall 1984).

Greyson, John. "Double Agents: Video Art Against AIDS." *Parallelogramme*, vol. 15, no. 2 (Fall 1989). *

Guest, Tim. "Intolerance: The Trouble with Social Realism." *Parallelogramme*, vol. 8, no. 1 (October/November 1982). *

Hill, Richard. "One Part Per Million." *Fuse*, vol. 15, no. 3 (Winter 1992).

Hill, Tom. "First Nations and Museums," *Muse*, vol. 6, no. 3 (Fall 1988).

Houle, Robert. "Sovereignty over Subjectivity." *C Magazine*, no. 30 (Summer 1991).

Huard, Michel. "Les Centres autogérés au Québec." *Parallelogramme*, vol. 11, no. 4 (April/May 1986). Translation in vol. 11, no. 5 (Summer 1986).

Keziere, Russell. "Ich bin ein Woodcutter: Kanada, Europa. Amerika," *Vanguard*, vol. 16, no. 1 (February/March 1987).

——————. "Ambivalence, Ambition, Administration." *Vanguard*, vol. 9, no. 7 (September 1980).

Kibbins, Gary. "The Enduring of the Art System." *Parachute*, no. 29 (December/January/February 1982–1983).

Klepac, Walter. "Paradigms, Miscues and Continuities: The Formal Impulse." *Vanguard,* vol. 12, no. 3 (April 1983).

Kleyn, Robert. "Canadian Art or Canadian Artists." *Vanguard,* vol. 14, no. 1 (February 1985).

Kwinter, Kerri. "Ontario Open Screenings: Six Days of Resistance." *Fuse,* vol. 9, no. 1/2 (Summer 1985).

Laing, Carol. "Nationalisms: Women and the State." *Parachute,* no. 52 (September/October/November 1988).

Lamoureux, Johanne. "Le musée en pièces détachées." *Public,* no. 1 (Winter 1988). *

————. "La statistique canadienne: A State Ethics." *Parachute,* no. 60 (October/November/December 1990).

————. "On Coverage: Performance, Seduction, Flatness." *artscanada,* no. 240/241 (March/April 1981).

Lessard, Denis. "Ironie, références et distances: six artistes québécois." *Vanguard,* vol. 14, no. 8, (October 1985). *

Lewis, Mark. "Concerning the Question of the Post-cultural." *C Magazine,* no. 8 (Winter 1985).

Lypchuk, Donna. "Famous Lies and Illustrious Disguises." *Parallelogramme,* vol. 11, no. 1 (Fall 1985). *

Martel, Richard. "Vers une nouvelle façon d'envisager le concept d'art québécois." *Possible,* vol. 5, no. 3/4 (1981).

————. "Ruses et procédures." *Inter,* no. 39 (Spring 1988).

Mason, Joyce. "Alter Eros: Was it good for you?" *Fuse,* vol. 8, no. 1/2 (Summer 1984).

McLachlan, Ian. "Censorship: The Frivolity of Power." *Parallelogramme,* vol. 8, no. 3 (February/March 1983). *

Morrison, Ann. "Off the Pedestal: Appearance vs. Content." *Vanguard,* vol. 9, no. 2 (March 1980).

Nemiroff, Diana. "Identity and Difference: Canadians at Stuttgart." *Vanguard,* vol. 12, no. 5/6 (Summer 1983).

————. "Bureaucracy Exposed." *Vanguard,* vol. 12, no. 7 (September 1983).

Nemiroff, Diana. "Rhetoric and Figure in Montréal Painting Now." *Parachute*, no. 27 (Summer 1982).

Nourbese Philip, Marlene. "Who's Listening: Artist, Audiences and Language." *Fuse*, vol. 12, no. 1/2 (September 1988).

——————. "The Multicultural Whitewash: Racism in Ontario Arts Funding System." *Fuse*, vol. 11, no. 3 (Fall 1987).

——————. "Gut Issues in Babylon." *Fuse*, vol. 12, no. 5 (April/May 1989).

Oille, Jennifer. "A Question of Place: Part I." *Vanguard*, vol. 10, no. 8 (October 1981).

——————. "A Question of Place: Part II." *Vanguard*, vol. 10, no. 9 (November 1981).

Oille, Jennifer and Dot Tuer. "Censorship in Canada: Case Histories; Ontario." *Vanguard*, vol. 15, no. 3 (Summer 1986).

Patton, Andy. "Civil Space." *Parachute*, no. 31 (June/July/August 1983).

Podedworny, Carol. "First Nations Art and the Canadian Mainstream." *C Magazine*, no. 31 (Fall 1991).

Pontbriand, Chantal. "OKanada." *Parachute*, no. 31 (June/July/August 1983).

——————. "Histoire et postmodernité: des exemples dans l'art canadien." *Parachute*, no. 47 (June/July/August 1987). *

——————. "Pour une muséographie canadienne." *Parachute*, no. 46 (March/April/May 1987). *

Racine, Rober. "Creér à rebours vers le récit." *Parachute*, no. 48 (September/October/November 1987).

Robertson, Clive. "Business and Culture." *Fuse*, vol. 5, no. 6/7 (August/September 1981).

——————. "Rhetoric on the Run." *Parallelogramme*, vol. 8, no. 5 (June/July/August 1983). *

——————. "The Story Behind Organized Art." *Fuse*, vol. 4, no. 6 (November 1980).

——————. "Video Structures: Back to Basic Memory." *Parallelogramme*, vol. 12, no. 5 (Summer 1987). *

Ross, Christine. "Vers un renouvellement vidéographique de la critique d'art." *Paralellogramme*, vol. 14, no. 3 (Winter 1988–1989). *

———. "Femmes Forces: Les enjeux du Musée du Québec." *Vanguard*, vol. 17, no. 1 (February/March 1988). *

Shuebrook, Ron. "Empathetic Witness: Halifax, N.S." *Vanguard*, vol. 10, no. 1 (February 1981).

Tenhaaf, Nell. "The Trough of the Wave: Sexism and Feminism." *Vanguard*, vol. 13, no. 7 (September 1984).

Town, Elke. "Luminous Sites." *Vanguard*, vol. 15, no. 3 (Summer 1986).

———. "We Like to Imagine." *Photocommunique*, vol. 8, no. 3 (Fall 1986).

Townsend-Gault, Charlotte. "Nova Scotia Revisited." *Vanguard*, vol. 14, no. 3 (April 1985).

———. "Culture of the Land Claims." *Vanguard*, vol. 16, no. 5 (November 1987).

Tuer, Dot. "The Art of Nation Building." *Parallelogramme*, vol. 17, no. 4 (Spring 1992).

———. "The CEAC was Banned in Canada." *C Magazine*, no. 11 (Fall 1986).

———. "From the Father's House: Women's Video and Feminism." *Fuse*, vol. 11, no. 4 (Winter 1987–1988).

———. "Gestures in the Looking Glass." *C Magazine*, no. 14 (Summer 1987).

Wall, Jeff. "The Site of Culture: Contradictions, Totality and the Avant-Garde." *Vanguard*, vol. 12, no. 4 (May 1983).

Watson, Scott. "Signing Off." *Vanguard*, vol. 18, no. 3 (April/May 1989).

———. "Surface, Ruin, Flesh: The Return of Romantic Values in Painting." *Vanguard*, vol. 16, no. 4 (Summer 1985).

Williams, Carol. "Sites of Intervention." *Vanguard*, vol. 16, no. 4 (September/October 1987).

Wood, William. "Sustaining Testimony: Under the Gaze of Criticism." *Vanguard*, vol. 14, no. 7 (September 1985).

Wood, William. "Skin Jobs." *C Magazine*, no. 11 (Fall 1986).

Young Man, Alfred. "Issues and Trends in Contemporary Native Art." *Parallelogramme*, vol. 13, no. 3 (February/March 1988). *

—————————. "Token and Taboo: Academia vs. Native Art." *Fuse*, vol. 11, no. 6 (July 1988).

Books and Catalogues

An asterisk (*) at the end of an entry indicates a bilingual publication.

Active Surplus: The Economy of the Object. Bruce Grenville. Toronto: The Power Plant, 1987.

Allegorical Image in Recent Canadian Painting. Bruce Grenville. Kingston: Agnes Etherington Art Centre, 1985.

Art et féminisme. Rose-Marie Arbour, ed. Montréal: Musée d'art contemporain, 1982.

Artists/Critics. Bruce Grenville and Jeanne Randolph, eds. Toronto: YYZ Books, 1985.

Art/Société 1975–1980. Marcel Saint-Pierre and Richard Martel. Québec: Éditions Intervention and Musée du Québec, 1981.

Artropolis: Exhibition of Contemporary British Columbia Art. Annette Hurtig, Ian Wallace, et al. Vancouver: Artropolis, 1987.

Aurora Borealis. René Blouin, Normand Thériault, et al. Montréal: Centre international d'art contemporain, 1985. *

Beyond History. Karen Duffek and Tom Hill. Vancouver: Vancouver Art Gallery, 1989.

Books by Artists. Tim Guest, ed. Toronto: Art Metropole, 1981.

Canada Video. Bruce Ferguson. Ottawa: National Gallery of Canada, 1980. *

Canadian Biennale of Contemporary Art. Diana Nemiroff. Ottawa: National Gallery of Canada, 1989. *

Contemporary Canadian Art. David Burnett and Marilyn Schiff. Toronto: Hurtig Publishers and Art Gallery of Ontario, 1983.

Decalog YYZ 1979–1989. Barbara Fischer. Toronto: YYZ Books, 1992.

Enchantment/Disturbance. Renee Baert. Toronto: The Power Plant, 1988.

Event Horizon: Essays on Hope, Sexuality, Social Space and Media(tion) in Art. Lorne Falk, Barbara Fischer, et al. Banff: Walter Phillips Gallery, 1987.

Eye of Nature. Daina Augaitis, Helga Pakasaar, et al. Banff: Walter Phillips Gallery, 1991.

Feministe-toi-même, feministe-quand-même. Nicole Jolicoeur, Isabelle Bernier, et al. Québec: La Chambre Blanche, 1985. *

Fiction. Elke Town. Toronto: Art Gallery of Ontario, 1982.

From Sea to Shining Sea. AA Bronson, ed. Toronto: The Power Plant, 1987.

Indigena: Contemporary Native Perspectives. Gerald McMaster, Lee-Ann Martin, et al. Hull: Canadian Museum of Civilization, 1992. *

Instabili: The Question of Subject. Christine Ross, Mary Kelly, et al. Montréal: Galerie Powerhouse/La Centrale and Artexte, 1990. *

Interior Presence: Projecting Situations. Donna McAlear and Robert Milthorp. Calgary: Nickle Arts Museum, 1989.

Issues of Censorship. Varda Burstyn, ed. Toronto: A Space, 1985.

Künstler aus Kanada. Bruce Ferguson, Glenn Lewis, et al. Stuttgart: Württembergischer Kunstverein, 1983. *

Land Spirit Power. Diana Nemiroff, Charlotte Townsend-Gault, et al. Ottawa: National Gallery of Canada, 1992. *

Legitimation. Renee Baert. Montréal: La Centrale/Galerie Powerhouse, 1989. *

Lumières. Claude Gosselin, Danielle Roy, et al. Montréal: Centre international d'art contemporain, 1988. *

Luminous Sites: Ten Video Installations. Merike Talve, Peggy Gale, et al. Vancouver: Video Inn and Western Front, 1986.

Mise en Scène: Kim Adams, Mowry Baden, Ronald Brener, Al McWilliams, Liz Magor, Jerry Pethick. Scott Watson, Lorna Farrell-Ward, et al. Vancouver: Vancouver Art Galley, 1982.

Museums by Artists. AA Bronson and Peggy Gale, eds. Toronto: Art Metropole, 1983.

Museums, the Public, and Anthropology. Michael Ames. Vancouver: University of British Columbia Press, 1986.

Northern Noises. Bruce W. Ferguson. Winnipeg: Winnipeg Art Gallery, 1987. *

OKanada. Pierre Théberge, Peggy Gale, et al. Ottawa: The Canada Council and Berlin: Akademie der Kunste, 1982. *

Paysage. Serge Bérard. Montréal: Dazibao, 1987. *

Performance by Artists. AA Bronson and Peggy Gale, eds. Toronto: Art Metropole, 1979.

Performance in Canada 1970–1990. Alain-Martin Richard and Clive Robertson, eds. Québec: Éditions Intervention and Toronto: The Coach House Press, 1991. *

Performance, Text(e)s & Documents. Chantal Pontbriand, ed. Montréal: Éditions Parachute, 1980. *

Pluralities/1980/Pluralités. Philip Fry, Willard Holmes, et al. Ottawa: National Gallery of Canada, 1980. *

Points de forces: Les centres d'artistes, bilan et perspectives. Marie-Josée Dauphinais, Lise Lamarche, et al. Montréal: Regroupements des centres d'artistes autogérés du Québec et La Centrale, 1992.

Pornography and the Urban World. Jean Gagnon. Toronto: Art Metropole, 1986. *

Pour la suite du monde. Gilles Godmer, Réal Lussier, et al. Montréal: Musée d'art contemporain, 1992. *

Psychoanalysis and Synchronized Swimming, and Other Writings on Art. Jeanne Randolph. Toronto: YYZ Books, 1991.

Public: Some Uncertain Signs. Mark Lewis, Janine Marchessault, et al. Toronto: Public Access Collective, 1988.

Remembering Postmodernism: Trends in Recent Canadian Art. Mark Cheetham and Linda Hutcheon. Toronto: Oxford University Press, 1991.

Repères: Art actuel au Québec. France Gascon. Montréal: Musée d'art contemporain, 1982.

Ruse historique: L'art à Montréal. Chantal Pontbriand. Toronto: The Power Plant, 1988. *

S.L. Simpson Gallery. Bruce Grenville. Toronto: S.L. Simpson Gallery, 1990.

Second Link: Viewpoints on Video in the Eighties. Lorne Falk, Peggy Gale, et al. Banff: Walter Phillips Gallery, 1983.

Sémiologie du langage visuel. Fernande Saint-Martin. Montréal: Presses de l'Université du Québec, 1987. English version *Semiotics of Visual Language.* Bloomington: Indiana University Press, 1990.

Songs of Experience. Jessica Bradley and Diana Nemiroff. Ottawa: National Gallery of Canada, 1986. *

Sound by Artists. Dan Lander and Micah Lexier, eds. Toronto: Art Metropole and Banff: Walter Phillips Gallery, 1990.

Stations. Roger Bellmare, James D. Campbell, et al. Montréal: Centre international d'art contemporain, 1987.

Struggles with the Image: Essays in Art Criticism. Philip Monk. Toronto: YYZ Books, 1988.

Subjects and Subject Matter. Elke Town. London: London Regional Art Gallery, 1984.

Thirteen Essays on Photography. Robert Graham, Keith Bell, et al. Ottawa: Canadian Museum of Contemporary Photography, 1990. *

Toronto, A Play of History (Jeu d'histoire). Louise Dompierre, Alvin Balkind, et al. Toronto: The Power Plant, 1988.

Toronto Painting '84. David Burnett. Toronto: Art Gallery of Ontario, 1984.

Un-Natural Traces: Contemporary Art from Canada. Bruce W. Ferguson. London: Barbican Art Gallery, 1991.

Vancouver Anthology: The Institutional Politics of Art. Stan Douglas, ed. Vancouver: Talon Books, 1991.

Vancouver: Art and Artists 1931–1983. Vancouver: Vancouver Art Gallery, 1983.

Vedute: Pièces détachées sur l'art 1976–1987. René Payant. Laval: Éditions Trois, 1987.

Vidéo. René Payant, ed. Montréal: Artexte and Vidéo 84, 1984. *

Video by Artists. AA Bronson and Peggy Gale, ed. Toronto: Art Metropole, 1976.

Video by Artists 2. Elke Town, ed. Toronto: Art Metropole, 1986.

Visions: Contemporary Art in Canada. Alvin Balkind, Gary Michael Dault, et al. Vancouver: Douglas and McIntyre, 1983.

Western Front Video. René Blouin and Peggy Gale. Montréal: Musée d'art contemporain, 1984. *

Whispered Art History: Twenty Years at the Western Front. Keith Wallace, ed. Vancouver: Arsenal Pulp Press, 1993.

Women Against Censorship. Varda Burstyn, ed. Vancouver: Douglas and McIntyre, 1985.

Yellow Peril Reconsidered. Paul Wong, ed. Vancouver: On Edge, 1990.

Zone of Conventional Practice and Other Real Stories. Cheryl Simon, ed. Montréal: Optica, 1989. *

A complete listing of contemporary art exhibition catalogues published in Canada since 1970 may be obtained in *The Catalogue of Catalogues* published annually by Artexte Information Centre. A bibliography of exhibition catalogues published in Canada from 1965 to 1990 is forthcoming.

TEXT SOURCES

Kass Banning, "The Mummification of Mommy: Joyce Wieland as the AGO's First Living Other," *C Magazine*, no. 13 (Spring 1987): 32–38.

Serge Bérard, "Rober Racine, ou le travail de déconstruction du dictionnaire," *Parachute*, no. 62 (April/May/June 1991): 18–23.

Varda Burstyn, "Art and Censorship," *Fuse*, vol. 7, no. 3 (September/October 1983): 84–90.

Michael Dorland, "A Thoroughly Hidden Country: *Ressentiment*, Canadian Nationalism, Canadian Culture," *Canadian Journal of Political and Social Theory*, vol. xii, no. 1–2 (1988): 130–164.

Guy Sioui Durand, "La censure tranquille," *Intervention*, no. 14 (February 1982): 5–7.

Bruce W. Ferguson, "Northern Noises," *Vanguard*, vol. 16, no. 6 (December/January 1987–1988): 10–13 and *Northern Noises* (Winnipeg: Winnipeg Art Gallery, 1987): 9–13.

Jacqueline Fry, "Le musée dans quelques oeuvres récentes," *Parachute*, no. 24 (Fall 1981): 33–45.

Philip Fry, "Concerning *The Wacousta Syndrome:* (More About What's Canadian in Canadian Art," *Parachute*, no. 43 (June/July/August 1986): 49–53.

Monika Kin Gagnon, "Al Fannanah '1 Rassamah: Jamelie Hassan," *Vanguard*, vol. 17, no. 5 (November 1988): 10–15.

Bruce Grenville, "Mapping the Surface: The Process of Recent Toronto Sculpture," *Parachute*, no. 47 (June/July/August 1987): 22–27. Revised from an earlier version published in *Mapping the Surface: The Process of Recent Toronto Sculpture* (Saskatoon: Mendel Art Gallery, 1986).

Walter Klepac, "The Order of Words, The Order of Things: Deconstruction in Contemporary Art," *C Magazine*, no. 3 (Fall 1984): 42–51.

Carol Laing, "How Can We Speak To Painting?" *C Magazine*, no. 25 (Spring 1990): 18–25.

Johanne Lamoureux, "Lieux et non-lieux du pittoresque," *Parachute,* no. 39 (June/July/August 1985): 10–19.

Philip Monk, "Colony, Commodity and Copy-right: Reference and Self-Reference in Canadian Art," *Vanguard,* vol. 12, no. 5/6 (Summer 1983): 14–17. Reprinted in *Struggles with the Image: Essays in Art Criticism* (Toronto: YYZ Books, 1988): 91–108.

Diana Nemiroff, "Par-al-lel," *Parallelogramme,* vol. 9, no. 1 (Autumn 1983): 16–19.

René Payant, "Le choc du présent," *Performance Text(e)s Documents,* ed. Chantal Pontbriand (Montréal: Éditions Parachute, 1981): 127–137. Reprinted in *Vedute: Pièces détachées sur l'art 1967–1987* (Laval: Éditions Trois, 1987): 301–315.

Jeanne Randolph, "The Amenable Object," *Vanguard,* vol. 12, no. 5/6 (Summer 1983): 31–33. Reprinted in *Psychoanalysis and Synchronized Swimming, and Other Writings on Art* (Toronto: YYZ Books, 1991): 21–35.

Christine Ross, "L'histoire d'une rupture," presented at the Universities Art Association of Canada conference held in Montréal, October 1990.

Marcel Saint-Pierre, "Idem," *ETC,* no. 1 (Fall 1987): 28–32.

Kim Sawchuk, "Shifting Fields: Art Within the Context of Colonialism in Canada; The Work of Don Proch," *Provincial Essays,* no. 8 (1989): 44–54.

Loretta Todd, "Notes on Appropriation," *Parallelogramme,* vol. 16, no. 1 (Summer 1990): 24–33.

Elke Town, "Prince Charming and the Associated Press: The Needlepoint Work of Colette Whiten," *Descant,* no. 59 (Winter 1987): 80–98.

Charlotte Townsend-Gault, "Kwakiutl Ready-Mades?" *Vanguard,* vol. 17, no. 5 (November 1988): 28–33.

Dot Tuer, "Video in Drag: Trans-sexing the Feminine," *Parallelogramme,* vol. 12, no. 3 (February/March 1987): 24–29.

William Wood, "The Difference of Times" and "Facing West," *West: Roy Arden* (Vancouver: Artspeak Gallery, 1988): 7–25.

CONTRIBUTORS

Kass Banning is a Toronto writer, film and cultural critic. She teaches cultural studies at York University and her writing has appeared in numerous anthologies and catalogues. She is a member of the editorial collectives of *Cineaction* and *Border/Lines* and is currently working on a book entitled *Race on Ice: Shading the Great North*.

Serge Bérard is a doctoral candidate at the University of British Columbia, Vancouver. He is also a critic and freelance curator and contributes regularly to *Parachute* magazine.

Varda Burstyn is the editor of *Women Against Censorship* (Douglas and McIntyre, 1985). She has been active with the National Action Committee on the Status of Women, working on issues related to reproductive and genetic technologies. She is presently working on a book on sport, gender, and politics.

Michael Dorland teaches at the School of Journalism and Communications at Carleton University in Ottawa. He was associate editor of *Cinema Canada* in the early 1980s and has edited a number of publications and written many articles on Canadian film and communications theory.

Guy Sioui Durand is a critic and freelance curator. He is co-founder and member of the editorial collective of *Inter*. He has written extensively on art and art institutions in Québec since the 1970s.

Bruce W. Ferguson is a freelance curator and critic living in New York City. Among the numerous exhibitions he has curated are: *Space Invaders*, 1984, *Northern Noises*, 1987, *The Impossible Self*, 1988 and *Un-natural Traces: Contemporary Art from Canada*, 1991.

Jacqueline Fry was director of the Département d'Afrique Noire at the Musée de l'Homme in Paris. After coming to Canada in 1970 she wrote many exhibition catalogues on Inuit, Indian, and African art, as well as on contemporary Canadian art. She taught in the Visual Arts department of the University of Ottawa.

Philip Fry teaches in the Visual Arts department of the University of Ottawa. He has published many texts on contemporary Canadian art in exhibition catalogues and in *Imposture* and *Parachute* magazines. He is currently working on a long term landscape gardening project.

Monika Kin Gagnon is a writer and critic living in Vancouver. She has written extensively on Canadian art in *C Magazine*, *Parallelogramme* and *Parachute*. She was co-editor of *Parallelogramme* and a founding member of *Border/Lines*.

Bruce Grenville was a freelance curator and critic in Toronto through the 1980s. He has organized numerous exhibitions including *The Allegorical Image in Recent Canadian Painting*, 1984 and *Active Surplus: The Economy of the Object*, 1987. He is currently curator of contemporary art at the Mendel Art Gallery in Saskatoon.

Walter Klepac is a freelance critic and curator working in Toronto. He has published numerous texts in *C Magazine* and *Parachute*, as well as catalogues texts on Ron Martin and Roland Poulin. He also curated *Reading: Public Signs/Private Acts* at the Art Gallery of York University in 1991.

Carol Laing is a practising artist and teaches at the Ontario College of Art, Toronto. She contributes regularly to *C Magazine* and *Parachute* and has written a number of catalogue texts on Canadian artists.

Johanne Lamoureux is Professor of Art History at the Université de Montréal. She has published many catalogue texts on contemporary Canadian art, and contributes regularly to *Parachute* magazine.

Philip Monk was a freelance curator and critic in the early 1980s in Toronto where he organized exhibitions such as *Language and Representation*, 1982 and *Subjects in Pictures*, 1984. He is currently curator of contemporary art at the Art Gallery of Ontario. *Struggles with the Image*, a collection of his writings, was published by YYZ in 1988.

Diana Nemiroff is curator of contemporary art at the National Gallery of Canada in Ottawa where she was co-curator of *Songs of Experience*, 1986 and *Land, Spirit, Power*, 1992 and was the curator of the *Canadian Biennial of Contemporary Art*, 1989. She was Québec editor of *Vanguard* magazine in the early 1980s.

René Payant was professor of Art History at the Université de Montréal and long time editor and contributor to *Parachute* magazine. His book *Vedute* (Éditions Trois, 1987) is a collection of his writings on art from 1976-1987.

Jeanne Randolph is a psychiatrist and art critic living in Toronto. She has published many articles on the relationship between art and technology, and has written numerous catalogue texts on Canadian artists. She was curator of *Influencing Machines* in 1984. A collection of her writings, *Psychoanalysis and Synchronized Swimming* was published by YYZ in 1991.

Christine Ross is professor of Art History at McGill University, Montréal. She has written many articles and catalogue texts that explore the conjunction of feminism, subjectivity, and video.

Marcel Saint-Pierre is a painter and professor of Art History at the Université du Québec à Montréal. He has published numerous texts in *Vanguard* and *Chroniques* and in exhibition catalogues. He is currently writing two chapters on art in Québec in 1960s for a book to be published by VLB Éditeur, Montréal.

Kim Sawchuk is a critic and writer living in Montréal. She teaches feminist theory in the Communications Studies program at Concordia University in Montréal and has written numerous texts from a cultural studies perspective, most recently in *Territories of Difference*, published by the Walter Phillips Gallery.

Loretta Todd is a Vancouver independent film and videomaker whose work focuses on the concerns of the Native artist. She has addressed this subject most recently in *Territories of Difference*, published by the Walter Phillips Gallery.

Elke Town was a freelance curator and critic in Toronto during the 1980s. Among the exhibitions she curated are *Subjects and Subject Matter* and *Fiction*. She was Ontario editor of *Vanguard* until 1987 and currently works for Telefilm Canada.

Charlotte Townsend-Gault is an art critic and anthropologist working in Vancouver. She was an editor of *Vanguard* magazine until 1987 and was co-curator of *Land, Spirit, Power* held at the National Gallery of Canada in 1992.

Dot Tuer is a writer and critic living in Toronto. She has written extensively on gender, sexuality, and video for *C Magazine*, *Parallelogramme* and *Fuse*, as well as catalogue essays on the work of Lisa Steele and Kim Tomczak, and Vera Frenkel.

William Wood is a doctoral candidate at Sussex University in Brighton, England. He was an editor for both *C Magazine* and *Vanguard*, has written extensively on contemporary Canadian art and was co-curator of an exhibition of the work of the N. E. Thing Company for the UBC Fine Arts Gallery in 1993.

INDEX

PHOTO CREDITS

Art Gallery of Ontario: Miller
National Gallery of Canada: Brown, Cadieux, Hassan, J. Scott, Snow, Wiitasalo
Robert McLaughlin Art Gallery: Wieland
Vancouver Art Gallery: Wall
Karen Bondarchuk: Peacock
Françoise Boulet: Fleming & Lapointe
Doug Curran: Adams
John Dean: Poitras
Ron Diamond: Goulet
Stan Douglas: K. Campbell
Denis Farley: Alloucherie, Magor
Yves Ferland: Jolicoeur
Sheena Gourlay: Frenkel
Monte Greenshields: Arden
Barrie Jones: Belmore
Robert Kezeire: Morgan, Sterbak
Louis Lussier: Racine
Peter MacCallum: Carr-Harris, Tod, Van Halm, Wainio
Ernest Mayer: Bond, Dean, Proch
Ellen McCluskey: Cameron
Trevor Mills: Lum
Tom Moore: Goodwin
Cheryl O'Brien: Gurney, Wiens
Ann Pearson: Mars
Alison Rossiter: Steinman
Richard-Max Tremblay: M. Scott
Henk Visser: Collyer

Photos were received from Shelagh Alexander, Eleanor Bond, Kati Campbell, Eric Cameron, Melvin Charney, Stan Douglas, Martha Fleming & Lyne Lapointe, Robert Fones, Vera Frenkel, Wyn Geleynse, Will Gorlitz, Michel Goulet, Janice Gurney, Jamelie Hassan, Nicole Jolicoeur, Ken Lum, Tanya Mars, Bernie Miller, Joey Morgon, Alain Paiement, Jan Peacock, Jana Sterbak, Carol Wainio, Robert Wiens.

We are also grateful to the following institutions for supplying images: Galerie René Blouin, Montréal (Cadieux, Goodwin, Racine, Steinman, Sterbak); Galerie Christiane Chassay, Montréal (Adams, Paiement); Galerie Brenda Wallace, Montréal (Pellegrinuzzi, M. Scott); S.L. Simpson Gallery, Toronto (General Idea, Snow, Tod, Van Halm, Wainio); Susan Hobbs Gallery, Toronto (Carr-Harris, Collyer, Meigs, Whiten, Wiens); Diane Farris Gallery, Vancouver (Lukacs); Galerie Rochefort, Montréal (Alloucherie); Art Gallery of Windsor, Windsor (Belmore); Walter Phillips Gallery, Banff (Arden, Poitras); V-Tape, Toronto (C. Campbell); Centre international d'art contemporain, Montréal (Magor).

Sight Lines: Reading Contemporary Canadian Art.
Edited by Jessica Bradley and Lesley Johnstone.

The production coordination was done by Lesley Johnstone,
with the assistance of: Martine Deslauriers and
Nathalie Parent (research); Donald McGrath
(translation); Marie Côté (text entry); Jennifer Allen
(revisions and copy editing); Edward Tingley
(indexing and final proofreading).

Sight Lines was designed by Angela Grauerholz
and Réjean Myette. The text was set in Garamond
(Book, Semibold and Bold) and Frutiger (Light and Bold).

Printed by Les Éditions Marquis Ltée.

Distributed by **Artexte Information Centre**
        3575 Saint-Laurent
        suite 103
        Montréal, Québec
        H2X 2T7
        Tel. (514) 845-2759
        Fax (514) 845-4345